UNSUNG
GENIUS

UNSUNG GENIUS

THE PASSION
OF DANCER-
CHOREOGRAPHER
JACK COLE

BY GLENN LONEY

FRANKLIN WATTS
New York □ London
Toronto □ Sydney
1984

Quotation acknowledgement:

Ruth S. Denis Collection,
Department of Special Collections, UCLA Library.

Arthur Todd Collection,
Department of Special Collections, UCLA Library.

Portions of this book have appeared in
substantially different form in *Dance Magazine.*

Photographs courtesy of:
Richard Gingrich collection,
pp. 178, 179, 184, 185, 189, 194, 197;
Florence Lessing collection:
pp. 180, 181, 186, 187, 188, 195;
Paul Stiga collection:
pp. 182, 190, 191, 192, 193;
Caricature © by Al Hirschfeld,
used by permission: p. 183;
Movie Star News: p. 196.

Library of Congress Cataloging in Publication Data

Loney, Glenn Meredith, 1928–
Unsung genius.

Bibliography: p.
Includes index.
1. Cole, Jack, 1911 2. Dancers—United States—
Biography. 3. Choreographers—United States—
Biography. 4. Modern dance. I. Title.
GV1785.C63L66 1984   793.3'2'0924 [B]   84-7447
ISBN 0-531-09765-X

CONTENTS

UNSUNG
GENIUS

THIS BOOK IS DEDICATED
TO THE MEMORY OF THAT
UNSUNG GENIUS JACK COLE

PREFACE

"The universe sparkles with miracles, but none among them shines like man." Jack Cole had some of his student dancers in the UCLA *Requiem for a Dead Hero* use the *barat natyam* gestures for that ego-enhancing observation from the mysterious East. Cole also wrote it as a heading in one of his notebooks but never got around to writing any of his own observations beneath it. Other headings were: "Erect he marches through infinite obstacles, beautiful and regal, whither no one knows," and "Truth, who loves him, casts off her veil for him alone."

Jack Cole's life was truly strewn with obstacles, some of his own making. And Truth may have shown herself naked to Cole, if to no one else, but he rapidly restored her veil. As a result of Cole's strong sense of personal privacy, his innate secretiveness, and his fondness for improving on already good stories, it has not been easy to reconstruct the record of his life or of his multiple careers—in cabarets, in films, in the musical theatre, and in teaching. My thanks must go to all mentioned in this book who helped reveal some aspect of Cole and his talents, whether their information was provided in first-hand interviews or in previously published—and unpublished—materials and letters.

Most important of all the people to whom I owe thanks for being able to complete this book on Jack Cole are William Como, Editor in Chief of *Dance Magazine*, and Richard Philp, Managing Editor. In 1978, Bill Como asked me to talk to Gwen Verdon, Florence Lessing, Lee Theodore, and others, to keep the memory of Jack Cole and his dance contributions alive. The finished manuscript was 100 pages long. There was no way *Dance* could run a feature of that length. It lay neglected in the editor's files until one day Richard Philp reread it and urged its publication in twelve monthly installments—unheard of in these times of rising costs. Bill Como and Richard Philp have been most supportive of the entire project, culminating in the publication of this book. The files of *Dance Magazine* were opened for me; I was generously permitted to quote both Cole and his critics from past pages of *Dance,* which gave Jack Cole one of the few awards he ever won. I am also grateful to the publishers of *Dance,* Jean Gordon and Robert and Roslyne Paige Stern, for their help and support of this project.

Permission to study and use materials in the Dance Collection of the Library for the Performing Arts in Lincoln Center, in the Special Collections of the University Research Library of the University of California at Los Angeles, and in the Theatre Museum, then housed in London's Victoria & Albert Museum, has been invaluable in investigating the life and work of Jack Cole. Paul Stiga has been most helpful in making available his collection of Cole's production papers. Elizabeth Tait, of Sotheby's, London, helped me trace Cole's papers sold at an auction. A number of Cole's friends and colleagues, interviewed for the *Dance* series or for this book, shared their personal Cole files of notes, reviews, and photographs; I am also in their debt. Bill Kenly, of Paramount Pictures, generously screened Cole's films for me from his private collection.

Brooklyn College and the Graduate Center of the City University of New York gave me a sabbatical so I could write Cole's story, building on the foundation of the *Dance Magazine* research. My agent, Sally Wecksler, encouraged me, as did my excellent and dance-loving editor at Franklin Watts, Jim Connor. He is himself a cinema buff and a Cole admirer; without those attributes, this book might never have been published. Unfortunately, I got carried away with Cole, and the original manuscript was about twice the length of this narrative. Jim Connor has pruned it carefully and thoughtfully. Nothing major is gone, but some wonderful anecdotes and quotes have had to be cut. So, my thanks also to those who contributed, only to have their comments and memories summarized or omitted. Jane Sherman Lehac was an especially helpful and frequent correspondent on Cole and on Denishawn, of which she is a veteran.

Jack Cole's wonderful dance library was dispersed at auction. Now, as a result of materials which surfaced during research for this book, UCLA will actually have a Jack Cole Collection as part of its Theatre Arts Library, curated by Audree Malkin. Both she and Professor Carol Scothorn, Dance Chairperson at UCLA, deserve thanks from all of Jack Cole's friends and fans for endorsing the project and getting it under way.

Cole had a fourth motto he inscribed in his notebooks. Along with the other three already quoted, his longtime companion John David Gray wanted it included "in anything that is said or done about Jack." It was simply this: "Doing a show can be fun. Remember that."

Glenn Loney
New York, 1984

INTRODUCTORY
NOTES BY
AGNES DE MILLE

Jack Cole was the first commercial choreographer to put a lasting stamp on the national style. A pupil of Denishawn, he developed jazz versions of East Indian and South American dances. Although his pieces were seen mainly in nightclubs and on Broadway (the notable exception being his *Requiem for Jimmy Dean*, done by the Harkness Ballet), he influenced many serious choreographers by his astonishing and vital handling of rhythm. His *Magdalena*, to music by Villa-Lobos, although short-lived, included dances that had an enduring impact. His nightclub acts and movies were unforgettable as well. From him stems the idiom of Broadway ballet, a vernacular style that requires enormous technique, in that it involves considerable classic training, plus acrobatic falls and many kinds of knee slides. This dance idiom is called ballet-jazz, and is taught as a separate technique in many New York schools. It has gone into the vocabulary of later choreographers—Robbins, first, then Bob Fosse, Michael Kidd, Herbert Ross, Gower Champion, Donald McKayle, and Peter Gennaro. In Hollywood, Jack Cole made some excellent dances that were filmed with great intelligence, chiefly because he himself designed the camera work and supervised it setup by setup.*

*Agnes de Mille, *America Dances* (New York: Macmillan, 1980).

Dear Mr. Cole:
I saw *Magdalena* last week and hasten to write you my grateful congratulations for some of the finest dancing I have ever seen. I don't remember having seen musical numbers which I thought were better staged, and knowing exactly the problems and labors involved in producing your effects, I sat with hanging jaw.

It was a bang-up job, and I wanted to stand and cheer at the end, as well as several times during the evening. The *Pianola* number is in a class by itself, but besides this, I thought the dancing around the madonna, the jungle ritual, and the little Spanish piece, which I felt must have been cut [down] from your original design, were enchanting.

I have never written before to a choreographer whom I did not know, but I am too excited to refrain. Is there any way of saving some of those dances so that we can go on seeing them, complete with their beautiful costumes?

Sincerely yours,
Agnes de Mille

1

GOING, GOING, GONE!

MEMORIES OF JACK COLE

LOT 184
Cole (Jack). Twenty-two costumes worn by Cole when he was a solo artist and touring America, Brazil, and Cuba during the late 1930s and 1940s, some costumes extremely decorative.

LOT 186
Monroe (Marilyn). Pair of white kid gloves and a sequined and ivory fan used by Marilyn Monroe in *Some Like It Hot,* in an Indian Lacquer box.

The gloves and fan were given by Marilyn Monroe to Jack Cole.

LOT 187
St. Denis (Ruth). Gold headdress worn by Ruth St. Denis in her Indian dances, decorated with silver and green sequins and gold and silver wire, on a hatter's dummy.

Height 505mm. c1925

J

ack Cole, Marilyn Monroe, and Ruth St. Denis—three important names in American performing arts and three very interesting personalities. What would their souvenirs bring on the auction block?

The scene was Sotheby's. Not the New York branch, Sotheby Parke Bernet, but the parent auction house, in London's New Bond Street. Dealers and collectors were bidding for the last items from the large collection the distinguished dancer-choreographer Jack Cole had assembled over a long career. Fascinated by the lore of the dance, an art to which Cole had devoted his hectic life, this gifted man had amassed an impressive collection of manuscripts, books, scores, photos, and art works chronicling the origins and development of dance across the ages. It was a collection that had dominated his spacious home in Los Angeles. He wrote to friends and dance critics and urged them to come and admire these remarkable treasures. More than once, he described himself as "inordinately proud" of the collection.

Jack Cole wanted his collection, especially his own papers and those of Ruth St. Denis, a lifelong friend and possible surrogate mother, to be preserved in the library of the University of California at Los Angeles. Close friends and former partners such as Gwen Verdon and Anna Austin Crane insist that was his intention. Cole died in February 1974, at age 62, still active as a choreographer and teacher, notably at UCLA. But in November 1979, in London, his dance treasures were rapidly disappearing into the collections of other dance lovers or into the stock of dealers in dance rarities.

In the previous summer, two days had been needed to dispose of 542 lots of Cole's wonderfully eclectic mass of dance manuscripts and first editions. On July 16 and 17, many of the items brought good prices. For the second part of the sale, on November 12, only one day was required to strew the remainder of Cole's dance archives—his papers, pictures, photos, and sketches—to the four winds. Among these were Cole's designs for settings of dance sequences in such Cole-choreographed films as *Down to Earth*, *The Jolson Story*, *On the Riviera*, and *The Thrill of Brazil*.

The irony of the sale was, however, that Jack Cole was virtually unknown or not remembered in London. Despite the London success of films with Cole choreography, and even on occasion with his own dynamic dance presence, bidders were cold toward Cole. Marilyn Monroe's gloves and fan were sold for £400, and later would probably bring much more from an eager Monroe cultist. Ruth St. Denis had in her time assiduously created her own cult, but now, in 1979, her glittering golden headdress, a vivid reminder of her dedication to the dance of the mysterious Orient, was no match for Monroe memorabilia. It brought £50.

And how much did Jack Cole's colorful costumes earn, those gaudy reminders of his triumphs at the Rainbow Room, the Chez Paree, the Copacabana, and Slapsie Maxie's? Nothing. They remained unsold. So did one lot of six hundred photographs of Jack Cole and his dancers, some taken by his friend the former dancer Marcus Blechman. Among the youthful faces in these photographs were such electrifying dancers as Gwen Verdon, Rod Alexander, and the late Carol Haney. No buyers. Nor was there a buyer for another lot of ninety-five photos, many of them recording Cole's choreography on Broadway and in films. A group of twenty-one scripts of musicals and films, some with Cole's notes on production details and dance sequences, brought only £30. But a heap of annotated scores for Cole's dances found no takers at all. Nor did a large collection of his personal papers, which included a photo album of his family, letters, passports, and visas.

Those artists who admired Jack Cole, especially those who knew his collection and how much it meant to him, were mainly working in New York and Los Angeles, or in retirement. Few, if any, knew of the London sales until it was too late. Such longtime friends and former Cole dancers as Florence Lessing, Ethel Martin, Gwen Verdon, and Anna Austin would surely have bid on the personal papers, to preserve them for UCLA.

Cole's seven huge, specially bound scrapbooks, crammed with memories, remained unsold, even though they contained some of his childhood letters and important correspondence from Ruth St. Denis and Ted Shawn, from the days when he was an alienated, disruptive teenaged member of the Denishawn Dancers.

Fortunately, after the auction was over, the scrapbooks were bought for the Theatre Museum at the Victoria and Albert Museum in London. Though there are few references to Cole's work in London—he staged the dances for *Kismet* in the West End as he had done on Broadway—the scrapbooks do contain a wide-ranging survey of the Cole career. The material may not be of much interest to British dance, cinema, and musical comedy buffs, but at least it has been preserved.

It's a loss that all the Jack Cole memorabilia could not be kept intact, available for enjoyment and research in a major American archive, whether at UCLA or the Dance Collection of the Lincoln Center Library of the Performing Arts. The consolation is that Cole's remarkable hoard of dance first editions and rare manuscripts by now have found their way into other dance collections. Those surviving artifacts and photos closely linked with Cole's work on Broadway, in nightclubs and casinos, and in motion pictures will surely find a haven in some dance archive or among the keepsakes of Cole fans and friends who know how to value his peculiar genius. Nothing has been really lost. It has only been redistributed.

The same may well be said of Cole's contributions as a dancer-choreographer. Dances that he created for Radio City Music Hall, for Broadway, and for the clubs are mainly preserved in photographs that can only hint at the dynamism of actual performance. Dance sequences he devised—and sometimes danced in as well—for Hollywood films are fortunately far better preserved, but the most memorable of Cole's choreography is not easily available for viewing. The same is true of most dances Cole set for TV shows. Cole's major club and Broadway dances were created before the advent of inexpensive, hand-held videotape cameras.

Despite these disadvantages, Jack Cole's work certainly survives, like his library, in redistributed form. Many of the

dancers with whom he worked have gone on to successful careers as dancers, choreographers, and dedicated dance teachers. Even choreographers who never worked with Cole have
been influenced by his experiments in linking the ethnic dance
of the Far East with the American jazz beat. Or by Cole dances
which were inspired by the music and dance of Latin America
and the Caribbean, or by creations which took their inspiration
from as far away as Africa and as near as Harlem. Some choreographers of note, such as Jerome Robbins and Bob Fosse, do
not admit any Cole influence in their work, but their colleagues
are often quick to point out instances of the Cole dynamic, even
if these men do not see it.

So it's not unfair to say that Jack Cole's work survives, redistributed in both those he trained and those he impressed. A
number of Cole's admirers regard him as "the father of American jazz dance." Some prefer to rephrase this as "the father of
modern American theatre dance." That's not to say that there
aren't several other leading contenders for the latter honor, but
hyperbole, after all, is an old attribute of the theatre. It is Cole's
posthumous misfortune, however, that outside the worlds of
the dance and the theatre, few today remember him or his work.

When Cole died in 1974, he was rapidly cremated. Close
friends learned of his death from obituaries in *Variety* and the
New York Times. There was no memorial service. In 1979, even
the memories were auctioned off. It cost a bidder only £35 to
buy Cole's treasured *Photoplay* gold medal, two gold Donaldson Awards, and a silver award from *Dance Magazine*. Like many
innovators, Cole was disappearing into the mists of time and
forgetfulness, despite the fact that he had worked in or on more
than a score of Broadway shows and some twenty-five films.

There are some dance purists who wouldn't award Jack Cole
many points for his contributions to popular entertainment. This
attitude may proceed from a misapprehension about the vari-
eties of artistic experience. Cole may have preferred a Columbia sound stage to Carnegie Hall, but that did not mean his work
and his dedication as a dancer or choreographer was any less
serious. In fact, from comments Cole made from time to time,

it's clear he was none too happy with Hollywood, but he could at least make a living there.

Considering the popular amnesia with which Jack Cole's considerable contributions have been rewarded, it is impressive, and encouraging, that one serious American choreographer who is generally recognized as having made major innovations in dance in the musical theatre, Agnes de Mille, is speaking out on Cole's behalf. De Mille's choreography in the 1943 *Oklahoma!* has become a landmark in American theatre history. Even people who swear they don't like dance have been known to conjure up golden memories of de Mille's dream ballet in *Oklahoma!* If a choreographer of the stature of Agnes de Mille finds much to admire in Jack Cole and his work, obviously it is time that attention be paid to this unsung genius.

"Cole was splendid!" says de Mille forcefully. Direct and outspoken, Agnes de Mille has never left anyone in doubt about her likes and dislikes. "Certainly he was a pioneer. He was the first important choreographer in the commercial sphere. He came along very early. He set the Broadway jazz style. That was his! Robbins took it up and made it even more popular and famous. But it was Cole's, the whole jazz idiom. He was first a pupil of Denishawn. Then he started doing East Indian dances to modern music. He had the lovely Kraft sisters to dance with him. Those were marvelous dances—and damn good dancers, too!"

De Mille suggests that a major reason Cole has not achieved the recognition he deserves as a pioneer of new dance forms for musicals and films is that much of his most innovative work was actually performed in nightclubs. Often, Cole's startling, striking dances were dismissed by some critics as being merely flashy entertainment for audiences more intent on drinking or being noticed by gossip columnists such as Dorothy Kilgallen and Walter Winchell. In the Art Deco ambiance of Rockefeller Center's Rainbow Room, both as a dancer and a choreographer, Cole could be much admired—but not taken seriously. Agnes de Mille points out, however, that at least one leading dance critic, John Martin, "really knew Cole's worth."

In fact, both Martin and the late Walter Terry, for decades America's premiere and pioneer critics of the dance, were aware of Jack Cole's very special talents as a creator and a performer. From time to time, Martin and Terry did see Cole's club work. They reviewed it with a clear understanding that they were watching something quite different from conventional supper-club dance routines.

In 1948, John Martin summarized Cole's talents in *Dance Magazine* thus: "Cole fits into no easy category. He is not of the ballet, yet the technique he has established is probably the strictest and the most spectacular anywhere to be found. He is not an orthodox 'modern' dancer, for, though his movement is extremely individual, it employs a great deal of objective material—from the Orient, from the Caribbean, from Harlem. Certainly, however, he is not an eclectic, for the influences that he has evoked have been completely absorbed into his own motor idiom.

"His art is strictly high-tension; it is nervous, gaunt, flagellant, yet with an opulent sensuous beauty that sets up a violent cross-current of conflict at its very source. The dancer, whether it is Cole himself or a particular member of his company, is a depersonalized being, an intense kinetic entity, rather than an individual. In this state of technical preparedness, which amounts almost to possession, he performs incredible movement, with a dynamism that transfers itself to the spectators as sheer motor enkindlement."

But it wasn't only in the Rainbow Room and on Broadway that Jack Cole wowed the audiences and won the respect of some serious dance critics. In Hollywood, he succeeded in convincing Harry Cohn, the tough, foul-mouthed head of Columbia Pictures, that it would be a good investment to set up a dance studio on the lot so a corps of dancers could be trained and kept ready for use in Columbia musicals. Instead of desperately trying to create something roughly resembling an ensemble for the brief span of a film's production, studio choreographers would now have a nucleus of talented, highly trained, attractive young dancers, skilled in a variety of dance forms and techniques. There had been nothing like this Jack Cole cinema dance workshop before in Hollywood, and there hasn't been since, either.

The *New York Times*'s dance critic, Anna Kisselgoff, remembered this in the obituary she wrote for Cole the day after he died. He was still training young dancers at UCLA, right up to the time he was suddenly felled by cancer. Kisselgoff gave Cole his due: "In the Forties at the Columbia lot, Jack Cole taught and trained an entire generation of dancers through a jazz-influenced style that came to represent American Show Dancing throughout the world and that was widely copied everywhere." She also noted the fact that jazz dance wasn't the only thing Cole's young dancers learned. Daily classes in strict Cecchetti ballet were the rule. Whenever possible, Jack Cole also had ethnic dance experts such as Uday Shankar and La Meri work with his group.

Among the young hopefuls, at one time or another, were such talents as Gwen Verdon, George and Ethel Martin, Carol Haney, Bob Hamilton, Rod Alexander, and Matt Mattox. All of them, working as dancers, choreographers, and teachers, have been able to redistribute some of the Jack Cole legacy, both in theory and in performance.

The American Dance Machine, founded and animated by Lee Becker Theodore (who created the role of "Anybody's" for Jerome Robbins in *West Side Story*) has been making the Cole heritage visible again. The Dance Machine is dedicated to the reconstruction and preservation of outstanding Broadway "theatre dances," on videotape and in live performance. In New York, Lee Theodore personally teaches daily classes in the dance "vocabulary" of the twentieth-century American musical theatre, with emphasis on Cole training and techniques to achieve maximum intensity, clarity, precision, and flexibility from the youthful ADM students.

In 1976, the Dance Machine received an NEA grant for a pilot project, the *Jack Cole Interface,* reconstructing as many "lost" Cole dance numbers as possible. The grant application was signed by such former Cole colleagues as Florence Lessing, Buzz Miller, Gwen Verdon, Bob Hamilton, Ethel Martin, and the late

Beatrice Kraft. A dividend of the reconstruction work is a twenty-five-minute film, *Recollections*, which is on file in the Library of Congress. It includes clips from Cole films and TV shows, as well as some of the American Dance Machine's reconstructions, performed by ADM students. This film also features reminiscences by Cole's former dancers. The concensus: he was a remarkable man and artist, though he was often difficult as a man and very demanding as an artist.

In 1982, the American Dance Machine, building on its *Recollections*, premiered a Jack Cole tribute, labeled a "musical fantasy" by Lee Theodore. Titled simply *Jack*, it opened in—of all places—Tokyo, where enthusiastic Japanese had welcomed an ADM training unit so that their own young dancers would be better prepared to perform American musicals. Wayne Cilento, who bears an eerie resemblance to Cole, starred. Irene Sharaff, who had designed outfits for shows choreographed by Cole, created the costumes, evoking the look of Cole's dancers in various memorable routines from the clubs, films, and Broadway. Theodore conceived and directed *Jack*, with one of Cole's favorite dancers, Buzz Miller, supervising. Shortly after this premiere, another Jack Cole protégé, director-choreographer Ron Field, let it be known that he, too, was contemplating a musical based on Jack Cole. It seemed that Cole's almost forgotten reputation would undergo a posthumous rehabilitation.

Lee Theodore had worked with Jack Cole on a *Ziegfeld Follies*—minus the flamboyant hand and ego of Florenz Ziegfeld—in the early 1950s. This ill-starred revue never made it to Broadway. Cole had danced in a 1943 edition of the *Follies* at the Winter Garden, but times and tastes had changed. As Theodore recalls, "It bombed. They left the scenery in the hallway at the Forrest Theatre in Philadelphia." Whatever the fate of that show—for Cole had relatively few personal failures as a choreographer—he certainly left an indelible impression on Lee Theodore. Her characterization of Cole may seem effusive, even excessive, but it's typical of the comments of those who worked with him: "I did work with that extraordinary man and had the privilege of seeing him in action. He was a *Creature*—not one of us. Either an Aryan or a God! He was an extraordinary dancer.

That unique, special talent was in everything that he did. A special energy. It was always there when you were in his presence, as it is with most great people." In retrospect, Theodore regrets some lost opportunities. Instead of bombarding Cole with questions about his concepts, his techniques, his hopes for American theatre dance, she never said a word to him.

"He used to thank me at the end of eight hours hard work. I felt very flattered. I worked very hard for him," she recalls. "A few months later, he wrote me to ask me to assist him on a film he was doing. I wasn't available." Lee Theodore frowns, shaking her head at this missed opportunity. "Stupidly enough, I didn't *make* myself available. So I never worked with him again. Which I much regret!"

It's not easy today to re-create Cole's choreography exactly the way he wanted it performed. Ethel Martin, whose husband, George, became Cole's much valued deputy and assistant on many shows, worked on the American Dance Machine's first program. If the reconstructions were to be effective, she insisted that it was essential to carry on the rigorous rehearsal sessions Cole put his dancers through. These occasionally made Broadway and Hollywood producers frantic, but before Cole would proceed to develop new choreography in the rehearsal period, the dancers would have a regular regimen of exercises and dance techniques to limber them up and prepare them for the tremendous physical and emotional challenges with which Cole would confront them in the dances.

"You look worse doing Jack Cole's work than anyone else's if you don't train," Ethel Martin insists. "It's something you cannot stumble through; it will look awkward. We trained for years and years. I worked with Jack steadily for 17 years, and on and off after that. He could call us all back. He had trained us. We spoke his language. From all over the world, he could call us back if he was doing a film or a show. The Jack Cole Dancers! Many people who did one Broadway show with Jack would then call themselves Cole dancers, but there was really only a small nucleus. Gwen Verdon was one. She's a fantastic disciple of Jack's."

For those who aren't sure if they have ever seen Jack Cole's choreography, whether on Broadway or at the movies or on TV, it may be helpful to list some of his more interesting credits. Cole's initial training and first performances were with the Denishawn ensemble, which was imbued with lofty, even ethereal metaphysical principles by the founders, Ruth St. Denis and Ted Shawn. So it was oddly appropriate that Jack Cole made his Broadway debut, dancing the role of an Olympian, in Molière's *The School for Husbands,* at Charles Frohman's Empire Theatre on October 16, 1933. This godlike impersonation did not come directly from Cole's beloved "Miss Ruth" St. Denis, but from two of her chief disciples, Doris Humphrey and Charles Weidman, who had found themselves barred from the metaphorical, and actual, Denishawn dance sanctuary. Their crime was labelled "disloyalty" by the paternalistic and mildly egomaniacal Shawn. Humphrey and Weidman had dared to question the Denishawn ethic and aesthetic; they had begun new explorations in American dance. Cole, ever a dissident and intolerant of authority and supervision, joined them.

Eager to make a living in dance, which at the height of the Depression was clearly not possible with the Humphrey-Weidman ensemble, Cole soon began performing his own exotic and exciting dances in supperclubs and casinos. Even though his choreography was often regarded as too good or too startling for nightclub patrons, it was noticed and admired, resulting in offers to appear in Broadway revues and musicals. In 1934, he was in the revue, *Thumbs Up,* at the St. James Theatre. The next year he was back on Broadway in *May Wine.* Cole and his ensemble electrified audiences in the 1942 *Keep 'Em Laughing.* In 1943, he choreographed *Something for the Boys* at the Alvin Theatre. Three months later, he was dancing in the *Ziegfeld Follies. Allah Be Praised!* was his next choreographic assignment, at the Adelphi Theatre. In 1947, the Shubert Theatre stage in Philadelphia resounded to his dances in *Bonanza Bound,* which was bound for Broadway but didn't make it. This was followed by the lavish *Magdalena,* based on Heitor Villa-Lobos' music, which began life as a West Coast production of Edwin Lester's Civic Light Opera. After bowing in Los Angeles and San Francisco, it opened at the Ziegfeld Theatre in New York on September 20, 1948, where its stay was sadly brief considering its many riches, not the least of which was the haunting, ingenious choregraphy of Jack Cole. Gwen Verdon and Jack Cole danced in *Alive and Kicking*, a 1950 Winter Garden revue, to which he also contributed some splendid dances.

A memorable success, also at the Winter Garden, was *Kismet*, choreographed by Cole in 1953. That was also the year of *Carnival in Flanders*, with Dolores Gray. Cole choreographed this production as well, but between Philadelphia and New York his name disappeared from the credits, to be replaced by Helen Tamiris. Another casualty in Philadelphia was the so-called "Fiftieth Anniversary" edition of the *Ziegfeld Follies* starring that notorious non-dancer Tallulah Bankhead. It limped onto Broadway the following season, minus both Bankhead and Jack Cole. *Jamaica*, with Lena Horne, was also enhanced with Cole choreography. When *Candide* was produced in London in 1959, at the Saville Theatre, Cole devised the dances.

Today it's commonplace to have director-choreographers. When Cole staged and choreographed *Donnybrook!*, a musical version of the film *The Quiet Man* in May 1961, there were relatively few who did double duty. Jerome Robbins had recently enjoyed a notable success with *West Side Story*, so Jack Cole may have thought it was time for him to show what he could achieve. For various reasons, *Donnybrook!* was not a financial success and was rapidly followed by *Kean* in the fall of the same year. Alfred Drake was the star; the Wright and Forrest musical was inspired by Jean Paul Sartre's drama about the tempestuous nineteenth-century British tragedian. Again Cole directed and choreographed, but again the show did not succeed.

Cole's luck changed with *A Funny Thing Happened on the Way to the Forum*, at the Alvin Theatre in 1962. This time, he didn't direct the book, but his staging of the musical numbers and his choreography greatly contributed to the enthusiastic reception the show received from both critics and the paying public. Cole and Drake worked together again in 1963 on a musical adaptation of that old melodramatic best-seller, *The Prisoner of Zenda*, now known simply as *Zenda*. Even with fiery Chita Rivera, it didn't have enough pep to get from California to New York. A musicalization of Ben Jonson's Jacobean comedy *Volpone*, called *Foxy*, arrived at the Ziegfeld Theatre in 1964, complete with Bert Lahr and Cole choreography. 1965 was the year of *Man of La Mancha*, with its memorable rape scene. Some Cole-watchers insist he had an affinity for devising danced rape sequences, but close associates regard this as calumny.

His last three efforts for Broadway all closed out of town: *Chu Chem* (1966), *Mata Hari* (1967), and *Lolita* (1971). These failures were not his fault, but they were blows to his pride and didn't enhance his reputation. At the time of his death, however, he was involved in pre-production discussions of another Broadway musical, which was subsequently dropped because, as his agent said, "no one but Jack Cole could have brought it off."

Especially on the evidence of the last few stage musicals in which Cole was involved, it might seem that those fans who insist he had few failures have been somewhat blinded by hero worship. But, even in the case of shows that did not reach Broadway, or have very long runs once they opened in New York, the failures seldom seem to have been Cole's. Often, his choreography was cited by critics as the one bright, inventive, redeeming quality in these productions. Since Cole had elected to work in the commercial theatre as both choreographer and later, director, that meant he had to accept the risks as well as the rewards. Unlike his work with his own Jack Cole Dancers in casinos and clubs, he seldom had major artistic control; instead, he had to tailor his contributions to the talents of others involved and to the whims of stars and producers.

From time to time, Jack Cole talked wistfully and earnestly with close friends in the dance world about founding his own company for the creation and performance of serious works. It never came into being, but in 1967 he did win praise for his choreography of Alberto Ginastera's opera, *Bomarzo*, premiered in New York by the New York City Opera, under Julius Rudel. That same year, the Harkness Ballet, defying Cole, performed the fragments he had rehearsed with the troupe of a projected but far from completed *Requiem for Jimmy Dean.*

A page in one of Cole's bulky scrapbooks features this clip from a newspaper story about him: "Jack Cole doesn't like Hollywood but he has to go back." For an artist who said he hated Hollywood, Jack Cole certainly managed—despite some epic outbursts and upsets—to function effectively there and to leave his distinctive stamp as a choreographer, and sometimes also as a dancer, on a number of films. This cinematic output runs from 1941, when he and his dancers appeared in *Moon Over Miami,* through 1960, when Cole worked for the last time with Marilyn Monroe. The film was *Let's Make Love,* and some colleagues who were close to Cole and Monroe on this film insist that it was Jack Cole, not some studio or Method Svengali, who really helped Monroe develop her screen personality, teaching her how to move and to project her lines and songs.

In the two decades bounded by *Moon Over Miami* and *Let's Make Love,* Cole also won the confidence and affection of a number of stars who came to depend on his sensitive understanding and his brilliant solutions for musical numbers and dance sequences that would maximize their potential. Betty Grable insisted that a major reason for her studio suspension was her refusal to begin a new film without Cole as her choreographer. Mitzi Gaynor was so grateful for what Cole had achieved choreographically for her in *The I Don't Care Girl,* she wrote him a note afterward, urging him to ask for her in *his* next film. It's true that Rita Hayworth was one of the dancing family of Cansinos, but Cole created for her some of filmdom's most inventive and sultry choreography. *Gilda* is memorable for movement; *Down to Earth* for its wildly jazzy neo-classic terpsichore.

Working with Ann Miller, Cole had the good sense to let her do her tap-dancing speciality, framing her with his more elaborate and intricate dance sequences. Other stars he worked with in films included Lana Turner, Lauren Bacall, Jane Russell, who remains devoted to Cole's memory, Gene Kelly, Marge and Gower Champion, Danny Kaye, Alfred Drake, Dolores

Gray, and the four-time Tony Award winner, Gwen Verdon, who became a star after training and dancing with Cole and working as his personal assistant.

Few of the films Cole worked on during the war years in Hollywood can be called great cinematic works of art. At that time, no one pretended that they were intended to be anything other than good, solid, popular entertainment. Cole's dances were certainly both popular and entertaining, but they often strove, in their unusual conceptions and their technical brilliance, to be something more than just a flash of color and a dash of flesh to help war-worried audiences pass an hour or two of temporary escape.

In the post-war euphoria and the growing material prosperity of the 1950s, fun and fantasy were still in demand, at least in the movie musical. McCarthyism, especially when it threatened the film industry, was hardly a nurturing climate for cinema musicals of *Angst* and social protest. Later, following their stage successes, film versions of *West Side Story* and *Fiddler on the Roof* would dramatically explore the wounds caused by poverty and racial intolerance. But these were not Jack Cole's films. Possibly his coaching of Marilyn Monroe is both symbolic and symptomatic of Cole's decision to follow a different road than Jerome Robbins.

Despite Cole's occasional attempts at serious choreography in popular entertainment media and his expressed longing to have a concert ensemble, deep down in his psyche, hidden from public view by his abrasive, aggressive, dominant, and demanding manner, Cole may well have feared to meet this challenge. For, despite his tough exterior, inside he was insecure, somewhat shy, and rather scarred by an unhappy childhood.

Whatever Jack Cole's inner fears and his insufficiencies as a creator may have been, he did devise some very exciting, imaginative, and dynamic dances for Hollywood films. If they haven't quite achieved the status of high art or its opposite, the nadir of "high camp," many have become part of America's popular cultural heritage. Among them are *Eadie Was a Lady, On the Riviera, Gentlemen Prefer Blondes, Kismet, Les Girls,* and *Some Like It Hot.* During the Golden Days of TV, Cole also choreographed production numbers for three major shows: the "Perry Como Show" (NBC), the "Bob Hope Show" (NBC), and the "Sid Caesar Show" (CBS).

Jack Cole never won a Tony or an Emmy. He did win the *Dance Magazine* Award twice: in 1943 for his dancing in the *Ziegfeld Follies,* and in 1955 for his choreography in *Three for the Show. Photoplay* gave him its award in 1945 for choreographing *The Jolson Story.* Cole won the Donaldson Award twice in 1950, for his dancing and his choreography in the Broadway revue *Alive and Kicking.*

How sad and bitterly ironic it was that these awards that meant so much to Jack Cole, which he would surely have wanted permanently preserved in a Cole Collection at UCLA, were being sold to the highest bidder in November 1979 in London, far away from the Broadway and Hollywood scenes of his choreographic triumphs. Far away from Cole's friends, who might have been able to save these awards as silent memorials of a remarkable creative artist who, at the last, was denied even a memorial service.

2

AGONY
WITHOUT
ECSTASY

GROWING
UP IN
NEW JERSEY

The best storytellers don't make good journalists. Even when their stories are drawn from memory, especially if these memories are intensely painful or embarrassing, the facts acquire a framework and decoration that make the actual events unrecognizable to anyone who was an eyewitness. Some testimonies of Cole's past have been discovered, but most of the details of Cole's childhood come from Cole, once or twice removed, as recalled by those who knew him after he'd left his native New Jersey behind him.

Who would be better than Cole at describing his lonely, painful childhood? Perhaps an impartial observer of that period would be best, because Jack Cole was a very good storyteller. Whether he was talking to friends in show business or to newspaper interviewers, he couldn't resist improving on previous versions of his experiences. Thus, he told one reporter that he was enrolled at Dartmouth when he first saw the Denishawn Dancers and decided to drop out of college and join Ruth St. Denis and Ted Shawn. Another journalist reported, however, that Jack Cole was a student at Columbia University when a glimpse of the Denishawn dance innovations made him an instant convert.

Even at the end of his life, Cole was fond of characterizing himself as homespun and "shanty Irish." Kimberly Kaufman, who studied dance with Cole at UCLA and wrote her M.A. thesis on him, noted this. At various times, he told some of his dancers about his "rowdy" Irish family in New Jersey. Cole's real father, however, possessed a rather Germanic name: Richter. Jack Cole was born John Ewing Richter, and later adopted the name Cole when his mother remarried.

In one of Cole's large, red-bound scrapbooks, there is a collection of unmounted family photos. Most of them show an infant Jack Cole in a white smock, being dandled proudly by his mother. Others show the family in the neat yard of a conventional house of the period. In another scrapbook, there is an entire page of Cole photos, dated in Cole's own hand. Under little pink nimbus labeled "1913" is a sepia shot of the infant Jack Cole and his smiling mother. Although some sources have given Cole's birthday as April 27, 1914, neither 1913 nor 1914 is correct. Shortly before this book went to press, Sister Irene Marie, the Archivist of Mount Saint Dominic, the convent boarding school Cole attended as a small child, found the attendance records for 1918 and 1919. Jack Cole was listed as eight years of age, with his mother residing in Manhattan on West 180th Street. That argued a 1911 birth year. A week later, a copy of Cole's birth certificate arrived from New Jersey's Bureau of Vital Statistics. It's official: Cole was born April 27, 1911, the son of Charles F. Richter, 29, a druggist, and his wife, the former Mae Ewing, 28. He was their only child, born at 37 Remsen Avenue, New Brunswick, New Jersey.

It is said that in the theatre only men grow older; actresses are ageless. Cole at least established a year in his private scrapbook. But he was to tell friends and journalists that he was younger than he really was. With older performers, a bit of fibbing about age is good business. Producers and directors are often worried about sudden illness or death in the midst of a Broadway run or the shooting of a film. Jack Cole, even when he was young, may have wanted to appear still younger. He may have liked the image of himself as a dance prodigy, for his talent soon proved prodigious when he departed from Denishawn.

Anna Austin Crane, who met Cole when he joined St. Denis and Shawn, heard many stories from him about his New Jersey childhood. One story he told Austin, who is preparing a memoir of Cole, was that his mother told him his real father had died. She remarried, taking a Mr. Cole as her new husband, and along with him, his lively family. In later life, Cole also told other dance associates that he thought his father had died until one day he got a call from his real father.

Letters and phone calls to Coles in the New Brunswick area, where the Cole family was centered, have so far located no one who knew the young John Ewing Richter or J. Ewing Cole. Cole's mother's family, the Ewings, did respond with memories of their famous relative. Paul Ewing was city attorney of

New Brunswick in the 1940s, and William Ewing currently works in the Sheriff's Office there. William Ewing says he met Jack Cole only a couple of times, but his brother and Paul Ewing, Jr., were better acquainted with him. While visiting Cole in Hollywood, Paul Ewing, Jr., met Marilyn Monroe and Tallulah Bankhead.

One of Cole's dance partners who met his mother has described her as "an old battle-axe." Cole's reminiscences to friends and associates over the years indicated an on-going guilty animosity. She was, after all, his mother, and Jack Cole had had a good, strict upbringing, first in a Catholic school and later in a military academy. Respect for one's mother was a cardinal virtue. Once, when Mrs. Cole was older and unwell, Jack Cole took a partner and friend to the hospital to visit her. Either to amuse his guest or to torment his mother, he took some of her street clothes out of the closet and proceeded to model them, mocking his mother's taste in hats and coats. Told of this seemingly gratuitous cruelty, Anna Austin responds: "But she was pretty stinking to him, too. She was no rose to him!"

Cole's mother had a special cure for hangover. In fact, the only confidence Jack Cole ever shared about his childhood with his longtime dance accompanist and arranger, Hal Schaefer, was the "Cole cure." He did it in a roundabout way. Schaefer had long been puzzled by Cole's method for eating eggs. At lunch in the studio commissary, Cole would often order fried eggs. Then, as Schaefer looked on in disbelief, Cole would cut around the yolk, pushing away the white portion. Cole ate only the egg yolks, heavily peppered. Finally, Schaefer had to know why. Cole explained that, when he was a child, he didn't realize that the yolk of an egg was yellow. This would seem another example of Cole's propensity for exaggeration in telling a good story. Cole insisted that his mother covered her egg yolks so thickly with black pepper that one couldn't see any yellow at all. Of course she didn't eat the white part, a habit Cole learned from her. It was Mrs. Cole's belief that black pepper and egg yolks would soothe her hangover, or so Jack Cole claimed.

At some time in his childhood, Cole was hurt and had to be hospitalized, a painful memory in later life. Accounts are confusing. Some Cole colleagues say he told them he'd hurt his leg or knee—which certainly troubled him in his mature years—when he was performing dances that subjected his knees to constant shock and abrasions. Jane Russell heard that Cole was told he'd never be able to walk again. Others believe Cole's eye had been hurt in an accident, and this was the reason for his being confined in a hospital. Whatever the cause, Cole told of his determination to get out of his bed and the hospital and build his physical stamina.

It's not clear whether Cole's eye problem was congenital or the result of some trauma in early childhood. Some friends think he was effectually blind in one eye; others disagree, saying he was able to see with both. Photos of Cole were very carefully posed so that the cast in his eye wouldn't make him look cross-eyed. He was always very sensitive about this. His early school letters reveal this concern. Young Cole wanted to get his eyes fixed. When Cole was with Ted Shawn, who was planning to launch his all-male dance troupe, Barton Mumaw was struck by the effect this physical defect had on Cole. He always was embarrassed by it. Mumaw now cannot remember whether it was the right or the left eye, but one was crossed toward the nose. "He always tried to keep his eyes shut," says Mumaw.

When Jack Cole was studying with Doris Humphrey and Charles Weidman, fellow student and dancer Eleanor King found him "a rather tormented young man." He was already a perfectionist, she says, but she believes his personal anguish was caused by the cast in his eye, "the result of being hit as a youngster." Rather than dwell on Cole's eye problems, Anna Austin remembers mainly that they were blue. Some other Cole dancers and co-workers cannot recall what color they were because he either kept his gaze directed toward the floor or let his eyes dart here and there, seldom looking at anyone.

A childhood disability such as crossed eyes can be a martyrdom, not only from the difficulties in seeing, but also from the taunts of children at school or in the neighborhood. Cole's childhood letters mention no close school chums at all. His youthful peers may well have made him miserable.

Jack Cole's mother, for whatever reasons, also does not seem to have been overly fond of him or overly protective. With the memory of the experience still fairly recent, Cole told Anna Austin of his dislike of the two schools in which his mother had successively deposited him. When a sensitive, partially handicapped little boy is sent off to a convent boarding school, as John Ewing Richter was, the act often argues either a disrupted family or uncaring parents. Even in later life, those who got to know Cole found that he was, initially at least, a very shy and very private man.

How shy and hurt he must have been when he was a boarding student at the Academy of the Sisters of Saint Dominic, in Caldwell, New Jersey. Whatever Mrs. Richter-Cole's real maternal feelings about her son, she did retain some of his letters from this period which Cole kept. They are spaced over the year of 1919, when he was eight. He already writes and spells fairly well for one so young. Some letters are awkwardly formed; there are some odd phonetic spellings. Sentences march along in pencil on ruler-drawn lines.

An early letter, dated March 5, 1919, thanks his mother for bringing him cake and candy. He is longing, and continues to do so, for letters. He promises to write to "Uncle Buck." He signs himself, "Your little boy, John," after assuring his mother that it is "lots of fun up here." Perhaps the good sisters of Saint Dominic read the students' letters before they were mailed. If Mrs. Richter's little boy was unhappy, he wasn't about to put that in writing. Later letters are filled with the urgency of his need for affection, maternal letters, new shoes, and an operation for his eyes.

Envelopes show that Cole was writing to Mrs. C. J. Richter, 705 West 180th Street, in New York City. One letter, to his Uncle Buck Ewing, is addressed to Mr. W. J. Ewing, 37 Remsen Avenue, New Brunswick, New Jersey.

There is a picture postcard showing a gloomy view of Grant's Tomb. Cole's message: "I am real well and happy. Hope you are the same." This is not dated, but it could also have come from Caldwell, rather than from the tomb. On May 21, he wrote to thank his mother for visiting him. His Uncle John had driven up in his car to see young Cole. He needed summer clothes.

He planned to get his mother some dogwood from the garden at Saint Dominic's. On June 4, he was busy with exams and begged his mother not to be mad that he was not writing. He had a nice communion day, he noted, and he needed new shoes. Although he was enrolled at the school as John Richter, this time he signed himself as "Jack."

Uncle Buck Ewing was something of a role model. On June 28, Cole wrote to tell him he'd had his hair "cut off." He now had a "pomp just like you." If this is a pompadour styling, popular at that time, he couldn't have had his hair shorn as completely as he suggests. Also, the doctor was going to change his glasses. On July 11, he wrote his mother from Lambertsville, where he was visiting relatives. He had had four teeth pulled, and Uncle Jack had sent him some new shoes, which would soon wear out.

Problems with his shoes would plague him, but Cole was more concerned about his eyes: "Write and tell me if you are going to get my eye ficked [sic]." Whatever the boy's anxieties, he always closed his letters with rows of X's to let his absent mother know how much he cared. Unfortunately, there are no letters from his mother in the collection, so the nature and degree of her caring for Cole can only be guessed.

On August 21, Cole wrote to his mother, at 158 Church Street, in New Brunswick. He had pulled out a tooth. Eva had brought him some toys from "Mt. Pocno." Betty had gone to "Asberre Park" for a few days. For a phonetic rendering, that's not a bad try at "Asbury." Obviously longing to be part of family life, instead of a boarder in a convent school, Cole asked, "How is George? Tell him not to be spooning to [sic] much with Nell." Among the letters, there is a card to his mother from Sister Victoria. A note from Cole included: "I'm so glad I'm going to get my eye ficked [sic]."

Writing on September 19, Cole reported he now had to wear his Sunday shoes because his old ones had worn out and no new ones had arrived. Lonely, he made enquiries about various family members and friends. On October 9, he told his mother that he was now serving at the altar. But there were no honors without responsibilities as well. Sister had told him he must have a plaid tie for Sunday. His shoes needed mending. Cole also notes: "I got a letter from Dad last week and answered it." Dad had sent him a scapular, but he "did not come up to see me yet." He closed with the unreassuring statement that he was "having a lot of fun."

There is no reference at all, earlier in the year, to his father, only to his uncles. On November 5, Cole was still impatient for a parental visit: "I have not heard from dad yet or he hasn't been up to see me." He was hungry for visitors—and he needed a new Sunday suit. The last of these 1919 letters is dated December 16. The bloodshot was gone from Cole's eyes, which could mean he had had an operation. His dad had sent him a box of candy. He had had to get a new pair of shoes, because he "couldn't wear the ones you bought me. They where [sic] to [sic] small."

The Sisters of Saint Dominic have been in Caldwell a long time. Their letterhead cites 1881. Unfortunately, school ledgers containing marks from past years date only from the 1920s. In response to a query, their archivist asked retired sisters if they remembered a young John Richter. The aged Sister Gerard recalled moderating the boys who boarded, among whom was John Richter. She remembered that he received "a book about show business" from his mother and was very happy with it. A ledger from that school year was found. In it is a record of the expenses John Richter had when he was at the convent. The two most frequent charges are for haircuts and shoe repair. He also needed shoestrings now and then, and he had his glasses repaired. The rest of the expenses are for books, pencils, note pads, and that plaid tie.

When Jack Cole reviewed his career for journalists or gossip columnists, he usually said nothing about his childhood. If he said anything, it would be that his father was a pharmacist in New Brunswick, New Jersey. Apparently, late in 1919 Cole was able to stay with his father, who must not have been with Jack's mother at that time, for Cole wrote to her of going to bed at nine every night and sleeping in his dad's bed. "I meet Dad on the train on his early weeks and come home with him." Cole had started a savings account and expected "to save my money." His Uncle Buck's little girl had died.

In Cole's scrapbooks, beneath the "1913" photo of him as an infant, there is a picture of him smartly outfitted as a cadet. Cole labelled this "1923." He was, however, already attending a military academy in 1921, again as a boarding student. The establishment was Newton Academy, in Newton, New Jersey. Enquiries addressed to the school were returned by the post office checked "Address Unknown." Cole himself preserved a visual record of this bastion of rigid discipline. It is a sepia-tone postal card. Newton Academy does not appear to have been a welcoming, nurturing environment for young boys whose parents didn't want—or couldn't have—them at home.

This card is addressed to W. Harrison Cole, 9 Central Avenue, Newark, New Jersey. The message: "Billy, am having a fine time. Don't forget to come up Sunday." Jack Cole may not have had as many visitors as he would have liked, but his academic work was prospering. A progress report sent to his mother, dated October 14, 1921, notified her that his class work was very good, while his deportment was merely good. He had not yet learned, apparently, how to behave like the fabled holy terror he would become. He had two marks against him—two shoes not shined. Newton Academy, after all, was in the business of molding disciplined minds and bodies. On this report, Cole is still identified as J. Richter, a name he was also to retain on passports. Returning to the United States after an engagement in South America during World War II, Cole had difficulties with immigration officials because of his German name.

There is a big difference in the handwriting of these 1921 notes compared with those of 1919. Now Cole's hand is quite graceful, not a childish attempt to draw the letters. In some ways, he may have been maturing rapidly, or at least learning how to shield himself from emotional or physical hurt from his fellow cadets. But Cole was still very lonely, especially hungry for parental love and some kind of family life. His mother must have been most unfeeling if she was not moved by this note of October 15, 1921: "Dear Mother, You sure did disappoint me by not coming up Sunday. The boys went to Sunday School and on a hike and I had to stay home because you were coming and then you didn't come. I was up in my room crying. Hope you are well. . . . Please come up next week. And won't you *please* send me more than two letters a week because I get so lonesome. Send me something like five letters a week." He closed his letter with four long rows of X's, all kisses for his mother. In addition, he told her that he also needed kid gloves and $1.25 for the Academy's Hallowe'en party.

The next day, there was another urgent note to his mother. He had to have that $1.25 for the party, "which is no more than fair." He needed a costume and a wig as well. Hallowe'en was drawing very near. Among these letters, there is an undated note to his mother that offers some interesting insights into the developing Jack Cole aesthetic, considering how important the right costumes would be to him when he began his career as a supperclub dancer. Cole instructed his mother not to get him an Indian suit. It was "to [sic] common a costume." The same was true of cowboy attire. Lest his mother take the easy way out and send him a circus outfit, he also condemned the outfit of tanbark funnymen in the same terms: "Or a clown is to [sic] common." Oddly enough, in later life, the dress, image, and legend of the clown Harlequin fascinated Cole, who must have seen himself as Harlequin, at least in one of the varied aspects of his complex personality.

There may be more information about Jack Cole's step-father and stepfamily in those personal papers offered for auction but unsold in London at Sotheby's. In the auction lots that have been examined, aside from the foregoing letters and photos, the only other family item is an obituary from the *New York Times*. It is dated December 9, but has no indication of year. In Boston, in Deaconness Hospital, Paul W. Ewing, aged fifty-eight, died. He had been city attorney of New Brunswick since 1938. He graduated from New York University Law School and was active in Democratic politics. This is surely Jack Cole's cousin Paul, who is mentioned in his letters to his mother.

Another very interesting document is preserved in the Cole scrapbooks. It is the commencement program for Columbia High School, South Orange, New Jersey. Jack Cole was among the graduates on the night of June 21, 1928, no longer an unwilling inmate of convent schools or military academies.

If one of Jack Cole's tales is to be believed, following the

South Orange adventure in education, he enrolled at Dartmouth College. The director of alumni records writes, however, "I find no record of this person." A different version has him attending Columbia University, when the magic of Denishawn drew him away from staid lecture halls, to sit at the feet of Miss Ruth and Ted Shawn, who were also given to lecturing on anything from esoteric Hindu rituals to health foods, as well as on all aspects of the dance and their importance in it.

In the spring term of 1930, Jack Ewing Cole was indeed registered at Columbia University, in the extension program. He returned only for the autumn term. But, as he amassed his impressive collection of dance manuscripts, first editions, and dance images, Cole was to school himself, becoming one of the best-informed dancer-choreographers in America.

When he joined Denishawn, Jack Cole met Anna Austin. Among his youthful confidences, Cole told Austin that his mother had not tried to stop him from dancing, but she made fun of it. As time passed, Austin recalls, even Cole's successes didn't seem to convince his mother that he'd made the absolutely right choice. Her attitude, says Austin, was: "When will you get a *real* job?"

Cole's mother may well have been something of a metaphoric cross for him to bear, but Barton Mumaw suggests that his stepfather caused him some suffering as well. There is nothing relating to the Cole brood, at least not identified as such, among the treasured keepsakes Cole stuffed into his scrapbooks for future mounting. Cole's childhood, about which so little is now known, affected him greatly. Very greatly, says Mumaw. "It affected his kind of [dance] movement, if you want to get down to it. If you look at some of Jack's movements, at the force in them and where it's directed, you'll see a lot of hurt and a lot of fight. It's aggressive, and there's deep resentment. Jack was a fighter, but it was fighting out of a fear of being hurt."

When Kimberly Kaufman was helping catalogue Cole's extensive library for the Sotheby's sales, she had the opportunity to examine Cole's archives. Eager for details of his personal life, she was surprised to find, as she phrased it, "notebook after notebook of blank pages." Cole intended to fill these with his personal memoirs, but he never found the time. Like the seven great scrapbooks, which are only partially filled, although they are stuffed with loose letters, photos, and reviews.

Cole didn't have the time for pasting up his own life or improving on his personal legend in writing—despite some near-desperate patches of idleness in his long career—because he was often deeply, intensely involved in some kind of major dance activity. Also, he was a hyperactive, impatient man, for whom the project of weeks or months of reflective writing must have seemed a chore fit only for extreme old age, which he was not to see. Jack Cole's real memoir is not to be found in reconstructing his personal life, but in the interviews he gave, in film sequences of his spectacular choreography, in pictures of Cole and his dancers, and in the memories they cherish of him.

3

DENISHAWN DAYS

A WORKING APPRENTICESHIP

fter the regimentation of the convent school and the military academy, followed by the freer atmosphere of public schools, and once his mother became Mrs. Cole and settled into her new life, Jack Cole had a taste of boisterous family relations and wider possibilities in education and in play. Impelled by his hospitalization, he worked at developing his body, and became a fine swimmer and athlete. He was not a trained dancer; indeed, he knew little of dance until his sudden revelation of its power through the dances of Denishawn.

Fleeing New Brunswick and South Orange, New Jersey, Jack Cole emigrated to Manhattan to study at Columbia University. When he wished to apply himself, he was an excellent student. But, when Cole decided to try to win acceptance to Denishawn, he left his classes at Columbia and worked on Wall Street in a bank. He soon won the approval of Denishawn's founders and stars, Ruth St. Denis and Ted Shawn. "Miss Ruth," as she was known all her life to generations of disciples and dancers, was also a fugitive from New Jersey. She had a special fondness for the young Cole and she may well have become a surrogate mother, giving him the attention, affection, and inspiration his own mother had failed to provide. Throughout his career, Cole was to keep in close touch with Miss Ruth, sometimes teaching dance for her at Adelphi College (as it then was) where she headed an innovative dance program, sometimes giving her subsidies to set down her memoirs and to make her life easier when she was no longer in the spotlight.

When Jack Cole first saw Ruth St. Denis and Ted Shawn lead their troupe in a program of lavishly produced and costumed dances, some bearing an oriental stamp, the dancers of Denishawn were the best-known American exponents of modern dance. In fact, they were virtually the only important ones. There was no major native ballet company, aside from the classically trained dancers working with the Metropolitan Opera.

American innovators such as Loïe Fuller and Isadora Duncan had certainly captured the popular imagination, it's true. But they had gone on to European triumphs—and, in Isadora's case, notoriety as well—leaving American stages behind. Loïe Fuller and Isadora Duncan helped pave the way for Denishawn.

Ruth St. Denis had already been dancing as a celebrated soloist when Ted Shawn, who was more than a decade her junior, met her and began the relationship that spawned Denishawn and resulted in an often stormy marriage, never dissolved despite a separation after the dissolution of Denishawn.

There are parallels in the characters and drives of Ted Shawn and Jack Cole. Shawn had also been hospitalized in his youth, paralyzed, unable to walk. He not only taught himself to walk, but he developed his body, of which he was later to be rather narcissistically proud. He became fascinated with the dance, as did Cole, and supported his explorations of its possibilities by performing and teaching ballroom dancing. Shawn's determination to learn more, to grow, and to create, drove him to Los Angeles and then to New York.

Joined in an often uneasy and unequal relationship with Ruth St. Denis, because occasionally Miss Ruth thoughtlessly patronized him and was, fleetingly, romantically unfaithful to him, Shawn gave direction, organization, and force to the company the duo developed. Today, it's almost impossible to understand how difficult it must have been for Denishawn to survive. Now, when it seems possible to find funding for almost anyone who wants to form a dance group, Denishawn's struggles seem unbelievable. But struggles they were, not merely for survival, but for success in bringing the vision of modern dance to the multitudes. Shawn and St. Denis's efforts were epic and unending.

Today, Denishawn is only a memory, even less than that for many who were born after the disastrous stock market crash of 1929. Vaudeville is also nothing more than shreds and patches for the memorabilia market. And yet, in the hectic 1920s, vaudeville was a thriving popular entertainment. Denishawn made itself known across the nation by appearing in vaudeville bills. For a season, Denishawn even toured as part of a *Ziegfeld*

Follies package. Although Miss Ruth often complained of the deadening routine of never-ending one-night stands, both she and Shawn responded to the challenge of bringing dance to America, mounting ever more costly productions. They made a lot of money, and they immediately spent it on elaborate costumes, settings, and special effects. This may have been financially improvident—indeed, it proved to be so—but the devotion both Miss Ruth and Shawn lavished on their art demanded such splurging. An often delighted and amazed American public was the fortunate recipient of this largesse.

When Jack Cole joined Denishawn, it was already beginning to disintegrate, even though Miss Ruth and Shawn tried to shield their young dancers from this awareness. It was Shawn who first recognized Cole's potential. And it was Shawn who put an often recalcitrant Cole through his paces, while Miss Ruth offered encouragement and exaltation. With some of the profits from the successful 1927-28 *Ziegfeld Follies* tour, Denishawn House had been constructed on land owned by Denishawn in New York's Van Cortlandt Park. There had been earlier Denishawn houses and homes, both on the West and East coasts. At the crest of Denishawn's popularity, there were Denishawn training centers in a number of American cities. But now the dream was dying. Miss Ruth and Shawn were living apart— although in the same mansion of dance culture, and this huge house had been built with most of Denishawn's resources invested in it.

Jack Cole came to Denishawn and the House in 1930. Anna Austin, already in the ensemble and a veteran of the *Follies* tour, remembers him as being about sixteen or seventeen then. Cole and Austin immediately became close friends; later, she and Florence Lessing would become his dance partners when he played the clubs. Typical of his time of life, Cole was irreverent and rebellious. Considering his haphazard, unsettling childhood, it's hardly surprising. Denishawn House was, however, hardly the place for irreverence.

Although Cole adored the prematurely white-haired Miss Ruth, her airs and graces must have, at times, amused him. Anna Austin recalls a Denishawn crisis, provoked by Cole.

Restive, he put a jazz record on the phonograph without realizing that Miss Ruth was in a nearby room discussing a projected program of religious dance with an Episcopal bishop. Despite the proximity of the clergyman, Miss Ruth rushed into the room where Cole was enjoying jazz. Shocked, she shouted, "Shut that damn thing off!" Later, before a convocation of the dancers, a very grave Ted Shawn fixed Cole coldly with his gaze and told them, "The Temple has been defiled." Austin swears it happened at Denishawn House, and she was there. Barton Mumaw, who joined Shawn later, reports that he had also heard about this event, but in a different context.

"Jack was quicksilver," Mumaw recalls. "At that time, Jack was very full of himself, but he did respect Ted Shawn. His nature was such, however, that he found it very difficult to get along with people who were . . ." Mumaw searches for the right word and settles for "normal." Today, he finds Cole's conduct understandable, even humorous. Then, it was seen as disruptive to the ensemble, and Shawn had to lecture Cole about his behavior. From surviving letters and reports, it's clear that Shawn had a real, almost fatherly affection for Jack, a feeling he maintained over the years, even though Cole mocked or disparaged him to others, such as their mutual friend Walter Terry.

Barton Mumaw verifies Shawn's regard: "He liked Jack, yes. Jack was one of the very few people from whom Shawn would accept criticism. Jack and I were the only two he'd permit to criticize his choreography. Oh yes, Shawn respected Jack. And Jack was much more generous about Shawn after he'd had more experience himself. He realized what it was to head a company and be responsible for them. But Shawn put up with Jack's disruptions as long as he could, and then he made an ultimatum: either Jack had to cooperate, or he had to leave the company. That was one of the reasons Shawn was such a good director. He had to be like a king."

Jack Cole's first public appearance with the Denishawn Dancers was in the Fourth Lewisohn Stadium Concert in August 1930. Cole preserved the program in his scrapbooks.

Despite Cole's relative lack of training—he'd been at Denishawn only two and one-half months at that time—he was able, according to Anna Austin, to take part in the opening number of the concert's second section, *Angkor-Vat*, a St. Denis dance. Cole posed in this dance sequence as one of the many thousands of carvings on this ancient Cambodian temple. Barton Mumaw, who had joined Denishawn about that time, had also rehearsed, but an injured ankle kept him from joining the frieze. Cole was also one of twenty-one men supporting Shawn in his *Group Dance for Male Ensemble,* with music by W. F. Bach.

Not all Denishawn dances were free-form confections of unstructured movement. In fact, among the most successful program offerings were Shawn's Spanish dances. Audiences also obviously enjoyed seeing St. Denis and Shawn in a romantic Vienneze waltz, although Miss Ruth disliked such stereotyped crowd pleasers.

During the 1930-31 tour, which followed the Lewisohn Stadium engagement, Cole was still learning specific dance steps, various Denishawn choreography, and group discipline. Miss Ruth was not on the tour, which was billed as "Ted Shawn and the Denishawn Dancers," with Ernestine Day partnering Shawn. Others in the troupe were Regenia Beck, Gladys Tinker, Phoebe Baughan, Muriel Barnett, Martha Hinman, Vivian Berman, Campbell Griggs, and Jack Cole. Mary Campbell was the accompanist. During the first half of the tour, from New York to Baltimore, Cole was in the ensemble.

In one of Jack Cole's scrapbooks, there is a page labeled "How It Started—1930." Among the photos Cole pasted in the book is one of Shawn and Ernestine Day in Cuban costumes for "La Rumba," part of the *Hispanic Suite.* There is Miss Ruth in two elegant poses, and a photo of Shawn, Weidman, and Humphrey in period costumes. There's also a program, dated December 22–26, 1930, for the Forrest Theatre (now the Eugene O'Neill), on 49th Street, west of Broadway, in Manhattan. This is a holiday offering, interrupting the tour, with Miss Ruth and Shawn together again. Jack Cole is listed in a nautch dance ensemble.

For the second half of the tour, the program was twice revised to include a number that featured Cole and Campbell Griggs in *The Camel Boys.* Whip-dancing and feats of skill with whips had long been popular vaudeville routines. In this number, Cole was dressed in baggy pants, clasped at the ankle. Bare-chested, topped by a white turban, Cole wielded a six-foot bullwhip. It's been described as a *tour de force* of gymnastic skills, with Cole snaking the whip along and then suddenly making it lash and crack across the floor. In this vignette, Cole was for the first time showing the amazing energy, the panache, and the trim but vibrant physique which would astonish audiences in nightclubs from coast to coast.

During the tour, Shawn asked Cole to help him manage the company's wardrobe. It's not clear exactly how it happened, but the two had a terrible battle about a costume Cole despised. In Walter Terry's version, Shawn told him that Cole didn't like an outfit made of felt that he had to wear. He refused to go on stage in it. Shawn insisted that he must do so. Cole angrily ripped and tore off the offending garment. Shawn pinned the ruined costume onto Cole, sticking him with some of the pins. Barton Mumaw says there's a basis of truth to the story, but even Shawn may have embroidered it in telling the tale to Terry.

In the spring of 1931, Ted Shawn was off to Europe again, performing in Germany and Switzerland, and accompanied by Mary Campbell, who was also fond of Cole. On May 25, Shawn wrote Cole from London's Park Lane Hotel:

> Dear Jack:
> When the picture fell out of your letter, I said, "Ah, Jack has fallen in love with one of Singer's Midgets, and this is the portrait of his beloved." Imagine my embarrassment when I discovered it was Jack himself at a tender age (if not in a tender mood).
>
> I know Mary has been writing you giving you bulletins of our doings and so you know all that. However, what she can't say is that I am as fond of you as ever, and simply cannot picture next season's tour without your funny face and disrupting doings. Seriously, I do want you both for the stadium this summer—then to live at the farm with Mary and me while we work on the fall

tour, and then the tour itself. How about it? And next spring, Switzerland, Germany, England, Prague, Vienna, Budapest, and points East!

Anyway, you can't get out of my heart, even if I never see you again. Once there, always there. And whatever you do, I'm *for* you, strong.

"Papa"

Cole must have been torn at this point between his affection and loyalty for Miss Ruth, who was going her own way, and for Shawn, who wanted to play papa to all of his dancing children, but especially so in Cole's case, if other letters from Shawn are to be believed. From Miss Ruth, he could always expect an outpouring of love and strong, if unfocused, encouragement. From Shawn, he was apt to receive instructions, correction, and even stern reproof, recalling his earlier experiences of authoritarian supervision. Shawn tempered his strong leadership with a real personal regard, but the rebellious young Cole surely reacted more against the restraints than responded to the benevolent paternalism.

Before long, Denishawn House would be lost because the mortgage payments could not be met. The Depression would take its toll on touring very soon, so the surpluses Miss Ruth and Shawn were formerly accustomed to pouring into new productions and the dance training facilities would no longer be available. Without the strong box-office attraction of the St. Denis and Shawn duo, it became difficult to lure audiences, especially in more remote locales. Shawn's concern for holding his ensemble together, after Miss Ruth's withdrawal, is shown in the care he took to woo the recalcitrant Jack Cole. Following his London letter, there was another on June 19, 1931. Again, Shawn assured Cole how much he wanted him to participate in the Lewisohn Stadium *Job* and to stay with the troupe for the subsequent tour. Cole could stay with Shawn and Mary Campbell at the New York apartment and also live with them on the farm. (This was Jacob's Pillow, in the Berkshires, near Lee, Massachusetts, which Shawn had acquired. It would give him a much-needed base for his future men's group, and it would become the center of major summer dance training and performance, making for itself an important place in the annals of modern American dance.) In order to support himself, Cole was to do some jobs connected with producing *Job*, as well as to help prepare the farm's old clapboard buildings for their new life and uses. But, Shawn stressed, Cole would have to agree to stick with it.

This last time the Denishawn Dancers, headed by Miss Ruth and Shawn, appeared together as of old was the final Fifth Lewisohn Stadium Concert in August 1931. Thousands flocked to the stadium to see the final Denishawn epic, *Job: A Masque for Dancing*, with a score by Ralph Vaughan Williams. And this was only the first segment of a three-part dance program, which included St. Denis's *Salome*, Shawn's athletic *Frohsinn*, St. Denis's *Dance Balinese*, four dances to American folk music, Schubert's *Unfinished Symphony*, and the admired St. Denis-Shawn duo *Idyll*, their last professional appearance together. This momentous bill of Denishawn farewells was climaxed by St. Denis's *The Prophetess: An Allegorical Dance-Drama*. No one could ever accuse Denishawn of sparing themselves or of giving short measure.

Vaughan Williams' *Job*, with a Geoffrey Keynes scenario, had been given an intimate production in London in July, but Shawn devised the choreography for this new *Masque*, for this was an American premiere at Lewisohn. He cast himself as Satan, using William Blake's vision of God's fallen angel as "a reptilian green figure with scales." More interesting than his own election of Satan is the role he chose for young Jack Cole, who appeared this time under the name of J. Ewing Cole. Elihu, he of the Dance of Youth and Beauty, was interpreted by Cole. This casting is especially intriguing in the light of Cole's brash, youthful criticisms of Denishawn.

How often must the patient and yet loving Shawn have suffered the rebellious, brilliant young Jack Cole bursting with spirit, exploding with suggestions and criticisms. But it took patience to get J. Ewing Cole ready to play Elihu, who at least in the biblical account, is full of good, wise counsel.

Both Shawn and Miss Ruth tried to find financing to move *Job* to a midtown theatre, encouraged, they said, by public response to this and the rest of the program. John Martin, dance critic for the *New York Times*, was not swept away, however, on the tide of popular enthusiasm that Miss Ruth and Shawn were momentarily riding. He said, in part: "The problem of reproducing in movement the peculiarly eloquent distortions of Blake is one which has never yet been successfully solved by dancers, and Mr. Shawn has in this instance arrived no nearer the goal than his predecessors. Mr. Shawn was the Satan; Paul Haakon, in his first appearance since his return from Europe, was seen in a very minor role as one of Job's sons; Arthur Moor filled the title role, and J. Ewing Cole, hampered by inane choreography, made a rather weak and ineffectual Elihu." Martin opened his negative review with the comment that the audience was of "surprisingly small dimensions."

Barton Mumaw, who played one of Job's Comforters, thinks that Martin had a real vendetta against Shawn then and later, when he began touring with his men's group, in which Mumaw was an outstanding soloist. "Martin fought us; he really fought us," Mumaw recalls. "He was entirely interested in Martha Graham and in Doris Humphrey and Charles Weidman. In the beginning, he wouldn't mention the men dancers, if he could avoid it. Ted once said Martin wrote that he never liked anything Shawn did and he never would. I didn't see that in print, and Ted may have exaggerated, but Martin certainly did not support Denishawn. And it was so important then. There was so little dance in America. I'd never seen a dancer until I saw Ted Shawn."

The experience of playing Elihu must have meant a lot to Jack Cole. Years later, he mounted in a scrapbook such keepsakes as *Job's* program notes, Shawn's letters urging him to participate, but not the offending John Martin review.

To keep his company together, to feed them, Shawn had to continue touring, even without the powerful audience magnet of Ruth St. Denis. The breakup in their marriage and dancing partnership had come somewhat earlier. Its cause, a very handsome male serpent in the uneasy Denishawn Eden, must have made Jack Cole think very hard about his feelings for Miss Ruth. As Shawn indicated in his autobiography, Miss Ruth had often undercut his authority and even his self-confidence as a dancer and choreographer. Some of this was thoughtless; some was deliberate. She always thought of herself as a genius, a distinction she did not grant to her partner and husband. She was heard several times commenting that Shawn would never be at peace until he had accepted himself as subordinate to St. Denis in talent and technique. What tore the delicate Denishawn fabric finally, irrevocably, was the arrival of an extremely good-looking man on the scene. Both Miss Ruth and Shawn fell in love with him. Shawn names him in his account of his own career, without extensive explanations of his real role. Up to this time, Shawn said that he had had no overt male relationships and also insisted he was not unfaithful to Miss Ruth, who was rather less worried about improprieties. To Shawn, it was very important that the public overcome any old stereotypes it nourished about male dancers being sissies. He and his male dancers had always projected vigorous, athletic, masculine images, in dances that surged with male power. But this new development in his private life, not only for its effect on Denishawn and Miss Ruth, must have puzzled the young Jack Cole, who like many sensitive male teenagers was trying to establish his own masculine identity. He was soon to evolve the tough, aggressive, even slightly sinister *machismo* image that won the admiration of gangster capos in whose clubs he danced and delighted the startled club patrons, who had never seen a dancer quite like Jack Cole.

In the fall of 1931, Ted Shawn and His Dancers, a new ensemble title, was offered to communities on the Eastern Seaboard and in the Midwest and South. There was a Smith College Workshop, with Jack Cole appearing in such works as *Extase, Rhapsody, Boston Fancy (1854)*, and *March of the Proletariat*. In Redding, Connecticut, on October 31, Cole and the rest of the troupe appeared in *Boston Fancy*—an extremely popular adaptation of square and other country dances—as a housewarming for "The Haven." Shawn headed the dancers, which included Anna Austin, Regenia Beck, Phoebe Baughan, Gladys

Tinker, Martha Hinman, Alice Dudley—later, like Austin, to be a Cole supperclub dance partner—J. Ewing Cole, Campbell Griggs, Lester Shafer, and Barton Mumaw. Mary Campbell remained Shawn's loyal accompanist.

This tour was to make an impression, as had prior Denishawn tours, on a number of young people. Especially interested, however, were two young men who previously had known little of dance. One of them was Walter Terry. On January 7, 1932, the ensemble performed in Memorial Hall of the University of North Carolina, at Chapel Hill. Terry was being introduced to both Shawn and Cole, not suspecting what each, in different ways, would mean to him during his long professional career. On February 27, in Miami, at the University of Florida, the head of the music department took a talented young novice composer, Robert Wright, to see the Shawn company. After the performance, Wright met J. Ewing Cole and was impressed with Cole's bearing and dynamism. Ten years later, when Wright and his partner, George "Chet" Forrest, were running the music theatre at Camp Tamiment, one of their best dancers, J. C. McCord, couldn't stop praising the talents of Jack Cole. Wright remembers he did not immediately make the connection. Later, when they were working together with Cole on revues for clubs and such Broadway musicals as *Kismet, Magdalena,* and *Kean,* that initial meeting would be recalled with amusement.

During the Christmas break in this 1931–32 tour, Miss Ruth sent Cole a photo inscribed: "To Jack with understanding and love, from Miss Ruth." This was a bond of friendship and respect that only death was to break.

The Depression had its malign effects on the tour. As Shawn noted in his autobiography, ". . . before we were halfway through the season, I smelled disaster . . . Our tour was cut short, and I, $5,000 in the red, was in need of a good forceful manager." But something important was to come out of this managerial and artistic travail, in part thanks to the successful reception given to three all-male dance numbers in the tour program: the *Rhapsody, The Workers' Songs,* and *Coolie Dance.* "While I struggled for survival," Shawn explained, "I became more determined that somehow I would form the all-male dance group that I had been planning toward for many years." This aborted tour had given him the confidence he needed; there was indeed a public for dances performed solely by men.

Despite the closure of Denishawn and its branches, despite the burden of debt, despite the rupture of a long personal and professional partnership, Shawn sought to give stability to his company and to play his favorite role of "papa" to the individual members. Just how much J. Ewing Cole and his fellow dancers knew or understood about the harrowing troubles Shawn was then undergoing isn't clear, but they certainly were themselves daily faced with privations and difficulties in playing to meager houses and in traveling from engagement to engagement. Nonetheless, Cole kept many reviews, photos, and souvenirs from this tour and mounted them in the scrapbook covering his early career. One of these shows Cole and dancer friends at the Shubert Theatre in Kansas City. Another photo is of later vintage; it shows a pleasant and apparently pleased man dressed in farm clothes, his foot poised on a shovel. Cole labeled it, somewhat ironically: "Campbell Griggs, Ex-Dancer." Considering Cole's own lifelong dedication to the dance, it's understandable that he should regard the defection of this friend of his youth with either amusement or contempt. Yet, at this time, he continued to be disruptive and unreliable, showing no signs of his later fanaticism about promptness, hard work, discipline, and perfection in technique and performance.

Shawn seems to have put up with a lot. One letter Cole preserved is addressed to "Dear Jewing," Shawn's idea of a clever commentary on Cole's pretentions to J. Ewing, instead of Jack, which he'd used initially with Denishawn. Shawn had some summer dates set, and he wanted Cole to be with the company. On either side of the letterhead, Cole pasted photos of men's activities at Jacob's Pillow. One shows some of the young male dancers at work in the nude. Shawn encouraged nude sunbathing during relaxation periods, when he would read philosophy, poetry, and other improving works to his charges. But he also liked the idea of working, rehearsing, and dancing in the nude. This was to become an ideal of Cole's, something he tried once with the men in his Columbia Pictures studio dance group—with hilarious results.

Before the hard work, the rehearsals, and the nude sunbathing at Jacob's Pillow in the summer of 1932, and following the Depression-caused termination of the troupe's tour, Cole appeared in New York with Ruth St. Denis and her company of dancers, at the Mansfield Theatre. Miss Ruth offered her suite of East Indian dances for a week, from April 23-30, 1932. Cole danced in the ballet *The Caves*, from *The Light of Asia*, according to Anna Austin, who, like Cole, remained close to Miss Ruth, despite the Denishawn split. Cole also repeated his tour whip specialty, *The Camel Boy*.

With so much missing, it is difficult to reconstruct Jack Cole's adventures and his professional growth during this period. Fortunately, Cole mounted in his Denishawn-era scrapbook a long letter from Ted Shawn, written apparently more in anger than in sorrow. Such a letter would have been immediately destroyed by many. It's interesting that Cole kept it so long, giving it effectually a place of honor in his memorabilia. No matter how cutting he may have been about Shawn, Cole was clearly impressed with his caring, with his insistence on obedience to the chief, and on discipline in rehearsal and performance. If at this time in his young life, Cole was mercurial, unpredictable, and unreliable, he soon discarded the last two attributes and before long became a severe taskmaster for his own dancers.

The letter is worth quoting in full, both because of the information it suggests about Jack Cole and for the insight it gives into the relationship between master and pupil, "papa" and surrogate son. This time, however, although the missive is addressed to "Dear Jack," it closes with a strongly drawn "Ted Shawn," more like a logo than a signature. No "papa" is signing this ultimatum. Shawn writes:

> I have been thinking much and deeply about the fundamental principles of my relationship to you, in fact to any and all men who may be my pupils, members of my company, and later, part of the men's group.

Something is wrong somewhere. In the last year, you have had (except for about two months) your living, and [for] nine weeks, a salary which exceeded your living necessities sufficiently to have paid your living for those two months. During this time you had training, creative activity, professional experience and prestige—not to mention such intangibles as my personal friendship, encouragement, and belief in you. Yet you became sulky, selfish, discourteous, inconsiderate, disobedient, resentful. After the summer had developed to the point where the programs were set and announced, and I would have injured myself in dismissing you more than I would have hurt you, you took advantage of this to act in a way which certainly deserved instant and irrevocable dismissal.

From the beginning, it had been pointed out to you, that relationship with me is unique and it cannot be compared to anything else, nor judged by any other standards. Although as leader and responsible party in the group, authority must be vested in me, I am not a parent against whom you rebel. I am a friend who offered circumstances enabling you to do the thing you most wanted to do in life—and your host. Although part of the time, I employed your services and paid you a salary, I cannot be considered as an ordinary employer, out of whom you get all you can, and give as little as you can. Ours is a co-operation, or it is nothing. Spiritually, mentally, physically, you must share responsibility, accept bad times as cheerfully as you accept good, and realize that bad luck happens to us all as a group, and not to me alone, with you holding me responsible for the results.

You came of your own free will and accord, because it was what you wanted to do—and I gave all I promised, and more, and gave it lovingly, freely, and happily. You in turn gave less than you should, and gave that irregularly and grudgingly.

If there is to be any future relationship between us—your attitude will have to undergo a drastic change, and you will have to convince me that the proper attitude entered into will last—and that it will not, in the midst of a season, revert to your past childish and cowardly behavior.

There is a performance October seventh in Pittsfield, others pending, scattered through the fall, and a compact tour beginning after January. The managers and public are interested only in me. What company I provide is entirely my own affair. The men's group is important as an idea and is independent of individuals. I would rather postpone it by far than deal with men who cannot be depended upon as to behaviour, loyalty, courtesy, and 100% co-operation all of the time.

If you want to work with me in the future it is up to you—I must be convinced that you can consistently deliver what must be delivered and that once decided, you are not liable to changes of mind in inconvenient midstream. I want to be convinced, but the convincing must be done by you.

If you wish to join wholeheartedly and without reservations, accepting my leadership, obeying because you believe in my fairness, then write to me definitely stating that you are coming on this basis.

I cannot, however, any longer offer room and board. You will have to support yourself during rehearsals. I will pay for each day's public performance one-sixth week's salary, the same salary as January-February of this year's tour. I believe that on this basis even for the coming twelve months you will more than earn your living—but I cannot guarantee that you will.

Let me hear from you immediately. If I do not hear from you by October first, I will plan the program without you.

Assuring you of my unchanged friendship and belief in
you, I am
As ever yours, Ted Shawn.

This had a sobering effect on Cole, who elected to remain with
Shawn and join the new men's group. It may finally have
dawned on him that the Depression, and not Ted Shawn, was
responsible for the curtailed 1931-32 tour. Having been at Denishawn on a scholarship, he was now in a different situation,
with fewer subsidies, fewer assurances. Shawn, determined to
survive and to realize his dream of an ensemble of male dancers,
took on a teaching assignment at a college in Springfield, Massachusetts. He was able to work with men's gym classes and,
from these students choose eight capable gymnasts briefly to
augment his core of men from Jacob's Pillow. He also taught in
Boston at Miriam Winslow's dance school. She had been an early
Denishawn pupil, as well as a personal student of Shawn's.

These two financial and artistic stop-gaps resulted in the
premiere program of Ted Shawn and His Ensemble of Men
Dancers, shown first at Springfield College and then to Boston
audiences at the Repertory Theatre on March 21, 1933. As
Christena L. Schlundt notes in her chronology, *Professional Appearances of Ted Shawn and His Men Dancers,* only a week before
this momentous but unheralded dance event, President Roosevelt had declared a national bank holiday, which, as she says,
"left audiences without streetcar fare, let alone the price of admission for a dance concert." The engagement of ten performances of three varied Shawn programs lost only $28. More
important, Boston reviewers hailed the dances and dancers. The
Transcript's critic, H. T. Parker, who had had harsh words for
Denishawn in earlier days, was enthusiastic: "A more masculine company than Mr. Shawn and his ensemble were hard to
imagine. . ."

Shawn's company roster was led by J. Ewing Cole, fol-
lowed by Barton Mumaw, Sterling Stamford, Frank Overlees,
Wilbur McCormack, Seth Goodwin, Francis Luoma, George
Panff, Peter Pretka, Clayton Shay, Clyde Shotzbarger, John

Seeley, and Lyle Welser. The faithful Mary Campbell accompanied, as usual, but she was soon to be replaced by Jess Meeker, as Shawn prepared for a fall tour with a newly formed men's group.

That summer at Jacob's Pillow, Jack Cole was still around. Anna Austin had been invited by Shawn to perform St. Denis's *Dance of the Red and Gold Sari,* among other numbers. Today, Austin remembers the sojourn as fun; it was also an honor, in that she was the first woman to be invited to perform at Jacob's Pillow. She says, "At mealtime, Ted would sit at the head of the table with his ideas and plans for developing Jacob's Pillow with the men's group. While Ted was talking, I'd get these pinches and pokes from Jack. I had a hard time keeping a straight face and appearing to be taking in every word that Ted was saying.

"While I was there, Jack and I enjoyed many walks through the woods. He told me then that he could not stay very long, as he intended to go out on his own, and that he missed very much being with Miss Ruth. The following fall, he was back in New York at the studio with Miss Ruth," Austin recalls. She also cherishes the memory of a proposal from Jack, for whom she had deep but purely sisterly feelings.

After that Massachusetts summer, if the materials that Jack Cole collected and saved are valid indicators, Ted Shawn's further career did not much concern him. Just as Shawn at various times had used and depended on the talents and strengths of others until he no longer needed them and could subtly or abruptly discard them, so it was with Cole at this time. Later Cole would prove himself very protective of his own dancers against outside pressures, like his mentor, although he could himself terrorize them at rehearsals.

4

WEEKS WITH WEIDMAN & HUMPHREY

USED, NOT TRAINED

F

or a dance novice like Jack Cole, it was unusual to be singled out in a major review by John Martin. There were, after all, a number of talented young dancers in the Denishawn cast for *Job* at Lewisohn Stadium. True, he did have a solo as Elihu, which necessarily made him stand out. It was most unfortunate, however, that Martin's initial criticism of Jack Cole was negative. But Martin didn't put all the blame on Cole. Ted Shawn's "inane choreography," Martin implied, was the real culprit.

Cole was a disruptive element in Denishawn even before the stadium dance concert. Considering his indecision afterward, when Shawn had to woo or scold him with missives to get him to consider joining the all-male group, it's possible that Martin's critique had made a deep wound in Cole's already insecure young ego. But, rather than blame himself, Cole had the authority of the *New York Times* to blame Shawn and his choreography. This may well have intensified Cole's criticisms and mutterings.

His departure was probably foreseen by Shawn, though during that fateful summer at Jacob's Pillow, only Anna Austin was allowed to know Cole's decision to leave. He may have been scouting for a viable base in Manhattan. He was to find it temporarily with two other famous Denishawn defectors, Charles Weidman and Doris Humphrey. Like Humphrey and Weidman, Cole took a great deal away from his experience with Ruth St. Denis and Ted Shawn. More, perhaps, than he realized.

Barton Mumaw points out some very specific things Cole had learned at Denishawn. As he puts it, "It was there that Jack, like Martha Graham and Doris and Charles, learned about the theatre in a way that dancers of today are deprived of. So many of the things the dancers themselves were responsible for are taken away by members of unions. When he left Denishawn, and Shawn, he already knew the importance of costuming, lighting, handling of 'props,' materials, and, despite his recalcitrance, the discipline required of the art."

It's ironic that Cole became such a stern taskmaster with students and his own professional dancers soon after. Shawn was a far more kindly, patient teacher-choreographer than Jack Cole would ever be. But there was one time when even he was pushed past the breaking point. As Mumaw recalls, "Jack could be so exasperating that there was no way to deal with him, except as a recalcitrant child who refused, stubbornly, to accede to the rights of others. It was this quality which goaded Shawn to physical retaliation. I don't remember the circumstances that led to so uncharacteristic a move on Shawn's part, but the argument culminated in a sharp slap on the face.

"Of course, they were both so shocked they stood staring at each other like instant statues, then broke and embraced, to the accompaniment of tears, for they loved and respected each other, no matter what the surface distortions," says Mumaw. This mutual regard was obviously something very special.

In his Denishawn days, when Cole was at his worst, if he'd hurt Miss Ruth, he'd always feel very sorry afterward. Barton Mumaw remembers how Cole would apologize and try to make it up to her. "When his sunny side broke through, it warmed all within its radiance," Mumaw notes. But, says Mumaw, "while he respected Shawn, he enjoyed his bedevilment of him, for Shawn was the Director, the Administrator, and the Disciplinarian, all forms of the authoritarianism so reprehensible to Jack at that stage. In later years, when Jack himself was the choreographer, director, and manager of his own company, he admitted his own tactics were based on Shawn's example."

In that summer of 1933, in the depths of the Depression, thousands and thousands of Americans were without jobs, without even minimum daily nutritional needs. Some feared they would never find work again. For Cole to leave the rural womb of Jacob's Pillow and the potential adventure and excitement of helping create a new chapter in American dance history with the men's group, a lot of courage and belief in his own dance potential must have been required. But there was always a clash of temperaments between Shawn and Cole.

So he set out to write his own chapter in the story of American dance. Ted Shawn was not pleased with the solution, Mumaw says, since he was really fond of Cole; he admired him as a person and for his talent as a dancer. Nonetheless, both Cole and Shawn realized there would always be friction between them. Mumaw thinks that at the hour of parting, Shawn must have given "a subliminal sigh of relief," as he blessed Cole and sent him on his way.

Out of the Berkshires and back in New York City, Cole's next haven was the group formed by Doris Humphrey and Charles Weidman. Although he had grown in technique and confidence through his Denishawn experience, Cole had not yet shed his tendency to be tardy, unreliable, and difficult. Weidman, a generous-hearted and very gifted dancer-choreographer, did what he could to help Cole survive and to encourage him as a performer. Weidman was well known for his sense of humor, which manifested itself in dance in a series of affectionate parodies of such distinctive figures as his former mentors, Miss Ruth and Shawn. At the very least, Cole must have found this appealing. He was not above travestying some of his beloved Miss Ruth's Indian dances himself. He was well aware that they owed rather little to authentic dances of the Orient.

Doris Humphrey especially—but Weidman as well—demanded of the dancers who joined them that they make themselves entirely free for training, rehearsal, and concert performances. This made it impossible for any of the devout young adherents to support themselves with regular jobs. At any moment, there might be an urgent call to rehearse for an engagement somewhere in Connecticut or Manhattan. Owing to the Depression, however, these performances weren't frequent enough to provide a living for the group. Letitia Ide Ratner, who was with the company at the time Jack Cole was also finding his dance identity, explains that there were odd jobs available to the dancers, such as modeling for art classes or for individual painters and sculptors. Eleanor King, also with Humphrey-Weidman at this time, confirms these economic arrangements.

Years later, Charles Weidman was to recall that Cole stayed at the studio because he had nowhere else to go. His pride made it impossible for him to accept direct charity from Weidman, who was only too glad to help this difficult but talented young man. Weidman conceived a face-saving, indirect form of subsidy. He would leave fifty-cent pieces around the studio in conspicuous places. When Cole found them, he could then afford meals— for less than five cents each!—in the long-vanished MacFadden Restaurant on 44th Street. This was an unspoken arrangement. Cole wasn't stealing; he knew perfectly well why those coins were lying around.

Cole was able to use the remainder of the money for lessons. He had already, at Shawn's insistence, studied the Cecchetti method of ballet training. Now he intensified his studies with Luigi Albertieri. Tired of and irritated with Ruth St. Denis's phoney dance compositions, Cole sought out experts. He went to La Meri for instruction in Indian dance. When he had the opportunity to work with Uday Shankar, a masterful exponent of Indian dance, Cole seized it. Later, whenever possible, he invited La Meri, Shankar, and others to demonstrate and teach techniques and dances to his own students and ensembles.

Gwen Verdon remembers this aspect of the training vividly. Her own mother had been a dancer and had taught both ballet and Denishawn technique for Ruth St. Denis in Los Angeles. Thus, Verdon was, as she says, "way ahead" when she auditioned for Cole. "I didn't realize that all this funny dancing I was doing as a kid was the same thing that Jack had learned when he was sixteen, with Denishawn."

Verdon comments on Cole's reaction to Miss Ruth's choreography: ". . . her idea of East Indian dance, [was] to go around 'goosing angels.' He knew it was not correct at all. That's why he studied with La Meri and Uday Shankar—and made all of us study with them as well. We had to read the *Bhagavad-Gita* to understand all the stories and characters. . . . But Jack also knew he had learned something from Denishawn. About the importance of costuming, even if it was for pseudo-Indian dance. When we danced with him, we had to do absolutely authentic dances, but in jazzy costumes, to jazz music. He learned the theatricality from Denishawn," Verdon insists.

While Cole was preparing himself for a commercial career as a dancer-choreographer, he was beginning to collect books and articles dealing with the dance. Although he'd dropped out of Columbia University, he would return to read dance tomes in the library. His interest in developing a definitive dance library was aroused at this time, but he had no place initially to stockpile his books. He was sleeping on a mattress on the floor at Weidman's studio. He was also, by several accounts, dressing in a style that was even more bizarre and shabby than the Depression dictated. Attempts to give him some conventional, if cast-off, pieces of clothing offended the Cole pride. Weidman and Humphrey reluctantly dismissed Cole from their company, not for lack of talent, but for his persistent failure to maintain company discipline, by not arriving on time for rehearsals and not discharging other responsibilities with enthusiasm and attention to detail. He was still, as at Denishawn, playing "Peck's Bad Boy."

Eleanor King's book, *Transformations,* documents the formative years of the Humphrey-Weidman collaboration in a personal account rich in anecdote. Asked to enlarge on the memories of Jack Cole, King says, "I knew nothing about Jack before he appeared at the Humphrey-Weidman Studio, 151 West 18th Street, circa '33—when he appeared with Doris and Charles and about ten members of the company in the Theatre Guild *School for Husbands,* dancing in the *Dream of Sganarelle* ballet. . . . I remember Jack as a perfectionist, and a rather tormented young man, possibly because of the cast in one eye. . . . I remember him sitting on a bench backstage at the Empire [Theatre] while we were waiting to go on, and he said, 'Everybody hates me.' Emotionally, he was quite insecure, which may explain his drive for perfection."

Doris Humphrey and Charles Weidman asked a lot of their dancers. Some were to complain later that they were "used, but not trained." Both Humphrey and Weidman, to keep the group together, with the aid of Pauline Lawrence, who completed a kind of dance studio *troika,* gave classes to earn money. They gave concerts of their works, when opportunities presented themselves. But it was a constant struggle to survive, let alone to choreograph creatively and find appreciative audiences and responsive critics. Group members, who also helped fill the communal "kitty" by teaching, even helped train each other, sharing special areas of dance expertise.

Letitia Ide recalls those frantic days: "You didn't get paid unless there was a concert. There was no regular pay at all. You couldn't take an outside job, but if you worked with them, you still couldn't make a living. That was the catch! It was difficult because the rehearsal schedule was irregular. But people did pose for sculptors and artists. A few may have worked at Macy's, but that was very tricky because the schedule varied so much and the times when there might be performances out of town. And we had to be ready to go!

"Doris Humphrey was very much loved by everyone in the company. But she was very serious; there wasn't much time for fun. It came to a parting of the ways for some, because things just got too rugged, too difficult. Some of the kids couldn't manage and had to leave. But I know they respected her. I'm sure they loved her, too," Ide insists.

In one of Cole's scrapbooks, there's an invitation to a party from Doris Humphrey, pasted in a place of honor. Ide says, "Oh, they had fun on holidays. They'd have parties. Charles and Pauline Lawrence did marvelous imitations of Miss Ruth. They were lovely hosts, and we had a few nice company parties, but it wasn't fun and games." From that period, 1933-34, Cole also preserved in his scrapbook photographs of such Humphrey-Weidman stalwarts as Ada Korvin and Cole's longtime friend, the erstwhile dancer and, later, dance-photographer Marcus Blechman. His image is captioned: "With toes bloody but unbowed." Several photos show the Humphrey-Weidman troupe in various dance routines; one is from the Broadway production of *School for Husbands*.

Having departed the sheltering Berkshires for the unfriendly pavements of Manhattan in the summer of 1933, Cole almost immediately found himself back on the stage of Lewisohn Stadium. The Humphrey-Weidman group had been engaged to perform in August with the New York Philharmonic. Cole was used as a supporting male dancer. He shared the stage with José Limon, Blechman, John Glenn, William Matons, Gabriel Zuckerman, and Gene Martel in the *Farandole,* which had been created for the Cleveland Opera *Carmen* production.

What a contrast between John Martin on Denishawn and on Humphrey-Weidman. On the latter, just seen at the Lewisohn Stadium, he pontificated: ". . . there is not an ensemble anywhere in Western Europe that is its peer; for it has the rare combination of two first-rate 'stars,' an unusually strong line of soloists, impeccable teamwork, and one of the most gifted choreographers of the day." Some 12,000 watched, stretching, as Eleanor King describes it, "north and south for two city blocks . . ." At least Martin this time didn't single Cole out for reproof. Later in August, the program was repeated with the Philadelphia Orchestra in Robin Hood Dell.

Doris Humphrey, always pregnant with dance ideas, had been physically pregnant as well, so preparations for the successful concerts were fraught with added worry. Some dance educators and critics were becoming disturbed by what they saw as a new direction as well. At Humphrey-Weidman, training began with a foundation of natural movement, which was then followed by studies in distortion and stylization, leading to choreographic creation and performance. This distortion, says Eleanor King, "as a means of emphasis, of accentuation, was an inevitable hallmark of Humphrey-Weidman composition." Unquestionably, it also had an effect on the impressionable Jack Cole, who would shortly be doing the most remarkable things with and to his body on the dance floors of smart supperclubs and gangster-run nightspots.

After a recent and not so successful dance involvement in a Broadway production of a pre–Leonard Bernstein *Candide,* the Humphrey-Weidman dancers soon found themselves with almost more remunerative Broadway work than they could handle. Weidman was contracted to create dances for *As Thousands Cheer,* which ran almost a year, and *I'd Rather Be Right,* which managed only three months. Dancers were divided between the two shows. And then on October 16, 1933, there was the *School for Husbands* for the Theatre Guild, in which Cole participated, playing an Olympian. Humphrey set the major dance, with Weidman playing a dancing master and Osgood Perkins as

Sganarelle, a favorite character of Molière's. The ballet was a wonderful mélange, featuring Egyptians and Olympians, as well as a passage with Weidman and Humphrey beautifully costumed as Harlequin and Columbine. The character of Harlequin later had an almost mystical appeal for Cole, and he used these *Commedia* characters and costumes in fascinating choreography of his own.

Eleanor King recalls Cole as "the most dedicated dancer of the boys, the most sophisticated in his acute sense of style, the one who demanded the most from himself and everyone else." Cole and his fellow dancers were rewarded with a run of fifteen weeks on Broadway.

This profitable skirmish with the commercial theatre, after the rigors of Denishawn one-night stands and endless high-mindedness about the dignity of the dance and the mission of the pioneers of serious new dance in America, surely had a marked effect on Cole. He had already been thinking about projecting his talents into the commercial arena, and he remembered that even Miss Ruth and Ted Shawn had not been too proud to appear in vaudeville and the *Ziegfeld Follies.*

This Theatre Guild confection was, however, no vulgar popular entertainment. Essentially, it was Molière's play, *School for Husbands,* enhanced by an imaginative playwright-inspired dream sequence. Well before Agnes de Mille's memorable dream ballet in *Oklahoma!* (1943), the decade of the 1930s would see Balanchine dream dances on Broadway, as well as this 1933 delight by Doris Humphrey.

Among the critical comments were Brooks Atkinson's judgment that the ballet was "self-consciously literary" and Burns Mantle's opinion that the show was "a thing of beauty and a joy for sixty minutes."

This exercise in bygone style and period charm was soon augmented by the December 1933 opening of the Palais Royale, a newly refurbished premises on Broadway between 47th and 48th Streets. Operating as a supperclub, with such talent as the Boswell Sisters and Emil Coleman's orchestra, the Palais Royale asked the Humphrey-Weidman dancers to do a dinner show before *School for Husbands,* followed by a later supper show. The dancers were no longer starving, but they were being worn down by the logistics of two moves per night, not to mention the contrasts between the two shows.

Jack Cole and Eleanor King danced the tango at the Palais. Cole saved the *Variety* review, which in part said: "Imagine their [the audience's] surprise when the Charles Weidman dancers came on. A nightclub troupe without a smile amongst them— but more astonishing yet, simply covered with clothes. Opaque clothes, too. And not to make their torso tossing more insistent either, because, incredible though it may seem, there was no torso tossing. The girls at the tables figured it must be the Rebellion. They were terribly impressed."

King recalls that tango. Earlier, it had been a duet for her and José Limon, danced to Bizet's *Andalouse*. But, because Cole was shorter than Limon, King had to dance with her knees bent all the time. Because of Cole's shyness about his eye problem, which made him look away from people or at the floor, there was an indirectness in his danced approaches to King. Weidman thought this made the dance more sexy. Even more titillating to the viewers was the M.C.'s announcement on opening night that Cole and King had just been married that morning. It wasn't true; it was said to raise audience expectations for an especially steamy tango. The M.C. confided that, until this moment on the dance floor, Cole and King had not been able to be together. This suggestive and false introduction made King want to "sink through the floor."

With holiday matinées during this Christmas 1933 season, there would be 2:30 P.M. curtains at the Empire Theatre; a 7:00 P.M. dinner show at the Palais Royale; an 8:30 P.M. performance back at the Empire, followed by the 11:00 P.M. supper show at the Palais, with a repeat performance at 12:30 or 1:00 A.M. Many New Yorkers didn't have the price of a sandwich then, but at the Palais Royale, large audiences were able to wine and dine in style. This conspicuous consumption fortunately made it possible for the Humphrey-Weidman dancers to survive at a more than marginal level.

The experience served as a concrete demonstration to Jack

Cole how one could stage serious dances in a nightclub and succeed. It also made it clear that, no matter how pure and elevated were Humphrey's motives and goals, she was not too proud to let her work be seen in a nightclub, as long as it was her best, performed with all that the dancers could give it. King remembers the strain of this dual engagement. During a rehearsal for the *Cotillion* number, she was crying from fatigue. Cole had developed knee trouble—which was to bother him intermittently later in his career—and he asked Humphrey if he could avoid rehearsing the second position balance in *Life of the Bee*. Other dancers would be perching on his slanted legs. "No rehearse, no perform," Humphrey told him.

Cole had been making expeditions to Harlem to sample the music, the dance, and other more sinister aspects of its unique nightlife. He offered Eleanor King a chance to smoke a reefer. She cautiously tried it, with no interesting or ill effects. Cole told her some of the contraband cigarettes sold in Harlem didn't have any marijuana in them. But he couldn't know which they were until he'd tried smoking them. A later Cole club choreography would be called *Reefer Madness*.

After the New York run of *School for Husbands*, encouraged by some admiring reviews, the Theatre Guild took the production and the Humphrey-Weidman dancers on tour, opening in Pittsburgh at the Nixon Theatre. Moving on to Philadelphia and the Chestnut Street Theatre, the troupe celebrated Eleanor King's birthday. Cole gave her a goldfish in a glass bowl filled with water. It was not the most practical gift for traveling performers, but, undismayed, she carried the goldfish bowl while colleagues took care of tips, tickets, and luggage.

A bitterly cold Washington winter ended the tour in the nation's capital after only a week there, with no hope of a promised Boston booking. But the Broadway experience had already done its damage. Dancers were lured by the steady salaries, so important in the grim days of the mid-1930s. Some of the Humphrey-Weidman regulars were ready to break free in any case. Cole this time did not have the option of leaving. He was dismissed for chronic lateness. He was an obviously talented dancer, but neither Weidman nor Humphrey would any longer overlook his lack of consideration for the rest of the company.

Cole already had formed some effective plans for his immediate future. He asked Alice Dudley, a St. Denis favorite, to become his partner in a nightclub duo. Manhattan's Embassy Club, operated by the notorious gangster Dutch Schultz, was their first engagement. Cole's venture into club work, which was to remain one of the three major arenas for his genius along with Broadway shows and Hollywood films, is a chapter in itself, spanning three decades. Even though Cole was well aware of the aesthetic damage the Broadway engagements had done to the Humphrey-Weidman company, he decided he liked eating rather than starving. Not only would he have a good and fairly stable income, he thought, but he would also have audiences he could astonish and delight with his technical virtuosity. He later insisted his decision was sound, that it was nonsense for a serious dancer "not to try his luck commercially . . ."

Nonetheless, Cole did not turn his back on serious work nor on further study. He continued reading and collecting dance books. He studied with experts, and he taught. It was a pattern of self-imposed discipline he was to follow throughout his career. No matter what his contractual obligations might be, Cole was always the teacher and taskmaster as well.

At this point in his life, Jack Cole found himself confronted with a choice. Two dance roads diverged. Serious modern dance, despite the gains made thanks to Denishawn, Graham, and Humphrey-Weidman, was still the less traveled path, and certainly far less well remunerated than the work of star dancers in musicals and revues. Cole decided not to take the less used road, and that made all the difference in his career.

Later, critics who early recognized his unique gifts blamed him for making such a choice. It mattered not at all that he was to spend much of his nonperformance time on serious study of dance, on training students, or on exhausting rehearsals and choreographing. Cole may not have been serving dance as high art in precisely the kind of temple dance purists would endorse, but his supperclub choreography was indeed fine art of

its kind. But what could Cole have done in any case? He preferred comfort to misery, eating to starving, working to waiting, and applause to silence. He could work in clubs; the recent
Humphrey-Weidman bookings had proved that. But his ego,
his temper, his eccentricities, and his apparent lack of discipline had all conspired to cut him off from two outstanding,
serious, noncommerical dance ensembles. He had no financial
reserves. He knew no craft or profession except dancing. With
his reputation for being difficult, would any other high-minded
dance company be eager to have Jack Cole on its roster?

He thought not, and he made his choice. But, given his
protean dance interests and his boundless energy, he didn't cut
himself off from Miss Ruth nor from such fellow dancers as
Eleanor King and Marcus Blechman, who was becoming an expert dance photographer. At the height of his early success as
a club dancer at the Rainbow Room and elsewhere, Cole still
found time to appear in the title role of Eleanor King's haunting *Icaro*. This was premiered on April 10, 1937, in the Sculpture Court of the Brooklyn Museum.

For several compelling reasons, Eleanor King decided that
Icaro was a drama for which she wished to create a dance. David
Diamond composed the score. King enlisted the cooperation of
such dance friends as Cole, his nightclub partner Alice Dudley,
George Bockman, Katherine Litz, and Ada Korvin. Cole was to
dance Icaro. Dudley was Phaedra. Kenneth Bostock was Icaro's
luckless father, Daedalus. Litz danced Ariadne to the Theseus
of Bockman. Three readers uttered the original Italian text—no
translation—with four musicians accompanying. King has re-
created the entire experience in *Transformations*. Wearing white,
Cole wielded wings made of aluminum moldings, which, says
King, flashed and rippled. The rest of the dancers wore black
practice outfits, with the classical pillars of the Sculpture Court
setting the scene of this "pre-Hellenic Dance Drama."

"In this choreographic production of *Icaro*," a program note
informed the curious, "the attempt has been to achieve through
a synthesis of movement, words, and music the fullest expression of the heroic drama." King remembers the audience as being
several thousand strong. A professional reviewer had this to say

about Icaro and Phaedra: "Jack Cole and Alice Dudley formerly danced with Ted Shawn and Ruth St. Denis. Cole gave an efficient performance, but Miss Dudley seemed not to have mastered her material fully. Both approached their new task with what appeared to be devotional respect."

Doris Humphrey had some thoughtful, positive things to say. Unlike St. Denis and Shawn, bitterly complaining of disloyalty when their flock had begun to scatter, Humphrey knew how to be generous and supportive. Ruth St. Denis was also in the audience, and her response, conveyed in a note to Cole, was very enthusiastic. She said in part: "You were simply superb! The scene with you and . . . Duds [Dudley] was marvelous! Both in feeling as well as technique . . ." She had very high praise both for Eleanor King's aims in *Icaro*, and for what she achieved. The work was repeated for an audience of a hundred in the much smaller space of Studio 61, in Carnegie Hall on May 2. *Icaro* won honorable mention that year from *Dance Magazine*, as it launched its first annual awards.

Even though Jack Cole had rapidly become a successful dancer-choreographer on the nightclub circuit, at this time he did not turn his back on serious dance concert efforts. They had been his initial exposure to the dance, and his apprenticeship as well. Now it was time for the boy to become a man, to demonstrate both his genius and his discipline.

5

COLE'S CAREER IN THE CLUBS

STREWING PEARLS BEFORE SWINE?

The Eighteenth Amendment to the Constitution of the United States instituted Prohibition. Carrie Nation had succeeded. But resourceful Americans who craved a drink could generally find one, as even more resourceful gangsters devised strategies to meet the need. In the 1920s, the speakeasy became a secretive rendezvous, where both socialites and serious drinkers could slake their thirsts and often enjoy the talents of some striking entertainers.

Then, in December 1933, Prohibition came to an end with the Twenty-first Amendment. For Jack Cole, correcting the Constitution couldn't have come at a more opportune moment. New clubs were opening; older ones were making themselves more chic. There was a need for flash and glitter, for entertainment that dazzled, but which didn't discourage drinking.

For his partner, Cole chose Alice Dudley, known as "Duds" to her friends at Denishawn, where she was, as Jane Sherman remembers, "one of Miss Ruth's most beautiful 'children.' " Preserved in Jack Cole's scrapbooks and elsewhere among his papers are a number of photos of the glowingly lovely young Alice Dudley, as well as duos with a pensive, saturnine Cole. Dudley's beauty shines so radiantly in these pictures that it's easy to understand the superlatives showered on her by cabaret reviewers. Following *School for Husbands,* Cole and Dudley were engaged to perform at the Embassy Club, on East 57th Street. Mobster Dutch Schultz ran the Embassy, and he obviously respected Cole's energy and seeming toughness. Not only that, Cole's choreography was so radically different from typical club acts, that even somnolent drunks sat bolt upright to watch Cole and Dudley make the sparks fly up from the dance floor.

Cole was later to reminisce about this initial booking. He was surprised that he'd been so quickly hired. True, the Humphrey-Weidman dancers had been well received at the Palais Royale, but now it would be just Cole and Dudley on their own.

Although Cole's interest in learning ethnic dance steps was insatiable at this time, he realized that authentic reconstructions would be too arty for patrons who had come to have a martini or enjoy a supper. Nonetheless, Cole decided to give the customers his best, in hopes that he might be able to astonish them enough to forget about their drinks or soups for the duration of the act.

With *Blue Prelude* and *Minnie the Moocher*, he certainly succeeded. Audiences stared at Dudley and Cole in wonder. Some spectators were annoyed by the sounds of bare feet slapping on the polished floor. But, since Dutch Schultz liked Cole's work, who were they to protest? Cole at first felt acute anxiety at being stared at. At Denishawn and with Humphrey-Weidman, he could always blend into the group. Now he and Dudley were alone in the spotlight.

Reports of their exciting dancing spread. The duo was engaged for *Caviar*, a cabaret revue produced at the Forrest Theatre in midtown Manhattan. This show opened on May 28, 1934, promoted as "The Brilliant Summer Musical Treat," with the "Most Stunning Chorus on Broadway." *Caviar*'s press agent advised the public that the revue also contained the "Most Daring Dance of the Century." This routine, presented in the context of a cabaret scene, was Cole and Dudley's duet *Appassionette*. The developing Cole style drew this comment from a cabaret critic: ". . . a matter of much violent and rather decadent jerking and posturing, seemed to find favor with the audience." If not with the critic—

The Dudley-Cole duo was also invited to appear on the vast stage of the recentiy opened Radio City Music Hall. *Satan's Serenade* was the first Radio City show for Cole in 1934. The format of these theme-revues, which accompanied major film premieres, was a fairly rigid sequence of dancing and singing numbers, related to some topical event, a holiday, or an interesting design concept. It's a formula that was still being used in the early 1980s, though minus the motion picture premieres.

Cole explained how he choreographed for his Radio City stints: "Our dances depended on what the big stage set was for that week. They might call and ask, 'What can you do in front of twenty sheets of plate glass?' It was the first time people were used to activate the scenery." When Jean Arthur and Joel McCrea were emoting on the Music Hall's giant screen in *Adventure in Manhattan*, Cole and Dudley were getting ready to amaze the audiences, sometimes 6,000 strong, in three or four shows a day, with a routine called *Triangles*. When Jean Hersholt appeared on screen in *Sins of Man*, the accompanying revue was *Smoke Shadows*. Robert Weede sang "Love Is Like a Cigarette," and Jack Cole and Alice Dudley danced to "Over a Cigarette."

On September 9, 1937, the Music Hall revue was labeled *Lantern Gleams*. Among the various lantern-linked routines was Cole's *Japanese Lanterns*, in which he performed a Japanese spear dance, probably inspired by Ted Shawn's. Cole had often been critical of the spurious ethnology of Denishawn choreography, but he was now finding, in his own work, that a riveting theatrical effect, interpolated into an otherwise accurately observed Hindu or flamenco routine, captured and held his audiences. In the vast reaches of Radio City Music Hall one had to be electrifying, larger than life, to project beyond the footlights. One reviewer noted of Cole's choreography in *Japanese Lanterns* that the spear dance was well executed. "Mr. Cole had good lines and did many showy leaps and difficult floor rolls, which might have been sensational in a smaller theatre." Other Cole admirers were to recall that the Radio City stage was just too big; even with Cole's tremendous vitality, his choreography didn't show to best effect at the Music Hall.

In 1934, the initial year of the Cole-Dudley partnership, there were a series of successes. Both theatre professionals and the public were becoming aware of the dynamic Cole talents. On December 27, 1934, a John Murray Anderson revue, *Thumbs Up*, opened on Broadway at the St. James Theatre, which ran nearly five months, fairly good in the midst of the Depression. "Zing Went the Strings of My Heart" and "Autumn in New York" were two musical hits in this show.

In the new year of 1935, *Vanity Fair*, as was its custom in celebrating both the justly famous and trendy new talents, published photos of the stylish Cole-Dudley duo from *Thumbs Up*, and judged: "Their dancing is intensely modern, dramatic, and striking in its great clarity of style. It seems certain that they are destined for continued success." The *New Yorker's* critic, the popular humorist Robert Benchley, also praised Cole and Dudley.

Significantly, Cole and Dudley, with Cole's distinctive, imaginative choreography, were not successors to those other famous dancing duos, Vernon and Irene Castle, and Fred and Adele Astaire. Cole was not remotely interested in ballroom dancing. Luckily, his surprising innovations were generally welcomed by audiences. So much so that Cole and Dudley were also invited to perform across the street from Radio City Music Hall at its rival, Roxy's Theatre.

Pleased with Cole's work at Radio City Music Hall, when the Rockefeller interests opened the art deco Rainbow Room at the pinnacle of the RCA Building, they invited Jack Cole and Alice Dudley to perform. Cole's work was so admired that even when he was engaged elsewhere, the Rainbow Room management begged for dancers trained and choreographed by Cole.

From various reports, working with Cole was never easy. It must have been especially taxing for John Roy, manager of the Rainbow Room, as well as renting manager for Rockefeller Center. Some gossip items reported that Cole and Roy were clashing fiercely. At one point, Cole quit cold, only to return after being soothed. Shortly before the May 1938 opening of a new Rainbow Room show, it was hinted in the gossip columns that Cole was ailing and might not be able to appear. Cole relented and offered some dances of Bali: *Play Dance* and *Love Dance*, not the usual nightclub fare. A reviewer thought Cole had "one of the best acts on a cabaret floor." Following this Rainbow Room stint, Billy Rose immediately engaged Cole for his Casa Mañana, formerly the home of Earl Carroll's *Vanities*, at 7th Avenue and 50th Street. One cabaret critic insisted that Cole's work in this revue was "the only worthwhile thing at Casa Mañana."

Cole took not one, but two new partners, when Alice Dudley and he parted. They were his Denishawn confidante, Anna Austin, with whom he'd set up a dance school and studio, and Florence Lessing. Austin and Lessing complemented each other marvelously in both looks and technique. What's more, they were perfect feminine foils for the sultry suggestiveness and the arrogant aggression of the Cole male dance-persona. In later years, although each went her own way professionally and personally, they both remained close to Cole and responded whenever he needed their help.

In addition to Cole's engagements in the late 1930s and early 1940s at the Rainbow Room, Radio City, Roxy's, and the Casa Mañana, Anna Austin has made a list which includes the Strand and Loew's theatres and the Plaza Hotel in New York, as well as Chicago's Chez Paree, Detroit's Book-Cadillac Hotel, the Latin Quarter and the Surf Club in Miami Beach and the Hollywood Hotel in Hollywood, Florida. When Cole was in Los Angeles, Ciro's and Slapsie Maxie's hosted his act. In San Francisco, there were engagements at the Fairmont and the Mark Hopkins hotels. When the United States was getting involved in World War II, in 1941, Cole, Florence Lessing, and Marian Lawrence went to Rio de Janeiro for highly successful performances at the Copacabana.

Only a few years after the shy, insecure, undisciplined, and disruptive Jack Cole had left Shawn and Humphrey-Weidman, an amazing transformation had occurred. He was feisty, assertive, aggressive, ferociously disciplined, and astonishingly creative. One journalist dubbed Cole "An American Nijinsky." Walter Terry, who ordinarily wouldn't waste his time on supperclub dancing, reviewed Cole's work with admiration and understanding. Initially, what had so amazed nightclub audiences was Cole's uncompromising insistence on the validity of ethnic dances as vital entertainment. In itself, this was revolutionary in cabaret programming. Cole's adaptations of Indian, Balinese, and Afro-American dance techniques were not intended to be museum-quality reproductions. It was necessary to heighten and theatricalize the dances.

One of the most arresting of the Cole theatrical effects was his knee slides. Anna Austin says these were first shown in *Georgia Revival Meeting*, danced to "Swing Low, Sweet Chariot." Cole dropped to his knees upstage and slid downstage on them twice. At the close of this dance sequence, all three dancers,

Cole, Austin, and Lessing, did knee slides. The knee slides were so successful that Cole often danced on his knees after that. From this and possible childhood injuries, Cole developed the knee trouble that was to plague him for years. But he suffered the pain, rather than surrender the effect.

Cole's most noted innovation, however, was the coupling of authentic ethnic dance with jazz accompaniment. Before Cole's experiments, no one had thought of such a thing; after these were rapidly praised by critics, many began to imitate Cole. A testimony to Cole's ingenuity in this matter, from the Broadway choreographer-director Donald Saddler, makes it clear that the initial idea was not Cole's, but that of Marcus Blechman. Saddler was a friend of Blechman's, though not of Cole's, when the two were Humphrey-Weidman dancers. Blechman wasn't, Saddler says, "a very good dancer. He was very musical, however, so he led the line in and counted the music. At that time, no serious dancer was appearing in clubs. Marcus had this jazz recording. He played it for Jack and said, 'Why don't you do what you're doing, this East Indian dance, but do it to this jazz?' That evolved into a whole new vocabulary of jazz dancing, for which we have to thank Jack Cole."

Florence Lessing confirms this version of the origin of "Jazz Dance," and is firm on this point: "In fact, our first rehearsals of the East Indian dance to jazz were held in Marcus's apartment. Then we had our first engagement at the Rainbow Room." Although Cole, emulating his Denishawn experience, at first danced the dances of India to ethnic music, he soon began to perform them to swing, with accompaniments by Raymond Scott and Larry Clinton, among others. It was not until 1942, according to Florence Lessing, that Marcus Blechman gave him the idea of performing various ethnic dances to a jazz beat. Cole's first public demonstration of this was his *Wedding of a Solid Sender*, danced to "Yes, Indeed." Benny Goodman's music was an inspiration to Cole in these combinations, as was the music of Duke Ellington. 1947 was the year Cole created the frenetic *Sing, Sing, Sing* choreography.

"I got to know Jack Cole at Anna Austin's studio," Lessing recalls. "She had been a Denishawn dancer, and she was teaching the East Indian work, à la Miss Ruth, so it wasn't terribly authentic. You know, lots of draperies, but not much accuracy. I joined the classes because someone had told me about them. I'd first seen Cole in a Spanish dance class. He was doing a cape dance, with a cigarette in his hand all the time. He had to do something aggressive. The teacher didn't like it, but you couldn't forget it.

"Jack very quickly took over Anna's classes. He said he was going to teach, and that was that. Then he abstracted it farther and farther from the Denishawn school. Once he had removed it from that influence, he made it more authentic. That's how Anna Austin and I came to dance with him," Lessing says. Among the dances developed at this time were *War Dance of the Wooden Indians*, which Lessing remembers as fun to do and very inventive. 1939 was the year of *Oriental Impressions*. In 1941, there was *Polynesian Faun*, inspired by *L'après-midi d'un Faun*, and *Latin Impressions*, given impetus by Cole's interest in Caribbean rhythms and movements.

As a Rainbow Room regular, Cole became a prized, pampered artist. Initially, however, things were different. Even though a featured performer, he had to take the service rather than the passenger elevator. Cole angrily referred to it as the "garbage" elevator. The management objected to his customary streetwear: moccasins, heavy woolen socks, dark green corduroy trousers, and gray flannel shirt. They weren't about to expose paying customers in evening dress to such sartorial atrocities. They did not much like Cole's monkish tonsure either.

Once Cole and his partners were on the dance floor, however, it was quite a different matter. Florence Lessing remembers how it used to be: "It was a very elegant audience. We had to put on evening dresses to go to the Ladies' Room. There was no provision for the performers, and the room was very formal. That was a nuisance, but it was such an elegant place! Not like clubs now. And because the audience represented a kind of quality, it was a pleasure to dance for them."

One of these spectators, at least, appreciated the quality and the origins of Cole's Rainbow Room work. This was Leticia Jay, who wrote an extended essay on modern American dance, saluting Jack Cole as the father of jazz dance. She reported: "The first modern jazz dancing that I saw was his 'Wedding of a Solid Sender' [1942]. It employed the principles of sharp dynamics and clarity of line characteristic of Bharata Natyam technique, without in any way suggesting East Indian type of dance . . ." Cole thought enough of this tribute to preserve it in one of his scrapbooks. Florence Lessing reports that the Lindy dance step was really the basis of *Wedding of a Solid Sender*, a lively, amusing salute to a flamboyantly dressed zoot-suiter.

Cole's audiences often saw him with naked, oiled torso, set off by gleaming loose pantaloons of gold lamé, with circlets of bells and rattles on arms and legs, and eyelids heavy with makeup and paste jewels. Or in a bolero, fluffy with bird feathers, dominating the trim lines of black flamenco trousers and a tight gold cummerbund. Or in a beautifully woven oriental silk *dhoti,* patterned with flowers and topped by a tightly wrapped torso cloth, reaching to his bare chest, with a flower over his right ear and a whisk in his right hand. Austin and Lessing, on the other hand, were seldom so exposed as Cole. He saw to it that their splendid costumes would move wonderfully with the Cole choreography and make the two attractive women even more fascinating, but always complement—never eclipse—the central Cole performance.

Shortly before he died, Walter Terry reminisced about some of the Cole shows he saw in the Rainbow Room: "To use a cliché, he was very cat-like in movement. He was small and very slight. At the Rainbow Room, I remember him doing not only the oriental dances to jazz, but also Harlem dances, in brown chinos, with bare feet and bare torso. I think he must have been the first to use Harlem rhythms that weren't done in terms of taps. In the Rainbow Room, something like *that!"*

Reviewers of Cole's club acts in those days often exhausted their fund of adjectives, trying to describe the physicality of Cole's movements. It was not unusual for Cole to race ferociously in one direction, only to reverse with equal energy in an instant. Or suddenly to leap straight up, as though he intended to shoot through the ceiling. Or downward, as though he hoped to pound a hole downward to the cellars.

Florence Lessing recalls a six-month period when the ensemble's performance schedule had to be broken owing to a strep infection in one of Cole's knees. Other than that, however, he always worked hard and steadily. Cole told Walter Terry that he'd been to see a doctor about his knees. The doctor asked him how old he was. The still youthful Cole told him. The doctor shook his head: "Well, you may be that young, but your knees are a *hundred* years old. You've given them that much punishment." Terry also remembered the six-month recuperation. "But he was brutal about his body, to keep the absolute steel-like perfection he had," Terry explained.

If Cole was severe with himself, he could be even more demanding of others with whom he collaborated. Almost everyone who worked with Cole has mentioned his temper, white hot and raging because of some failure in technique or some infraction of discipline. But Cole's was a temper which would later, damped down and turned off, often be replaced with a needling joke or a sardonic smile. The harvest of Cole's hair-trigger emotional responses, as can be imagined, has been an ambivalence toward Cole as a person, even at this distance in time. Cole provoked some real love-hate feelings in his dancers, but, in retrospect, these are modified by the admission that Cole was right to demand what he did, considering the stunning results in performance.

The results were memorable. Buzz Miller, who was a later dancer-colleague of Cole's, comments on Cole's peculiar genius in concocting nightclub choreography so original that there was nothing with which to compare it: "Jack wasn't a person who just did dances. He was very conceptual. You could see Jack's stamp on every show, film, or nightclub act. You could sense his mood from the way a piece was danced. It's said he never did a concert piece, but he really made concert pieces out of everything he did, whether for nightclubs or Broadway. He brought serious work to places which before had nothing but girls in plumes-and-bananas to offer. And he and Agnes de Mille also did that for the Broadway musical theatre!"

One reason Cole's choreography was so distinctive, no

matter what the ethnic basis, was his fanatic insistence on clarity and precision in movement. Nothing sloppy, nothing tentative, nothing improvised in the manner of Ruth St. Denis. In the clubs, as well as on Broadway and in films, perfection—and nothing less—was Cole's acceptable standard of performance. Fortunately, both Anna Austin and Florence Lessing gave Cole what he demanded on the dance floor, and they were both fond of him as well.

Lessing says she could withstand some of the outbursts of temper because: "Jack and I were very good friends. We'd dance the evening performance, and then go out social dancing for the rest of the night, especially to the rhumba clubs." She also realized that the flashes of Cole ire soon passed. But both orchestra leaders and club patrons learned to fear Jack Cole's righteous wrath. Walter Terry recalled an incident involving the Rainbow Room's Eddie Le Baron, whose band was accompanying a difficult Cole choreography. Cole stopped mid-dance and said, "You have your way of counting. And I have mine. Why don't we have a conference and see if we can't come to some sort of an agreement? Then we can get on with this show!" He said that right in front of the audience, said Terry, sighing at the memory.

This was not an isolated or unusual occurrence. Another time, Terry had taken Miss Ruth to the Rainbow Room to watch Cole's East Indian dances. Things weren't going well with the conductor. Cole was clearly furious. "At intermission," Terry said, "we could hear him way backstage, screaming invectives. Miss Ruth was talking to me about something, but broke off to listen. 'Dear,' she said, 'I think the vibrations are wrong. I'd better go back.' Cole told me afterward that he'd told the conductor that the man could neither count nor conduct. He told the manager of the Rainbow Room that he wouldn't do the second act. He'd even told one of the Rockefeller brothers, who owned the building, that they could throw him in jail for the rest of his life. He'd prefer that, to dancing with that idiot with the baton. At this point, Miss Ruth came in. 'Now, dear, what *is* it?' she asked." Cole told Terry how he sat down and told

St. Denis how wrong the beat was, how far off were the rhythms. "She just sat there," Terry reported, "and said, 'Yes, dear. Yes, dear.'

"After Cole finished a detailed account of what was wrong with the music," said Terry, "Miss Ruth looked at Cole and said, 'I know exactly how you feel, only with me, it's *Life!*' Cole looked at her in astonishment, then burst out laughing. He told me, 'I thought, oh, what's the use?' and went back on and did the second act. But that will show you something about Cole's moods. He was an odd mixture of emotions. When Miss Ruth was on tour, he even took care of her parrot, Dada, who was a miserable beast."

Buzz Miller confirms Cole's temperament: "If the musicians weren't playing the right tempo, he'd start stomping. You wouldn't believe where this creature was coming from. It was like some wild animal on the floor, when he got angry. If the musicians were too slow, he'd do the whole number three bars ahead. He'd finish it and stomp off—not missing a beat—with the musicians still playing away. Sometimes he was possessed, chasing a conductor around in his Indian costume!"

Anna Austin usually managed to escape the famed Cole wrath. Terry called her a "very good dancer, a very attractive dancer." He'd discussed her talents with Cole, who told him that Austin would get bored with the dance routines after a while. According to Terry, "After six weeks in the same show, Anna'd begin to notice friends in the audience. In the middle of a number, she'd wave to them, do something to let them know she'd seen them. Jack told me: 'Except that she made me laugh, I would have killed her.' " Today, Anna Austin is understandably annoyed at Terry's tale. She says, "I did *not* wave to anyone in the audience, and I only started getting bored after doing the same dances for *ten* weeks. But it's true that Jack never yelled at me. I think that's because we had a deep love for each other."

Once, some Rainbow Room patrons got a show no one had expected, least of all Jack Cole. His dressing room was just below the observation deck of the RCA Building. There was a terrace adjoining, opposite the bank of elevators rising to the deck above. Before performances, Cole would exercise on the terrace. If the weather were nice, Cole would warm up for his act completely nude. Customarily, the elevators took tourists right up to the observation deck, but one evening, the doors opened at Cole's floor. There, in all his sinewy masculine glory was the sweat-glistening Jack Cole, facing the astonished out-of-towners. Cole told friends that he then took a very deep bow, facing downward until the doors had closed. He said that night those tourists had got more for their money than the patrons of the Rainbow Room.

Gwen Verdon, who worked the clubs with Cole in the late 1940s, also has some tales of Cole bravado. Chicago's Chez Paree, she remembers, was really run by Murder, Inc. And, as with Dutch Schultz at the Embassy Club in New York, the gangsters thought Cole was terrific and his act a knockout. "They thought Jack Cole was the most extraordinary thing they'd ever seen! If you were noisy, they simply put you out. If you were really raucous, and they couldn't budge you without making a big commotion, the head-waiter—and I saw this happen—would put a salt-shaker in a napkin and tap the guy on the head. He'd pass out, at least until the show was over.

"That's why Jack worked all the nightclubs, from Florida to Vegas. The mob really liked his work. I mean, Bugsy Segal thought Jack Cole was the greatest thing that ever hit Vegas. But he always said, 'I wouldn't want to meet Cole in a dark alley.' They all said that about him, because he was kind of weird-looking. The more you knew Cole, though, he became absolutely beautiful," Verdon says.

Although many of the clubs were run by gangsters, says Florence Lessing, Cole and his partners were always treated with the greatest courtesy and respect. Owners and managers recognized Cole's work as something very special, even if some of the patrons did not. Lessing says, "Jack got these people to stop eating and drinking by sheer force of personality and intensity. He had this knack. That's one of the most valuable things I learned from him: how to command an audience's attention.

He did it not only through these sharp changes of direction and level, and his strong physical action, but also by doing *nothing*."

There was, for instance, very little dance movement in *Babalu*, one of Cole's *Latin Impressions*. ". . . an absolute minimum of movement," Lessing stresses. "Jack and I walked a bit, stood, or sat, but we never lost eye-contact. There was a very intense personal thing going on. That held the audience. But even in a dance with a lot of action, Jack would suddenly stop and turn his head very slowly—or just gyrate his hips very slowly. Everything would be very silent, very quiet, after great outbursts of energy. That's what I mean by Jack Cole's wonderful dynamics. You can use this in any kind of dance," Lessing observes.

There were times when audiences saw The Jack Cole Dancers, instead of Jack Cole and His Dancers. He was still appearing with supporting dancers in the late 1950s and early 1960s, but in 1938, very early in his supperclub success, he had to form a Jack Cole group without the master-dancer at its center. Cole's dances at the Rainbow Room had won him an engagement with Billy Rose at the Casa Mañana. But the Rainbow Room's manager wanted Cole's dances, even if he couldn't have Cole himself. So Cole formed the Ballet Intime. He engaged and trained Ernestine Day, an erstwhile Ted Shawn partner, Letitia Ide, Fe Alf, Eleanor King, for whom he'd danced *Icaro* the year before, and George Bockman. The numbers programmed for the six-week engagement were *Begin the Beguine, Pawnee Indian War Dance*, Ravel's *Bolero*, and *Georgia Revival Meeting*, with its knee slides.

The high point of the Ballet Intime's choreography was the *Georgia Revival Meeting*. The music Cole used when he, Austin, and Lessing had first performed it was "Swing Low, Sweet Chariot." Initially, the melody was played in traditional tempo; then it was syncopated, jazzed up for a smashing finish, in which George Bockman had to do the Cole knee slide, his body inclined away from the audience, while the women frantically shook their skirts. Ovations were unusual in the Rainbow Room, but this dance earned them. A cabaret critic found the routine the most exciting moment of the evening.

In 1940, Cole and his partners, Austin and Lessing, were the first dance team to be featured on a live television broadcast from New York City. This new medium was indeed an infant—in fact, a World's Fair novelty to most people—but Cole was able to project his club dances effectively on it. New York audiences weren't the only ones clamoring for Cole and his routines. He also made a hit at the Chez Paree in Chicago, to which he returned a number of times. In August 1942, his opening was saluted by a Hirschfeld caricature depicting Cole as a zoot-suiter. There was also a Hirschfeld sketch of Cole with Lessing and Austin. The *Chicago Times* headlined its Cole story: "Marihuana Frenzy in Harlem at 4 o'clock in the Morning." Among the offerings on the program were Cole's *Reefer Man*, *Reefer Joint at 4 A.M.*, *Wedding of a Solid Sender*, *Nanigo*—a Cuban witchcraft dance—and some East Indian dances.

In Cole's scrapbooks he usually didn't bother to indicate the dates of critiques. A review from the early 1940s at the Chez Paree gives an idea of how Cole was received in the Windy City: "Jack Cole, who carries the entire burden of the Chez 'midstream' changeover show, is even more startling than he was two months ago. He is a young man with an incredible imagination which constantly reveals new facets with every subtle turn of his head. His absorption might be called fanatical. His animalism makes you squirm, but his penitent's face is hypnotic."

At this period, Cole was performing with four women and three conga drummers, according to Chicago reports. A gossip item, with no date, appears in a Cole scrapbook: he has had his *fourth* engagement at Chez Paree in less than a year.

Singer Dolores Gray met Cole very early in her own career. She was much impressed with Cole and his partners, Austin and Lessing, and recalls: "I always found his work fascinating because he had this fabulously elegant style that was his alone. He had a slight cast in one eye—and he always wore jewels over his eyelids. It made him look far apart from anything one would see in the ordinary world. He became a very arty figure. His appearances were always very startling because they were so colorful and his dancing was so strong. Then he'd suddenly disappear, never to come back."

In the thick of Cole's Hollywood film-making, a major studio strike brought production to a halt and contracts weren't renewed. Cole then made Hollywood audiences sit up at places like Ciro's and Slapsie Maxie's. He took his dancers on the road again. Florence Lessing was his partner in January 1947 when the troupe of eleven opened at Chicago's Chez Paree. There were three shows nightly, with Tony Martin and Pearl Bailey heading the bill. One reviewer commented on Cole's oriental dances, ". . . although movements are stilted routine, it doesn't lack grace and agility." A newspaper photo-feature bore the headline: "Dancer Spoofs the Public and It Pays Off." Using native dances with a swing band was regarded as a clever gimmick, though by this time it was hardly a novelty with Cole. Among the numbers that captured this reviewer's interest were what he called a *Cuban Love Dance, Persian Market,* and *Wooden Indian,* and he wrote about *Persian Market:* "Miss Lessing and Cole scurry through an imaginary market-place with dead pan actions, leaving the emphasis on fast foot and arm business."

This critic was certain Cole was putting something over on his Chicago audiences. Cole was kidding the public, he insisted. ". . . heavy dance made palatable," he reported. He liked the troupe, which included Carol Haney, as well as Lessing. The calypso singers and native drummers in the West Indian numbers also won praise, but this reviewer was not to be fooled. He told his readers it was ". . . one of the finest hoke jobs of the interpretative school, à la Martha Graham, with much of it way over the average cafe audience head. However, table-sitters appreciated it even as a straight job."

Hollywood must have seemed a closed chapter for Cole. There were to be no more films for Columbia Pictures, so Cole had asked the members of his studio dance ensemble if they'd like to join his nightclub act.

Rod Alexander remembers: "There were dropouts naturally, leaving George and Ethel Martin, Carol Haney, myself,

Bob Hamilton, Ruth Godfrey, and Alex Romero. He then brought in Florence Lessing, with whom he'd danced before, to be his partner. With very little time and a great deal of hard work, we prepared two East Indian dances and two Afro-Cuban dances." In Chicago, they worked on a dance to Benny Goodman's "Sing, Sing, Sing." Cole and the three men, says Alexander, "kicked, spun, slammed, and slid on our knees for seven minutes in true Jack Cole style. It was a tremendous hit with the audience."

This number and the others repeated Cole's Chicago success in New York at the Latin Quarter, run by Lou Walters, father of the TV personality Barbara Walters. Then it was back to Los Angeles and Slapsie Maxie's, where, Alexander reports, Cole began having temper tantrums with orchestra leaders again. Once, he slammed his makeup hand-mirror against the wall in frustration. A shard cut his hand. Carol Haney was now Cole's partner, and it was back to New York for another engagement. Cole was contracted to choreograph a new musical, *Bonanza Bound*, so he told Rod Alexander he would have to take his place. Unfortunately, Cole was too busy on the musical to teach Alexander his own routines. He had to master them on his own. Cole also forgot to tell the others about the new arrangement.

They were booked into a Florida club and would have to be in top form, without Cole there to drill and scold them. Alexander, with no car, found it almost impossible to round them up from their unaccustomed freedom—sunbathing on the beaches—for requisite rehearsals. *Bonanza Bound* proved the misnomer of the 1940s. It wasn't even bound for Broadway, as things turned out, closing out of town and losing, not winning, a bonanza. That brought Cole to Florida and his dancers after they'd been performing for several weeks. Cole took over; he imported Gwen Verdon to replace Carol Haney. Bob Hamilton was also leaving, as was Alexander, who had to be in New York for rehearsals with Helen Tamiris on *Inside U.S.A.*

Gwen Verdon says she first auditioned for Jack Cole when she was underage; she was already a very young mother, but she was too young to work in clubs so she was fired. As soon as she was old enough, in 1947, however, Cole took her back.

Because there was gambling in the Florida club where Cole's dancers were performing, Cole saw to it that Verdon had a chaperone. He also insisted that she finish school through correspondence courses. She earned her high school diploma. As she now says, "Three more credits, and I'd have an M.A. in social work! That's all because of Jack Cole." Although Verdon was replacing Haney and was prepared to do all she had done, at least in terms of body movement, she had to work hard. "I learned all the East Indian dance. Whenever Uday Shankar was in town, we'd have a group study class with him," she says.

Buzz Miller, who soon joined the club act, remembers that Cole ". . . liked to get up every day and dance until he was silly. We worked extremely hard. He could go over one bar for days, until everyone was absolutely exact. We were all strong as bulls because we worked from 11 A.M. till dinnertime. And we'd have three shows that night. I was in the nightclub act until 1950, when he broke it up.

"Nightclub audiences then were good. Cole had a terrific following, people who appreciated what he was doing. It wasn't your ordinary nightclub act at all. When I first went to California, a friend took me to see it. I was overwhelmed. It blew my head off. I couldn't have known that, in a couple of weeks, I'd be in the act," Miller comments. "In *Sing, Sing, Sing,* we'd do these slides and slams into the floor. Then we'd go right back up. I don't know how to describe it." Buzz Miller had become a member of Cole's dance nucleus, and he was much later to teach the Cole Technique for the American Dance Machine.

In 1947, Cole was getting back into his stride as a full-time club performer. A columnist noted that Cole and his troupe ought to get more than the $2,500 per week paid by the Latin Quarter. Cole used nine dancers, it was reported, and they presented sixteen minutes of dance, including the East Indian "jive ballet," West Indian calypso, and the zoot-suiter. In March, the *Times*'s John Martin had reviewed Cole's Latin Quarter show, noting his Hindu dancing to jazz music as "a curiously amusing combination, which has taken on the status almost of an established form." Martin said, "Besides being a good dancer, Mr. Cole is a good choreographer and a good showman."

Jack Cole may have told his studio dance group, of whom he was always protective, that the film contract with Columbia had come to an end, but it also appears that an initial reason for reactivating his club act may have been the rigors of protracted studio strikes. In his scrapbooks, Cole pasted this title six times on one page: "Cole Takes a Vacation from Films." On another page is a Cole complaint, cut up into separate words and scattered over the surface: "The stars don't know how to dance." This is from a tart Cole interview. Although an ad for the Latin Quarter of April 6, 1947, says Cole's current engagement must come to an end because Sophie Tucker begins a run on April 14, Cole told interviewer Frances Herridge that he had to be back in Hollywood on April 13. He told her he didn't want to return to the movie industry strike. He clipped a printed newspaper paragraph about this and included it in a complicated scrapbook collage, featuring photos of himself and Lessing. The paragraph read: "Jack Cole doesn't like Hollywood but he has to go back."

Whatever Cole thought of the motion picture industry—and he could be cynical and scathing by turns—he found his work valued when he and the company performed in Hollywood clubs. The *Los Angeles Times* noted that Cole was virtually unknown when he was working on films. A three-months-plus engagement at Slapsie Maxie's in 1947 made him famous. An engagement at Ciro's on Sunset Strip in the late 1940s drew Hollywood's elite. A critic commented: "The dancing as a whole was excellent, the costumes imaginative, and the music couldn't have been better." Supporting Cole were Gwenneth Verdon— who in this period spelled her name several ways before she settled on Gwen—Marie Groscup, Patricia Toun, Carl Ratcliff, and Richard D'Arch.

One of the more arresting Cole full-page doodles in his scrapbooks is related to Ciro's. A photo of the club, with signs advertising Cole and his singers, dancers, and musicians— "Ciro's Fun Festival . . . Jack Cole . . . Continuous Dancing Two Bands"—has been cut out to resemble a huge billboard, mounted on spindly black pillars. Two of these are also burdened with immense reticulated feet, as though the skin had been peeled from Cole's soles to reveal the brutally punished muscles and nerves. A very shaky pile of images of Freudian significance stand beside this Ciro's sign, atop a brick fireplace. Inside the arch of the fireplace is Cole in a picture from his 1950 choreography *Harlequin's Odyssey*, so the Ciro's experience was still weighing on him in the 1950s—or whenever he got around to pasting up this scrapbook page.

Slapsie Maxie's was another Los Angeles showplace for Cole and his dancers. Slapsie Maxie Rosenbloom, a former boxer, was the semi-celebrity titular host. George Martin remembers playing there after a Chez Paree engagement, when Lena Horne was on the bill. Dezi Arnaz was conducting the band. "It was this little club over on Wilshire Boulevard. Gene Kelly, Van Johnson, Judy Garland—they all came. The minute the act started, they'd get up from their tables and go back to stand up and see better." *Variety* found this June 1947 show "more concert-hall than night-club style." Robert Wright and George Forrest, who had come to admire Cole as an artist and value him as a friend, were present at a Cole opening at Slapsie Maxie's. Wright says, "I remember Gene Kelly getting down to kiss Cole's feet. He said, 'Daddy, without you there isn't anything!' It was some opening night! Kelly told Cole that he had all the ideas, 'the rest of us just follow you.' "

Cole preserved a Hollywood note from Tony Martin, who'd once been on a Chez Paree bill with him. Martin asked him to come over to his table for a minute. Cyd Charisse was with him and admired Cole's work. There is also a 1948 telegram from Cole's lawyer in New York to the owners of Slapsie Maxie's, Jerry Brooks and Sy De Vore. Cole was angry about his billing. Once, Cole got angry at one of their patrons. Hal Schaefer swears Cole rushed into the restaurant's kitchen, grabbed a cleaver, and chased the offending diner out onto Wilshire Boulevard, still dressed in his scanty costume and jewelry.

Although early in his club career Cole was still struggling with shyness, Hollywood taught him the value of good public relations. He retained no press agent, otherwise his stories might have been less extravagant and more consistent. While at the

Chez Paree in Chicago in 1948, he told a *Daily News* interviewer he was a Dartmouth graduate and a former college hockey player. He did give Miss Ruth credit as his *guru*, and he admitted that he was fond of children, flower gardens, dogs, and jewelry. The *Daily News* writer described Cole's art: "He dances like a demon from the celestial frying pan of Baal, the sun god. His head darts forward and withdraws on its serpentine neck as if taking aim for its hidden fangs. His body wriggles amid almost superhuman strides. His arms and hands weave sinuously. But his eyes! They glare menacingly beneath rotating eyebrows from a bronzed, hook-nosed face that reeks of brutality with a capital Biff! B-r-r-r-r!"

This *News*-man also described Cole's visage as a "panther puss" with "Boris Karloff squinters." After confiding that even Cole's own dancers seemed afraid of him, not to mention ringside customers who "shrink under his hard-bitten gaze," the reporter hazarded the pun: "It's like taking one high-Baal too many!"

Another Chicago writer, Ann Marsters, had this to say of Cole's face, studied during the "weird gyrations of his East Indian dances" at the Chez Paree: "The bony, vicious, unflinching hardness of it. The cruel eyes glinting from the darkened skin. The brutality of his whole expression.

"This is enough to frighten customers into attention. They look, they wonder—and they scarcely dare turn away. After all, a man with a face like that might be capable of taking violent revenge, should you happen to offend him," Marsters suggested. Offstage, however, Cole proved to be "a nice, gentle, pink-faced Irish lad with a fine sense of humor . . ." Cole explained his savage manner as a defense. Male dancers, he said, already had several strikes against them. Those who wore jewelry and a skirt—or *dhoti*—as Cole did in his Indian dances, were asking to have tomatoes thrown at them.

Florida mobsters liked Jack Cole and his dancers quite as much as their patrons. Cole was a good drawing card. Wright and Forrest used him in shows in 1946, 1947, and 1948, and recall: "We built numbers around Jack. One year we did *Anna and the King of Siam*, based on Margaret Landon's book; this was before the musical version called *The King and I*. We did *Pink Champagne*. And we did a show called *Spring in Brazil*." Cole then knew his worth; he was one of the most highly-paid dance acts, but he paid his own dancers out of his weekly fee. Wright and Forrest were determined to have Cole in one of their shows, after his earlier success with them. Cole told his agent, Jack Davies, that he wanted $7,500 a week. This wasn't coming out of Wright's or Forrest's pockets; they were creating songs and putting the show together. The man who paid the bills was the casino owner, a mobster with a terrifying reputation. He guaranteed Cole would be in the show. When Jack Davies told him of Cole's insistence on more money, this Mafioso asked, "How much does he want?" Davies told him. The godfather's answer was curt and pointed: "Tell him he gets $6,500, or he dances from now on in a cement kimono." Bob Wright explains, "That was a *lot* of money then."

When it was snowing in New York, January in Florida was the height of the sunny season for the rich, the criminal, and the elderly. In Cole's scrapbooks a page is devoted to Florida 1948. There are photos of Cole, Verdon, and his friend David Gray on the beach. There are costume shots, a map of Florida, pictures of seashells, and Cole's decorations in red ink. Rave reviews extol Cole's art and technique. On this bill at the Colonial Inn, Joe E. Lewis is the comic, and he's judged a letdown by reviewers, who call Cole the climax of the show. That season, Kay Thompson and the Williams Brothers opened in Miami at the Copacabana. Cole took his company to see them, but they couldn't get in.

One of Cole's dancers, George Martin, later to be a trusted assistant choreographer, regretted missing out on the Thompson act. But he did get to see B. S. Pulley perform in Miami, a distance from Hollywood, as the guest of their gangster employer. One of the chorus girls at the Colonial Inn was the mobster's girlfriend. She and Ethel Martin had danced together in *Something for the Boys* on Broadway. Her sinister swain invited her, the Martins, and some other Cole dancers to drive down to Miami for Pulley's show. "We got in this big black Cadillac," Martin says. "They looked back, and we were being followed, so we flew down the road. I was about 23 and had no idea about gangsters. We could have been gunned down."

The following January 1949, Cole and troupe were booked into the new Norman Bel Geddes–designed Copa City in Miami; the old Copacabana had burned down. Xavier Cugat and his Orchestra and Kay Thompson were on the bill. George Martin, who greatly admired Thompson and who would be dancing with her the next season, when Cole dissolved the act, discovered that the public was really flocking to see Jack Cole and His Dancers. "They couldn't have cared less about Kay," he says. Gossip-hawk Dorothy Kilgallen was quick to report to her eager readers that Thompson and Cole were feuding. Thompson demanded, it was said, that Cole's jazz dance be removed from the program, on the ostensible ground that it wasn't really authentic East Indian. Kilgallen suggested that Thompson found it too tough to follow Cole's act. If so, she wasn't the first, nor the last, to feel that way.

At the close of the 1950s, while Fidel Castro and his guerrilla fighters were gathering strength, a luxurious new casino-hotel was constructed in Havana. It was the Havana Riviera, designed to compete with casinos in Miami and Las Vegas. Jack Cole was asked to present the first half of the premiere show, with Ginger Rogers featured in the second part. Cole's troupe included Gwen Verdon and the future director-choreographer Ron Field. Cole sent Hal Schaefer to Cuba in advance of the ensemble. Schaefer had to pick out the house band and a smaller relief band for the hotel. The big band was to be in a Las Vegas format, playing all the shows.

Schaefer describes the hotel as a "multi-multi-million-dollar" complex of gambling, entertainment, gustatory delights, recreation, and relaxation. It was, he says, backed by another major mobster. If this Mafia power was in the habit of reporting his taxable income, he could have used the Havana Riviera as a huge tax loss. During the initial engagement, with Ginger Rogers and Jack Cole's Dancers and Singers and Hal

Schaefer and His Quintette, Castro came down out of the mountains and invaded Havana.

Cole's group at this time was in top form. A memorable feature of this last show in Havana was a number in which Cole danced in a central position, as a beautiful woman in a glamorous gown artfully moved around him, always facing front. Then, at the climax of the dance, as she finally turned to look at Cole, pandemonium broke out in the audience. They at last saw what he had been leering at all through the routine. The woman turned to reveal her naked backside. The dress was held together behind by delicate chains. One of Cole's friends explains: "Jack thought the Cubans liked plump rumps. He said, 'It's all that sugar they eat.' "

Fidel Castro's revolutionary program for his *Cubanos* did not include gambling, catering to rich foreigners, or ogling women's bare bottoms. Cole and company departed on one of the last flights out. "There were teenagers with machine guns in the streets," Schaefer remembers.

Although Cole was fond of criticizing Ruth St. Denis and Ted Shawn for the lack of authenticity in their oriental dances, they at least made a tour of the Orient and the Indian sub-continent, where even their fantasies of Asian dance were ecstatically received. They also seized every opportunity to study native dances from local experts in those traditions. Cole did not take his dancers to the Far East, but it would have been interesting to observe the responses of such audiences to Cole's far more authentic routines, especially when coupled with jazz. Shirada Narghis, writing in *Dance* in 1945, surveying the influence of Indian dance in America, singled out Jack Cole. She praised Ruth St. Denis's intentions, La Meri's mastery of authentic techniques, and Jack Cole's adaptations of them. "An exceptional example is Jack Cole, who performs authentic Indian dance techniques to swing tempo without loss of the general dignity of the art. This is the final proof of the universal appeal of the world's oldest dance form," she asserted.

Perhaps Cole was going "stir-crazy" in Hollywood; in the 1940s, he would occasionally announce to interviewers that he was going to assemble a company and tour Europe. When he unveiled *Harlequin's Odyssey* in 1950, he thought it would make an attractive centerpiece for a foreign tour repertoire. No European tour ever materialized, so Ted Shawn was still ahead of Cole in that. Cole did, of course, work in both London and Paris on films and shows. And there had been expeditions to Brazil and to Cuba. Josh Meyer, who succeeded Jack Davies as Cole's agent, says he didn't travel much because he was in demand in New York and Hollywood.

Jack Cole's last hurrah on the international scene was a memorable engagement in Beirut, Lebanon, when it was still untroubled, prosperous, and widely known as "the Paris of the Middle East." Meyer arranged this engagement with the Paris-based impressario Charlie Henchiz, who produced lavish shows for the Casino du Liban, about twenty kilometers outside Beirut. "Don't be misled because it was Beirut," Meyer cautions. "Some of these shows were bigger than Las Vegas spectaculars. They were really tremendous." Cole was intrigued by the challenge of mounting what he called a "tits-and-feathers" show.

Choosing Ethel Martin as his assistant, Cole flew to Paris to assemble and train his troupe. Cole also wanted companionship, so he summoned from New York his personal friend and professional masseur, Ernie Eschmann. Originally, Eschmann thought he was going to see all the Paris sights, help Cole out when he could, and return to New York in a few weeks. When it was time for the Cole company to depart for Beirut in a charter plane, Eschmann found himself on board. Cole promised him he'd be back in the United States by Christmas. Ethel Martin, who wanted to be home with her family for the holidays, had the same hopes.

The Beirut-bound plane made a detour to Milan to load the costumes that had been made there. Seats were removed and replaced with huge costume boxes. "They looked like coffins," Eschmann recalls. The image was given added force when the captain used the intercom to tell Cole and his artists, "We've taken on extra weight. We're going to try to take off, but we're not sure we'll make it." Ethel Martin groaned, and Eschmann told her he had a confidence to share with her when they reached Beirut. When they landed safely, he revealed that Henchiz, who wasn't on the flight, had insured the plane and passengers for $1 million.

Eschmann remembers being especially impressed by the headliner, Maggie Burke, who learned all the steps Cole had set for the troupe. Cole made sure that Ethel Martin went home before Christmas. But in Beirut, the sun was shining, and Cole could see orange trees from the casino hotel window. Just like Los Angeles. He asked for orange juice, but the hotel didn't have any. So Cole moved to a hotel in the heart of Beirut that did have orange juice. He was driven out daily to the casino by a maniacal Lebanese chauffeur named Zak. Eschmann says he seemed to *aim* at opposing traffic, to show how *macho* he was. Once he purposely rammed another car. Cole would cheer him on: "Get another Christian today! Pave your way to Heaven!"

The decade had come to an end, and it was the end of an era for Jack Cole, as well. Shortly before he and his company left Paris for Beirut, Richard Nixon's election to the presidency was announced on the radio. At Cole's hotel, the concierge asked him, "What does this mean?" Cole answered, "This means disaster." The year was 1971. In 1974, Jack Cole would be dead.

But not forgotten, certainly not by his dancers and those who worked closely with him. One aspect of Cole's work in the clubs went unnoticed, except by insiders. That was his skilled management of his act, rather like Ted Shawn, making sure there were a string of bookings, the best working conditions, and better-than-average salaries. Cole always valued his own work highly and made his gangland employers pay him well. They respected his art and his toughness. Cole's agent, Josh Meyer, who initially worked with Jack Davies, Cole's first agent, says, "It was our job to demand and get whatever the traffic would bear, including working conditions and facilities. Cole relied on us to get the best. If we hadn't, he wouldn't have stayed with us for very long. A beginner may perform in less than adequate circumstances. Not Jack Cole! His dancers were unique, possibly the finest dance group of its kind around. We didn't accept bad offers. We were in the position of demanding and getting."

One advantage of Jack Cole's wild temper, says Meyer, was that you always knew where you stood with him. "He was not an even-tempered man. He'd fly into a rage if he thought someone was misusing him. I got along with Jack because he was bluntly honest. He could be brutally frank, and that didn't make a hit with a lot of people." Meyer, and Davies before him, made arrangements for the Jack Cole Dancers for so many weeks at a set fee. The employer and the agent didn't have to worry about the details of how Cole paid his own dancers and musicians. Meyer thinks Cole may have had verbal agreements with them, but among Cole's papers is a contract dated April 23, 1950 for his dancers, for an engagement at Ciro's, seven days a week, two shows nightly, at $125 per week minimum, good money in those days.

George Martin believes that Cole kept rather little of his own big fees. "Jack wanted the best, the most expensive costumes. He made a lot, but he paid it all out. We always traveled first-class with the club act. We toured two years in the late 1940s, and we always went Superchief—with bedrooms. Cole paid for the travel; we paid our own living expenses." Cole also made sure that his dancers weren't earning less than they had at Columbia Pictures.

One highly decorative but obsessive page in the Cole scrapbooks underlines Cole's worries and concerns as a business manager for his troupe. The page is covered with groups of dollar signs: $$$$$$$$$$. There are myriad cutouts of photos of heads, feet, and hands of Cole's dancers. Written over and over are their names: Buzz, Gwen, Florence, Bob, Rod, Alex, Harry, Carol, George, Ethel. Also repeated are India, Cuba, Africa—sources of Cole's ethnic inspirations. And city names such as New York and Chicago; club names: Chez Paree. *Sing, Sing, Sing* is repeated, as is the phrase "Secret Agent." The period this complicated doodle-collage covers is January 1947 to August 1949. Cole's obsession isn't just with the dollars he was making, nor with his valued dancers. There is line after line of repeated listings of such things as agent's fees, baggage, cleaning, costumes, orchestra, music, rehearsal halls, all the many expenses Cole had to cover with the dollars that were rolling in during this frantic touring. It was wearing him down, and by 1950 he was glad to be able to break up the group and give up club dates for a while. His companion, David Gray, certainly helped him with production, but Cole always had to oversee all aspects of his operation.

Even when the club act wasn't his own, Cole brought his best ideas to its production and his most intense concentration to such important details as orchestrations, costumes, and lighting. Betty Grable, Mitzi Gaynor, and Jane Russell begged Cole to create club acts for them, which he did with pleasure and panache. He was fond of them, both as performers and friends. He knew their real strengths very well, and their limitations, which he managed to minimize.

On October 22, 1958, *Journal-American* columnist Gene Knight reported that Jane Russell would shortly be opening at New York's Latin Quarter. As Jane Russell remembers, what proved to be a solid success for her could have been either a disaster or a last-minute cancellation, had it not been for Cole's coming to her rescue. Russell was already long famous for her sultry role in Howard Hughes's film, *The Outlaw*. More recently, she'd been praised for her work in *Gentlemen Prefer Blondes* and *Gentlemen Marry Brunettes;* in both films, Jack Cole had helped her make the most of her talents. Now Russell had just recorded a solo album, and her agency was projecting a Las Vegas booking for her in a special act. Their idea was to test it in New York first, and they insisted on having someone who was under contract to them devise the act and direct Russell in it. Russell had begged for Cole from the start, but the agency was adamant. Unfortunately, their candidate had no ideas and finally put the blame on Jane Russell. "I can't work with you," he told her. "There's no way we can put an act together." He walked out on Russell. She'd hoped for a month's rehearsals. There were only two weeks left, and not the ghost of an act.

"That goddamn idiot!" Cole exclaimed when he heard of Russell's difficulties. "He simply doesn't know what to do." Cole told her to come to his hilltop home. Russell brought along her new album and two others she'd made with Connie Haines, featuring Negro spirituals. Cole played the records, immediately picking tunes for Russell's act. From the spirituals, he picked four songs and made a medley of them. "He paid a great deal of attention to the pacing of the show," Russell says. "Not too many 'slows' in a row." Four days into rehearsals, Cole conceived the idea of a chant to lead into the spirituals, beginning slowly and culminating in wild intensity. Back in New York, Hal Schaefer was making orchestra arrangements from tapes Cole and Russell were sending from Los Angeles. Schaefer would tour with Russell when she took the act to Europe.

Cole set up five numbers for Russell, several of them with Ron Field and two other men as backup dancers. The dancers wore solid black. There was now no time to make special gowns for Russell, so Cole searched her closets and found two of simple cut, but with enough beading to make them shine in the spotlight. One red; one black.

One reason Cole liked Russell so much, Schaefer explains, is that, though she wasn't a trained dancer, she loved good jazz. In fact, her secret passion had been to be a jazz singer. Cole loved that about her, and her feeling for jazz illuminated her singing. As Schaefer says, "Whenever she sang, it was swinging, bright, and 'up'—very nice! And she looked good! Jack gave her some very effective movements. It was a very nice, appealling act. She had a bit to say about her film career, but mostly she sang. Jack was a wizard with people who weren't great dancers!"

At the Latin Quarter for their final dress rehearsal, Russell and Cole found the stage filled with girls working on routines for a new show. They refused to get off the stage. Russell remembers, "We sat and sat and sat. Finally Jack was so upset that he got up and started to fly down the stairs. I went after him and begged, 'Jaaaack! Please don't leave!' We'll get them off, but I'll never be able to do the act unless you're here. He said, 'OK, but *get them off!*' "

Galvanized, Russell shouted at the astonished girls, "Get off *now!*" They fled, but there was so little time left that Cole and Russell could only rehearse the beginnings and endings of the numbers, setting the lights, and making other technical arrangements. Russell was to open that very night; there was no time for her to run through the show completely. In effect, she made her Latin Quarter debut cold. It was a success; Cole even came to see the opening, something he usually avoided. Cabaret critics were admiring of Russell's performance. It was, she notes, "a very chic show." Her numbers, of course, were part of a larger stage show, as was the case in Las Vegas.

Without the backup dancers, she toured Europe, accompanied by Hal Schaefer as her orchestra conductor. They had to have police escorts everywhere they went, says Schaefer. "Every time Jane walked in or out of a public place, they'd mob her. They sat on the roof of her car. She was the great *star!* So she really didn't have to do much. Her being there was enough." Russell loved it all. "I was a big curiosity. The Italians went wild, hollering out of the balconies in the theatres. The Spaniards were fabulous audiences. You could hear a pin drop, they were so silent. But if they liked you, at the end they made a big commotion. They were my favorite audiences." It might have been enough for Jane Russell just to stand on stage and look beautiful. Jack Cole wasn't going to let her settle for that. He knew her strengths as a performer and he helped her make a charming show from them.

Cole's career as a dancer-choreographer for nightclubs and stage shows ran from the mid-1930s to the dawn of the 1970s, more than a generation. Despite the managerial problems Cole may have had over the years, he had the continual satisfaction of being reviewed as a very serious dancer and choreographer. For an artist who longed for the critical acceptance that had come to St. Denis and Shawn, Martha Graham, and Doris Humphrey and Charles Weidman, it was perhaps greater praise to be acclaimed for daring to do authentic ethnic dances in supperclub arenas.

Again and again reviewers marveled, not only at what Cole and his dancers did, but also at the fact that club or casino customers actually enjoyed Cole's riveting but demanding choreography. Often, Cole's contributions were singled out as the best things in the shows; the same was to happen with a number of the movie-musicals he choreographed.

In 1943, two oddly contrasting judgments on Cole's work came from gossip columnist Dorothy Kilgallen, and from Margaret Lloyd, of the *Christian Science Monitor*. Kilgallen thought that Cole's "legs behave like Nijinsky's, but his mind works like Joe Doakes'." She praised Cole for taking the *art* out of dance and giving it a "hotfoot." Cole's forays late at night into Harlem, his gleanings from the daily papers, had inspired works exploring the underside of urban ethnic culture, such as *Reefer Man*, which made an interesting contrast to East Indian and Latin ethnicity. Cole had made all of this rich variety of dance experience into dynamic entertainment, instead of academic research projects. That was something Kilgallen could admire. Lloyd was austere and severe with Cole: "There remains more than a tinge of diabolism in his inversions, a perverse audacity in his deviations from the norm." But she was, after all, writing for the *Monitor*, which preferred to endorse the things of the spirit, rather than those of the flesh.

To the end, Walter Terry remained a staunch admirer of Cole and his work. He found it to be of a very high order. "He literally mastered the East Indian dance. He learned the authentic gesture and the authentic use of the body and the head from La Meri [the American dancer, Russell Meriwether Hughes]. . . . The spinoffs from his work are incredible! A lot of people thought of it only as Hindu dance being swung, but there were the Harlem and Caribbean dances, too."

That other dean of dance criticism, John Martin, considered Cole's art gaunt, nervous, and flagellant, yet with an opulent, sensuous beauty. For Martin, Cole was a depersonalized being, an intense kinetic entity, rather than an individual. That was also true of the ensemble. Such a state of preparedness was, said Martin, close to being possessed. Other values he noted: an incredible movement with a dynamism which transfered itself to the spectators; smoldering reserves of energy; no fears of falling or sliding on foot, knee, or back.

Martin observed that Cole's taste was "fairly exotic, his curiosity wide, and his experimentation eager and bold." Cole was well aware of the value of pauses, inhibitions of movement, and the movement of one small group against another. And all of these effects were accomplished, said Martin, with a great deal of pictorial skill. He summed up Cole's talent: "It is a neurotic quality, if you will, but there is undeniable genius in it."

6

EVOLUTION OF COLE'S TECHNIQUE

FROM STUDENT TO TEACHER TO CHOREOGRAPHER

Enjoying his initial successes in New York's supperclubs, Cole did not save himself during the day. As he was to do all his life, he used up excess nervous energy, kept his body trim, and mastered new dance skills with daily studio work. Anna Austin had her own New York studio. A dancer who was then a student remembers the day Jack Cole came to class and ended by teaching it. Austin and Cole decided to share studio responsibilities. They opened the joint venture at 52 West 72nd Street. Because Cole "had no patience with beginners," Austin taught them, leaving the advanced classes in technique to Cole. Cole was dancing professionally with Alice Dudley at the time, but the bond of affection and respect Austin and Cole had forged in their brief Denishawn association made them effective teaching partners.

Even Ruth St. Denis, who had given Austin her blessing as a teacher of Denishawn dance, came to admire Cole's talents as an instructor. In 1935, her personal and professional life in disarray, Miss Ruth began taking daily lessons with Cole. She was fifty-five and still learning—ironically, from a former pupil. To her diary, she confided: "To see me struggling with a barre is a sight, but it is doing me a world of good."

Considering Jack Cole's busy schedule of teaching and performing at this time, it's a measure of his love for Miss Ruth that he was her partner in one of her Rhythmic Choir ventures. On December 20, 1936, at Calvary Church, Fourth Avenue and East 21st Street, St. Denis presented *A Christmas Pageant—Birth and Rebirth*. The program described the production as a "rhythmic ritual." Assisted by Calvary's choir and Sunday School, St. Denis and her dancers offered a two-part invention. The first was *The Masque of Mary*, featuring Anna Austin as Mary and Don Begenau as Joseph. Edwin Strawbridge was the Angel Gabriel, and Virginia Miller, the Angel of the Star. The Three Kings and the Spirit of Asia completed this cast.

Calvary's rector, the Reverend Samuel Shoemaker, introduced the second part, *Rebirth*. In this section, flesh struggled
with spirit, much as it had been doing in Miss Ruth's own life.
Appropriately, Jack Cole represented The Temporal Self, with
St. Denis as The Eternal Self. The sequence of danced events,
related to a text read aloud, was: The ascent of the Eternal Self
through life towards the Eternal Gates, accompanied by the
symbolic choir of earth figures; The Struggle; The Ultimate Surrender; The Realization (Revelations 21:1–6); Dance of Praise
(Psalm 150); and The Spirit of Asia, followed by the children
from the East. No one in those days talked of a Third World.
At Christmastide, it was perhaps enough to give the three kings
of the Orient a place on the program. Miss Ruth, however,
managed metaphorically to bring all the cults of Asia to the holy
cradle. What the cynical young Jack Cole thought of all this can
be imagined, but he did it for love of Miss Ruth.

By the following year, Cole already had popular successes
at Radio City Music Hall and the Rainbow Room to his credit.
But, possibly inspired by Miss Ruth's dedication and his own
experiences at Denishawn and with Humphrey and Weidman,
Cole was also making an effort to create and perform serious
dance works.

Shortly before Eleanor King's *Icaro*, however, Cole and Anna
Austin gave a dance concert in Studio 61 at Carnegie Hall. It
was an outgrowth of their studio work; they called themselves
the Ruth St. Denis Dancers. Miss Ruth lent more than her name
to the venture. She announced the dances—divided into oriental and modern—and filled in pauses with reminiscences and
backgrounds for the choreography. The dancers also used some
of her own costumes and props. Among the exotic numbers were
two St. Denis nautch dances, as well as Javanese and Siamese
impressions. Cole choreographed a modern solo for himself inspired by Baudelaire's *Les Fleurs du mal*. He also devised *The Irish
Wake*. A review preserved in Cole's scrapbooks said of this: "very
stirring, its choreography simple but expressive. Once the
dancers chanted prayers as they moved, which was fitting,
though a trifle inexpertly handled." Curiously, nearly thirty years

later, Cole would be recapturing Irish movement and atmosphere as director-choreographer of the Broadway musical *Donnybrook!* Florence Lessing, who later danced in *The Irish Wake,* says she found it deeply moving, exciting to perform every time the group did it.

The generally admiring concert review, dated March 7, 1937, notes that both the oriental and the modern dances were performed with ". . . finesse by the attractive group, with Anna Austin and Jack Cole as the leading dancers. Miss Austin, who uses her hands and arms gracefully, is best in the more delicate art of the Eastern numbers, while Mr. Cole is more suited to the modern idiom. Though he did the Eastern numbers very well and quite in character, he has not yet acquired enough variety of mood. He has obviously absorbed some of Shan-Kar's [sic] mannerisms." What Cole had actually mastered—not merely absorbed—were not mannerisms but authentic body positions and movements.

Cole got another checkmark from the critic: "The costuming throughout was very good; my only criticism is Mr. Cole's predilection for the nude." A different critic, rather hostile, had other ideas. He pointed out that the performances were, after all, done in a famous dancer's studio to audiences of fellow dancers. A lay audience, he was sure, would have rewarded Cole with jeers for his efforts at serious choreography. True, Cole's dance was faithful to Baudelaire's poetic text, but that only meant that it was, necessarily, morbid and decadent. It symbolized, he said, "a futile attempt at release from thralldom." Cole performed with a red rose at his feet. Dressed in a white suit, Cole also had a dead-white face, with brown lips and heavy-lidded eyes. His body filled with lassitude, he danced barefoot—as was his custom. For this alienated critic, Cole was "a symbol of vague sexuality."

Following this Austin-Cole dance concert, Ruth St. Denis found it necessary to correct an erroneous report, published in *Tempo.* Although she had served as mistress of ceremonies for the event, she was not part of the new company nor had she danced. Rather, she had only "talked to the modest audience."

Her efforts, she said, were to demonstrate that she was "back of them."

Fortunately for Miss Ruth, desperately casting about for artistic fulfillment and earned income, her Rhythmic Choir and what she called "Temple Evenings" had found two important admirers. The president of Adelphi College, Dr. Paul Dawson Eddy, and his wife, Isabel, were much impressed. Mrs. Eddy even joined the St. Denis Rhythmic Choir. Miss Ruth had just undergone the humiliation of having to audition for a variety show the bandleader Xavier Cugat was organizing. Cole, who sometimes worked with Cugat, may have suggested this as a stopgap, but St. Denis felt she'd made a fool of herself.

Dr. Eddy, a humanist and an enlightened educator, surely realized how wrong it was that such a distinguished, charismatic, creative artist as Ruth St. Denis had no regular income and no proper place to work and perform, largely because she was not a hardheaded business manager. St. Denis' difficulties at this time must also have stiffened Jack Cole's resolve to make a real living as a dancer, even if it meant abandoning the concert stage for the supperclub arena.

The farsighted Dr. Eddy invited St. Denis to found an innovative Department of Dance at Adelphi College. Until her death in 1968, it was to sustain her and provide a frequent haven in her peripatetic existence. Miss Ruth knew quite well how little talent she had for organization or for the daily supervision of classes and the counseling of students. She was excellent as a source of inspiration, however, and her loyal friends became Adelphi's initial dance faculty. Anna Austin taught oriental dance, including a number of Miss Ruth's specialties. Don Begenau instructed the Adelphians in social dance, very useful in Garden City and elsewhere on Long Island. Jack Cole and Ada Korvin shared responsibility for modern dance classes.

"To be honest," Miss Ruth wrote, "I do not give much more than my name and the loan of my art objects and costumes to it." With candor, she admitted, "Jack and Anna do the rest." And it was just as well. Although she could entrance classes with her lectures, laden with mystical pronouncements, and with demonstrations of her noted dance solos, she found it difficult to analyze—and through analysis, teach—why and how she performed these dances. Anna Austin knew, however, just how to achieve the St. Denis effects.

At this time, Cole was performing nightly in Manhattan, where his celebrity was growing. He spared himself neither on the nightclub floor nor in the Adelphi classrooms. This was dubbed Cole's "Jekyll and Hyde" period. Along with a profusion of favorable reviews for his club performances, Cole also preserved some Adelphi memorabilia. One item was a gossip column note that Cole had been asked to head the Modern Dance Department at Adelphi College. True, Cole was teaching modern dance, but Miss Ruth was the departmental head. The college position, it was reported, was a result of Cole's successes at the Rainbow Room. Considering Dr. Eddy's initial interest in a St. Denis–led dance program as a result of church performances, this is a curious switch of secular for sacred. Eddy had even urged Miss Ruth to emphasize religious dance in the Adelphi curriculum.

Dance critic and historian Don McDonagh notes, in his entry on Cole in *The Complete Guide to Modern Dance*, that Cole "made his discovery of combining Hindu dance gesture with thirties jazz and swing music when teaching at Adelphi University." Actually, Adelphi would not become a university until the 1960s, and Cole made his discovery elsewhere, in Marcus Blechman's apartment, according to Florence Lessing and Donald Saddler.

Among Cole's souvenirs are photos of Adelphi classes, mingled with shots of Miss Ruth in and out of costume. On one page of a Cole scrapbook, there is a large newspaper feature about the Adelphi adventure, titled "Heel, Toe, Away They Go." There's no date or author indicated. A subhead reads: "Out at Adelphi College in Garden City, Ruth St. Denis Is Doing Things With the Dance and the Curriculum . . . She Hopes To Turn Out Not Just Dancers But Educated Dancers Like It's Never Been Done in College Before." Photos show a black-clad Ada Korvin leaping across the lawn, arms high over her head as she beats on a drum head. Other pictures depict Adelphi students, also in black, leaping, kneeling, and doing backbends. The article is filled with inspirational and rather visionary comments by Miss Ruth, hoping for dance miracles in the groves of academe. Jack Cole, it's announced, is to head the Adelphi summer school in dance, supervised by Ruth St. Denis.

The image of Miss Ruth supervising anyone as well-organized as the maturing Jack Cole is amusing. Actually, Cole was helping her organize the work of the department. In 1938, in addition to his commercial success at the Rainbow Room and Casa Mañana, Cole apparently found time to perform with the women of his Ballet Intime at the Dance Theatre of the YMHA at Lexington Avenue and 92nd Street. A reviewer commented on the stunning *West Indian Impression*, with its smartly executed large sweeping movement and beautiful costuming: "The combined efforts of Jack Cole, Letitia Ide, Fe Alf, Eleanor King, and Ernestine Day, all dancers with forceful styles, made this number really powerful."

Meanwhile, out at Adelphi College, it wasn't all lawn-leaping and back-stretching. Ruth St. Denis wanted to do something special to put the new dance program in the New York spotlight. Her solution was to plan a dance concert, under the favored Adelphi rubric of "Festival of the Arts," for October 28, 1938. This was to be the formal opening of the Dance Department—followed by a November 11 concert to launch a companion Music Department.

Adelphi College duly presented "Ruth St. Denis and Her Staff" in a program that began with three "Music Visualizations" by Miss Ruth: *Claire de lune, First Arabesque,* and *Catedral engloutie,* all danced to Debussy's compositions. Next came the department's "Modern Group," with Cole again dancing the role of Icarus, based on Eleanor King's more complex *Icaro.* This sequence was limited to an encounter among Icarus, his mother Erigone (Ada Korvin), and his beloved Phaedra (Florence Lessing). A program note explained: "The reason for doing this dance at this time is that these are stirring days of a universal effort on man's part to fly, not merely with his mechanical inventions, but with his whole being out and over the forces of today that are parallel to those in the time of the Greek legend."

Which is only a more inflated, St. Denisian way of saying that this *Prayer to Nike* was symbolically an anti-Fascist dance.

Part I ended with an offering by the "American Indian Group." As she had done for Ballet Intime, Ernestine Day drew on her childhood experiences and choreographed *Pawnee Indian Dance*. Part II opened with St. Denis performing her *Black and Gold Sari* and Anna Austin in two of the nautch dances. Jack Cole was featured in the third offering of the "Oriental Group." In *Shiva Instructs the Gods,* Cole impersonated Shiva demonstrating the art of dance to a gaggle of Hindu gods, played by Adelphi students. Program Note: "Shiva, it is understood, created the worlds by dancing, and this vast symbolism of rhythm he is imparting to the gods."

Following this, Cole, Austin, and Lessing gave their *Impression of a Balinese Lelong*. Don Begenau and Eugenie Foley represented the "Social Dance Group," animating a waltz and a tango. Miss Ruth brought the program to a close in Part III, with *Kwan-non*, a solo in which she related this aspect of the Buddha to the tender compassion of the Madonna. This work was chosen to represent the "Religious Dance Group." Interestingly, although there were already a pianist, a percussionist, and a trumpeter engaged for the concert, Jack Cole brought along his own accompanist.

In the Cole scrapbooks there are a number of photos of a springtime 1939 Adelphi College production, conceived—and almost abandoned shortly before its opening—by an alternately excited and frustrated Jack Cole. Before he reached the breaking point, he wrote to Walter Terry, then working as dance critic for the Boston *Herald* (1936–39). Cole said, "I hope you come down to see the new work I'm doing with the college dance students and with Miss Ruth in it. I'm taking the Bible—a part of it—and treating it as a primitive mystery. Miss Ruth is the leader of the chorus." Terry was reconstructing this letter from memory in the late 1970s, so Cole may have presented Miss Ruth's role differently in the actual letter.

Eleanor King notes that Cole invited *her* to be chorus leader of this adventurous work. Neither King nor Terry have identified it with a title, but Gwen Verdon, who heard about it much later, says Cole called it *The Legend of Jesus Christ*. This was prefaced by the phrase: *A Primitive Mystery*. As King explains it, "Yearning to do something more sacred and less secular, Jack saw a mystical vision of Miss Ruth as catalyst for blending rites of Osiris with the Passion of Christ." In fact, King reports that there were two choruses, one of professional dancers and one of Adelphi College students. Cole conceived of both Miss Ruth and Eleanor King as chorus leaders, but, in the event, Miss Ruth also took upon herself the burden of suggesting Christ crucified.

This was a very ambitious project for the dance program and for Adelphi, because Cole had commissioned a Broadway composer, hired union musicians, and ordered commercially-made theatre costumes. What was beyond the meager departmental budget, Cole provided from his club earnings. He had, after all, learned the lesson of not stinting on production values from Miss Ruth herself. If the scrapbook photos are to be trusted, though, the values were basically concentrated in the handsomely cut long, flowing Greek gowns, and in the lighting. The scenic environment was nothing but a bare stage, with a simple curtain behind it.

Cole wasn't wasting any money on King or the other dance professionals. Unlike the thoroughly unionized musicians, they danced for the love of it, which was certainly no novelty for any of them. They did it for Cole, and for the opportunity to be working with the now legendary Ruth St. Denis.

Cole, never one to spare his friends honest appraisal or a malicious quip, in his letter to Walter Terry urged: "You must come because Miss Ruth is trying to look like a modern dancer and learn how to count." In the prime of Denishawn, St. Denis hadn't cared about counting; she danced her celebrated solos the way she felt them at the moment, which meant that they were seldom the same twice in succession. She even discouraged her Denishawn charges from coordinating the movements with the music with a rigid system of counts. *"Feel!"* she would tell them.

Terry got a written account from Cole of the results of this practice; Cole reported that he told Miss Ruth he couldn't per-

mit her to improvise. He was a disciplinarian, and she was setting a bad example for the student dancers. In front of the entire
company, or so he told Terry, he called Miss Ruth "a broken-
down old hag, who'd never learned how to count." As Cole
told the tale, Miss Ruth threw herself down on the stage and
screamed and beat the floor.

"The girls in the group were dressed in stylized Greek costumes, with Cretan wigs made out of leather," Terry recalled,
from Cole's letter. "Jack flew out of the Adelphi College Theatre down that street in Garden City that leads to the railroad
station—followed by sixteen girls in Greek garb, all of them
yelling: 'Mr. Cole! Mr. Cole! Please come back.'

"Jack said, 'My timing was wrong. I got there just as the
train pulled out, so there I was, standing on the platform with
sixteen Greek girls. So naturally I went back. Miss Ruth and I
kissed and made up.' "

It's a very amusing story. Cole must have told it wonderfully, and many times after the event was only a dim memory
for most who saw the dance ritual. Walter Terry told it with
special relish when he came to the "old hag" invective. Nonetheless, Eleanor King's memory of this occurrence, in the context of the feverish rehearsals, sounds much more like what really
must have happened. Of course it's entirely possible that he did
call Miss Ruth an old hag, but, from King's recollection, it's clear
Cole didn't tell the whole story. He must have avoided sharing
the core of the tale with Terry, because it was a problem which
was to afflict him as a choreographer all his life. Cole worked
on dances a few steps at a time, getting each one absolutely
right, before moving on to the next movement sequence. Dancers
frequently had no idea of the total shape the dance would ultimately acquire, or of its possible meaning. Some malcontents
now and then suggested that Cole didn't know these things
either; that he was composing as he went along, hoping it would
all turn out looking effective.

A week before the scheduled premiere—to which the college had invited not only local luminaries, but important people from New York as well—the musicians, the performers, and
the costumes were brought together for the first time. Cole was

also performing every night at the Rainbow Room. His act was exhausting, yet he was commuting to Garden City on Long Island daily to work on the dance. He was under a lot of tension, and he had not yet choreographed an ending for the composition. At one point in the rehearsal, as the cast accustomed itself to the full-skirted gowns, Miss Ruth paused to ask Cole a few questions. As King tells it: "Jack dear, we have different ways of working, I know. You are a perfectionist who likes to proceed step by step; I like to have a clear concept of the whole before I begin to move. I have two questions, dear, so that I can perform my part better. Can you tell us how we are to speak with the solo instruments, do we come ahead of the oboe or the trumpet, or under it, or after it? And just what is the conclusion to be, so that we can gauge our tension in the work as a whole?"

These are perfectly reasonable concerns. But, as King recalls, they infuriated him. "He walked a perfect circle of rage, raised his shoulders, shouted: 'I'm through with the whole thing!' and walked out." Such behavior was not surprising to those who knew Cole. Not only had he threatened to walk out of nightclub performances, he had menaced those he considered as his antagonists with violence. At least he didn't hit anyone at Adelphi. The girls duly rescued Cole from the railroad station, as he had told Terry. King can't recall how the ritual dance was finally concluded, nor did she ever read a review of it. But, from the experience, she came away with a high respect for Ruth St. Denis, who was equal to any vocal or movement demand. Miss Ruth, King decided, was more professional than Jack Cole.

Terry later confirmed Cole's account with one of the dancers, so both versions are aspects of the same event. "Jack had a terrible temper," Terry said. "He was a perfectionist. I did see that performance. It was really brilliant. I'm sorry it's been lost, because it was so moving, the audience was in tears."

Cole must have found himself overcommitted, with rehearsals and performances in New York and daytime teaching duties on Long Island. On October 10, 1939, Miss Ruth sent him a note, which said in part: "I don't want to be the least bit pompous or stuffy about the matter, but I feel that the Dance Dept. is getting a little snarled for lack of a better method of correlating its activities. . . . So hereafter will you please send me a brief note or phone as to what your next plans are and what your emergency slip-ups seem to have to be, and I will try to do my best to adjust matters all around. . . . I do not pretend to know the details of your theoretic or practical teaching . . . but I am responsible for the smooth running of the Dept. . . . You understand I cannot do this unless all plans for the department are sent to this desk. If and when I make mistakes, I shall be only too happy to be checked about it. . . . Yours always affectionately . . ."

She wrote in her journal at this time, "I realize that this 'war' between Jack and me is the same as all wars between egotists. I want so much to put into living practice the law that hatred never ceases by hatred but only by love." Unfortunately for Miss Ruth's admirable ambitions as a healer and a peacemaker, Jack Cole was busily armoring his own insecurities, not with love, but with the appearance of being mean and tough. Later in life, when Walter Terry accused him of mellowing, he explained that he was getting older and it took a lot of energy to be evil.

When Jack Cole had engaged his studio ensemble at Columbia Pictures in 1944, he had a remarkable core of handpicked dancers to teach. He could put them through gymnastic exercises, Cecchetti ballet, ethnic dances, and Cole Technique until they were ready to drop. Despite his sarcasm and occasional sadism, they were devoted to him. To study with Cole, however, if one wasn't one of Cole's own dancers, the student had to offer a challenge—as well as meet the challenges Cole set for him or her. Gwen Verdon gives an example: "He taught at the Eugene Loring school, but he didn't like the students. If he had Valerie Bettis or someone like that in class, then he liked teaching. But if he didn't have someone of that talent, he'd have me teach the classes. He said he was bored."

Among Cole's papers are lists of important dance books he thought dance students should read and lists of Hindu dance postures. There are also notes on primitive dances and imitative magic, as well as Cole's commentaries on John Dewey's *Art as Experience.* One Jack Cole jotting leaps off the page: "The amateur does not exist in oriental art." Cole well understood the significance of a lifetime spent perfecting and performing traditional dances and rituals in India, Siam, Java, China, and Japan. He was offended, occasionally enraged, by students who were halfhearted in their efforts, or by those who, although vital and full of enthusiasm for mastering techniques, had no intellectual curiosity about the historical or religious roots of the ethnic dances they were learning.

Gwen Verdon says Cole wasn't just a teacher; he was an *educator.* He drilled his own ensembles mercilessly to get the steps right, the sequences fluid, and the tensions extra taut. But none of this was done, she says, without thought for what lay behind the movements. "Whether it was in dance, or theology, or how to go through a revolving door properly, Jack was an educator. He had a theory that everything was interrelated, and, therefore, knowing as much as possible would make you better at anything you did. How you felt about yourself, he thought, would have an effect on the kind of dancer you could be. He'd only hire people for his group who he felt were really students. You know, the kind of person who, if he lives to be 104, will still be taking a college course in some subject. Cole wanted to work only with people who had the appetite to learn about everything."

Cole's goal both in training and in performance was perfection. He pushed his dancers to the limit to achieve it. That meant commitment had to be total and unending. Barton Mumaw, who assisted Cole on the film version of *Kismet,* says he was entranced by the manner in which Cole instructed his dancers in the complicated coordinations of the East Indian technique he was using. "He stretched movement and action to the nth degree," Mumaw explains. "This exaggeration of movement, plus a steely control, are the hallmarks of his way of dance."

Mumaw watched Cole give the dancers, in effect, a detailed dissection of each movement, with a physical demonstration. Each movement was studied and mastered. "The dancers learned at a snail's pace until perfection was achieved. At ensuing rehearsals, the movements were repeated exactly, but at a slightly faster tempo. This progression went on and on until fingers, toes, arms, legs, torsos, and heads, not to mention eyes and eyebrows, were moving at lightning speed. However, there was no diminution or change in the slightest degree from the original slow movements so deeply etched into the dancer's bodies. Jack's attention to detail could be maddening. I remember the day when all that was accomplished was one eight-measure phrase, and his delight with the final solution—and our discomfiture."

From his earliest club appearances, Cole's use of exotic Asian dance movements was a vivid novelty. The technique of learning and teaching them, which he'd perfected, enabled him to make something very special of Afro-Cuban and Harlem dance steps as well. Cole and his dancers weren't by any means the only ensemble able to tango, rhumba, or conga. But no one, not even the best of the real Latins, could perform these dances like Cole and his troupe. Obviously, linking East Indian steps and poses to a frantic jazz beat made what was basically painstakingly authentic into a new dance form. When Cole did the same for the rhythms of Harlem and Latin America, there also an astonishing transformation took place in the dances.

Cole's catholicity in ethnic tastes, coupled with his flexibility as a dancer, made anything possible. Buzz Miller insists that Cole's Technique can be applied to a wide range of dance areas. Although Cole preferred to work in his three main ethnic areas, the Irish dances in *Donnybrook!* also appealled to him. Miller points out that the classical ballet he did for the New York City Opera's *Bomarzo* was "a crazy little jewel!"

Explaining Cole as a teacher, Buzz Miller calls him a "coiled spring. He had tremendous energy inside him. His *port de bras* was fantastic. When I started teaching instead of performing, I found that what I really had to teach all came from Jack Cole. All of it!" He muses: "Today, who could sustain a Cole program for a whole two hours?" Outlining Cole's contributions, Miller says, "What he gave me was a legacy that's hard to cope with, because people just don't understand it. They have the wrong conceptions of jazz. You have to work very hard to really cut it. So it throws them . . .

"Lee Theodore has this piece called *Vocabulary* in the American Dance Machine's repertoire. It's just sections of Cole's work—steps. But it's a rather sensational little ten-minute thing," Miller says. Unfortunately, it's so difficult to master, there wasn't time enough to prepare it for a Broadway ADM engagement in the two weeks of rehearsal allowed. The young dancers couldn't get it right in so short a time.

"The biggest problems with Cole's work are achieving *Placement* and *Isolation*," Miller explains. He arches his back forward in a curious curve, at the same time inclining it towards the left. "See? Like this—but you have to be absolutely precise in taking the position, and you have to *hold* it. As with Cole's East Indian dances. That's placement, and it has to be used in all the other dance forms as well." This is the equivalent in singing of hitting the note exactly, not sounding it a quarter-tone off and sliding up or down into the right pitch. That, in dance, has become all too common: sliding into the correct position, making adjustments, which makes movement look sloppy, tentative, undefined.

"Watch Gwen Verdon when she dances. Notice how precise her body placement is, and yet how open, how easy she seems to be with it. Unlike some dancers, she's never vague in her movements, never sloppy. Cole's work wasn't like disco-dancing. If you're making an arch, nothing else moves! Now that takes a lot of muscle; to hold the position and make sure nothing else is wobbling or wiggling," says Miller.

"Only in a very, very few situations did Cole ever do a dance under pressure, when he knew there really wouldn't be enough time for rehearsals. As a rule, he'd say, if you cannot do it well, you've got no business being on stage dancing anyway. Today, it's not so much a problem of dancers watching the clock during rehearsals. No, when dancers are on stage in front of an audience, they want to look good," Miller insists. "The problem now is to get them wound up enough. To bring them to that pitch of excitement and preparedness where they can do the dance expertly."

Buzz Miller is a slight, intense dancer-teacher, with a charming manner. He has none of the fury of Cole, but he still demands the utmost of his dance students. When he announces a class in Cole Technique, he says, people are excited at the prospect and sign up. After one session, many don't return. It's too demanding, too exacting. "Who *needs* to work that hard?" Miller echoes his dropouts. "Right! No one needs to work that hard. But there is a real reward for them at the end of the course. But, not everyone can or will wait for it."

Although Miller became expert in all three of Cole's dance specialties, his first important assignment with Jack Cole was the Broadway musical *Magdalena*, which drew heavily on the Afro-Cuban, the Latin American dances. Days of unremitting effort were needed to set Cole's choreography. Every little articulation of any part of the body had to be absolutely right. Miller had never danced this way before, with so much use of isolation, learning to make each finger move quite separately of the others. Learning to make movements very strong, very controlled, and very cool. Learning to isolate even the movements of eyes and eyebrows.

"I was thrown into this work with no preparation," Miller recalls. "I did it very badly until I came to understand it—the reason for it." Cole explained the symbolism of even the smallest gesture of the hands or face in oriental dances, for instance. Understanding the tradition was a great help to him.

Florence Lessing, who mastered all this a decade before the advent of Miller in the Cole ensemble, stresses the importance of Cole's notion of *Isolation*. It requires, she says, a great deal of concentration and control. The dancer has to be very intelligent to be successful in mastering the technique: "So many parts of the body, so many muscles moving in opposition to each other, and each in isolation from the other!"

Each dance form uses special body muscles, so that in one kind of dance different groups of muscles will be used than in others. Cole's East Indian dance training is an excellent way to learn how to isolate muscle movements, Lessing suggests. She explains: "Modern dance will use the torso more than ballet does. Ballet uses the legs and feet more than does modern dance. What is wonderful, then, about East Indian training is the tremendous isolation of the quick head action, above, and the quite separate sinuous action of the arms and hands and fingers. All of this in a matter of seconds. To me, it's one of the most intricate forms of dance."

Florence Lessing also pays tribute to Jack Cole's dynamics: "In those sudden, rapid changes of direction—shooting forward and then jumping suddenly upward, for instance—you could see Cole's tremendous sense of dynamics, so interestingly juxtaposed. He managed switches from something sustained to something very abrupt wonderfully well. From the abruptness, he'd move into something very flowing, followed perhaps by a potent pause. He'd be using all the aspects of the art of dance: rhythm, tempo, levels, patterns . . ."

British director-choreographer Malcolm Goddard, who danced for Cole both on stage *(Kismet)* and on film, notes that Cole found it very difficult to discover English dancers who could meet his standards of performance. "Dance in British musicals," Goddard explains, "does tend to be different from American. It's always been difficult for a man to dance in England. It was considered not in good taste. You know, *'Men* don't dance!' Today, that's certainly changing. But after World War II, there weren't enough men who wanted to dance, so dance students were taken from the classroom too soon. Weaned into the theatre, if you like.

"Our dancers don't have the energy American dancers do. Energy is habit-forming! But it's not instinctive in an English dancer. We're not *hard* enough. We are capable, of course; we do the American shows. We will come up to the demanded level, but you do have to demand, and that usually is not done," Goddard admits. "Our training isn't as broad in show-dance as is most Americans'. . . . When I worked with Cole, from 1954 to '56, I knew my body wasn't ideal for his work. I wasn't really tall enough, and my body wasn't as limber as it once was. Not as disciplined. I managed, through guts and determination. It would have been, for me, wonderful to have started with Cole at fourteen, not at twenty-five.

"With Cole, you learned how to do everything. Today, many TV and show dancers are only good for disco. And producers want them to look young, so they are taken from training too soon. In the time of *Can-Can* and *Guys and Dolls,* every dancer had to learn *double-tours, grand pirouettes, coupe jeté,* tap dancing—everything! Now lots of dancers find it difficult to do disco correctly. Or jazz.

"Classical dancers are trained to move *out* or away from the ground. Jazz dancers move *into* the ground! It's that African thing. That's what Jack Cole gave us: One minute you were working into the ground, but the next, you were aloft, doing a *double-tour.* Suddenly, you'd been pulled out of the ground! That was quite a challenge, but that's what choreographers are there for—to challenge you," Goddard insists.

"In a Jack Cole show, a man was acting and then began to dance, and he danced the same way he was acting—in character. The author had written words to fit the character, so why shouldn't the choreographer give him movements to fit the character? Dance grows out of natural movement, but with a special visual style, and with synchronizations. The body has to hit good shapes instinctively. That's the difference, I think, between being a dancer and an actor," says Goddard thoughtfully.

"Jack Cole colored my life. After working with him, I became a different dancer. I became aware of different things, possibilities. He taught me things about audience sight lines which are terribly important. . . . If you are looking out into a large, deep auditorium, and you are blinded by the spotlights, where do you look? How do you fix your focus? You have to establish eye contact with the audience, when in fact you cannot see it. That takes a special technique and intensity of gaze which you must have. But the most important things Cole taught me were the *functional* things about dancing—dancing like a real person. You dance like a real waiter, stenographer, or cook, if that's what the character is. You do not dance like a dancer! It may take actors years to learn to act well, but all dancers, deep down, are actors. Or they ought to be. Good dancers can *think* themselves into the role or character. Unfortunately, in British musical productions, that's just not done enough. It's not encouraged or demanded," says a regretful Malcolm Goddard.

Fortunately, Jack Cole's techniques have been exported. Not only did Cole leave his mark on Goddard and other British dancers, but Matt Mattox, a stellar Cole student, veteran of eight years and seven Cole musicals, is currently teaching his own adaptation of Cole's work with jazz dance in France. He told *Dance* readers about his experiences with Cole: "You always did everything full out. You never marked the movement. By doing this, you gained stamina and strength." In this, Mattox echoes other Cole disciples. "You also learned to do everything to a precise count. It was because of this that his ensemble work was so neat and clean. Those of us who adored him never marked anything, even if he said, 'Mark it, fellas.' " Mattox found Cole's choreography hard to classify; it wasn't ballet and it wasn't really modern. Just the same, the Cole technique was "the strictest and most spectacular to be seen anywhere," and the modern influences, by way of Denishawn and Humphrey-Weidman, were also apparent.

Mattox admits, "No one could dance like Jack; we could only try to assimilate his way of dance. I watched him like a hawk, trying to learn how he isolated his movement so specifically . . ." Mattox managed to emulate Cole, but it took him a long time to realize what had been happening to his body in the process. Mattox mastered the Cole style, seeing in it tendencies toward both modern and jazz dance. And, even though blacks had unquestionably originated jazz dancing, he thought Cole's evolution of it was unique. By 1956, Mattox was teaching Cole style, with Cole's approval. For two years, he taught everything he says he could remember, but then he decided it was time to develop his own method, inspired by Cole's work.

In 1963, when Jack Cole was choreographing the Broadway musical, *Foxy*, which starred Bert Lahr, Clayton Cole asked him about jazz dance for *Dance Magazine*. What did the putative father think of the form's recent evolution? Jack Cole roared: "It's gone silly!" When asked for a clear definition of jazz dance, the response was that anything danced to jazz music should qualify. Did that mean, then, that a classical choreography, performed to a jazz beat would in fact be an example?

"No," Jack Cole said, "because it would lack the essence of

jazz, which is its *feeling*." Curiously, even though an important aspect of jazz is its bursts of free-floating instrumental improvisation, Cole saw no necessity for matching these with concurrent dance improvisations. His dances, timed to the split second for performance in clubs, films, and Broadway shows, had to be accompanied by set orchestrations, allowing no mid-performance musical surprises for his dancers.

"Jazz is urban folk music," Cole insisted. This was an idea he was fond of expounding. It is, he explained, the great articulation of the inarticulate. Cole didn't mean illiterate. "By inarticulate, I mean those who lacked the technical training necessary to express themselves through formal music. This was really their heart's blood, and naturally it reflected the society that gave it birth. Jazz has always remained accessible to the urban, technically untrained folk. It always must, or it will lose its validity."

At that time, despite the peculiarities of "Third Stream" jazz and the particularities of "West Coast" jazz, Jack Cole thought jazz was still accessible. He insisted that its dance form should remain that way as well. The formalities of classical ballet, he thought, were not accessible to urban folk. Cole protested urban innocence: "The man in the street cannot go on *pointe*; he can't pirouette. Whenever I see someone come out and go through a 'swinging' routine with a second position in it, I know he's left the track. Also, of course, the feeling of *in*articulation wouldn't be there."

For Cole, then, anything unsophisticated, danced to jazz music, as long as the movement corresponded to the *style* of the music, could be called jazz dance. But it was not the most precise of definitions. Cole was convinced that ballet dancers were least able to pick up the jazz style. At auditions, he revealed, he asked new dancers to snap their fingers in rhythm. This showed him whether they could keep time; many could not, he found. It also revealed the presence or absence of "true jazz feeling." Because of their orientation toward linear design, ballet dancers tended to *assume* the feeling, to do it from the outside. Cole preferred "a less formal person," one who was more concerned with individual expression, instead of seeing himself as part of a great tradition.

Real jazz dancing, in Cole's view, used to be seen in the 1920s and 1930s in dance halls; in such dances as the Camel Walk, the Charleston, and the Lindy Hop, Cole saw all these as inspired by African dance. He found them "filled with authentic feeling." The root of all the various elaborations was the Lindy step, according to Jack Cole. "Whatever is danced in the name of jazz dancing must come from the Lindy," he insisted, "necessarily theatricalized and broadened for the stage, of course."

If jazz itself was urban folk music, then jazz dance was, for Cole at least, urban folk dance. In the 1960s, however, he'd detected a trend toward "pop" music in dances that were presented as jazz-inspired. The term "modern jazz dance movement" also bothered Cole at this time. He didn't want it credited to him, he told interviewer Clayton Cole. "I never used the turned-out leg—in that sense, I'm closer to jazz dance." Then he made an important distinction: ". . . my real concern is not with jazz, but with a form of stylized theatre dance, which uses syncopated rhythms. I certainly believe that jazz music can well be used for dance, but let's not limit it to any one style, and let's not call it jazz dance."

Searching for a better name for the Jack Cole "show-biz" choreography, Cole mused: ". . . let's settle for Broadway Commercial, or something like that. To me it's rife with sentimentality; it's self-indulgent, but one thing else it is—it's *commercial*. It fits in with the—stuff—on television and such kindred 'artistic' endeavors. Maybe it helps orient a dancer to the harsh realities of hoofing for a buck. . . ."

7

COLE CREATES AT COLUMBIA

RITA HAYWORTH & ANN MILLER DANCE

Jack Cole was the only man in the world who wouldn't take a phone call from Marilyn Monroe. So says director-choreographer Ron Field. Because Cole had helped Monroe shape the screen persona she projected so successfully, she came increasingly to depend on his cinema expertise and his personal understanding as her own insecurities began to overwhelm her. Field remembers once having to lie to Monroe that Cole was not there, when she called for some reassurance and he didn't want to talk to her.

Marilyn Monroe was not the only superstar who adored Cole and wanted him as her choreographer. He, in turn, adored these sex-goddesses and used his special skills to enhance their images and add luster to their legends. Most of them were not trained dancers, but Cole knew how to design movement for them that created the impression on screen that they were sisters in spirit to Ginger Rogers. Among the talents who profited from working with Jack Cole were Betty Grable, Rita Hayworth, Dolores Gray, Ann Miller, Mitzi Gaynor, and Jane Russell. Alone among this stellar roster, Ann Miller, supremely confident in her tap dancing, may not have felt a debt to Jack Cole and his choreography, though his genius illuminated two of her films. That Hollywood's sex-goddesses—the world's sex-goddesses, virtually—adored Cole and demanded him as their choreographer, says Ron Field, made it possible for Cole to achieve as much as he did with their films. "They wouldn't work without him," Field emphasizes. "They *empowered* him! . . . When Rita Hayworth empowered Jack Cole at Columbia, he got everything he wanted from Harry Cohn. At Fox, Betty Grable and Marilyn Monroe empowered Cole . . .

"When that didn't happen," Field recalls, "Cole would go crazy. He otherwise had to answer to too many people who didn't understand him. Nor did they care to understand him; nor did they treat him like the artist he was." In fact, although Jack Cole worked on some thirty films, in Hollywood and abroad, the only memorable thing about some of them is the Cole choreography. Other far less talented men, for whom the title "dance director" is, as Cole more than once insisted, entirely appropriate, were summoned to stage dance sequences in big-budget cinema blockbusters. They knew how to engineer large-scale imitations of the Busby Berkeley masses of precision dancers on acres of sound stage settings that were increasingly sumptuous and vulgar.

Jack Cole had no interest in imitating anyone, especially Busby Berkeley. He also hated the idea of spectacular "dance numbers," inserted here and there in a film, possibly as colorful and welcome relief from the vapidity and overfamiliarity of the plot developments. Cole strove for an integration of plot action and the dance, notably at a time when Agnes de Mille's *Oklahoma!* choreography was inspiring the same kind of revolution on Broadway.

Seen today on the Late Late Late Show on television, Jack Cole's choreography stands out, often by itself, not because Cole didn't try his best for integration, but because the films on which he worked—even ones with very big budgets—frequently had plots that would never have won either a Pulitzer Prize for literary excellence or an Oscar for cinematic effectivensss. As George Martin says, "It was great fun, dancing in 'B' musicals!" Of course they weren't all, by any means, B pictures. Time passes, however, and tastes change.

There's an old Chinese/Russian/French proverb: "You can't step twice into the same river." If you try it with the River of Time, you run the danger of getting caught in the undertow. Seeing Cole's dances now, in old film reruns, viewers may feel they are looking at artifacts from another age. And so they are; you really had to have been there, sitting in darkened film theatres in the 1940s and 1950s, escaping from the rigors of daily life into the magic world of the movie musicals.

Busby Berkeley had his legions of imitators. Cole wasn't one of them. But Cole had his own imitators, even in his own time. It's not unfair to say that Cole's earlier work in major American city supperclubs had already made its mark on young dancers and choreographers who understood exactly what Cole's innovations meant to film and television, and how they could be adapted and abstracted. Cole's special kind of imagination, his bizarre fantasy, his erotic aggressiveness in dance movement, his sense of novelty: all these were unique when Cole came to Hollywood. Before long, however, Cole, as well as Berkeley, had his clones. After all, it's often said that imitation is the sincerest form of flattery. It's also the cheapest.

"When I first came to California and the movies, I was exploding with enthusiasm," Cole explained to performing arts critic and historian Arthur Todd in the early 1950s. For an article, he wrote: "I saw no reason why dancing and musical numbers need be so pedestrian and unimaginative, so pretentious and dull, so enormous and hilariously stupid. After a little experience, I was astounded that they came off as well as they did. The front office and the script entirely govern the point of view and the style of the production. As long as we must deal with the backstage or entertainment story—and literally at that—just so long will the dance production remain at its present level." It irked Cole endlessly that the bogus realism of most films forbade an ordinary milkman from bursting into song and dance, unless, of course, he was played by Gene Kelly. Film audiences knew that sooner or later Kelly would dazzle them with his twinkling feet, no matter what his role. It seemed Cole's fate to be assigned to films built around Broadway, vaudeville, or Hollywood studio situations.

Since Jack Cole had first come to public notice, he had been given screen tests at least once a year. Finally, in 1941, he was called to Hollywood for a handsome sum, by the standards of those wartime austerity days, to create an authentic American Indian dance with Florence Lessing and Anna Austin. They had been performing in Detroit when the summons came. Until this moment, Cole's employer had been indifferent, Cole said, to his presence. Once he realized Cole intended to depart, he made a tearful scene, outlining the pitiful effects of his possible bankruptcy, a direct result of not having Cole and his dancers on the bill. Cole reluctantly bought back his contract for $600.

Cole, Lessing, and Austin flew immediately to Hollywood. Without a chance to rest, they went directly to the Fox studio where *Moon Over Miami* was being filmed, with Betty Grable as its sexy female star, partnered by a dashing Don Ameche. Other dancers were already in rehearsal. Hermes Pan, a popular Hollywood choreographer—for whom Cole had little regard as an artist—was devising the film's dance sequences. One of the show's songs was a ditty called "Seminole," which had been envisioned as a climactic production number. Because of Cole's reputation as an expert in ethnic dance, he seemed an ideal choice to create this number and perform it with his highly trained troupe.

Cole and his dancers were supposed to perform a lively and interesting Seminole ceremonial ritual in a sound stage replica of a Seminole village. Because it was Cole's first Hollywood film, this cinema novice collected and saved a horde of production photos and snapshots of the set and the number in performance. Thatched huts and palm trees backed the dance, which was adjusted to a large ceremonial bonfire in the center of the arena. Cole saw to it that a trampoline was also on hand.

Later, Cole swore he exaggerated not at all when he said that the makeup people had turned him out looking so much like an axe that "you could have buried me in the nearest woodpile." His partner Florence Lessing was even less lucky. The makeup experts colored her blue—the picture was in Technicolor—because they thought that might look very chic in a color film. Then the dancers waited the entire day for a call. None came. At 7:00 P.M. Cole left in anger for his hotel. He was followed posthaste by a studio emissary, begging him to return with his troupe the next morning.

The next day, Cole demanded his music for the dance and a room in which to rehearse. He was given the set for Tyrone Power's *Blood and Sand*. Cole was to retell this story often, so there are several versions, with differing embellishments. The account he gave much later to film critic Arthur Knight depicts the Seminole Indians' ethnic dance as being very little different from that which he found in the heart of Brazil's Matto Grosso. The Seminoles, he said, made a dreary little shuffle in one direction, grunted "hut," and then shuffled in the opposite direction, with another grunt.

Deciding that a Betty Grable musical deserved something more exciting than this kind of ethnic authenticity, Cole drew on his creative powers. Talking to Helen Dzhermolinska of *Dance Magazine* in 1942, not long after the filming, Cole made no mention of shuffles and "huts." He did, however, note that he had expected some music based on the Seminoles' monotonous thumping of drums and the plaintive obligato of a reed flute. When he was handed "Seminole, I love you . . ." he was horrified, but no one listened to his outcries in the din of filmmaking. At least Cole could draw on authentic Seminole dance for his inspiration; he had performed his own act in Florida and had had the opportunity to watch the Seminoles shuffling. The heart of his choreography would, of course, be performed by Cole, Lessing, and Austin. But, because this was to be a big production number, there were also back-up dancers.

He went to the general rehearsal studio to see what they were doing. He found several score of big, sturdy California lovelies, dressed in skimpy skirts and some beads, stolidly repeating: "One, two, three, kick! One, two, three, turn . . ." This time, Cole's protests were heard. The dance director worked out some compromises. But Cole still had to perform his impressive choreography to the forgettable melody of "Seminole" and spring six feet from a board to the ground. This stunning effect had to be repeated for the cameras for over three hours, take after take. Cole swore that he had to walk around in a semisquat until his thighs and knees recovered from the shock.

When the filming was completed, Cole learned that he had managed to break not just one, but four major Production Code rulings. Studio editors cut the Seminole dance sequence to ribbons, Cole later reported, but even with that cinematic surgery, Cole's choreography was finally shown in only four of the then forty-eight states. When the film opened in New York at the Roxy in July 1941, the *New York Times* judged *Moon Over Miami* "a very average musical comedy," despite the presence of Betty Grable. Neither Cole nor his sensational Seminoles were mentioned in the review. Cole's choreography was rated as too erotic by the Hays Office, which enforced the Production Code.

An article on Legion of Decency strictures regarding cinema choreography is preserved in Jack Cole's scrapbooks.

In disgust, Jack Cole returned to Manhattan, and not for the last time. Even after he established his home in Los Angeles in 1943, he was to maintain a New York apartment, an occasional refuge from studio struggles and the sunny unsophistication of Southern California. Harry Cohn, the ruthless and forceful chief of Columbia Pictures, lured Cole back to Hollywood with assurances of greater control and a very good salary. One of Cole's first assignments was on *Cover Girl* (1944), starring Rita Hayworth and Gene Kelly. Seymour Felix was the film's choreographer and Cole came in only at the end to "tidy up" some things.

That same year, MGM released a new version of *Kismet* starring Marlene Dietrich and Ronald Colman. The Kraft Twins, Beatrice and Evelyne, were featured in a dance specialty. Cole received no credit for his work, but he listed *Kismet* among his films when he tallied them for Arthur Todd. Once, discussing how he surmounted peculiar obstacles in film choreography, Cole noted that he had devised dance movement for Dietrich shortly after she'd recovered from a leg fracture. The *New York Times* made no mention of Cole, nor of a previous Dietrich indisposition, but it did make a point of the effective display of the famous Dietrich limbs.

Tonight and Every Night was Jack Cole's first major film effort for Columbia, completed in 1944 and released March 1945. The proud boast of London's notorious Windmill Theatre, both in wartime German bombing blitzes and after World War II, was "We Never Closed!" Small wonder; the Windmill was an intimate West End theatre that specialized in tableaus of lucious nude girls. Their nakedness, relieved by costume props such as spike heels and pert top hats, was legal as long as they didn't move. This was the theatrical reality that *Tonight and Every Night* sanitized as the "Music Box Theatre," sans nudity.

The script, directed by Victor Saville, was based on Leslie Storm's story, *Heart of a City*. The plot involved the courageous efforts of the Music Box ensemble to entertain Allied troops and besieged Londoners during the Blitz. For some reason, known best to Harry Cohn and Columbia's contract department, no attempt was made to cast or suggest British performers. Rita Hayworth and Janet Blair played attractive performers in the company. Hayworth fell in love with pilot Lee Bowman; Blair, with a fellow dancer, played by Marc Platt, fresh from his Broadway triumph in *Oklahoma!* Blair and Platt would die in an air raid. Hayworth, reunited with her airman, would valiantly refuse him to go on cheering the troops with her singing and dancing. Songs were by Sammy Cahn and Jule Styne.

Cole shared choreographic credit with Val Raset. But, as George Martin recalls, "Mickey Raset was the original choreographer, but he didn't do anything. He was a real old-fashioned Hollywood choreographer." Martin had just met his future wife, Ethel, dancing in *The Yellow Rose of Texas.* Raset wanted some jitterbugging in the new film. George Martin begged a reluctant Ethel to come to the audition. She said she couldn't jitterbug, then the most popular and frenzied of jazz dancing. Martin promised to "throw her around," and Raset hired them. They were part of the film's initial skeleton crew of dancers. They worked with Raset on part of a number for *Tonight and Every Night.* Harry Cohn came to see it; the next day, Martin remembers, Jack Cole was assigned to choreograph the picture.

Partnering Rita Hayworth had not been part of Cole's plan. As was to happen with Ann Miller in *Eadie Was a Lady* and with Betty Grable in *Meet Me After the Show,* Cole had to step in and dance in the film. As he told Arthur Todd, "Actually, I have never danced in pictures myself by intention—only to stay on schedule when accident threatened disaster to the budget. A sprained ankle caused me to partner Miss Hayworth . . ."

One of Jack Cole's novelties was a dance sequence in which characters in a newsreel stepped out of the frame to get involved in the production number. In another routine, the Music Box ensemble was sitting backstage when the grating voice of Adolf Hitler came over the wireless, rasping and ranting his determination to bring Britain to her knees. Aroused by this furious Teutonic rhetoric, Marc Platt began to mime the speech in dance. Cole choreographed it on a stairway—another challenge. There was no musical accompaniment; only the hated voice of Hitler. This was to become typical of the innovations and risks Cole introduced into musicals.

Francine Ames Kuney was one of Cole's core of dancers at Columbia. Showing stills from *Tonight and Every Night,* she says, "Here's Shelley Winters in that Hitler number. They're all sitting around listening to the radio before Marc begins to dance. Here's Marilyn Johnson, and Mrs. Sylvester Pat Weaver [before her marriage to the longtime head of NBC], Ethel Martin, myself, and Jewel McGowan. Shelley and Mrs. Weaver were contract players, not dancers."

Although the film was beautifully filmed in Technicolor, with some stunning costumes by Marcel Vertes and Jean Louis, the settings for the dance sequences were unusually restrained, compared with most Hollywood musicals of the time. From the first, Jack Cole knew what he wanted in terms of dance areas, surfaces, and levels for his production numbers. He had very clear ideas about the cut, construction, and colors of the costumes—and what kinds of interesting movements and actions they could inspire. Perhaps it was just his choreographer's vanity, though it could also have been Harry Cohn's hawkeye on the budget, but dance settings in *Tonight and Every Night* were suggestive, partial, even abstract, rather than solidly, ponderously splendid. This system of selectively setting a dance's scenic milieu is a distinctive Cole trademark, though he was not always able to employ it. Cole understood why some choreographers welcomed tons of scenery and gauze veilings for their production numbers; the mediocrity or inferiority of what they churned out for the cameras had to be overwhelmed by the sets and costumes so audiences wouldn't notice so clearly how devoid the dances were of originality, relevance, or vitality.

Francine Ames fondly remembers one sequence from *Tonight and Every Night* in which the girls in the ensemble were costumed as English nannies, taking their infant charges for pram rides in the park. "Suddenly, the park is invaded by all these American sailors! We rip off our cloaks, and there's a big jazz dance!" Ames says. Cahn and Styne had musically posed the question: "What Does an English Girl Think of a Yank?" Jack

Cole provided a frantic, erotic answer, in case anyone was in doubt.

One of the Music Box's specialty acts was Professor Lamberti, demonstrating his sleight of hand, with a slyly naughty Rita Hayworth assisting him. Lamberti was puzzled by the peals of laughter his act seemed to be eliciting from the audience. What he could not see was that his female helper was doing a make-believe striptease behind his back. This suggestion of a strip was almost the only indication in the film of the nature of the real Windmill's entertainments. Ames says, "Rita did a lot of stuff with the curtain that Jack had got directly from burlesque. He was influenced by some women in burlesque who were infamous and famous as well. How often he would go to study them! Rita was working the curtain, waving it back and forth between her legs. If the times had permitted, he'd have done a lot more. He was always intrigued by a dancer who was famous for twirling tassles on her breasts in opposite directions. He believed in muscular control. He was furious with women who'd adjust their bra straps in class, or pull on their shorts or tights. He claimed we should take classes in the nude, and we'd learn to control our muscles; that we didn't need bras. This was so ahead of its time. . ."

In 1946, almost immediately after the war was over, Francine Ames went to London. One sight she very much wanted to see was the famous Windmill Theatre. She hailed a taxi and told the driver her destination. He was appalled: "Oh mum! You don't want to go *there!*"

For Cole, the biggest dividend in working on the film was the creation of his own dance studio at Columbia, with a core of Cole dancers under annual contract. If Harry Cohn was churning out musicals and he wanted quality dancing, Cole convinced him there was no way to get it in a matter of days with dancers auditioned off the streets. Cole's experiences with *Moon Over Miami* had made that all too clear. It was true, of course, that studios did maintain singers and dancers under contract, but they were expected to be readily available for publicity or even for use as scene-swelling extras. Cole insisted his dancers were to be freed from such non-dance chores. He got his way.

After Cole had convinced Cohn he needed his own studio ensemble, he held auditions. Dancers he liked working with in *Tonight and Every Night* were in effect charter members—people such as Ethel and George Martin and Francine Ames. Rod Alexander, Alex Romero, and Bob Hamilton were selected by audition. As George Martin remembers, Harry Cohn assigned Stage 10 to Cole and had the studio built. "And then did we work! Every day from nine o'clock. When we weren't in production, we worked from 9:00 to 5:00 P.M., doing nothing but dancing. . . . He insisted we have $125 per week. Broadway was then paying dancers only $60 a week. I think at that point in Cole's life, he probably thought: 'I've got it!' Here was Harry Cohn paying all the bills. He had us locked in that room working away, but none of us would have not wanted to do it."

When the studio was launched, Cole's methods were the bane of union representatives. "Hollywood unions always had very strong rules about rest periods," says Martin. "And you didn't do this; you didn't do that. When we started working with Jack—especially Ethel, I, and Paul Steffen, who were very close—we never stopped working. Take the breaks? We didn't care. We'd get told off by the union guys, but it was such a challenge that we never stopped, and that carried through."

There were twelve in the initial studio group, according to Rod Alexander: six girls and six boys. In addition to Francine Ames and Ethel Martin, there were Gloria Maginetti, Ruth Godfrey, Nita Bieber, and Patricia Cummings. Gwen Verdon was a later addition. The six boys were Martin, Alexander, Romero, Steffen, Bob Hamilton, and Charles Lanard. For specialty work, Cole could call in such talents as Anita Alvarez, Harriet Ann Gray, and Paul Godkin.

"Every day we studied body mechanics for about two hours," says Alexander. "Then ballet for two hours, then lunch, after which we studied different ethnic forms of dance, including some tap. That was the general regimen." Rod Alexander believes he had to work harder than the others. "I was the least experienced. We got to know Jack during this time as well as anyone could get to know him. He was a mystery, moody at times, and at times humorous. But always the consummate dancer-choreographer and driving force. He would often, when he was angry, beat the drum for class and call out the exercises or demonstrate. When things did not go well, he would beat the drum harder and harder until the soft end of the drumstick came off and flew through the air. Then he'd throw away the stick and beat time with his hand. Finally, he'd walk away in disgust.

"Once a girl fainted in class. We continued to dance, leaping over her body. We were too frightened to stop, yet wondering why we didn't. She eventually revived; the class continued. There were times—mostly in the afternoon—when he wanted to try new movement. We followed him through several combinations, over and over, endlessly. He was tireless," Alexander says.

In Jack Cole's scrapbooks, there is a cartoon that makes mild fun of the Cole regimen. It shows bruised and bandaged dancers, collapsed in a heap on the floor. The caption: "I guess we're going to have to modify the choreography a bit." Over this satiric illustration, Jack Cole wrote with a bold felt-tip: "JACK COLE STUDIO."

Francine Ames Kuney emphasizes another value of the studio group for Cole. Not only did it give him a permanent nucleus of highly trained dancers, but it also gave him a ready pool of assistants who could help teach the steps and routines to other dancers, engaged from film to film for large-scale numbers, for which Cole might use another forty dancers. "So the look would be there," says Ames. "We didn't have to do all that junky between-pictures stuff the starlets had to do."

Among her memories of the Columbia dance studio is Cole's insistence that his dancers wear sneakers in rehearsals. "I think he was the first to have dancers do this," she says. "There really weren't that many kinds of shoes for dancers then—only the ballet shoe, the toe shoe, and the 'natural' sandal, a piece of suede and a T-strap, but no sole. Jack wanted us to get the feeling of our feet grabbing the floor. We did a lot of difficult things.

If a number required high-heels, we'd shift to them in rehearsal, but most classes and all the jazz dancing was done in
sneakers."

Looking back, she now marvels at that period at Columbia.
Harry Cohn liked and respected Cole and gave him everything
he wanted. "We had our own sound stage for rehearsals," she
says in wonder. "No one could touch it, no matter what the
budget for a film."

"Harry Cohn was so smitten with Jack's talent," says Ethel
Martin, "that he readily agreed to let Jack set up his unique dance
workshop. . . . Considering how careful Harry Cohn was re-
puted to be with money, it was amazing that he did this for
Jack. But it's curious, too, how Jack seemed to appeal to people
like Harry Cohn." George Martin believes Jack Cole had a very
special quality of attracting people: "From the Mafia on down,
I don't think there was a person who wasn't fascinated with
him. Look at Harry Cohn! That evil s.o.b. obviously thought he
was terrific." Martin says the ensemble members were mostly
around twenty years old at that time. "We thought of him as a
father, but he couldn't have been more than fourteen years
older," he guesses.

Surveying his career in the early 1950s, Cole called the studio "the ideal situation that happens to all of us once in a while."
He wrote of it with pride, ". . . because it was and is the only
such case on record." According to Cole's count, it lasted three
and one-half years, and he was permitted to hire sixteen dancers,
or so he wrote. Since he began with twelve dancers, in using
this figure he may have been counting those who joined the
group later, like young Gwyneth Verdon.

Verdon admits, "I was there only *briefly*. I wasn't old enough
to work in movies. I was seventeen. But I lied about my age,
and they found out. Well, first of all, I saw Jack Cole in a nightclub and I went backstage to talk to him. I told him I'd do anything to work for him. So he said, 'Come to the studio.' I guess
he thought I was funny, but I got the job. I was so willing to
work, and he admired that as much as he admired talent."

Between the major Columbia musicals that Cole choreographed, he later told Arthur Todd, ". . . there were innumer-

able 'B' pictures for Columbia, as well as ethnologic, period, or atmosphere chores for non-musical pictures." Sometimes these could be as simple as offering expert advice on historical accuracy; Cole was, after all, building a remarkable dance archive. He wrote Todd bluntly: "It is really the most important of my dance activities in California . . ." Cole put his collecting before his film work or his non-studio teaching at Eugene Loring's school.

Cole's studio school was an innovation, but, at the same time, a unique instance. After several years' absence from Hollywood sound stages, he was not again encouraged to set up a similar group at studio expense in the 1950s. Another Cole innovation, with more staying power, was his method of having a skilled artist present at dance rehearsals to make rapid, detailed sketches of the various important moments in the dances, from the point of view of key camera positions. These were usually executed in color. They permitted the set and costume designers to coordinate their contributions with the choreographer's dance imagery and compositions. "This is something new, and what I hope is a step forward," Cole was to say. "Too often in the past, the director didn't even see the set till he moved onto it, while the scenic and costume designers never saw the dancers at all . . ." From these swiftly-sketched color impressions of the nature of Cole's new choreography, the designers could then draft their own drawings so that these could be built in the studio shops. In planning new routines, Cole also made his own preliminary sketches, paying special attention to the areas and levels to be used in the dances.

At the Sotheby's Cole sale in November 1979, many watercolor and gouache drawings of sets, costumes, and dance scenes were auctioned off. Among the films represented were *The Thrill of Brazil*, *Down to Earth*, *The Jolson Story*, and *On the Riviera*. Considering Cole's care in building his dance collection, this instant dissolution is sad, but in his later years, he did lend such treasurers to those he thought would profit from being able to study them.

Released in 1945, *Eadie Was a Lady* spotlighted the vibrant talent of Ann Miller, famed for her endurance, speed, and style as a tap dancer. Taps were not tops with Jack Cole, but he was assigned to the film, and Miller unquestionably was the star of it. She had an avid public, and her films drew well. So, if she wanted to tap, Cole would just have to find a way to enhance her specialty with his own somewhat wider dance palette.

The fable involving Eadie, like Cole's previous Columbia gem, was set at least partially in a theatre. To be precise, "Foley's Variety Theatre," home of burlesque, as sanctioned by the Production Code, not as actually presented in America's seedy surviving bump-and-grind houses. Initially, Miller was shown as the stuff stars are made of, even in the rear of the chorus. She fairly glowed with vitality, enthusiasm, and charm.

To make sure that movie audiences didn't miss the initial point about Miller's talent and radiance in the chorus, both Cole and the film's director, Arthur Dreifuss, told the women in Cole's ensemble to "cool it!" The film's first big production number, described by Francine Ames as "that jazz-piano number," had a set in effect designed by Cole. It was, says Ames, "a series of platforms and steps that we worked off. . . . The whole dance was designed around those levels. There was no real scenery. He wanted platforms so people could jump, and it would look like there was real height there." Cole partnered Miller, stepping in at the last minute. He was a sleek piano player in a virtually invisible bar. Cole wore striped shirt, black bow tie, and flared black trousers. The jazz beat in "I'm Gonna See My Baby" fired up his stripe-suited male dancers and his dancing girls, clad in diaphanous black. Miller dominated the frenzy, however, spraying impudent sexiness all over the set. A sequined knee-length dress, slit at one point almost to the waist, a black feather boa, and very high-heeled shoes heightened the effect. Miller could tap all she pleased, but Cole knew how to complement her routines with his own brand of jazz dancing which blended effectively. For the title number, the Gay Nineties provided a production theme. The number was performed in a small club-theatre proscenium. The set was little more than a white Victorian cast-iron fence, a white cast-iron deer, and some white branches against a white background. Four of Cole's men were in Victorian sporting outfits, with straw boaters. Four of the women partnered them, in long black sequined skirts, tight white blouses and big Victorian hats. Miller made her entry bursting through a Gay Nineties poster. She did some taps, but the dance was largely composed of elegant movement patterns, with extended arms. For the film's Greek finale, Cole's women dancers were clad in free-flowing—but nonetheless clinging—white gowns, draped and fastened just as they had been 2500 years before in Attic Greece. They were partnered by bright young college lads, resplendent in white suits and straw hats. There was some blinking of lights to indicate thunder and lightning, followed by a dance sequence with umbrellas, now surely one of the hoariest of choreographic clichés. Outfitted in a short black sequined costume, Miller dazzled as she tapped.

Whatever their wartime worries about boys overseas or sugar shortages at home, movie audiences got full dance value for their money in *Eadie Was a Lady*. Francine Ames says of some of the numbers, "It was 'acceptable' burlesque. We couldn't do erotic burlesque." In fact, these early cinema dances had some of the special Cole qualities that would continue to distinguish his work. There was very little male and female dancing together, very little touching. Rather, Cole's dances often suggested a contest, or a conflict, between his men and women.

Those were the days of the double-feature: the main attraction—such as a musical—followed by a Grade "B" Western or adventure film. The bait was sweetened with the obligatory cartoon, a newsreel, and a comic short, a documentary, or a brief filmed encounter with a big band, fronted by some talented dancers. Cole made many such shorts for Columbia. In them, he could manage to sneak in some dance novelties the censor would certaintly have cut in a major film.

Cole's next big musical for Columbia was *Tars and Spars*, with Alfred Drake, brought to Hollywood on the crest of his *Oklahoma!* fame, playing a handsome Coast Guardsman smitten with Janet Blair. Although the picture opened in New York at Loew's State in February 1946, it was completed in 1945, and planned when the United States was still at war. V-E Day and V-J Day were already almost historical echoes; peacetime was upon the nation. The critic for the *New York Times* didn't even mention

Jack Cole, at least not by name: "Alfred Drake, who went from *Oklahoma!* to Hollywood, and Marc Platt, out of the same Broadway show, impressed us as being in need of a tunesmith and a choreographer, respectively." The manic mugging of a young comedian, Sid Caesar, pleased some of the other critics. Caesar and the film's title were almost the only survivals of the original Coast Guard show which had toured American theatres in 1944 and 1945.

The *Times* was partly right about *Tars and Spars*. Still, Cole did use some very original ideas for this trite script. Alfred Drake, under contract as a romantic leading man with a fine singing voice, was one of the first non-dancing film stars Cole would use in ingenious ways in effective dance numbers. Drake is sure he had met Cole before this film—as was Cole—but neither could remember where that might have been.

Drake's prior dance efforts were, as he says, "not at all like the sort of thing he [Cole] was doing. We did have a marvelous scene, Marc Platt, Sid Caesar, and I. There was a song and dance in a moment of great elation. It was supposed to take place in the radio-shack of the ship we were on. It was a wild one! We did all sorts of things.

"I came home aching every night from muscles that hadn't been used that way before. But it really turned out exceedingly well. We were all very pleased and proud of it. Sid was even less a dancer than I. It looked very, very good. And, of course, it was cut!" Drake laughs, but he still sounds disappointed that the choreography wasn't shown. "Cole was so good at handling people. Marc, of course, was a dancer, and Jack knew what he could do with him. But he was marvelous at handling people who weren't trained as dancers. He could make you do things which were quite amazing!"

One of those amazing things involved specialty dancer Anita Alvarez and Cole's ensemble. The production number, set in a carnival shooting gallery, was amazing in itself. More amazing was the fact that Alvarez was not killed when she fell off the set, which was almost twenty feet high. Francine Ames still remembers it vividly: "Jack was really horrified. It was quite dangerous. In fact, I got stunt pay on that set. I had to be up at the top of the set, with my legs hanging down as a moving target in the shooting gallery.

"It was very surrealistic," she recalls. "The dancers were either *arms* or *legs*. There were holes cut into the set for arms and legs to stick through. The arms had very elegant gloves on them. The legs had very beautiful shoes and hose. Those were the moving targets!" Asked if this idea of Cole's—letting marksmen draw a bead on human appendages apparently detached from any visible owners—didn't seem a bit sadistic, Ames responds thoughtfully: "Well, it was *Jack*, you see!"

On March 15, 1946, Rita Hayworth filled the giant screen of Radio City Music Hall, acting, singing, and undulating in *Gilda*, opposite a visibly agitated Glenn Ford. Charles Vidor directed and got his credit; Cole choreographed and got none. He devised some sultry, seductive dance movements for Hayworth, to heighten the effect of her songs, presented in a casino club. They were not novelty turns—if one overlooks a whip as a prop—nor were they strenuously choreographed "productions." The *Motion Picture Herald* noted that the film "provides three occasions for Miss Hayworth to entertain with songs of the blue variety and with a variety of dance which may be described as provocative, if not downright hot."

Virtually enshrined as the Hollywood Love Goddess, the alluring Hayworth sent male temperatures soaring almost everywhere *Gilda* was shown, especially with her rendition of "Put the Blame on Mame." Over at the *New York Times*, its conservative film critic, Bosley Crowther, wasn't tuning in; if Crowther found any merit in Rita Hayworth, it was not in her artistry, and he crushingly commented: "A couple of times she sings song numbers, with little distinction, be it said, and wiggles through a few dances that are nothing short of crude."

On September 6, Jack Cole's choreography for *The Thrill of Brazil* was unveiled at the Loew's State Theatre in Manhattan. Again, as in *Eadie Was a Lady*, Ann Miller starred and tapped. A dividend for Cole came from an unexpected source: Arthur Murray. The man who had taught many Americans "dancing in a hurry" presented his Annual Achievement Award collectively to the Jack Cole Dancers for their "electrifying routines" in Columbia's *The Thrill of Brazil*. The *New York Times*, however, was still not handing out awards of any kind to Jack Cole.

Actually, unless the *Times* reviewer, Thomas M. Pryor, had really done his homework, he couldn't have known that Jack Cole was involved in *The Thrill of Brazil*. Dance credits went only to Nick Castle, whom Cole hired to supervise Miller's tap dances, and to Eugene Loring, who set the rest of the dances, except for the frantic Cuban finale, devised by Cole with intimations of Voodoo ritual. Rod Alexander says Cole would call on Loring when there were too many films on the production agenda. Cole was a painstaking choreographer but also notoriously slow. If gossip columnists were to be believed, there was danger that somebody's blood might be spilled in the early days of production. Cole treasured a clipping which confided to the world: "Ann Miller is terrified of her new dance instructor, Jack Cole, a guy so on the temperamental side that, when he became disgusted with his last pupil, he left the studio for three days and came back with his head shaved. Ann's knocking herself out to prevent any similar outbursts."

Actually, Ann Miller was a thoroughly self-confident Hollywood star, a match—if not more than one—for Cole and his infamous temper. Cole left her to the tender choreography of Nick Castle and concentrated on the Cuban finale, while S. Sylvan Simon, the hapless director of this farrago of entertainment specialties, tried to keep the film moving along so viewers wouldn't pay too much attention to the plot. Again, this was one of those films where the characters could reasonably and realistically be expected to be involved in dance sequences. It might have made no sense to the front office and the millions of movie fans, but Cole longed for a film in which quite ordinary people in prosaic situations could suddenly be swept up in exciting and imaginative dances, even in fantastic and surreal ones. But, if he wanted to do what Agnes de Mille had done in *Oklahoma!*, he should have stayed on Broadway.

The following month, on October 11, 1946, Columbia opened *The Jolson Story* at Radio City Music Hall. It starred Larry Parks and Evelyn Keyes. Part of its novelty was provided by Jolson's own singing voice, issuing apparently from Parks's opened mouth. Parks spoke the lines himself, unfortunately, and the vocal disparity was noticeable. Fortunately for Jolson, if not for the viewers, Columbia had no intentions of telling the real, full Jolson story with any deep fidelity of detail. As a result, Bosley Crowther's *Times* critique now seems accurate, if not downright benign. He thought the songs were better than the talk. As for the plot, it was a "fat and fatuous tale." For Crowther, the story and its screen visualization were done with "such obvious and hackneyed fabrication that they are likely to make the sensitive squirm."

The irony in this is that *The Jolson Story* grossed $8 million, making it Columbia's most financially rewarding production at that time. The only films to exceed the grosses of *The Jolson Story* in 1946 were *The Best Years of Our Lives* and *Duel in the Sun*. It won six Oscars in a year of other interesting musicals: *The Harvey Girls, Blue Skies, The Road to Utopia, Ziegfeld Follies, Till the Clouds Roll By,* and *Margie.*

Before shooting got under way on *The Jolson Story*, Cole's dancers were allowed to listen to Jolson's voice as it would be heard on the completed sound track. Rod Alexander recalls, "Jolson's voice was superb, even though he was an older man at the time. I don't know whether it was due to improved sound equipment, or his voice was really better."

In rehearsal, Jack Cole worked with his augmented ensemble, and his assistant coached Larry Parks, who was not a dancer. Francine Ames says, "He said it himself: he couldn't walk straight with any grace at all. They literally taught him to move. He moved like Jolson, and Jolson used to come on the set to see how it was going. He was very pleased with what Larry was doing. He worked his behind off to learn to mimic Jolson and move as he did."

Jolson also watched Jack Cole's dance numbers with an eagle eye. "They never danced like that in my days in show business," he said. Rod Alexander thought about this comment, but even today he's not sure whether it was a genuine compliment for Cole, or a typically snide Jolsonian dig.

There was a Rainbow Room scene, in which Jolson was a customer but was recognized and asked to step onto the floor and sing. Cole's dancers also performed in the sequence. Their flamboyant costumes from a Cole South American number just filmed were reworked for this scene. Zebra-striped hip sashes were replaced with gold lamé. Different headdresses were created. Harry Cohn was not about to waste money on production costs.

One of the Jack Cole archival treasures which was dispersed in the 1979 Sotheby's sale, LOT 178, included twenty watercolor and gouache settings for dance scenes, costumes, and sets in *The Jolson Story*, as the catalogue states, "the majority mounted, *some with Jack Cole's library stamp on verso of mounts*, various sizes, 1946; Photographic reproductions of his dance settings, 105 in all, *black and white*. . ." What appear to be seven of the Jolson series are preserved in a private collection of original American set and costume designs in Brooklyn. Arranged in sequence, these watercolors outline the cinematic development of the Jack Cole choreography for "The Spaniard Who Blighted My Life," a number Jolson once performed in a revue.

Francine Ames considers "The Spaniard" a rather innocuous song, "but Jack made a comedy out of it." There were several singers with semi-solo roles. Larry Parks really couldn't dance, but he could mime the song. Cole's comic conceit for this production number was to hire an extremely tall model, Helen O'Hara, who was well over six feet. Cole had wardrobe provide her with built-up shoes with high heels and a very tall headdress. Carmen Miranda's celebrated cranial cascades of fruit were as foothills to the Everest of O'Hara's headgear. As a result, she towered over Parks's little Spaniard, who adored her. To vary the action, Cole introduced a cart, pulled by a donkey suit filled with two Cole dancers. Señoritas leaned from picturesque balconies laden with potted flowers. Ames was very fond of this sequence: "It was quite charming, but a rather long number. It's cut entirely when they show *The Jolson Story* on TV."

Alfred E. Green, the director of *Tars and Spars*, staged the film. *Variety* found Cole's dances excellent; *Dance Magazine*, long a Cole booster, judged them "among the most zestful sequences in the film."

The last of Cole's pictures for Columbia was *Down to Earth,* a sequel to—not a remake of—*Here Comes Mr. Jordan.* This supernatural gentleman had the power to interfere in the lives of mortals, which he did again in this film, which opened September 12, 1947 at Radio City Music Hall. It was once more a Technicolor musical, set in a theatre, permitting a natural, logical excuse for dancing. Rita Hayworth, as the elegantly lovely Muse of Dance, Terpsichore, looked down to earth and the Athens Theatre, where a producer, played by Larry Parks, was preparing a quasi-Greek dance, but swinging it.

At the Athens Theatre, the show was called *Swinging the Muses.* Cole must have been in heaven—or on Olympus, at least—with this show. The set was a collage of Greek columns, and classical overtones pervaded the atmosphere. Adele Jergens was playing Terpsichore in an earthly manifestation. The plot required Hayworth to be furious at this jazzy travesty of her art: "Doesn't the theatre belong to me?" she asked her sister Muses. Cole and Harry Cohn got two production numbers for the price of one, as Hayworth came down to earth and rapidly replaced Jergens in the show. Just as Ann Miller dazzled from the back row of the chorus in *Eadie Was a Lady,* so did the radiant Rita completely eclipse the charms and talents of a furious Jergens, who left the show.

Hayworth seemed both elegantly ethereal and wonderfully, warmly human in this film. Her beauty and vitality fairly vibrated and shimmered. Having Hayworth whirl as she danced, hair and skirt flying, helped the image. Cole's choreography for Hayworth showed her to remarkable advantage.

The plot required Parks to fall in love with his new star, which he did with gusto, if not great acting. Thespis, the Muse of Drama, hadn't come along with the Muse of Dance. Terpsichore found herself torn between Parks and a talented dancer in his revue, played by Marc Platt. In "This Can't Be Legal," she tried to sort out the dual attraction of the men, in music and dance artfully arranged by Jack Cole.

Cole was taking no chances on the effectiveness of a major production number with classic allusions aplenty, and more than a slight suggestion of a Martha Graham evocation of ancient

Greece. His assistant on *Down to Earth*, Harriet Ann Gray, was also cast as Cole's leading "classical" dancer, a foil for Rita Hayworth. Years later, Gray was to tell researcher Kimberly Kaufman that this was the first use of modern dance in a Hollywood musical. She added that the film, because it was considered a classic, was being preserved with other cinematic treasures in an Alaskan storage vault.

Bosley Crowther, who reviewed *Down to Earth* for the *Times*, generally admired Cole's dances, which was generous, considering his previous reservations about Cole's choreography—even when he didn't know it was Cole's. Of this classical sequence, he wrote: "A neo-classical hodgepodge of leaping and gliding girls and boys, labeled (we believe) a Greek Ballet is also a pictorial thing." It was indeed visually strong, but initially it wasn't clear whether Cole was gently spoofing a Graham work or was seriously trying to evoke a starkly tragic dance.

Francine Ames says this was "the challenge-ballet, in which the masks of Tragedy and Comedy competed. . . . Tragedy is represented by women on *pointe*, and Comedy is represented by men and women doing jazz dance." These latter dancing comedians wore straw hats and red-satin costumes. Ames recalls, "There were arches and forests of leafless trees. The ballet took place in this sort of empty space, a fantasy space." The setting Cole had called for was graced by fragments of classical architecture, with a great slanting central dancing area, apparently paved with large stone slabs. Flanking this were a series of ramps and platforms, and even bases of Greek columns, all offering the dancers a variety of levels for flowing, changing movement, but especially suited to choreographing two rival groups of dancers, challenging each other. On one side was the dark dourness of the tragic muse; on the other, the gay, rambunctious, jazzy muse of comedy. In case any viewers missed the point, there were elegantly stylized masks of Comedy and Tragedy, against which Hayworth posed. Cole even used visual quotes from classic friezes and statuary in some of the dance movements.

Cole danced with his chorus and with Hayworth. Carole Haney was also in the group; it was one of the few films she made with Cole. When she joined the studio, unlike the veterans who had had to slave and sweat to master the Cole techniques, Haney seemed to fall easily into them. "As though she'd been doing it all her life," one Cole dancer remembered. Another dancer in *Down to Earth*, Dorothy Roberts, told all to an interviewer. The report was headlined as "Film Chorus Girl's Day Means 8 Hours of Labor Set to Music." Roberts began by rerunning memories of her life as a Broadway dancer—flowers, stage-door johnnies, after-show nightclubbing, all the glamorous things associated with being a chorus girl. Jack Cole had, however, changed all that for Dorothy Roberts. She trained, rehearsed, or performed on the set from 9 to 6, with an hour for lunch, she revealed. But the work was secure, and the pay certain.

Roberts confirmed Cole's constant forebodings about training female dancers. "We all like dancing better than any other kind of work, but it's work just the same. Few of us expect to make a career of it. Ninety-five per cent of the girls want to marry, settle down, and raise families." These cinema dancers, she said, averaged twenty-two years of age, with career expectancies of only four or five years. Roberts did say that the male dancers, in contrast, seemed hopeful of careers in show business, of becoming actors, or even stars like Gene Kelly and Marc Platt. Cole himself added a footnote to the interview: "There is no type of dancing these youngsters aren't capable of doing. They have talent, training, and solid technique. In *Down to Earth*, for instance, they do classic ballet, then a swing version of the same ballet; adagio dancing is used, and there's a waltz, a clog, tap, and ultra-modern jive. They're working with famous dancers like Rita Hayworth and Marc Platt, and they just have to be good."

Cole's reference to Platt is interesting in the light of comments by George Martin, who was in the troupe. Martin says, "Jack Cole *made* Marc Platt with that one film, *Tonight and Every Night*, and then he proceeded in the next to destroy him. . . . It's the only time I saw him really cruel. I always found his criticisms funny: 'You dance like your ass is made of Venetian glass.' I'd fall over laughing. But he hurt Marc, just by criticizing him in front of his fellow dancers." Toward the close of the film,

Cole created a big production number, set in an imaginary "Gramercy Park Playground." One of the varied dance movements in this lively but complicated choreography required Martin and Rod Alexander to perform that old Cossack step, crouching on their heels and thrusting out alternate legs. It is fiendishly difficult to do, and absolutely exhausting when it has to be done and done and done for retakes. During this dance action, Marc Platt was involved in a different kind of dance movement.

But, remembers Martin, "He kept goofing, after Jack had been needling him. Being young, after four takes of this, I made some remark about Marc's getting his act together, or something less modern. Jack turned around and whipped at me: 'Don't you *ever*—' I thought I was being smart. . . . It was a big lesson for me. Never again did I vocally criticize a fellow dancer in rehearsal."

George Martin insists that Cole's attacks on Marc Platt in this film were the only instance of real Cole cruelty he can remember. Cole did try the same tactics later on Matt Mattox in *Carnival in Flanders,* but Mattox wouldn't let him get away with it. Cole respected dancers who would stand up to him. At one point in dance rehearsals for *Down to Earth,* however, Cole playfully needled Hayworth. Then married to Orson Welles, she was over three months pregnant when she performed Cole's strenuous dance routines. "Jack had her endlessly spinning around on a low Greek pillar or pedestal. Finally, she collapsed, and Jack came around and whispered, 'Oh-oh! Overpaid again!' " Martin found that funny, as Cole was obviously very fond of Hayworth and admired her courage and stamina. Francine Ames also recalls working with Hayworth as a pleasure: "Rita was a very classy lady. If things didn't go right for her, she'd let the dancers rest and work it out for herself." Cole confided to a New York friend, Ernie Eschmann: "Basically, she's a good dancer, but lazy when the cameras aren't on her. In rehearsal, she'd just go through the motions, but when the cameras were on, boom! she'd come out with it. And when she got started, then I got started, and the director said, 'Mr. Cole, hold it! *She's* the star.' "

Perhaps the angry Olympian gods were watching all the

preparations for this film that would invade their privacy. Filming almost began with real tragedy. Rod Alexander remembers that the picture should have shown the Nine Muses descending to earth in a special platform suspended on cables. As an Olympian page, Alexander was riding escort on the platform with the nine girls. Suddenly, the hitch on the cables slipped, and the platform began to lurch downward faster and faster, hitting the floor with a crash. Alexander jumped free, he recalls. The girls went down thuddingly with the platform. Fortunately no one was hurt, but the jinxed platform had to be cut.

Theatre Arts, then America's leading theatre magazine, had good things to say about Cole's work in *Down to Earth*, but with restraint. Its critic understood that Cole had to choreograph two kinds of dance in the film. One kind was intended to show the bad taste of the producer-director that caused Terpsichore to come down to earth. The other kind of dance was Cole trying to do his utmost. As *Theatre Arts* viewed the film: ". . . Cole has staged his own best vein of sly take-off. The choreographer has had the difficult assignment of laying out certain sequences in the kind of bad taste which proclaims itself and yet stays within the framework of possibility, and certain others which approach the artistic but only attain the arty. To characterize these so clearly that the context is plausible, but the comment is always apparent, takes not only skill, but standards of taste of a sort that are rare in any medium, and almost non-existent in films."

No wonder Cole put that review in his scrapbook!

8

RETURN TO LOTUSLAND

COLE'S SECOND SPATE OF FILMS

J ack Cole doesn't like Hollywood, but he has to go back." Clipped from a newspaper interview, that telling comment is pasted on one of Cole's scrapbook pages as a suggestive caption to a photo-collage of Jack Cole and Florence Lessing in costumes from his *Latin Impressions*. Cole is himself entangled in heavy cords he also controls, as a kind of puppet-master; the cords extend to images of Lessing atop thin poles. The Freudian significance of this far from unconscious scrapbook busywork is provocative. Even more so than another scrapbook page on which the printed legend is "The stars don't know how to dance."

With the postwar growth of unrest at Hollywood studios and the eruption of strike actions, Cole and his dancers found themselves in difficulties. George Martin remembers Cole telling the group that the contracts had not been renewed; for those who wanted to continue with him, he proposed forming a new club act which would tour America's major nightspots. This activity kept Cole and his dancing colleagues busy into 1950, when he began working in films again, with Danny Kaye in *On the Riviera*. In March 1947, however, Cole gave a curious interview to Frances Herridge. He told her he'd left Dartmouth for Denishawn, which was incorrect; he'd been at Columbia University; even his dates were wrong. He said that, before the studio strike, he'd been making $1,500 per week at Columbia Pictures with fourteen dancers in his studio group. Cole told Herridge that he didn't like Hollywood, but he was tied to it by a seven-year contract. He had to go back.

His home was in Los Angeles, high in the hills. He had more than studio reasons for returning. Also, with engagements at Ciro's and Slapsie Maxie's, Jack Cole and His Dancers could make a living outside the film studios and maintain a Los Angeles base. Touring was a necessity, however, if Cole was to provide his dancers with steady incomes. What happened to Cole's alleged seven-year contract is unclear. If his Columbia contract dated from 1943, which seems likely, it should then have run through 1949. Already in 1946, he had taken his dancers out to perform for nightclub and casino audiences. Robert Wright and Chet Forrest remember him doing a Florida summer engagement. After talking to Herridge, Cole did indeed return to Hollywood. That was in the spring of 1947, but after the September opening of *Down to Earth,* there weren't any more Cole choreographic credits on Columbia films. When Cole's film career resumed in 1950, it was with Fox.

Looking back on the relatively brief life of his Columbia dance workshop a decade later, Cole told a reporter that it ended in 1948. This was "A PERIOD OF GREAT EMOTIONAL STRESS," as Cole indicated in one of his scrapbooks. That legend appears on a very complicated Freudian doodle-collage Cole executed on a full page. The message is drawn on a board, tacked to a strangely composed pillar. The pillar supports a cornice adorned with a poster from Florida's Copa City, advertising Jack Cole and His Dancers, Xavier Cugat, Henny Youngman, and others. A huge cutout photo image of Cole's face, sad and enigmatic, is pasted on part of the Copa poster. Below this is Salvador Dali's crucified Christ, with pictorial emendations in Cole's hand. And that's only *half* of the page!

The film work was coming to an end. Cole and his company had already been performing outside the studios. He knew he could make a living for himself and them if he kept up the strenuous touring routine he'd had before coming to Hollywood. But he didn't like it; it was exhausting and repetitive. Even appreciative casino audiences weren't serious about dance—drinking, gambling, and coupling were their primary motives in coming to the clubs. There was tremendous, tiring responsibility involved in touring with a troupe of dancers and musicians, plus costumes and props. Cole also began working actively in the musical theatre again. But failures were disheartening, and even success didn't provide a steady income.

Well-paid club dates and a lucrative Hollywood contract had accustomed Jack Cole to a standard of living—coupled with a high standard for his dancers, as well—which he was not prepared to abandon, even though developing a serious concert group at this time might have strongly appealed to him. If there was to be no work for the group in films, then their sporadic touring would have to become full-time again.

Even though Cole saved a Christmas card from the Harry Cohns in his scrapbooks—it showed two charming toddlers— he nourished a grudge about the way his affiliation with Columbia ended. A decade later, he told an interviewer for *Dance Magazine* that, while he'd made a lot of money out of dance, he'd also lost a lot. "With the late Harry Cohn, in Hollywood, I must have lost over $100,000, sticking my neck out for his dancers during the time of the labor union troubles. One hundred thousand dollars may not seem like a lot of money to you," Cole told *Dance*'s reporter—to whom it must have seemed a fortune—"but I felt it!"

In 1947, before all the grim realities of leaving films and returning to the club circuit had come into focus for Cole, he wrote almost euphorically about dance in films. He was writing about dance potential, not the actuality, when he wrote: "The future of dancing in the medium of motion-pictures presents many exciting problems. The larger possibilities of dance as expressive movement have been only remotely explored due, largely, to the limitations of the 'front-office' point of view. Excellent dancing has been wasted because of the choreographer's awkward use of the camera. Artful dance direction has been frequently distorted by the cameraman's complete ignorance of and disrespect for dance as an art form.

"A subject can only be rendered in any medium by approaching it with an informed mind, sympathy, and understanding. Therefore, let us hope that the minds who plan motion-pictures become aware of the large possibilities of the dance, other than the spectacular and the decorative, that the choreographer learns to use the camera as the remarkably fluid instrument it can be, and also that he becomes aware of its severe limitations, and that the cameraman learns to look at the dance as an expressive and communicative form," Cole urged.

Two remarkable advantages for both audience and choreographer in filming dance, rather than seeing it live on stage,

Cole wrote, are that the cameraman seizes the spectator "by the back of the neck and forces him to regard the dance from the point of view intended," and that the camera enables audiences to see sequences of movement from entirely ideal positions. But, Cole implied, those were possibilities that were not always taken advantage of. Also, the bulk and the cumbersome nature of the camera and its attendant transport mechanisms offset some of the advantages, owing to the difficulty encountered in keeping pace with the dancer moving through space.

At that time, with Technicolor still evolving and other big screen effects yet to come, Cole was concerned that most of the opportunities for choreography occurred in color, rather than in black-and-white films. Color, Cole believed, was "curiously unkind to dancing. In color, strong and rapid movement becomes vitiated, decorative, or coldly impersonal, a strange paradox in the medium which takes pride in its lifelike quality."

The camera, Cole thought, had proven more than kind to mediocrity, while it was "savagely unsuccessful in transmitting highly personal and stylistic artistry." Cole also blamed dancers and choreographers as well as those behind the camera. Aside from making some effort to distort movement patterns to stay within range of the cameras, Cole argued, most choreographers had made few other attempts to take advantage of the camera's possibilities.

Jack Cole frequently complained about the cinematic use of dance as mere decoration. He especially despised Busby Berkeley's dance sequences for "using people like wallpaper." Nor did he like the idea of fitting a dance into a set-composition designed to show off the stars, or the set itself, with no thought for the spatial possibilities a choreographer might wish to develop. That, of course, was related to Cole's continuing demand for integration of dance with the other elements in the picture from the earliest stages of planning. He was infuriated by the Hollywood practice of intercutting a non-dancing star into the footage of a vital choreography. Cole wanted the songs and dances artistically integrated. If the star couldn't dance, then Cole would devise some interesting attractive movements or poses he or she could use to make the song more effective, more meaningful, as the dancers complemented and enhanced both song and star.

Of course, what Jack Cole really wanted was much more than that. He wanted the entire film to have "an integral rhythm." He often made the distinction, for those who cared to think about it, between a film with dance *in* it and a "motion-picture that dances wonderfully." His experiences with Ann Miller, for instance, still rankled him years later in 1968, when he told Ric Estrada of *Dance Magazine* how he hated the nickelodeon concept of a girl coming out to show the audiences how fast she could tap-dance. Miller was famous for her speed and endurance as a tap artiste, but, to Cole, this was hardly dance as an art form.

Busby Berkeley may have become a legend, and his massive production numbers High Camp, but Cole saw no reason to perpetuate mindless precision or a huge body count for its own sake. To Cole, such dance routines were the "birthday cake" choreography of the 1920s and 1930s.

When Cole hit his stride in the 1950s, he was much more in control both of his own resources and of the technical elements with which he had to work. Thus, Agnes de Mille could confidently state in *America Dances:* "Jack Cole made some excellent dances that were filmed with great intelligence, chiefly because he himself designed the camera work and supervised it setup by setup."

Twentieth Century–Fox wasn't in the business of choosing its film scripts from the writings of the great masters. Operating on the principle that old plots are best, possibly because audiences would feel at home with them, *On the Riviera* was based on a play by Rudolph Lothar and Hans Adler. Originally in German, the play had been produced on Broadway in the 1930s. Then Maurice Chevalier starred in the work in Paris, where it was adapted as *Folies Bergère.* In 1941, it was filmed as *That Night in Rio,* with Don Ameche in the leading role. Fox's Technicolor version enlisted the writing talents of Valentine Davies and Phoebe and Henry Ephron. No one was thinking about creating great art; a profitable and entertaining film was the goal. The more profitable, the better. Considering the number of transformations Lothar and Adler's original play had survived, apparently Fox executives either did not know or didn't care about that old folk saying: "Familiarity breeds contempt."

Danny Kaye was at that time a very popular star. Fans loved his irrepressible impersonations, his seemingly rubber face and agile body, his machine-gun delivery of patter songs that would have delighted Gilbert & Sullivan. The script was a vehicle for Kaye, nothing more.

Cole choreographed the dances and staged the songs. Most memorable of these was "Popo the Puppet," written by Kaye's talented wife, Sylvia Fine. In this virtuosic number, Kaye was a giant puppet, dressed in a colorful Commedia dell'Arte clown's outfit, a Harlequin on the ropes, as it were—not unlike Cole's own vision of himself in his scrapbook imagery. This same year, 1950, Cole had created his own semi-serious dance, *Harlequin's Odyssey*, so the tragicomic clown was very much on his mind. Cole used the puppet image again in *Kean*. In the song and dance, Kaye was strictly limited in the area in which he could perform, since he was supposed to be only a puppet controlled from above by an unseen puppet master. Actually, as a newspaper account disclosed, there were eight men overhead, manipulating the ropes to help a counterweighted Kaye "dance on air," as the report phrased it. Flanking Popo-Kaye on either side were two musical clowns, played by Cole dancers Ellen Ray and Gwyneth Verdon. In clown makeup and gaudy costumes, they had cymbals attached to the insides of their knees, making sardonic clashings every time they brought their legs together. They also had tambourines in both hands, to add to the rhythmic din, punctuating Fine's clever lines.

A major production number, "Rhythm of a New Romance," used a score of Cole-trained dancers, many showgirls, lavish sets, an obligatory staircase, and Kaye and Verdon dancing. Both Spanish and Indian dances were incorporated, with Rosario Imperio featured as a Spanish dancer. One of Cole's souvenirs was a note from Sylvia Fine, accompanying her revisions of the music and lyrics. She alerted him: "I will get in this afternoon to see you, hold your hand, and audition for the part of the castanet."

On the Riviera was one of those Cole pictures in which he performed without any kind of billing or fanfare. He did not include it in his definitive list for Arthur Todd certainly, and it was not a major effort. He was just filling in. When he watched the film with a New York friend, Ernie Eschmann, Cole told him: "Oh, I'm back there, in the background." Eschmann says, "He'd never told me that before. He said one of the guys got sick. 'So I went in for him, but I don't know what I'm doing. I was just filling in.' " He gave Eschmann some other inside information about his dancing as well: He didn't like to wear hats when he danced, and he tended to scowl from the mental concentration and muscular effort required to achieve all his incredible isolations and placements. When he danced for the cameras—and the actual sound track music would later be dubbed—directors or assistants would plead, "Smile, Jack!" On one occasion, they held up paper money, waving it and pointing at it, saying, "Jack! Oh, Jack!" And Cole made some extra money by smiling at the camera.

Time was very pleased with *On the Riviera*, which it considered "the best cinemusical" since *On the Town*. This was partly thanks to Jack Cole's dances. The *Hollywood Reporter* reported: "Jack Cole's stylized dances (with Kaye doing excellent impressionistic hoofing) are a welcome change from stereotypical terpsichorean forms—making intriguingly different Sylvia Fine's imaginative lyrics for 'Popo the Puppet' and 'Happy Ending.' "

Cole's return to Hollywood was not without its problems. His reputation for being difficult if not impossible to work with had preceded him. Although Cole would use a Wigman drum to beat time for ordinary dance rehearsals, it was essential when working on a film to have a rehearsal pianist. Not only would this accompanist give the dancers the daily musical cues they needed for learning the choreography, but he also had to create the music for the dance sequences himself. Cole Porter and Richard Rodgers were much too busy to bother composing dance

music. Lionel Newman had to take care of the problems connected with Fox musicals. He had sent Cole some eight potential accompanists, and Cole had flatly rejected them all. Newman was desperate.

Fox had a young musician under contract. He was a jazz
pianist, and he'd played with a number of big-time bands and
famous singers: Peggy Lee, Billy Eckstein, Vic Damone, Harry
James, Boyd Rayburn, Tommy Dorsey. But he wanted to settle
down, and Hollywood seemed a good place to find a steady
job. His name was Hal Schaefer. Newman sent him to audition
for Cole in an empty rehearsal hall.

Schaefer went up to meet "this wild-looking man." Cole
knew his background and that he was tired of touring. "Cole
asked me to sit down at the piano and play some blues. 'What
tempo?' I asked. 'About a medium tempo.' I began playing, and
after a little while, he started to dance. It sounds like the movies, but this was for real! I had many, many years with Cole,
and there's much I don't remember, but this, our first meeting,
was outstanding. I'll never forget it! Cole was dancing, nod-
ding his head, shaking it: 'Yes!' I was noted for my swing, for
my strength, my beat. Cole didn't like the studio pianists—
people who were namby-pamby, 'vanilla,' or too refined. The
beat was Number One, foot-stomping. The beat had to be
steady, and it had to swing."

Inspired by what Cole was doing, Schaefer found his musical fantasy was expanding, the beat getting more intense. Finally, Cole went over to the phone and called Lionel Newman.
"I found him. This is the man for me!" It was the beginning of
a collaboration—sometimes stormy—which would last more than
a decade. They worked together in Hollywood, as well as on
the club acts Jane Russell, Betty Grable, and Mitzi Gaynor would
take to Las Vegas. Schaefer helped Cole with the choreographic birth of the musical *Kismet* on the West Coast. In New
York, he worked with him on *A Funny Thing Happened on the
Way to the Forum.*

Before coming to Fox, Schaefer had been an arranger for
vocalists and big bands, as well as a pianist. This proved in-

valuable to Cole, for the dance music was customarily devised by the dance accompanist—not by the composer of the score—whether the show was on Broadway or on film.

"As Jack put it, the composer had created 45 seconds of music to get through a chorus. 'Now,' he'd say, 'what am I going to do to get through seven more minutes of dance? I'm not going to repeat that banal piece of music!' That's the way Cole would talk," says Schaefer. Cole told him, "I have to have someone to work with me, to take a thread of the song and develop it." With film scores, however, perhaps because the songs were less interesting than those in many Broadway shows, Cole often wanted Schaefer not to use the song-theme at all, but to get as far away from it as possible.

"Unless it was Borodin, as in *Kismet*," Schaefer explains. "Most of these scores weren't outstanding. They were functional, suitable for the vocal requirements, but not for Cole's dances. . . . You go with the choreographer, give him what he wants. Often the dance music leaves the original melody. It's a new part of the score—but Sondheim didn't write it! I left the original music farther behind with Cole than with any other choreographer."

Most dance numbers would run about seven minutes, so Hal Schaefer had to devise a musical interlude longer than many of the songs. He emphasizes a fact of which most non-dancers are not aware: Different choreographers—if they're really good, and not just imitators—have different dance languages, different vocabularies, different steps, different ways of moving and carrying the body. Some, like Bob Fosse, often create their choreography on their own bodies; what *they* cannot do is not apt to appear in their dances. Others are very good at exploiting the talents of other gifted dancers. Still others specialize in certain dance areas, such as ethnic, modern, or tap. The dance composer-arranger, says Schaefer, has got to be able to speak or at least understand the various dance languages of the choreographers with whom he works—or they cannot work together. Cole's potential vocabulary was limitless; he often boasted his dancers could dance anything. Cole alumni largely agree with this. So Schaefer had to be extremely versatile.

"I can't tell you how Cole visualized his numbers, but a good deal came from the music I fed him. He wasn't set in what he'd choreograph before he began rehearsals," Schaefer points out, indicating one of Cole's problems in completing choreography for deadlines. "He worked from the music. Oh, he'd have a general thing in mind—a tune, a rhythm. He'd say, 'Do you know this thing by Satie?' Or a Delius thing. Once in a while, he'd bring in a record. He'd play an excerpt and say, 'I want the *feeling* of music like that. In that genre. Sit down and start to play something!' I wrote a waltz for a movie we did in the style of Ravel. Jack had all these dancers coming in with candelabra. Very elegant!

"I don't know where Jack got his ideas from. He was the most inventive of choreographers. The most of any I've ever worked with. In *On the Riviera,* one of the most inventive numbers was 'Popo the Puppet.' . . . Jack designed it all, including the puppet theatre. He was always drawing sketches of things the way he wanted them. I think it was in *Farmer Takes a Wife* that Betty Grable and Gwen Verdon did that number with pie plates on their feet. In *Meet Me After the Show,* there was a number called 'No-Talent Joe.' Remember that? He used all these muscle men, and Grable did the dance. In those days, everyone was still doing Busby Berkeley numbers. All very cute, and in precision. In unison. All vanilla. Some of the numbers in *Gentlemen Prefer Blondes* are outstanding. You never knew what was going to happen next in a Cole dance. . . ."

David and Bathsheba, a Fox epic also released in 1951, was not a musical, but Cole was assigned to create a dance of Near Eastern parentage and sinuous, erotic overtones for a banquet for King David and his guests. Gregory Peck impersonated this adulterous monarch, with Susan Hayward playing the tempting, seductive Bathsheba. Gwyneth Verdon, choreographed by Cole, served up a spicier dance course than anything the Israelites could find on the king's dinner table. As choreography was not an important feature of the film, the *New York Times*'s critic saw no reason to mention it.

Meet Me After the Show, handsomely filmed in Technicolor, was yet another of those stories with a show business mainspring. Betty Grable and MacDonald Carey, the screenplay decreed, had been married for seven years, but the marriage was now in trouble. Suspecting Grable might have the famous "seven-year itch," Eddie Albert and Rory Calhoun made themselves available. Grable was type-cast as an entertainer; Carey was her husband the producer. Albert was a singer, while Calhoun was nothing but a handsome lay-about beachcomber. Naturally, virtue and the bonds of holy matrimony finally triumphed.

To keep audiences from falling asleep as the plot tediously unfolded, Jack Cole devised some very inventive dance sequences. Producer George Jessel should have been grateful to him. Grable's mother, Mrs. Lillian Grable, certainly was. Sharing secrets with Grable's many fans in a magazine article, "Daughter Knows Best," she told Jane Keasher: "Betty loved working with dance director Jack Cole, because he not only gave her some of the most spectacular routines she's ever had, but allowed her to use her comic ability."

Jack Cole treasured these homey confidences—several copies of them—in his scrapbooks, along with this intriguing gossip item: "Jack Cole is Betty Grable's new dancing teacher. He keeps her so busy she hasn't been able to pick a horse all week." Also among Cole's souvenirs are some photos of body builders. A shot of one muscle man has on its back Cole's penciled list of leading Hollywood male models, with their heights and telephone numbers. There's no date on the photograph, so it could be the record of auditions Cole held for the "No Talent Joe" sequence in *Meet Me After the Show*, or a number with Jane Russell in *Gentlemen Prefer Blondes*. Or Cole may have had other uses for these muscle-bound athletes.

"No Talent Joe" was a favorite with the film's reviewers. Again inspired by sculpture and architecture of ancient Greece and classical Rome, Cole outfitted his line of beefcake behemoths in gladiatorial array. The set was dressed with classical motifs, including elegant stylized horses, whose bodies curl into urns where their hindquarters ought to be. Torches, diaphanous drapes, and even some of the body builders initially frozen in statuary poses suggested at least neoclassical Hollywood, if not the historical antiquity which so fascinated Cole. Athletes posing and flexing muscles, with Grable on hand to stroke and pinch and sing, amusingly animated a vocal number which otherwise would have been senseless and probably tasteless as well.

A feature in the *Los Angeles Times* Sunday Supplement, "Betty and the Biceps," showed some shots of this number's beefier moments, arrested against what looked rather like a home gym from *The Last Days of Pompeii.* The Joe of the song title was played by 265-pound Arthur Wolge, also seen in *Quo Vadis.* Joe not only let Grable explore his muscle system, but his fellow athletes flexed their pectorals and made a living bench for Grable to grace with her own muscles. Today, there are those who would probably find this lacking in taste.

In Britain, the film was accompanied by the customary printed program. On the cover of *Picturegoer* was Grable hugging a huge polar bear. This was Cole's distinctive prop for an intentionally raffish routine, "It's a Hot Night in Alaska." Grable was attired in a cowgirl outfit, complete with pistols, and underneath her skirt, to be flashed to the roistering, crude audience was a sign: "Welcome American Legion." She was supported by a group of male dancers in rough Alaskan garb. Grable sang the song, suggestively amusing in its way, with an equally suggestive sexiness, which had all the marks of mechanical simulation. This was one of those difficult numbers, designed to look slightly sleazy—pandering to the elemental tastes of the bar's patrons—which, at the same time, had to be fun to watch, the audience knowing that the people who made the picture also knew just how tacky this song-and-dance sequence was.

One of the show's more impressive numbers in terms of "production values" was "Bettin' on a Man." The point of this song, it developed, was that a woman is safer betting on a horse. Men always prove so unreliable. Gwen Verdon and Jack Cole— with what looked like horsetails—pranced frenetically on an upper level in silhouette. Below, male dancers, throwing their arms up ecstatically in the air, pounded the floor with their agile feet. Grable strutted her stuff, supported some of the time by a glittering piano.

One Cole image for the opening title number, with Grable

in the spotlight, was certainly worthy of Busby Berkeley at his best: A huge black-gloved hand and arm slowly descended, a giant diamond bracelet around the wrist. In the open palm was the lovely Miss Grable, plumes on her head and trailing yards of ostrich feathers. It was visual overkill, but that's what these Technicolor musicals were all about.

No stranger to the theories of Dr. Freud and the possible significance of dreams, Jack Cole choreographed the film's most extended and elaborate dance as an unusual mixture of performance and dreamtime fantasy. The framework of the production number was a stage show in which Grable had the lead, but she also had her mind on other things as well. The curtain disclosed a fierce battle among slum kids, with Grable and Verdon holding off some marauding boys—buckets over their heads like helmets—with cap pistols. Vanquishing the boys, they dug into some garbage cans, finding boxing gloves and a sash. Feminine Grable wanted to dance with tomboy Verdon, who'd rather fight. Verdon took a boxing stance; Grable imitated a toreador with the sash. They performed a lively, jazzy dance in character. Then they climbed a tree, hitched across a backlot on a clothesline, and looked down. Cole had already used this part of the sequence on Broadway in 1950, in the revue, *Alive and Kicking*. Marie Groscup and Verdon played the kids in that version.

Because Grable was dreaming, it was an easy matter for the two ruffians to look down from a rooftop onto an arched terrace, where elegant, formally dressed folk were swirling about to the measures of "La Valse." Grable's fantasy grew more elaborate, with stairs, black-masked men bearing candelabras with long streamers, bare branches, and endlessly whirling women in full-skirted gowns. Eight couples in pink and white waltzed with abandon; then Grable made her appearance, lovelier than all the rest, waltzing effortlessly until the curtain fell.

Time thanked choreographer Cole from rescuing the picture from "the burden of its mail-order plot." It noted the notable assist from dancer Gwyneth Verdon. "The musical numbers— rain in the desert—are as usual handled quite nicely," *Time* reported. The melodies were not distinguished, though Grable gave "Bettin' on a Man" what *Time* called "a thorough barrel-house going-over." *Time*'s critic felt the call of the Yukon though; he liked "Hot Night in Alaska" best: ". . . Miss Grable cavorting exaggeratedly in a small-time, deliberately tacky floor show . . . yelling her head off about the time she melted Alaska. Doubtless she did, too."

Lydia Bailey had its premiere at Roxy's Theatre on May 31, 1951. It was a 20th Century–Fox film, but it was no musical. The locale, for once, was not a theatre or a nightclub. It was Haiti, during the struggles of the black population to free itself from the hated French planter-colonials. There was only one dance number in the film, but it also was realistically motivated. Haitians called upon the powers of voodoo to defeat their enemies. Jack Cole went to Haiti to study authentic voodoo rituals. His research was apparently successful, for the *New York Times* commented: "A voodoo dance on the plantation grounds makes a compelling spectacle, as does the climactic scene, in which the Haitians burn the embattled city."

Jean Negulesco directed a cast featuring Dale Robertson, Anne Francis, and William Marshall. Unfortunately for Cole's intentions, the impact of the ritual dance was continually vitiated by Negulesco's—or the film editor's—decision to intercut the dance sequence with shots of watchers' faces, filled with foreboding and terror. Dialogue also interrupted the insistent drumbeats and chanting, which steadily increased in tempo. As the frenzy of the dance increased, participants became possessed by spirits and fell to the ground, rolling about in ecstatic trances. Cole and Carmen de Lavallade shared a brief dance duo. Dancers carried sacrificial chickens and knives; at the climax of the ritual, the chickens were bloodily slaughtered to propitiate the gods.

Even when the circumstances seemed most favorable for the introduction—without excuses or gimmicks—of authentic ethnic dance in a Hollywood film, it was reduced, as in *Lydia Bailey,* to the level of a gimmick itself, a momentary sideshow to heighten the audience's excitement and suspense. It's true that the film was not intended as a factual documentation of Haiti's struggle for independence, nor as an archival reconstruction of ethnic dance. It was designed to entertain, but that end would have been even better served if the ritual could have been performed complete, because it would have been more powerful. Obviously, Negulesco and others were afraid audiences would rush to the toilets or the popcorn concession if they had to look at a serious, threatening dance for longer than two minutes at a time. Nonetheless, *Lydia Bailey* gave Jack Cole an opportunity to show Fox—and film audiences—something of his familiarity with dance lore.

Capable talents at Twentieth Century–Fox were probably well aware of Cole's expertise; some had surely seen his remarkable dance library and art collection. One example of Fox's use of Cole's knowledge is an April 10, 1952, memo Cole sent to producer-writer Lamar Trotti, who was at the time working on a new film, *Stars and Stripes Forever*, a musical biography of America's March King, John Phillip Sousa. Cole didn't choreograph, but he did offer advice which suggests he would have accepted the challenge.

In the script, as it then was, Debra Paget was required to replace an opera singer who failed to show for a Sunday afternoon John Philip Souza concert at the Hippodrome Theatre in New York. Cole was adamant that Paget's proposed number should not be conceived in terms of a musical featuring pretty girls. In Cole's view, Fox and every other major studio had already exhausted this kind of musical number, especially when based on songs and performance styles of the periods from 1880 to 1920. Cole's shrewd objection to the dominant musical modes of these years was that they lent themselves only to satire or caricature, both of which would be in the wrong spirit for one of the very popular Souza Sunday Concerts. Cole noted that the popular music of that time was either cheaply sentimental or noisy ragtime. Apparently, Cole did not see Souza's famous band as equivalent to Alexander's Ragtime Band!

Drawing on his own archives, Cole pointed out that a Souza concert would not be, in any case, a huge vaudeville or a girl show. Instead, he thought it ought to be presented in the projected film as a dressed-up, theatrical performance of popular musical "classics" of the time. Cole's vision was a remarkable blending of historical authenticity with the eminently theatrical. He proposed a dignified concert arrangement of Afro-American revival and camp-meeting songs. He didn't mention such groups as the celebrated Fisk Jubilee Singers, who performed the old Negro spirituals with great dignity and deep sincerity, but he may well have been thinking of them.

This would, of course, be no Hollywood "Uncle Tom" show, either in costume or movement. Instead, Cole saw the production number rather like an American image by Rockwell Kent, a master of native genre scenes and especially skilled in the woodcut. The movement patterns would be those of a chorus for a Greek drama. Cole was certain it could be done without giving offense to any religious group. He sent Trotti some traditional lyrics, noting it would give Fox the opportunity to offer on screen a kind of dance presentation never before shown.

What other choreographer under contract to Fox, or elsewhere, for that matter, could have created this Sousa concert number with effective integration of vocal music and dance, generating an honest and fervent excitement? Clearly, there was only one logical candidate to stage this number. Trotti didn't take the bait, however. When the film opened, reviewers generally found the biography boring; the only real interest was generated by Sousa's music.

About this time, dance critic Arthur Todd asked Cole for an accurate list of the Hollywood films he'd choreographed and in which he'd appeared, as well as some comments on the problems he'd found in choreographing for the cinema. The substance of Cole's response appeared two years later in a piece by Todd in *Dance and Dancers*. Cole's original letter is preserved in the Special Collections of the University Research Library at UCLA. It's worth quoting some passages to convey not only Cole's ideas but also the force with which he expressed them.

He made the point that he had never intentionally danced in any film after *Moon Over Miami*. Subsequent appearances, either in major dance parts or in the men's chorus, were last-minute arrangements to keep the shooting on schedule. Cole wrote Todd: "I have been invited a great many times to dance, and I would like very much to do so—but so far the occasion has never been suitable."

He continued: "I have very definite, determined, and hopeful views on dancing and choreography for the screen, but for the moment I think we must all be patient." This call for patience, coming from the eternally impatient Cole, struck a curious note. Cole then reviewed his hopes, in coming to Hollywood in the early 1940s, to reform the routine and boring use of dance in films. He soon learned that it was a miracle Hollywood achieved as much as it did, considering how pictures were actually made.

At this point, he mentioned a very popular dancing-singing-acting star, Gene Kelly, who was openly a great admirer of Cole, both as dancer and choreographer. "Parenthetically and with no recourse to personalities," Cole noted, "one of the few people who are in a position strong enough to effect a change is Mr. Gene Kelly. Mr. Kelly is a dancer, a star with contractual power of direction. . . .

"I mention this because the qualifications of the star as a dancer directly affects the quality of dancing and choreography in a picture. Ten times out of ten, the central role in a musical number must be performed by a performer who can only be classified as a talented amateur and a great many times not even a talented amateur. The architecture of the entire number must be designed with those limitations in mind. The miracles that sometimes happen are truly miracles and could happen only in the movies. The list of unsung heroes that sweat, strain, and curse to bring forth this mediocrity is long—set designer, costume designer, musical arranger, cameraman, and dance director. I speak at length of this executive lack of direction because any major change for the better in choreography for pictures must be effected by a change of view in this department."

Todd also asked Cole to outline what he thought were the differences between theatre and film. Because Cole had been accused by some of not knowing the difference, his reply is of interest: "The great difference at present . . . is one of fantasy and realism. When the curtain goes up in the theatre, the audience is actively agreeing and participating in the act of make-believe. On the screen, documentary realism takes over, and we believe that what we see is really there. This point of view is not implicit but has come to be accepted. Therefore, on the screen people only dance if, 1.—their job in life is that of entertainer: movie, theatre, nightclub, television. U.S.O. 2.— someone dreams, thereby excusing our flight from reality. 3.— the character happens to be Fred Astaire or Gene Kelly, in which case the audience has conditioned itself, and the author need make no explanation for the movement fantasy that may ensue.

"Dance in the theatre must be unified and sustained—not so on the screen. What would be disaster in New York can be mildly successful in California. The camera offers enormous latitude to the choreographer if he learns its powers, its whims, and its evils. Like all mechanical devices, if exploited for its own sake, it becomes tasteless and violently intrudes itself on an imaginative performance. For the choreographer it has the exalted power to force the audience to have his point of view at all times, and points of view completely impossible in the theatre. By the same token, the difficulty of obtaining presence on the screen is enormous. Movement always appears to be under glass, the strange paradox of seeming not real in a medium that is real above all else. In color the difficulty is doubled. It is hard to get a sharp edge around rapid and brilliant movement. The camera obliterates stress and strain, and all kinetic drama is lost. Dynamics are lost, and movement outline in space is emphasized. It has the power to make mediocre dancers seem brilliant and strong, and brilliant dancers seem weird and disoriented.

"Dance numbers usually occur after a considerable amount of the story has been told in medium and close shots, with intermittent long shots to establish geography or cover violent movement. Since there is usually a minimum of movement in a musical picture outside the musical numbers, it means that there has been a minimum of long shots. That is, the audience has become conditioned to the communication by large half-figures and even larger heads. When the dancer arrives with his necessity for full-figure photography, he inevitably becomes smaller in scale and begins to lose importance with the audience, unless we move in to a half-figure, at which point our movement quality becomes vitiated and almost non-existent.

"The opportunities for pure dance as such have been, up to now, very scarce. Dancing on the screen is usually the development of a song number. If the songwriter has his way, it will be confined to a rhythmic charade of his lyric. Here again the business end of the machine rears its ugly head. There are not many 'Rodgers & Hammersteins' who are eager to write 'lyric theatre,' a musical play—in which the 'play is the thing.' Most have their eye on record sales, juke-box and radio performance. What is suitable for a non-visual medium with an adolescent audience is pre-eminently unsuited for a visual medium that is trying to reach a more mature audience.

"For the screen, soloists and very small groups can be handled successfully. Large groups lose their importance through the distance from them necessary to keep them in frame. Here again we are not up against a natural mechanical barrier, but rather an executive point of view that fails to provide in the script for any demonstration of group experience. The sale of erotic charms of a single personality cannot be made when hidden in a group at some point distant.

"For the immediate future, greater coordination between writer, director, and dance director (for musical pictures, the dance director, a properly equipped one—very rare—should be the director) so that the picture as a whole sings and dances and is not a unit intermittently interrupted by more or less successfully fitted-in musical and dance interludes. Characters, situations, points of view that allow for fantasy, imagination, vitality and movement development: in other words, allowing dance and movement to communicate and be an integral part of the structure, rather than a decorative embellishment."

Cole's next film task was not a step forward in the direction of the integration of dance and plot he hoped for; it was Franz Lehar's Viennese operetta, *The Merry Widow*, two paces backward into a beloved but antiquated musical genre, where the dances were indeed embellishments, with the waltz obligatory.

Lana Turner was chosen to play the widow, a marriageable millionairess. With a flick of the typewriter keys, the MGM scriptwriters turned this heroine into an American, saving Turner the artistic agony of trying to impersonate a Central European. The handsome Argentine Fernando Lamas was to be her Danilo. Lamas told a columnist about the fears he and Lana Turner had when they learned that the notorious Jack Cole would be their choreographer. "We thought he might beat us or something. Instead, he has been as nice as could be. Maybe he gave up to begin with and decided: 'Can't make two professional dancers out of these people, so I might as well make two friends.'" Not only did Lamas suggest an off-set chumminess that's not easy to believe, but he also congratulated himself and Turner on their performances in Cole's choreography: "But the funny thing, on top of it, we look pretty good."

Curtis Bernhardt directed, but without the wit and panache of the immortal Ernst Lubitsch, whose 1934 *Merry Widow* was already a screen classic. Bernhardt had the dubious advantage of Technicolor. Its opulent hues replaced Lubitsch's sense of style. Joseph Pasternak produced the film, and *MGM News* credited him with giving Jack Cole his first cinema acting assignment. While Cole was putting the dancers—and the stars— through their paces, rehearsing the all-too-familiar "Merry Widow Waltz," Lana Turner made a series of candid photos of her choreographer in action.

But let the MGM publicists tell this charming story: "As a surprise for Cole, she made the finished film into a strip showing the various real life facial expressions. When producer Joe Pasternak saw it, he insisted that Cole was just the type of actor he needed for the role of the harrassed station-master in the film's story.

"And that is how a noted modern dance director becomes an old-fashioned gentleman, thanks to Lana Turner." Despite Cole's remarkable skills as a dancer, he was not, in any sense, a trained actor. Of course that didn't really matter very much in Hollywood, when the director, the camera, and the film editor could construct a performance, if it were not otherwise forthcoming. Fortunately, this was a small role, virtually a "cameo." Later, in *Designing Woman,* Cole would have a much larger, more demanding role; it would be agony for him.

Several years later, when Cole relived some of his experiences in *The Merry Widow* for film critic Arthur Knight, his complaints didn't focus on his thespian involvement. Rather, he raged against the "hopelessness" of trying to fight studio attitudes. Cole's favorite movieland whipping boy was "The Front-Office." The standard attitude of film executives, he said, was: "We've done it this way for twenty years, and we're not going to change things now." Perhaps they should have listened to Cole; he was constantly urging them and his directors to explore new ideas, new ways of telling the story, new ways of integrating music, movement, and dance, new ways of using the camera.

Cole told Arthur Knight that working on films like *The Merry Widow* was what periodically drove him back to the Broadway stage. Even Cole's club dates must have been a welcome relief from the frustrations of battling the front office and devising dances for stars who couldn't dance. What Cole said he found in the theatre, as opposed to films, was quite simply "freedom."

Reading Cole's published statements it's apparent that in the approximately two decades Cole worked in motion pictures his range of complaints didn't vary much. The bogus realism of the films continually bothered him. As he told Knight: "They want everything realistic. Everything has to show. When I staged the waltz for *The Merry Widow* a few years ago, I tried to capture the soft, gay atmosphere of another century. Then we went on the set, and it looked like the interior of an ice-box. I begged for pink color filters, for shadows. Shadows on Lana Turner? They thought I was insane."

On this, as on many films, Cole said, the studio way was to call in the wrong choreographer—then called the dance director—for the kind of picture being made. Of course, he wouldn't be assigned to the picture until the end of the planning phase, well after the script had been finished. There would

be, by that time, no opportunity for the dance director to suggest moments in the story that could logically, artistically, even
cleverly, be developed into dance sequences. Cole didn't dwell
on this, but the scriptwriters were usually journeymen with little appreciation of dance in its various forms, or of its potential
for revealing character, advancing plot, or establishing mood and
atmosphere. That didn't prevent them from indicating in their
scripts moments where the action could pause, while a dance
sequence was inserted. Cole hated this practice, and it's a tribute to his tenaciousness and forceful criticisms that he was increasingly allowed to participate in film planning at earlier stages.

"If they have confidence in you," he admitted, "you might
be called in when the script is only two-thirds done. Then you
still have some chance of influencing the character development, of creating an integration of your dance sequences and
the story line."

Before the advent of Jack Cole on the sound stages, dances
often had only the most tenuous relation to the film plots. Cole
had some modest suggestions to share with readers of *Dance*
for making cinema dance more effective: "My feeling is that the
dance director should work with the film director on the three
or four minutes that immediately precede and follow the dances,
to create a smooth transition from one to the other. Something
of that effect was created in the old Astaire-Rogers movies. They
created characters for whom dancing was the most natural thing
in the world—and it became the most natural thing in the world
for everything to move aside to let them dance. You still get
something of that in the old Astaire films, and in Gene Kelly's.
You expect them to dance. More often, though, the dance sequences are simply inserted without either preparation or logic
or, worst of all, consistency of style."

The *Hollywood Reporter* liked Cole's choreography, and it
agreed with his frequent complaint: ". . . stars could have been
better dancers." *The Merry Widow* opened at Loew's State in New
York in September 1952. Bosley Crowther of the *Times* thought
this the best *Widow* production he'd seen. Lamas looked fine,
and Turner, to him, seemed interested and haughty. There was
nothing grudging in Crowther's compliments for Cole, either:

"The dancers and the choruses are handled with dash and verve by Jack Cole." For once, this was a *Times* review Cole would want to put among his keepsakes. Crowther continued: "You'll look far to see anything more lusty and gusty in this line than the swish of the can-can dancers, in brilliant black-and-red at Maxim's—or anything more handsome and graceful, with the nice play of lights and shades, than the pink, white, and gold waltzing couples in the final number."

William Hawkins, also a Manhattan film critic, agreed with the *Times:* "Jack Cole has done a striking job with the dances. Only once is there a can-can, and instead of the conventional full-skirted high-kickers, he has crowded the screen with long-legged, precise dancers who give the French music-hall numbers a startling, mad, and modern wickedness." Indeed he did. Gone were the cumbersome skirts with yards of rustling ruffles. Instead, a pert, sexy Gwen Verdon and her sister-dancers were wearing form-fitting leotards, with perky bustles of ribbons perched on their posteriors. Long gloves and huge cartwheel hats, set off with a single large flower on each, completed their provocative, revealing costumes. It wasn't exactly "period" costuming, but it clearly pleased the critics.

From this cinema can-can, it was an easy step for Cole's trusted assistant, Gwen Verdon, to a live one on Broadway, in the long-running musical, *Can-Can.* Verdon won one of her four Tony Awards for this performance, a testimony not only to her undoubted talent but also to Cole's training. He'd permitted her to take time off from work to fly to New York for a *Can-Can* audition. He didn't expect her to come back with a leading role, apparently. Cole was momentarily upset, then glad for his protégé's good fortune. He had cause to regret Verdon's departure. She was the best of partners, the most willing of dance experimenters, and always certain to shine in her cinema specialities. More than that, she was devoted to Cole and would spend hours coaching the stars in their routines, which she and Cole had worked out beforehand. Even when she was one of Broadway's major stars, Verdon always stayed in touch with her friend and mentor, dropping in on rehearsals to give a helping hand when possible. Cole inspired that kind of loyalty.

But before she fled Hollywood, Gwen Verdon made important dance contributions to *The I Don't Care Girl*, which starred Mitzi Gaynor as Eva Tanguay, a celebrated star of vaudeville and revues. The title referred to a song Tanguay was identified with, "I Don't Care."

By the 1950s, there were few moviegoers who remembered Eva Tanguay, so Fox's decision to film a musical biography seemed a risky choice. Darryl F. Zanuck, head of 20th Century–Fox, wrote Cole a long memo about the abilities of the performers in the picture, urging him to make the most of their talent. He may have been trying to convince himself, because the picture, as of December 5, 1951—it wouldn't be released until 1953—was in serious trouble. Zanuck's memo dealt with new musical numbers, noting that a final determination would have to be made when they looked at the picture the next time, because Fox might have cut a little too deeply in some spots. Later in the memo, he worried about the added cost because of this terrible mistake they had made.

On December 21, in a memo to the producer, George Jessel, with copies to Cole and Lloyd Bacon, the film's director, Zanuck stressed his concern about the added costs, insisting on a better title than *I Don't Care*. He didn't like it because it sounded insignificant and small. For Zanuck, it did not have the feeling of a musical. Zanuck wanted to use the title of a *famous* song; it would help immensely. He thought that Cole might use such a song in one of the new production numbers, and the picture could take its name from that. Zanuck emphasized that he didn't want to limit or handicap Cole in any way. He liked the replacement numbers Cole had outlined, but the title remained an important problem, considering what the enormous cost of the picture would be as a result of the retakes in the new sequences.

Darryl Zanuck was trying to see the brighter side as well. In his December 5 memo to Cole, he noted that they had a number of people with real talent. He pointed out that Mitzi Gaynor was certainly a talented girl, recalling her work in *Golden Girl*. He told Cole they must agree that she had enormous talent. David Wayne could do anything Fox wanted him to do.

Oscar Levant had certain limitations, but he too had proved in *An American in Paris* that he could do a lot of things.

Zanuck suggested that instead of trying to design *big* or lavish production numbers, Cole should try to concentrate on numbers that would bring out the talent of these performers.

He was not, he said, talking about any intimate little show stuff, but he hoped that, with the possible exeception of the Ziegfeld spot and the finale, Cole could try to get the wonderful intimacy that he achieved in *Meet Me After the Show*. Although Cole's numbers looked big and lavish in that picture, on reflection, Zanuck observed, they were very intimate numbers that exploited the people effectively.

A great deal would depend on the songs they picked. These ought to be numbers which would give Cole an opportunity to show off the talent. As if to encourage Cole in this massive effort to save an endangered film, Zanuck reminded him of how effectively he had handled modern character numbers against painted scenery and changing sets. Zanuck believed audiences were no longer at all interested in big, lavish production numbers with a lot of people. Frequently, they laughed at them. Audiences were now interested in the talent of the cast.

As released, *The I Don't Care Girl* was a film-within-a-film in which the producer of the real film, George Jessel, appeared as a film producer in the process of finding out who Eva Tanguay really was, by talking to those who knew her and reconstructing her life and her great songs.

Several reviewers noted the choppiness of the film, with production numbers that didn't have any logical relation to plot development. Worse, some of them were anachronistic; they didn't belong to the period in which the real Eva Tanguay had appeared. For that matter, there were those who maintained that she had never been a *Follies* star, as she was in the film. Despite these reservations, Cole's numbers did win some praise.

As well they might, with a stunning Gwen Verdon even dancing aloft in the distance behind the star in W. C. Handy's "Beale Street Blues." Sinister gamblers in shades of lavender entered the 7-11 Club in this number, going upstairs, where the floor was marked off in various games of chance. Their women, led by Verdon in pink fedora and voluminous shocking-pink ruffled skirt—an idea from Cole's South American explorations—danced up a storm. And there was a very inventive sequence danced behind a wall of empty wine bottles.

Seymour Felix set some tap routines, but the rest of the dances and musical staging was Cole's handiwork. He staged "I Don't Care" twice, possibly to make the song more important to the audiences—and to Darryl F. Zanuck. Gaynor did it initially as the young Eva, a flurry of black feathers and feverish, joyous energy, reaching out from the stage to an enthusiastic audience. Later, "I Don't Care" was reprised in a thoroughly modern, even surreal choreography, which suggested events in Tanguay's troubled career. The sequence opened with two black cats leaping into the frame with a screech, followed by black-garbed, slinky catmen. Gaynor appeared in a yellow space in a yellow costume, molting black feathers. Cole used his beloved platforms and an inclined runway. There were elevated railway tracks and cutout engines animated by dancers, and telephone lines stretching into the distance—all against the yellow background. There were puffs of flame as Tanguay's costume abruptly changed colors. There were ladders and ornamental pipe railings on the ramps and platforms. Jets of gas burst from these at the close, with a curtain of flame in front of Gaynor.

Matt Mattox and Marc Wilder were among Cole's dancers. Recently, Mattox recalled this number for *Dance Magazine*. Although there were some decorative railings, he noted that some of the ramps and platforms had no guardrails. Part of the sequence required Gaynor to dance up a flight of steps, followed by her male admirers. At the top of the platform, she was to turn and execute a high kick. Two dancers would then perform a back-somersault, being caught by six strong male dancers. Gwen Verdon, with whom Cole had created the dance, used to take Gaynor's place in some rehearsals, when Gaynor was needed for other shots.

To illustrate the degree to which Cole's dancers responded to his challenges, Mattox cited a camera run-through: "Gwen was doing Mitzi, and Marc Wilder and I did the movement for all the other boys. We arrived at the top of the stairs; Gwen turned and kicked out at us, and Marc and I fell backwards, forgetting there were no boys waiting to catch us. Marc ended up rolling backwards down fourteen stairs, and I fell onto my back after passing through seven feet of space. We had put ourselves into the action so thoroughly that we forgot there was no one waiting to catch us. . . ." Mattox and Cole's other dedicated disciples never "marked," just going through the motions in rehearsal, even if Cole said it was all right. They always danced full force, whether in rehearsal or in performance. Mattox says it was because they all respected Cole as a master and wanted him to be able to see in rehearsal how his dance sequences would look on the screen.

Sheilah Graham wrote in the *Daily Mirror:* "They don't know whether it's the tan makeup or Jack Cole, but Mitzi turned up sexy as the 'I Don't Care Girl.' " When stars were pleased with the help that had been given them by talents like Cole, really pleased, they'd often ask to have such people work on their next film. Mitzi Gaynor knew very well what Cole had done for her—and how he'd helped save the picture. She sent him a note, which he saved in his scrapbooks. It was a reversal of the usual star-routine:

Dear Jack,
Thank you for all you have done for me. —You've spoiled me for anyone else. *Please* ask for me on your next picture—

Love, Mitzi

Jack Cole and Betty Grable were together again for Fox's *The Farmer Takes a Wife,* which opened in New York at the Globe Theatre in June 1953. Cole worked hard to provide appropriate and lively dances. Well he might. Grable was telling columnists that her long suspension by Fox was a direct result of her insistence on having Cole choreograph *Meet Me After the Show.* Studio bosses contended that Cole was too expensive. Grable didn't go into details about the costs, but it was well known that Cole's fees were high. His demands for perfection in his dancers and adequate rehearsal time as well must certainly have added to the cost of using Cole. Gwen Verdon was in this film.

In Cole's private papers, he kept a color-feature from *Collier's*, October 25, 1952. It was titled "Three Girls in a Tub," with photos by John Florea. The other two girls, in addition to Grable, were Jan Sterling and Rhonda Fleming. They weren't in the same tub; theirs was on the set for *Pony Express*, another exercise in nineteenth-century nostalgia. Florea caught Grable in a hip-bath, clad in a pink body stocking so she'd look nude under the suds. Thelma Ritter was helping her bathe in the film, but between takes, Cole and makeup man George Lang were crouching at her side in conference, getting ready for her number, "When I Close My Door." Cole was genuinely fond of Grable, and she made no secret of her admiration for him.

Critics were more restrained in their admiration for the film. In the *Hollywood Reporter*'s judgment, after a year's absence Grable was not returning to the screen in an auspicious vehicle. *Farmer*, it seemed, didn't adapt well to the musical genre. Cole's work was not admired: "The dance routines are unimaginative." In fact, the film, for the *Reporter*, was ". . . a mediocre musical with so-so entertainment values that will have to be carried most of the way by Miss Grable's marquee strength."

No matter; Cole had helped Zanuck and Fox save a costly picture, in *The I Don't Care Girl*. If *The Farmer Takes a Wife* had turned out to be an Erie Canal potboiler, Cole had again demonstrated his sensitivity to the needs of the movie musical stars, to their insecurities and inadequacies. Despite the high price he put on his talents, he was a wise choice for Fox when it was time to make two fabulous, famous ladies of show business, Jane Russell and Marilyn Monroe, look just as fabulous in cinematic dance sequences.

Above: Photograph of Jack Cole by Marcus Blechman. Right: Anna Austin, Cole, and Florence Lessing, in the Persian Room of the Plaza Hotel.

Above: Florence Lessing and Cole in Nice
Goin' *(1939). Left: Cole's "East Indian
Dances" as performed in the 1930s.*

Above: Cole's "Wedding of a Solid Sender," with Becky Lee (right) as his bride. Right: A zoot-suited Cole in an Al Hirschfeld caricature.

*Above: Florence Lessing, Cole,
and Anna Austin in* Moon over Miami
*(1941). Right: Cole and Carol Haney,
at the time of* Bonanza Bound!, *in
a photo by Marcus Blechman.*

To Tampico:—
Who is married
To Tito. I wish
you much happy
in your stone
house.
David
16 19..

Above: A rehearsal of "Latin Impressions"
at Chez Paree. Back row, left to right:
Bob Hamilton, George Martin, Alex Romero,
Rod Alexander; front: *Florence Lessing and Cole*
(on floor). Left: Photograph of David Gray, Cole's
longtime companion, by Marcus Blechman (1946).

Above: A rehearsal of "East Indian Hunting Dance" at Chez Paree. Left to right: *Ethel Martin, Ruth Godfrey, Florence Lessing, Carol Haney, Bob Hamilton, Alex Romero, Rod Alexander, and George Martin, who were the nucleus of Cole's Columbia dance workshop. Cole is in front.*
Right: Cole with Larry Parks, Rita Hayworth, and Marc Platt, stars of Down to Earth *(Columbia, 1947).*

Above: "The Broken Pianolita" number in Magdalena *(1948). Right: Cole oversees* Alive and Kicking *rehearsals.*

Above: Cole and Gwen Verdon in Alive
and Kicking. *Left:* Cole and Gwen Verdon at
rehearsals for Alive and Kicking (1950).

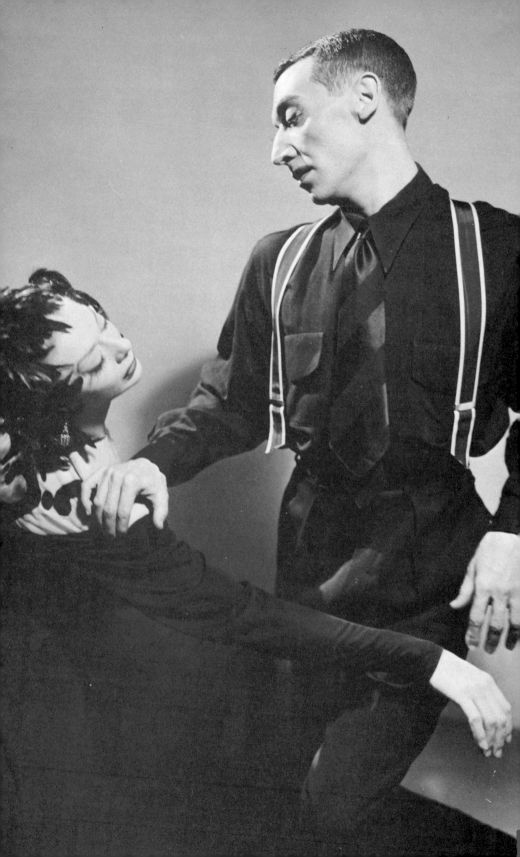

Above: Florence Lessing dancing "Rahadlakum" from Kismet *(1953). These knee drops ruined the knees of Cole and his dancers! Left: Cole and Gwen Verdon performing "I Didn't Want Him" from* Alive and Kicking.

Above: Cole and his dancers on the
television show "The Hollywood Palace."
Left: Cole and Marilyn Monroe
rehearsing "My Heart Belongs to Daddy"
from Let's Make Love *(1960).*

9

MEETING
MARILYN
MONROE

COLE HELPS
CREATE
A LEGEND

Long after her death, one of Marilyn Monroe's co-stars, after a hard day of giving interviews to promote a film of his own, grew increasingly irritated as journalists bombarded him with questions about Monroe. His film, his talents, his opinions, it seemed, weren't nearly as interesting. Everyone was fascinated by the legend of Marilyn Monroe. "I should have told them," he confided to a press agent after this ordeal, "that she was a dumb broad who couldn't act for beans."

If that were true—as some close observers suggest it was—then Fox was only type-casting her when it chose Monroe to play Anita Loos's equally legendary dumb blonde, the innocently unself-conscious gold digger Lorelei Lee. Carol Channing had, of course, created the definitive, enduring image of Lorelei when she opened on Broadway, December 8, 1949, in the musical version of *Gentlemen Prefer Blondes*, with its cautionary ballad, "Diamonds Are a Girl's Best Friend." Channing made the role her own.

Casting Monroe as Lorelei, rather than the performer who had made the role not only memorable on stage but also part of the lore of American show business, might seem incomprehensible. It wouldn't be the first time, however, nor the last that Hollywood would do this. For Fox, Marilyn Monroe was box-office dynamite. Unfortunately, her talents were limited, though God and genetics had generously endowed her body. The problem was to find a cinematic vehicle that would maximize her largely latent comic abilities and show her fabulous form to the greatest titillating advantage.

The obvious role for Monroe was that of the incredibly, delightfully dumb Lorelei Lee, the "little girl from Little Rock," who had an uncanny knack for separating rich admirers from their wealth, without giving up much on her side. As Lorelei's Little Rock chum, Dorothy, Fox chose Jane Russell, a statuesque beauty who had won fame in Howard Hughes' *The Out-*

law. It was a pairing made in Hollywood heaven; even Bosley Crowther crowed in glee about the stars' inherent magnetism and luxurious coquetry. The film proved a money-spinner, winning some $5 million for Fox.

Marilyn Monroe's performance as a singer, a dancer, and a deadpan comedienne was hailed. Some astute critics realized how much of her success, at least in the dance numbers, was owed to Jack Cole. Few knew what he had been doing behind the scenes to prepare her for the role, helping her develop her sensuous walk and breathlessly sexy mode of speaking, as well as giving her the best coaches to work with when he was busy on other aspects of the film project. One Cole intimate, Marcus Blechman, after seeing the finished film, wrote a note to Cole: "Your 'Diamonds' number is very effective from the point of view of cinematic composition. But Marilyn Monroe is not my particular answer to the death of Eleanora Duse."

Cole—and certain 20th Century–Fox executives—had no illusions about Monroe's extant abilities at that time. The immediate problem was to make this film work with the available talents Monroe and Russell had already demonstrated. If Cole could explore Monroe's potential and develop it, so much the better.

Hal Schaefer proved invaluable in this training. Schaefer considers himself to be one of the top vocal coaches and singing teachers; he's certainly earned his credits, considering the stars he's trained or improved. As he says, "This expertise came about because of Jack Cole. When we started to work with people like Monroe, Grable, and Russell, Jack didn't like the way they sang. . . . So Cole asked me, could I help Marilyn with her singing? Could I help Jane? I became Marilyn Monroe's vocal teacher—and Jane's. And I worked with Betty Grable and Mitzi Gaynor. Since I was already composing the dance music which Cole was choreographing, I also worked on the vocal parts, so we didn't lose any of their energy in the work," Schaefer explains. For him, it took time and patience—and love— but Monroe and Russell were so eager to learn and so grateful for the help Cole and Schaefer were giving them, that he found it a pleasure. Were there any temperamental outbursts at being taught, considering the fact that the ladies were already stars? No, Schaefer says.

"With singing, stars have the least amount of confidence in what they're doing. You don't presume to tell them how to say a line maybe, but they have the most anxiety, the most fear, when they have to sing. They don't really know how they're doing it; they are most insecure about singing. They aren't familiar with the way they sound. They can't call on it, control it, the way they want. . . . Most stars are insecure—unless they are Barbra Streisand, whom I discovered when she was seventeen. Even when she was seventeen, Barbra Streisand was never insecure. She was right, too, but she's one in a million."

Hal Schaefer explains Cole's method of developing the dances with Monroe and Russell: "He'd rehearse, setting up a routine for Marilyn or Jane—or both of them, but he'd work out the dances with Gwen Verdon. He'd formulate them. He'd be Marilyn; he'd do her movement, and Gwen would watch and memorize that. Then Gwen would do the dance while Jack stood back and studied it for camera angles and whatever. Then Gwen would teach Marilyn the moves when she came in to rehearse.

"Well, Marilyn couldn't move like Gwen, so Jack would have to be *very* patient. Nor could he talk to Marilyn the way he'd talk to some of his dancers." Hal Schaefer indicates, as have many Cole dancers, with indelibly etched memories of some Cole verbal image of their dancing, that such comments were often profane and frequently bordered on the obscene. "He was very close to that sometimes. . . . but for some reason, Jack liked both Marilyn and Jane. He liked them personally, and maybe he thought they were doing the best they could. Some people he didn't like, and for them, it wasn't easy getting along with Jack Cole.

"Jack, Jane, and I spent a lot of time together. We got to be friends. Jane's a wonderful woman, very straightforward, no nonsense. Marilyn lived a different life, so we didn't see her much socially. But we hung out with Jane." Today, living in Sedona, Arizona, Jane Russell has fond memories of Jack Cole. "I adored him!" she says. "You know, all his feistiness, and all the rest of it, I just adored. In *Gentlemen Prefer Blondes*, he was extremely patient with me and Marilyn. As he was in *Gentle-men Marry Brunettes,* which I did with Jeanne Crain.

"He was very tough on the dancers, but he knew that we were *nudniks.* He had the patience of Job. He would go over and over and over it with us, until we were actually doing it from *habit,* rather than from memory—or ability. Then he also had Gwen Verdon working with us. She was his assistant on both those pictures. So they worked the dances out before-hand, using our natural movements. They worked all that out before they got to us. . . . Then, when we came in, we were able to do everything he showed us. But we didn't think we'd ever remember it, so he had us do it so many times that we *did* it! It was like driving a car—after you learn how, you don't think about it anymore.

"When he was working with the boys, then Gwen would put us through our paces. Often, I'd get tired, after we'd worked for a certain length of time. Marilyn was tired, too, but she'd want to stay for another hour, or an hour and a half, and Jack would stay with her. And he'd tell me: 'I knew she wasn't learning one thing during that time.' But he'd say to me, 'Fine, baby! Go home!' I'd say, 'Jack! My eyes are crossing!' But Mar-ilyn would want to stay and go over it again and again. She wanted to have it down, to have confidence. And very sweetly, Jack stayed with her. He was darling with her. But I can un-derstand that with dancers he expected a great deal more," Jane Russell says.

Angry or frustrated stars have been known to have under-lings fired from a picture when they have the power and their threshold of irritation has been reached. Such an idea, Russell says, "would never even enter my mind! I think Jack had a dif-ferent tack with stars anyway. He loved working with Rita Hayworth. She was a dancer, and I know she adored him, too." Russell pauses, searching for an image or experience to explain her fondness for Jack Cole. Then she says, "I had a very snotty father, so I just adored Jack. I understood him, and I laughed at him. And I thought he was marvelous. He was very sweet with Marilyn, who probably didn't know anyone else like that."

It was in the midst of rehearsing *Gentlemen Prefer Blondes* that Jack Cole's assistant, Gwen Verdon, got the chance to audition in New York for *Can-Can*. She was working on the "Two Little Girls from Little Rock" number when the call came. As she recalls, Cole told her benevolently, "Go ahead, honey. You'll have a free weekend in New York." She remembers being terrified, for she had to sing for Cole Porter, the show's composer. "Can I dance first?" she begged. In retrospect, she still thinks that audition must have seemed like a disaster. But when the ordeal was over, Abe Burrows, the director, got up on the stage and called Verdon "Claudine." She knew then that she had the part. That part was to help her win a Tony.

When Verdon got back to Fox and *Gentlemen Prefer Blondes*, Cole asked her indulgently how the audition had gone. She told him she'd been hired for the musical. "He punched me," she recalls. When he'd calmed down, he was glad for her, but losing Verdon as an assistant made his work with the stars harder. That's why he was glad later to have her back between—and sometimes even during—her own shows. Cole was, of course, in the audience when *Can-Can* opened on Broadway.

Cole choreographed three big production numbers for *Gentlemen Prefer Blondes*, as well as two smaller ones. Even though Howard Hawks directed, Cole's stamp on the musical staging is everywhere apparent. To open the film, Cole devised a song staging for Monroe and Russell, in "Two Little Girls from Little Rock," which made effective use of their bodies—sensuously, glamorously clothed—in walking patterns, made more personal with uncomplicated hand and arm gestures that enhanced the lyrics. Cole used a staircase and ramps for this number, which was costumed in red and white, with an intense purple background.

Ethel Martin believes Cole's solution to one big production number, featuring Jane Russell, was nothing short of brilliant. Not only was Russell tall, but she was also a big-boned, generously proportioned star. But how to back up a Jane Russell song with the lean, lithe, and less than towering Cole dancers?

"We used the Olympic team," Martin recalls. "We also had boxers; gymnasts of all kinds. . . . Jack figured that was the only way to make a woman as big as Jane Russell look feminine—to surround her with muscular athletes." The song was called "Ain't There Anyone Here for Love?" Russell was crossing the Atlantic with her chum Lorelei, on the prowl for adventure. She wandered into the ship's gym where the Olympic team was keeping itself in trim with a regimen of exercises. Kimberly Kaufman, who studied dance with Jack Cole at UCLA just before his death, recognized some of the exercises: Cole had incorporated them into every one of her technique classes with him. What impressed her most was how the various athletic activities in the film were coordinated with the rhythms of the song. The muscle men were not dancers, but their workout became a complex choreography, replete with weight lifting, push-ups, chin-ups, boxing, rope skipping, and physical drills. In addition to the visual dividend of this gymnastic precision, which made the number effectively a dance routine, Cole presented all this narcissistic cultivation of the male body as an ironic counterpoint to Russell's lovelorn lament. Here was one of the world's most desirable women, begging for some attention, surrounded by men who had eyes only for themselves.

"Diamonds Are a Girl's Best Friend" was the musical's climactic number, large-scale, complex, and nearly ten minutes long—three minutes more than major dance sequences customarily were. The focus of attention was on Marilyn as Lorelei, singing this innocently cynical and very popular song. To avoid putting too much stress on her, however, Cole choreographed so that his dancers could help her carry the number. Pink and black dominated the scene, and Cole used set devices, props, and movement effects he'd already made something of a trademark in earlier films.

But nothing was ever simple with Cole. There was often an element of camp or sophisticated parody in his cinema dance numbers that only the well-attuned could hope to appreciate. For untutored viewers, the numbers may well have looked lush and lavish. But for others, already hating Hollywood excesses, such sequences could easily seem pretentious and ultimately tasteless.

Matt Mattox found the dancing just as brutal as that in *The I Don't Care Girl*. The suffering proved worth the effort, for as

Mattox told readers of *Dance:* "Jack opened my eyes to a new kind of dance. It reached down and grabbed your insides and made you aware of an emotional experience within yourself and with the people you worked with."

Cole's playful sense of parody apparently eluded the *New York Times's* Bosley Crowther. When the film opened at the Roxy in mid-July 1953, he wrote: "Except for one plush production number, in which Miss Monroe sings that candid refrain, the theme song of the gold diggers, 'Diamonds Are a Girl's Best Friend,' there is not much class to this picture." He did, however, find the ladies buoyant and the costumes colorful. He also singled out ". . . Miss Russell's violent chant to a he-man love, sung for a bunch of squirming athletes . . ." as well as ". . . her rendering of a torrid shimmy . . ."

Fortunately, most film critics were dazzled by Cole's dances. One review that Cole kept for his scrapbooks said in part: "The leading ladies can sing with pulse, and they can not only dance but have been given some striking dance patterns. The vivid, jazzy choreography of Jack Cole is one of the highlights of the picture. Furthermore, Miss Monroe's 'Diamonds' number is a superb example of the way the camera itself can become one of the most expressive of the dancers."

Rod Alexander explains Cole's success with non-dancers in two ways. First, Cole was one of the very few dance directors who could put together a series of dance steps so that they flowed from one another in such a way that it was both fun and exciting to execute the steps. "That's probably why he was such a favorite of Rita Hayworth, Betty Grable, and Marilyn Monroe. He also did a great job of coaching Alfred Drake in *Kismet* and Richard Kiley in *Man of La Mancha.*" Second, Cole had "tremendous patience" with those who weren't really dancers. "He had the ability to repeat a movement ad infinitum until it was perfect. This patience was also present when he was teaching," Alexander observes.

Another former Cole dancer, Francine Ames Kuney, concurs: "Jack Cole was a genius at staging movement. He could take non-dancers and get them to look like they were doing something rather important." Francine Ames insists that the Cole dance sequences shown in *Gilda* and *Gentlemen Prefer Blondes* are masterpieces. Even Marilyn Monroe's minimal dancing is memorable, she believes.

Robert Wright and Chet Forrest know a lot about films and dance directors. As Bob Wright says, "We worked with them all, from Busby Berkeley to George Balanchine." They observed Cole at work and marveled at what he was able to do when he took famous female stars in hand. Rita Hayworth was an outstanding example, in the opinion of Wright and Forrest. "Yes," Wright admits, "she did come from a dancing family, but her experience was very limited. We knew her first in 1937 and saw what she became. She was, initially, the most delicate, the most retiring, the shyest!"

Wright thinks about Cole's special gift for working with the stars: "The identification of the movie ladies with Jack was a very real thing. You can't call it choreography, but he was a *superb director*. He could create a female who was irresistible. Look at Marilyn Monroe! Look at Gwen Verdon! Look at Mitzi Gaynor!" Wright and Forrest knew her as Mitzi Gerber, when she was one of a flock of children in their very successful musical, *Song of Norway*, a fictionalized biography of composer Edvard Grieg, using some of his musical themes. Gaynor was a protégée of the West Coast producer, Edwin Lester. Wright and Forrest used her again at sixteen in *Gypsy Lady*, a wedding of two Victor Herbert operettas, *The Fortune Teller* and *Serenade*. Lester was later enamored of a failed Broadway show, *Flahooley* (May 1951). He revived it in California for his Civic Light Opera series with the new title of *Jollyanna*. Initially, it had Bil Baird puppets and the four-octave voice of Yma Sumac. In Los Angeles and San Francisco, the new ingredient was Mitzi Gaynor.

Jane Russell's early patron, the multimillionare aviation enthusiast Howard Hughes, was a major backer of the Lester revival. He'd taken an interest in young Mitzi Gaynor and her career, though her mother was seldom far from her side. Hughes had Jack Cole brought in to do everything he could to help the show. One evening, so the story goes, Gaynor invited Cole to join her, her mother, and Hughes in the Fairmont Hotel's supperclub. Hughes admired her dancing, but he didn't dance himself. Cole could round out the party and be her partner. Gaynor and Cole were the sole couple on the dance floor. Hughes had bought out the club, complete with its floorshow, so he wouldn't have to be stared at by the curious or celebrity-seekers. Cole remembered it as a very strange evening.

Dolores Gray, who worked with Cole in *Carnival in Flanders* on the stage and *Kismet* and *Designing Woman* on the screen, was another star whom Cole helped. Recently, Gray has been performing in *42nd Street*, and she's still a big fan of Jack Cole's. "He once said, 'Really, Dolores, you should have been a dancer!' I said, 'I know, I know. I love it and I understand it, but my body just isn't trained to do it.' " He told her he wanted to start a class with the lady stars he loved the most. Gray recalls, "It never came to pass. When I was working at Metro, he said, 'You really should train, Dolores, because you move and you understand.' I said, 'I know, but I always sang so well, I didn't have to.' He said, 'That's too bad!' "

Dolores Gray agrees that Cole was a master in devising movement that was just right for individual stars. But was he—as critics suggested, surmising from seeming aggression against women in some Cole dances—really aggressive toward women? "Not at all!" Gray is emphatic. "If he could see that you understood what was needed, but the body couldn't quite do it, then he was very patient. He'd work endlessly to help you."

Hal Schaefer notes that the stars' regard for Cole wasn't confined to the rehearsal studio or the sound stage. "Women were *nuts*, crazy, about Jack. I'm talking about very strongly attracted to him. Whatever Jack's sexual preferences were, they couldn't care less. That's the way they reacted to him, including Marilyn Monroe. And Jane Russell. Betty Grable thought Jack Cole was the cat's meow—or pajamas."

Cole's concern for Marilyn Monroe, Dolores Gray agrees, may have been a mixture of admiration for the talent he saw in her, as well as sympathy with her for the ordeal of her celebrity and the constant pressures of film-making. She says, "I think he saw reflections of himself in a person with gifts and talents, but unbelievably shy—who wanted to express it, but didn't know how." Was it possible, then, that Jack Cole really created the image the public came to adore as Marilyn Monroe? Gray says fervently, "I believe that! I believe that!"

Monroe came to depend on Cole more and more for advice and coaching. It's true, however, that she made herself dependent on a variety of people at this time, so there are a number of claimants for the role of Monroe's guru or image-shaper. Hal Schaefer remembers how Monroe would surround herself with a coterie of admirers and advisors, who'd want to remake her in their image. Then she'd drift to another group of adulants and suppliants. Jane Russell remembers a time when Marilyn Monroe was living in New York. "She had a way of going from one group to another, and she wouldn't see any of the old friends. There'd be a whole new group. But she wouldn't work on a picture if there was dancing or singing unless she could work with Jack, or have his advice. She'd call Jack and get him to come and work with her. Or she'd come out and work with him.

"He tried to call her once in New York," Jane Russell recalls, "and he got a very British-sounding female on the other end of the phone who told him that Miss Monroe was not available. He got very annoyed. But it was true—you could not reach Marilyn when she was in another group. They surrounded her. Agents, secretaries, God-knows-what, but you couldn't get hold of her. I was complaining about that to Jack. I'd been in New York, but I never reached her. He said, 'It's so stupid and wrong of her to do that.' He said, 'I'll tell you what I did.' Monroe had called Cole, and he was returning the call. He got this British secretary who was so grand. So he finally said, 'Listen! You tell Baby Doll that Jack Cole called! And if she doesn't call me back in ten minutes [here Russell's voice rises to an angry shout], *never call me again!*' And he hung up the phone. In ten minutes she was on the phone, crying. He just said, 'Look, honey! Get rid of those people. Your own friends cannot reach you. And they are so snooty and uppity and so *teddibly* grand. You don't need that, and it isn't doing you one bit of good.' From then on, he never had any trouble getting through," Russell says.

Hal Schaefer is one of those Monroe friends who thinks she

must have tried to reach him on that final fatal night. He explains Cole's attractiveness to Monroe, Grable, Russell, and the other stars: "I think it was his strength, his independence, that made women nuts about him. So whatever he said to Marilyn was all right with her. She may have been difficult with others, but not with Cole."

Some months later in 1953, *How to Marry a Millionaire* opened, with Monroe, Betty Grable, and Lauren Bacall. It wasn't a musical, and it carried no Cole credits, but two of the stars owed something in their performances to the skills of Jack Cole. The third would later work with him in *Designing Woman*. Even Monroe films that had nothing to do with Jack Cole, some of his colleagues suggest, profited from Monroe's private coaching with him. In 1954, Cole was to work twice with Monroe on Fox films. The first was *River of No Return*, with Monroe, Robert Mitchum, and Rory Calhoun. Lionel Newman and Ken Darby provided songs; Cole choreographed. This picture was followed by *There's No Business Like Show Business*, which was a curious case.

It was conceived as a Technicolor musical blockbuster, a family album of Irving Berlin hits, with a cast including Ethel Merman, Dan Dailey, Donald O'Connor, Mitzi Gaynor, and Johnnie Ray, all as an irresistible household of vaudevillians. Marilyn Monroe was also starred, cast as a nightclub singer involved with Donald O'Connor. Robert Alton, a widely admired Hollywood dance director, was asked to choreograph. Monroe, again insecure, begged to have Jack Cole stage her big number, "Heat Wave." Gossip columnists hinted at a feud between Alton and Cole because of this. But it was, after all, a film packed with musical numbers; Alton had more than enough to do himself. For that matter, Cole had engaged Nick Castle and Eugene Loring to help him out as well. Having Castle help Ann Miller perfect a tap routine in a Cole film was no different from having Cole help Monroe in an Alton film. In fact, after the rumors of feuding appeared in the local press, Alton called the dancers together, says Jerry Gotham, now choreographer for the Light Opera of Manhattan, but then a company dancer. Alton said there was no truth to the tale about a feud between him and Cole. He was pleased to have Cole working with Monroe—as well he might be.

The *New York Times's* Bosley Crowther was not so pleased with the results; he wrote of Marilyn Monroe, "whose wriggling and squirming in 'Heat Wave' and 'Lazy' are embarrassing to behold." Many of his fellow critics, however, thought "Heat Wave" was torrid, sultry, provocative, and a variety of similar adjectives.

What impressed Matt Mattox about this number was the ingenuity Cole used to prepare for the entry of his star, rapidly building suspense and excitement. "The first thing you saw," he told *Dance* readers, "before Marilyn made her entrance, was all of us boys flying through the air, elongated, filling the space of the screen, one at a time, two at a time. But what the audience didn't see was how we landed—on mattresses, off-camera. And in an instant after hitting the mattress, we had to jump up and build a gymnastic pyramid and look towards where Marilyn would make her entrance."

Working with Monroe in such films, Cole had to keep always in mind the restrictions of the Production Code. In his scrapbooks, he preserved the guiding rules of the Legion of Decency, which was filmland's moral watchdog. Should Cole be tempted to draw on his many hours of spectator-time spent in burlesque houses, and integrate bumps and grinds into his cinematic choreography, he had to remember to avoid erotic, obscene forward bumps. Cole could, in fact, use a bump, if it were bumped rearward. And grinds could be done sidewise, but never with a rotary motion. Undeterred by the Legion, Cole continued to help Monroe undulate provocatively and radiate sexuality on screen.

Betty Grable's first new musical in two years was *Three for the Show*, which opened in New York at the Roxy in February 1955. It was a Columbia remake of their 1940 film, *Too Many Husbands*, this time in CinemaScope and Technicolor. Cole choreographed, and again he and the front office had to keep an eye on the Legion of Decency. What bothered the Legion was the basic plot premise. Grable was a bigamist through no fault of her own. The Legion of Decency thought this was worth a rating of C—death at the box office—until some aspects of the plot were adjusted and one of Cole's dances was made less objectionable.

"How Come You Do Me Like You Do?" teemed with Cole trademarks: a bright-red background, ramps and levels, dancers moving in silhouette, and male dancers thrusting their arms upward with flashes of energy. Grable had a dream fantasy, set by Cole in a male harem, where she was absolute queen. There were even tonal hints of Borodin, foreshadowing the score of *Kismet*. The men were clad in full red satin trousers and red fezes. Otherwise, the rest of their masculine attractions were exposed to Grable's interested gaze. Lattice-towers served as cages, with men on tap for each day of the week. In Saturday's cage, Jack Lemmon and Gower Champion, both attired in yellow, competed for her favors. To the music of Hoagey Carmichael's "Down Boy," Grable then enjoyed the close company of both men at the same time. For this number, the harem males wore little black Vandyke beards, which Cole himself favored now and then.

Strains of *Swan Lake* introduced another dream ballet. There was an impressive flight of deep-blue stairs. From an upper platform, files of men bearing candelabras swept down. Women in long gowns performed a romantic ballet, with a central foursome of Grable and Lemmon and Marge and Gower Champion. One element in this elaborate dance fantasy was inspired by an old French print Cole had in his personal collection. It showed two women dueling over a man, with their seconds and doctors also represented by women. Cole thought this an amusing idea, a spoof on the whole dream sequence, but at the same time, using two levels and the stairs, it could be "a big, luscious ballet confection." Intended as a "sophisticated take-off," it was marred in the editing and cutting. Cole insisted it had become "serious," which was not what he wanted at all.

Cole showed a lot of choreographic and theatrical invention in this film. Even the credits were backed by an elaborate Cole Harlequinade. The *Los Angeles Examiner* voted for Cole's work: "The production numbers are worth the price of admission . . ." Writing for the *New York Times*, February 26, 1955,

A. H. Weiler admired the Champions and the waltz ballet. He found Grable's style polished in the harem sequence. She also pleased him in "I've Got a Crush on You" and "a torrid Caribbean-type fandango to the sensuous rhythms of 'How Come You Do Me Like You Do?' " All the aspects of show business Weiler found to be "spirited stuff." Like the Legion of Decency, he did not like "the stickiness of the major premise."

Such fine moral considerations did not prevent *Dance Magazine* from giving Jack Cole its first annual award for choreography in 1955. It was presented in the spring of 1956 and honored Cole for *Three for the Show, Kismet,* and *Gentlemen Marry Brunettes.* Cole, who never won a Tony or an Oscar or an Emmy, treasured it.

Gentlemen may prefer blondes, but it's said that they marry brunettes. Cole was engaged by United Artists to provide choreography for a film that was only by the implication of its title a sequel to Fox's big hit with Marilyn Monroe and Jane Russell. *Gentlemen Marry Brunettes* had Russell again crossing the Atlantic, this time to perform in Paris with her cinema-sister, Jeanne Crain. Scott Brady impersonated a theatrical agent who had lured them to the banks of the Seine. Two dividends for Cole were a trip to London, where part of the film was shot, and, of course, to Paris.

There he nearly fell off the Eiffel Tower. Cole was staging a song performed by an amorous Brady and his glamorous quarry, Jane Russell. Instead of faking it on a sound stage, they were at a lofty level of M. Eiffel's imposing World's Fair leftover. Cole wanted the camera farther away from the duo, so he pulled it back on its track, not noticing that this extended over the edge of the platform, high above Paris. Cole heard a jolt; the camera had come to a stop. It was just right. Cole said, "This is where I want it." Then he looked down—and down and down. He froze and had to be inched back onto the platform by an assistant. For the rest of the shooting, he told friends later, "I stayed ten feet from the edge."

Relaxing from performing in *Can-Can* on Broadway, Gwen Verdon had rejoined Cole for this film. Art Buchwald, who was then the resident wit of the *Paris Herald-Tribune,* interviewed

Verdon for his column. Both she and Jane Russell would be seen in a Dior fashion show in the film, she told him. Because of her success in *Can-Can*, Buchwald asked her how she learned to perform the dance. She replied, "Jack Cole. He learned it from watching early motion pictures." At first, Verdon said, she thought the can-can was vulgar, but then Cole had told her to "dance it like a lady athlete." After that, Buchwald reported, she had no problems about performing it.

The Eiffel Tower wasn't Cole's only problem with *Gentlemen Marry Brunettes*. Assembling and rehearsing a group of dancers in London, he found it almost impossible to discover any male dancers who could do his kind of dancing. One who did pass the test was Malcolm Goddard, later a director-choreographer. Goddard auditioned, although he knew his body was already too old to do some of the things Cole would expect. He auditioned three times before Cole decided to hire him. One day, he remembers, Cole and Verdon demonstrated a rhumba step for the young English dancers. Cole asked for volunteers to copy what they'd done. "Typically English, we said nothing. So Jack said, 'Well, Malcolm, you do it with Gwen.' I did it, foot-perfect. They were all amazed. Jack asked, 'How could you pick it up so fast?' " Goddard didn't betray his secret. It was a rhumba-twist, which he'd already learned when he mastered ballroom dancing.

United Artists used Technicolor and CinemaScope for the lackluster plot, drafted by the film's director, Richard Sale, and coauthor Mary Loos. Even with Cole choreography, a Dior fashion show, and Jane Russell and Jeanne Crain, the *New York Times* dismissed the film. At best, it was "a Cook's Tour of Paris and the Riviera," the *Times* man suggested. The musical numbers had "stereotypical renditions."

Cole had already done some choreography for a non-musical version of *Kismet* in 1944. Then, in 1953, with an Alexander Borodin–based score by Wright and Forrest, a new musical adaptation opened on Broadway for a run of 648 performances, followed in London by a run of nearly 600 showings. Alfred Drake had made the role of the beggar-poet Hajj his own on stage. So it was only natural that for the movie version of this big musical hit MGM would cast Howard Keel in the role.

The Middle Eastern setting of the story, Baghdad in an earlier, simpler age, lent itself to scenic opulence, something Hollywood could do far better than Broadway. Unfortunately for the fate of the film, most of the artistic attention seemed to have been concentrated on lavish decors and pretty people lolling around in them.

Some of Cole's Broadway sequences, adapted for the screen, retained their power to excite and please. "Baubles, Bangles, and Beads" still worked, as did Cole's nuptial procession choreographed for "Night of My Nights." Whenever the three Princesses of Ababu—Reiko Sato, Patricia Dunn, and Wonci Lui—went into action, Bosley Crowther of the *Times* found that "the current starts flowing." The *Hollywood Reporter* called *Kismet* a spotty picture but had praise for Cole. Some of his dances, it seemed, were "like *Prince Igor* performed in jazz." This was hardly surprising, as Borodin's opera, *Prince Igor*, had been Wright and Forrest's musical inspiration.

"Kismet" means Fate, and as fate would have it, few critics who panned or faintly praised the film could resist commenting on the irony of the title. Writing in *Dance Magazine*, film reviewer Arthur Knight had no laurels for the director Vincente Minelli; whatever excellences the picture had were owing to Cole's work in creating the dances and staging the musical numbers. Knight admired Cole's decision to put some whirling dervishes in the background while Howard Keel sang the opening number, "Fate." Cole also won praise for the movement he worked out for the citizens of Baghdad, thronging a busy bazaar.

Cole's contributions, Knight wrote, almost made up for the film's other deficiencies. As he said, ". . . Cole's energetic, angular, pseudo-Oriental routines possess a wit and urbane sureness, a cleanness and precision visible nowhere else in this handsome, heavy, and stupendously dull production." Dolores Gray, who played Lalume in the film, remembers some of the agonies of production. There was trouble shooting the

"Not Since Nineveh" sequence. It was set on the studio back-lot, she says, "but in June, in Culver City, which is near the sea, it's the foggy month!" Cast and crew spent an entire week on "Nineveh." The dampness affected sets, costumes, lighting, and Gray's spirits. Even the camels got in the way. Gray re-members doing several takes of the number that she thought were wonderful. "I'd say, 'OK, is that a wrap?' And Cole would say, 'Unh-uh.' I'd say, 'What?' He'd say, 'The motor wasn't *really* going. Now come on! Plug it in!' " Gray recalls. She, like Cole, has always rehearsed full out, never holding back, never mark-ing, she says, unless it was a technical rehearsal or final dress, when one needed to save some energy for opening night. Cole admired that. Despite all their efforts, though, Gray thought the results looked disappointing on the screen; it was too dark. "But we had to wind it up and finish it."

One Cole staging that won wide praise grew out of "Bag-dad," a song of welcome in which Gray greeted the three Prin-cesses of Ababu, who had come to the city as possible candi-dates for the hand and heart of the young caliph. The princesses had some striking movements as they introduced themselves with shields and swords. As Gray urged the trio of beauties to stay in Baghdad, two handsome retainers began to dance, demonstrating some of the city's attractions. With its shift into a powerful jazz beat, using full orchestra, the sequence became visually and aurally quite exciting. As of old, Cole employed the movements of Indian dance. The hand gestures were au-thentic, even if the music was not.

Wright and Forrest had written a special song for Gray, one not in the Broadway show. Called "Bored," it inspired Cole to develop a curiously erotic dance movement for Gray to use while singing it. It was performed for her, so she could see how it looked, how it worked. Neglected by her husband the Wazir, Lalume found herself bored to the point of frustration. So, as she sang her song, she was caressing an unresponsive retainer. "One was practically raping the man, but yet one didn't look at him," she says. Cole showed her himself how to do ara-besques down to the floor, sliding over on the man's sturdy body. "I'll never be able to do that," Gray protested. "Yes, you will! I'll teach you," he replied. When they'd done a couple of takes with the camera, to make sure it was worked out, Cole told her it would then be done in one take. "The cameras will make about seventeen moves, but you just keep going until we call cut," he ordered. Gray was supporting herself in this sequence with her left arm around the retainer's neck, since he could not move or support her in any way. Halfway through the filming, her arm was going limp. She had to stop. Lights didn't work; cameras didn't make the right moves. It had to be taken from the top again and again. Every time Gray pleaded with Cole: "I can't hang on any longer," he'd come back firmly: "Oh yes you can!"

Dolores Gray was very fond of Cole. There were no fights during the filming of *Kismet,* she says, but she did have a little confrontation on the last day of shooting a harem number, "Rahadlakum." Gray felt the placement Cole and Minelli had agreed upon in this scene, to be seen on the screen in CinemaScope, would not show her effectively in the song—half of which she'd already lost to Howard Keel, whom she was trying to seduce in this number. Cole wanted to protect his dancers, who were the Princesses of Ababu in the scene. Gray said, "I'm not worried about your dancers; I'm worried about my performance." Minelli sided with Cole. Cole told her, "I wash my hands of this." So did Minelli, adding, "If you really feel so strongly about this, Dolores, then you rehearse it and you shoot it!" She did just that, but told the producer Arthur Freed she was also willing to shoot it Cole's way and let them decide which was best. Freed decided against the extra time and cost. Dolores Gray's staging, instead of Jack Cole's, for "Rahadlakum" was seen by millions.

Not long after this, Dolores Gray heard that MGM would make a sophisticated comedy in which there was a role for a red-haired woman who could sing. The film would not be a musical, but it was to be directed by none other than Vincente Minelli; Jack Cole was set to choreograph a sequence in the film as well. Did Gray have a chance for the part she wanted?

She dyed her hair red, leaving nothing to Minelli's imagination. When Gray appeared to audition, he told her to go to wardrobe for costume fittings. No audition, and no hard feelings. She was cast in *Designing Woman* and she would also be working again with Jack Cole, who was functioning both as choreographer and a character actor. He played Randy Owen, a frantic choreographer. There was one production number, involving Dolores Gray. Performing "There'll Be Some Changes Made," Gray sang and danced, backed by a male ensemble. To make the number something special, Cole drew on his own years of frustration in trying to get good dances well-staged and filmed. In effect, Cole was giving audiences a satiric glimpse of the technical problems involved in getting a handsome production number to look not only wonderful, but effortless as well.

Cole's vision of dance-director Randy Owen was that of an obsessive, frantic eccentric. There were, in fact, a few touches of Cole in this cinema portrait. At one point in the action, Cole pirouetted around a musical producer's office, tossing bolts of fabric into the air as he explained his ideas for costumes. *Dance's* critic Arthur Knight reported that he also slithered around at a fashionable party in what seemed a parody of a Jack Cole dance. The climactic moment of the film showed Cole saving the star, Lauren Bacall, from a gang of hoodlums, with feet flying, using all his dives, slides, falls, rolls, and jumps from the Cole Technique. It was a bravura performance, designed to show that Randy Owen, despite some catty intimations about his manhood, was more than a match for such brutes.

Although Cole had already had a small role in *The Merry Widow* before he accepted the Owen role, he consulted his psychiatrist, who urged Cole to try it. Cole was more than equal to any challenge as a dancer, but acting apparently terrified him. Minelli later revealed that Cole threw up immediately after he finished any scene in which he had to speak.

Also released in 1957 was MGM's *Les Girls,* with Cole Porter's last score, which was hardly up to standard. It also proved to be Gene Kelly's last major starring musical for MGM or anyone. He was a fan of Jack Cole's, who was the dance director, and Cole admired his work as well. The musical was interesting but uneven.

George Cukor directed; it's rumored that he and Cole didn't

work well together. The girls of *Les Girls* were played by the gifted comedienne, Kay Kendall; Cole's friend Mitzi Gaynor, and Taina Elg, a talented Finnish ballerina. Because Kendall was not a dancer and "Les Girls" had been a singing and dancing act in Paris, Cole worked especially hard with her, achieving astonishing results. She looked a veteran trouper in the film. But there was a lot of work to be accomplished, dances to be developed, musical numbers to be rehearsed and filmed. Cole, it's said, gave most of his special attention to Kendall. Elg, after all, was a trained dancer, and Cole thought Gaynor could work it out for herself, or so it's been reported. Gaynor was hurt by Cole's apparent neglect, after their collaboration on *The I Don't Care Girl*.

Reviewers singled out several of Cole's dance numbers for attention. In "Why Am I So Gone About That Gal?" Kelly and Gaynor danced and sang a takeoff on the Brando film *The Wild Ones*. Kendall, Gaynor, and Elg all performed a number called "Ladies in Waiting." *Variety* thought Cole's dances were brightly staged, praising these two numbers, as well as a Kelly and Elg duo, "The Rope Song."

Marilyn Monroe, increasingly filled with anxieties about the demands made on her by directors, wanted to work closely with Jack Cole. His last two films were made with her: *Some Like It Hot*, released in 1959, and *Let's Make Love*, premiered in 1960. *Some Like It Hot* not only offered the femininity of Marilyn Monroe, but also the comical, awkward, adopted femininity of Tony Curtis and Jack Lemmon, playing in drag.

Cole was given no credit for his work with Monroe. She performed "Running Wild" and "I Wanna Be Loved by You," but there was no elaborate movement or staging. Donald Saddler confirms that Cole did indeed work with Monroe on the film, at her insistence. "Cole worked from a human behavioral standpoint, enhancing Monroe's femininity. . . . He understood how to give her things to do which could work—and which were right for her screen personality. She never really *danced* on the screen. But what she did, she did in her way better than anyone else could have done it. Jack Cole preserved that 'IT' quality she had!"

Marilyn Monroe made *Let's Make Love* for Fox. It was released in September 1960, premiering in New York at the Paramount Theatre. It was Cole's screen farewell as a dance director, though he didn't realize that would be the case. Cole preserved an article about the filming of this fable of a Franco-American millionaire, played by Yves Montand, who becomes an actor, only to fall in love with a pretty off-Broadway performer, which was Monroe's role. Several photos showed Monroe rehearsing with Cole, who was quoted about her chronic lateness.

Just before Cole accepted this assignment, he had considered working on Frank Loesser's fey and ill-fated Broadway musical, *Greenwillow*, which starred Tony Perkins. Something went amiss, so Cole began working with Monroe, preparing her for *Let's Make Love*. His frequent assistant George Martin helped him. He'd seen them work together on a film set, but, since her vocals were pre-recorded, Martin had never before watched Cole work so closely with Monroe. He had, however, been present when Cole was coaching Rita Hayworth and knew how close they were. Cole, Martin, Monroe, and Peter Matz were in a rehearsal studio on Sixth Avenue, as he recalls.

"We were working with Marilyn on 'My Heart Belongs to Daddy.' Matz was a very big arranger then. . . . Marilyn was married to Arthur Miller at that time. . . . It was fascinating sitting in the room, just Matz and I, as Cole taught Marilyn how to sing 'My Heart Belongs to Daddy.' I really contend that that persona she showed in her film musicals was Jack Cole. He grabbed on to something in her. She followed everything he gave her. Phrasing! He did it for her at the piano, with Peter. Jack couldn't sing, really, but he worked it all out for her. The gestures, the walk. All of it!"

In 1983, when director-choreographer Larry Fuller, one of Jack Cole's former dancers, staged a show called *Marilyn!* in London at the Adelphi Theatre, Cole was used as a goad with which to prick him. Ned Sherrin, reviewing the musical for *Plays and Players*, suggested that Fuller was studying staging in the School of Harold Prince—for whom Fuller had, in fact, previously choreographed. Said Sherrin: "If he was keen to be derivative of anyone in his steps for the Monroe character, Jack Cole would have been a better inspiration."

Cole's swan song—or, more appropriately, dance—as a film choreographer went largely unnoticed. And not just because no one, including Jack Cole, knew that's what it would be. *Variety* judged Monroe's performance to be spirited, lending liveliness to Cole's staging of "My Heart Belongs to Daddy." The song, *Variety* noted, was followed by "an age-old choreography pattern of the star bouncing over and being swung aloft by dancing boys." *Playboy* was kinder to Cole: "Credit Jack Cole for the knockout musical numbers."

Fortunately, most of Cole's film choreography has survived. TV nighthawks are occasionally treated to a film in which Cole actually danced. Musicals for which he only choreographed are also to be seen in television reruns. What no one has done yet is to organize a film festival of musicals and other motion pictures with Jack Cole's dance direction on display. But to give new life to Cole's art, to share the color and vibrancy of it all, as captured on film could be dangerous because such a concentration of energy and excitement might drive audiences crazy.

Although Cole designed a number of notable dance sequences for television, the medium constantly devours new materials, so older triumphs have been shoved aside, forgotten, or even lost. In 1940, for instance, Cole and his partners Anna Austin and Florence Lessing danced in what Austin insists was the first live TV broadcast from New York of that kind of performance. In 1950, Cole was choreographing for the "Bob Hope Show" on NBC, using his own troupe in the Cole repertory of East Indian and Latin-American dances. Cole's dancers appeared on "Your Show of Shows" and Sid Caesar specials on CBS. They were also invited to perform on "The Ed Sullivan Show." Possibly his last major TV show was a 1965 "Hollywood Palace" broadcast.

Unfortunately, in the 1950s TV was still a novelty. Everyone was curious but hoped that it would get better. Only a few surmised that they were actually watching the Golden Age of Television, that commercial pressures would gradually remove from it all the inventive daring and genuine excitement and vitality of live revues with big production numbers. There was no Museum of Broadcasting then to save films or tapes of shows, so today there is no video library of Cole choreography on file at the Museum. In searching for such visual records when she was preparing her American Dance Machine reconstructions of Cole choreography and the videotaped *Recollection of Jack Cole*, Lee Theodore gained access to CBS's own surviving tapes and films. "They were *gone!*" she says. "We got to the end of one, where a Cole number should have been, and it was gone. Someone had cut it off and taken it away."

10

THEATRE DANCE ON BROADWAY

COLE MAKES A DISTINCTIVE CONTRIBUTION

I n 1933, Jack Cole made his in-
auspicious Broadway debut as a member of the Doris Humphrey and Charles Weidman troupe, in the Theatre Guild production of Molière's *School for Husbands*. The star of this charming
and beautifully-designed revival was the popular star Osgood
Perkins.

In *School for Husbands*, in which he danced the role of an
Olympian, Cole failed to catch the critical eye of Brooks Atkinson, theatre "maven" for the *New York Times*. Cole's chum
Marcus Blechman was listed at least in Atkinson's review as
impersonating a bear. It was the depths of the Great Depression, but, oddly enough, it was also a Golden Age in the New
York theatre. This production was only the second Theatre Guild
offering in a season of sixteen projected theatre events.

It was an exciting, even daring, era in American theatre,
though bank closures and tax foreclosures on property everywhere testified to the desperate financial situation. Fortunately,
there were theatres that did, at least in their upper levels, offer
inexpensive seats. Both theatre and films were good, if temporary, avenues of escape from the harsh economic and social
realities of the times. For some, theatre was preferable because
it was live. In any case, it was more appealling to many, especially its colorful musicals and stage revues, than an evening's
program of serious modern dance. This lesson in artistic sup-
ply-and-demand was not lost on Jack Cole. *School for Husbands*,
supplemented with cabaret appearances at the Palais Royale
farther up Broadway, was keeping the Humphrey-Weidman
ensemble alive.

However astute Brooks Atkinson was in recognizing genuine talent in new playwrights and promising performers, he
cherished fairly traditional notions about the kind of dancing
appropriate for Broadway entertainments. Of *Thumbs Up*, Cole's
next bow on Broadway, he didn't mention Cole and his partner, Alice Dudley, but he had this to say about the revue's

dancing: ". . . the dancers go through their paces with the gusto of the old days, before art crept into this corner of musical revue producing." *Thumbs Up,* opening on December 27, 1934, was intended to capitalize on the festive season. Staged by John Murray Anderson, the revue ran for twenty weeks, not bad in bad times.

After the show closed, Cole and his beautiful young partner performed in St. Louis at the Summer Operetta. Cole saved a photo of this Midwest adventure, as well as mementos of the next musical theatre engagement, *Venus in Silk,* which tried out in October but didn't get to Broadway. Audrey Christie played Nina, and Cole was cast as Raki, a gypsy. *Variety* reported: "Best break of all goes to the dance team of Cole and Dudley . . . but that's no fault of the book."

This misfired production was rapidly followed by another operetta, *May Wine,* which opened December 5, 1935. Cole and Dudley were specialty dancers. One reviewer thought their routines showed the influence of Germany's leader in modern dance, Mary Wigman. Since one of their two numbers was a rhumba, it must have been something special, if it was done with a Wigman twist. Al Hirschfeld, the theatrical caricaturist, liked the duo well enough to portray them with his bold brush strokes. The *Times* review listed Cole and Dudley but had no comment on their dancing. It wasn't exactly a Viennese operetta, but Sigmund Romberg's score gave it that flavor. *May Wine* earned 213 performances, so it did find an interested audience. Sometime during 1935, says Anna Austin, Ruth St. Denis was engaged by the Shuberts to choreograph a revival of *Rose-Marie,* but Jack Cole actually did the work for his beloved Miss Ruth.

This was the period when Cole and Dudley were really beginning to catch on in the supperclubs. In August 1937, Cole took time out from midtown Manhattan to perform as "an entrancing Harlequin" in a production of *Princess Turandot* at the Westport Country Playhouse. Filmland's Chinese charmer, Anna May Wong, was the princess with the deadly riddle. Meanwhile, the Cole-Dudley duo had become a favorite at the Rainbow Room.

In 1939 Cole joined Mary Martin, who'd been featured at

the Rainbow Room, in the out-of-town tryouts of a new musical, *Nice Goin'*. It was based on the popular 1933 farce *Sailor, Beware!* Anna Austin was also in the company. She insists that it was during the show's Boston run that Cole hurt his knee badly. "He jumped off a springboard and, as he landed, twisted his knee. He had to be taken to the hospital and was laid up for eight weeks. When he got back to New York, he still could not dance. That's when he decided to have his eye operation," Austin explains. One of Cole's eyes was crossed—though none of his dancers or friends seems certain which one it was. Some say Cole told them he was blind in one eye. Others believe it was only impaired vision. In the early 1970s shortly before his death, he told UCLA student and admirer, choreographer Spider Kedelsky that he had difficulty seeing. Kedelsky found this hard to believe, as Cole never seemed to miss anything in a range of 360° in his classes.

Austin emphasizes, "One eye would go out of focus, so the operation straightened that out. He could see very well with both eyes." She thinks it's possible that Cole may have tried to give the impression he couldn't see well even if it wasn't so. It's not clear why he would have wanted to do such a thing, however, since he despised being pitied or patronized.

After the Hollywood fiasco of *Moon Over Miami*, Cole was back on Broadway with his dancers on April 24, 1942. The show was *Keep 'Em Laughing*, at the 44th Street Theatre. Among the talent on hand were Zero Mostel, Paul and Grace Hartman, William Gaxton, Victor Moore, and the "Incomparable Hildegarde," as she was known to nightclub and nationwide radio audiences. Jack Cole and His Dancers must have made no impression at all on Brooks Atkinson. The *Times* didn't mention them, even unfavorably. On the other hand, the distinguished theatre critic John Mason Brown, of the *World-Telegram*, found Cole and his dancers "both skillful and exotic." The *New York Post*'s Wilella Waldorf noted: "Jack Cole and his troupe adapt East Indian style to jazz tempos with interesting results." Walter Terry, reviewing the show for *Dance Magazine*, admired Cole's dances for their skill and theatricality. He especially liked two Hindu routines, set to swing music but performed with authentic gestures. These, he said, were ". . . no more violent nor virtuosic than the traditions of Hindu dance allow." Considering the intense nature of Cole's choreography, the tremendous concentration and energy they required, and the unsmiling seriousness with which they were often danced, it's a tribute to Cole's talent that no one pointed out that the revue was titled *Keep 'Em Laughing*.

Something very important happened to the American musical theatre in 1943, but it wasn't Cole's next show, *Something for the Boys*. Opening on January 7, it was a solid hit, thanks to the songs of Cole Porter and the boisterous "belting" singing style of Ethel Merman. The landmark musical of 1943 was still two months away. On March 31, Rodgers and Hammerstein's *Oklahoma!* opened at the St. James and launched a new trend in American musicals. *Something for the Boys* may have been overshadowed up at the Alvin Theatre, but it ran for a very respectable tally of 422 performances.

Lewis Nichols, reviewing for the *Times*, explained how Jack Cole's dances and dancers fitted into this tale of comic military-civilian misunderstandings and amorous skirmishes: "Anita Alvarez is on hand to lead the Spanish dance, without which no musical show set in Texas would be considered legal." Burns Mantle judged Cole's dances "superior." Already an admirer of Cole's, the *Post*'s Wilella Waldorf praised Alvarez's Spanish number and emphasized: "Jack Cole's dance numbers are unfailingly attractive." Later, Cecil Smith, a historian of American musicals, singled out Cole's choreography in the show in his book, *Musical Comedy in America*. He wrote: "Jack Cole's dances were a stroke of genius. Without being mere drills, they were built out of military formations for a big party scene, which maintained similar regularity of design by employing square-dance figures." This use of the square dance not only harked back to the Denishawn dance, *Boston Fancy-1854*, in which Cole performed, but it also anticipated Agnes de Mille's innovative use of American folk dance just two months later in *Oklahoma!* Cole was more in tune with the times than he knew.

Cole didn't have to be everywhere his dancers were, so it was possible for him—and some more of his dancers—to be the mainstay of a new *Ziegfeld Follies of 1943*. This show was not exactly as much of a tribute to the late, great Florenz Ziegfeld as it was an undisciplined playpen for the egotism of the comic star, Milton Berle. Ilona Massey and Arthur Treacher were also featured, but Berle was everywhere, even insinuating himself into a line of chorus boys. Cole's dances excited Berle's admiration; he thought they looked like a jam session at the Taj Mahal.

Composer-lyricists Robert Wright and Chet Forrest, who'd worked at MGM since their early twenties, had left the studio. John Murray Anderson staged this Shubert *Follies* and asked for their help. "When they were in trouble in Boston, they remembered us. Bob Alton was choreographing the show, but Jack Cole was the dancer, so we got together again," recalls Wright. Wright and Forrest were called in by Murray Anderson mainly to help Arthur Treacher. In his comic prime he was the quintessential English butler. In this *Follies,* unfortunately, he was being eclipsed by the irrepressible Milton Berle, not to mention some inadequate performance material.

When Wright and Forrest were heavily involved in Tamiment, a union-sponsored summer music theatre, one of their young dancers, J. C. McCord had constantly talked about the genius of a dancer called Jack Cole. His sister, Nancy McCord, had been featured in *May Wine*, the 1935 show in which Jack Cole danced. "He was his god," Wright recalled. "I wondered, can this be the shy Jack Cole I once met? The *small* Jack Cole? He was a giant on stage, of course, but off, he always seemed small to me. His bones were small. I'm only 5' 9", but I felt big next to Cole. When he was on stage, I felt *that* high." Wright's thumb and forefinger nearly come together as he indicates the effect this dynamic, demonic dancer had on an incredibly shrinking songwriter. "Jack was *hard* to get to know. When I was fifteen or sixteen, I'd played piano for Sally Rand, the fan dancer. Jack was fascinated. He couldn't get over this, that one of the writers, who wrote for Nelson Eddy and Jeannette MacDonald, also knew Sally Rand."

This *Ziegfeld Follies* had a little bit of everything but what most impressed the critics was the contribution of Jack Cole and his ensemble. Cole performed his *Wedding of a Solid Sender* and *Hindu Serenade*. The first was inspired partly by Cole's nocturnal adventuring in Harlem and in part by the wartime zoot-suiters, who were largely young men from the urban ethnic poor, mainly blacks and hispanics, but not exclusively so. One of the popular songs of the day described, in jive talk, the kind of suit a smartly dressed zoot-suiter should wear. In Cole's dance number, he wore a suit with exaggerated shoulders, mile-wide lapels, extra-long jacket, the whole of it vibrating with bold vertical stripes. He also twirled the obligatory yard-long key chain. Cole had made good use of the time he spent in Harlem dives, smoking reefers, picking up the urban folk dance he so admired, and taking note of black sartorial splendors. In this frenetic dance, as the zoot-suiter's bride, dancer Becky Lee matched Cole's energy and seeming abandon, although every movement was precisely planned and executed. The duo was backed by the Cole ensemble.

Cole's *Hindu Serenade* was a dance setting related to songs interpreted by Ilona Massey and Jaye Martin. Cole called on Anna Austin and Florence Lessing to join him in the dance, which he also costumed. Dance critic Don McDonagh describes this work: "The resplendently costumed man is seated at the center of the stage with one leg tucked under him and the other extended and bent at the knee. One hand rests confidently on his thigh and the other droops casually over the knee of the bent leg. . . .

"Suddenly the man rises and begins an exhausting, sinuous, and frantic dervish dance that has him alternately lost in ritual postures and whipping his supple body like a possessed jazz dancer. The three women [behind him] are a decorative frieze for his energetic and engaging dancing. . . . The piece ends with a decorative frenzy combining high voltage energy and the ritual hand gestures of traditional Hindu styles," McDonagh explains.

After the show opened at the Winter Garden on April Fool's Day in 1943, the critics were not terribly kind, except to Jack Cole and His Dancers, who were the high point of the evening for many. Lewis Nichols, of the *Times*, remarked: "Jack Cole has some moments of the inspired, angular dancing for which he is quite properly renowned." Ward Morehouse, writing in the *New York Sun,* observed: "Jack Cole's dance routines, particularly *The Wedding of a Solid Sender,* are eerie and fantastic and exceptionally well done." The man in the *Herald-Tribune*'s free seats, Howard Barnes, said, "Jack Cole does some fancy stepping in a jive wedding number."

This hodge-podge of variety entertainment may have borne Ziegfeld's name, but it had little in common with his lavish revues. Writing in *PM,* threatre critic Louis Kronenberger reported a pre-show conversation between the director-playwright Moss Hart and his colleague, the playwright Lillian Hellman. Hart was heard exclaiming, "Who'd have thought that we'd see another *Follies?*" Hellman, whose wit was often caustic, responded, "What makes you think we will?"

A year later, Cole was involved in an even more mindless production, *Allah Be Praised!* It opened April 24, 1944, at the Adelphi Theatre, where it didn't survive a full three weeks. Alfred Bloomingdale was the producer, who was reported once to have asked a drama critic what he thought. The solicitous reviewer replied, "Al, keep the store open nights!"

As had already happened to Cole so often in the supperclubs, his work was singled out for praise, almost as if to shame the other entertainers. He was to have the misfortune to be involved in more than a few Broadway flops from which he and his dancers could walk away, heads held high, with critical kudos. Considering all the widely varied elements and personalities that go into the making of a Broadway musical and as a result all the things that can go disastrously wrong, Cole can hardly be blamed for the choices he made on Broadway. When he agreed to work in or on a musical or revue, he and the rest of the creative team always had the highest hopes for success. It's well worth remembering that seldom, even in the most miserable turkey of a show, did Jack Cole come off with less than very good reviews.

Among the talent Cole had to work with were the Kraft twins, Evelyne and Beatrice, whom he also used as supperclub partners. Anita Alvarez was praised for her part in a slow-motion baseball game, a Cole novelty called *Katinka to Eva to Frances*. Burton Rascoe, who was quite anti-Cole in the *Follies*, executed an artful, graceful 180° turn; Cole's choreography he found "fetching," with special praise for "The Persian Way of Life." This began as a song, interpreted by Mary Jane Walsh, which developed into a Cole dance with Alvarez, Mary McConnell, and the Cole ensemble. John Chapman, of the *Daily News*, also praised Cole's work, as well as that of the Krafts and "a small gamine named Anita Alvarez." The *Times*'s Lewis Nichols concurred about the dancing talent and the dances, "which move briskly in the angular manner of Jack Cole . . ."

The energy levels Jack Cole had to maintain at this time—especially when he was heavily involved with his Columbia Pictures dance workshop and choreographing for films—must have been impressive. Colleagues describe him then as like a tightly coiled spring, but that isn't an image of Cole that changed much over the years. Occasionally, there was an enforced idleness, when he couldn't get a film assignment, or plans for a Broadway musical fell through. If his dancers were threatened with unemployment, however, he'd make sure that the Jack Cole Dancers—with or without Jack Cole—would have nightclub engagements.

During Cole's Columbia years, he'd receive letters and telegrams from New York proposing a variety of new musicals. One, dated December 3, 1944, asked Cole to consider choreographing a musical based on *The Firebrand of Florence*, a drama about the adventurous, boisterous artist Benvenuto Cellini. It must have aroused Cole's interest, especially because Cellini was a real rebel as well as a great artist-craftsman, something like Cole, who was himself to be described one day as a "Renaissance Man."

Almost a year later to the day, on December 5, 1945, Cole's New York agent, Jack Davies, sent him a wire with the news that Rodgers and Hammerstein's new musical production, *Annie Oakley*, would star Ethel Merman. Cole was invited to choreograph. When this Broadway classic finally opened as *Annie Get Your Gun*, with a hit parade score by Irving Berlin, Helen Tamiris was the choreographer. Rodgers and Hammerstein were merely the producers of the show. The previous summer, on July 18, Dorothy Kilgallen's producer-husband, Richard Kollmar, sent Cole a telegram begging him to choreograph his new project, to be called *Slightly Perfect*. Given Kollmar's tastes and skills, Cole must have realized that any perfection the show might have would be very slight indeed.

In 1947, Cole found a busy respite in New York, rehearsing a new musical called *Bonanza Bound*. That, financially, was certainly the hope of its creators, Adolph Green, Betty Comden, and Saul Chaplin. Jack Cole was their choreographer, renewing an old acquaintance made when Comden and Green were young comedians on a Rainbow Room bill with him.

1947 was also the year in which Gwen Verdon says she became "legal." Cole called her, asking, "I hope you've kept yourself in condition?" Verdon said she had. Cole then ordered her to get on an airplane and come to New York. "You can be in a show," he promised. The show was *Bonanza Bound*, which had such talents as George Coulouris, Hal Hackett, Adolph Green, and the gifted dancer Allyn MacLerie in its cast.

Set in the Alaskan Klondike, circa 1898, the show was also set to open in Philadelphia at the Forrest Theatre on Christmas night, 1947. In fact, the musical's opening scene was described in the script by Comden and Green as "a beautiful Christmas-card-like snow scene of the frozen north. Hills and trees, blue, blue sky and sparkling snow. . ." This icy idyll was shattered by a rough prospector bursting on the scene, crying, "Gold! Gold!"

The famed Klondike Gold Rush was on—and it remained for director Charlie Friedman and Jack Cole to make it all happen on stage, including the dancing girls and other camp followers who streamed northward in search of fortune. To whet the appetites of New Yorkers for the new musical, Cole took time out from rehearsals to discuss the show's problems with veteran theatre journalist Vernon Rice. Rice began his report by warning his readers that Cole was no man to mince words. In fact, he said, "not a word of it can you print in a family newspaper." Rice hastened to assure his public that Cole's manners were otherwise all one would expect of a decently brought-up "average American." Cole's curse, it seemed, was frankness, and he was very frank about that Klondike gold-strike with Rice.

Rice had already seen some of the rehearsals, discovering that many of Cole's dancing girls were what were euphemistically called "ladies of the evening." Cole, he admitted, called them something far more frank. Cole told him, "The girls that got to Alaska were tired and beat up. I've got a problem in trying to get that tired feeling into the dances, without having the dances seem tired."

Already noted for his interest in ethnic dances, Cole admitted he'd hoped to include an authentic Eskimo dance in the show. At the turn of the century, however, or so Cole told Rice, Eskimos were in the habit of taking off all their clothes when they danced. Of course, he may just have been pulling Rice's leg—or parka. "There isn't time between the first and second acts to distribute a brochure explaining the habits and customs of the Eskimos, so I've substituted a Totem Pole Dance," Cole said. He refrained from commenting on the Freudian phallic potential in dancing round such a monumental wooden erection.

Cole's biggest problem was not, however, with the dances or dancers. He was also staging the musical numbers. He found that: "Men singers are against all movement, and women singers get so carried away that they think they are Diosa Costellos. You end up having them lined up like the Music Hall Glee Club." Extremely nervous, though he tried to disguise his fears and anxieties with his tough talk and generally macho manner, Cole admitted to Vernon Rice that he was in his "liquid period." Working on a show, he found he could not keep solid food down. "Always I see in my mind the producers stalking the halls with the investment hanging heavy over their heads," Cole said. So he kept a liquid cycle going: coffee, orange juice, milk, soup, scotch, and celery juice.

Shortly before the company moved to Philadelphia for the opening, Cole was pushing his dancers hard, to make up for time he'd lost training some of them to dance. This was to be his rehearsal pattern until his very last days teaching at UCLA. Before he could work out choreography, he had to prepare his people in Cole Technique so they could execute the steps and movements. Isolations and placements were not easily achieved. "The dancing schools," Cole complained, "spend all their time stretching their legs and forget to make dancers of them." Only Dick Reed of Ballet Theatre and Gwen Verdon, in Cole's opinion, had arrived with sufficient technique to pick up Cole's dance cues as he gave them.

Cole's choreographic timing may have been all right, but the show died before reaching Broadway. *Bonanza Bound* was no "Big Bonanza."

Looking back on that show today, Gwen Verdon thinks Cole was modifying his methods of choreography. She says, "He couldn't do what he had done with those ballets which were performed in isolation from such concerns. It just couldn't look like *dancers* doing a ballet. Instead, they had to look like human beings, people who belonged to the place and the time of the musical. Townspeople, or whatever. The dancers had to fit in. They couldn't look like ballerinas waiting for their cues."

Ethel Martin stresses Cole's skilled adaptation of his broad ethnic dance know-how to the needs of Broadway musicals. Even more important to Martin, however, is the fact that Cole's choreography was always on the leading, even the cutting-edge of innovation. Sometimes, he'd want to try a dance that was too experimental, too advanced, or by Broadway's standards at that time, too shocking.

The following year, 1948, Cole created his most memorable choreographic and musical staging for the lavish and most unusual musical, *Magdalena,* with a lush tropical treasure-house of musical themes by the Brazilian composer and musical ethnologist, Heitor Villa-Lobos. It was, says Agnes de Mille, a generation before its time. Whatever its problems about timing, many who saw it couldn't believe what they were seeing and even today still talk about this show with wonder. But, as with many things which arrive before the public is ready for them— if ever—*Magdalena* failed financially. After an exciting West Coast tryout, with ecstatic reviews from the San Francisco music *and* drama critics, *Magdalena* opened in New York at the Zeigfeld Theatre on September 20, 1948. In eleven weeks, it was over.

Backstage at the Philharmonic Auditorium in Los Angeles, these telegrams were waiting for Jack Cole on the night of July 26, 1948:

MY DEEP RESPECT TO YOU JACK AND THANKS   I WOULD
HAVE BEEN COMPLETELY LOST WITHOUT YOU— JULES DAS-
SIN—

I THINK YOU ARE WONDERFUL AND THANK YOU FOR HELP-
ING ME   SUCCESS TO YOU TONIGHT   LOVE— SHARAFF—

The director and the costume designer of *Magdalena* were quite properly grateful to Jack Cole. Together with the composer, Villa-Lobos, and his lyricist-adaptors, Wright and Forrest, Cole was the most responsible for the unusual achievement of this production. Unfortunately, the New York critics certainly weren't as ecstatic as the San Francisco critics, who went verbally wild about the show's score, its lavish Howard Bay settings, its fantastic costumes, its talented cast with *trained* voices—Dorothy Sarnoff, John Raitt, Irra Petina, and, perhaps most memorable of all, Jack Cole's astonishing choreography.

No one was very happy about the show's book, set in Colombia. It involved an Indian worker's revolt in an emerald mine, a pious peasant girl's attempts to convert her feisty boyfriend to Christ, and the excesses and repressions of a South American general. The title referred not to some abandoned woman or "Magdalene," as they were once called, but to the mysterious and mighty Magdalena River, which winds and twists its way from the southwestern Cordilleras of Colombia through the land toward the northern coast, where the waters disgorge into the Caribbean.

Magdalena cost producer Edwin Lester and his Civic Light Opera one-third of a million dollars to mount, then an unheard of sum for a musical. After its Los Angeles and San Francisco openings, he had cause to think he was right to splurge, right to pay Villa-Lobos the largest composer's advance ever in the American musical theatre. John Hobart, drama critic for the prestigious *San Francisco Chronicle,* was tremendously impressed with both the daring of the show's concept and its stage visualization. He found that the much ballyhooed *Magdalena* was "an evening of unrelieved magnificence."

Whatever Jules Dassin brought to the stage direction in terms of vision, role interpretation, and line readings, the whole show had Cole's unique movement stamped upon it. John Hobart paid tribute to Cole's visual animation of *Magdalena:* "No doubt the jungle has been idealized for musical-show purposes; one suspects that the real Muzos [a Colombian Indian tribe] never wore such spectacularly beautiful costumes . . . nor ever indulged in such extraordinarily exuberant dances.

"For *Magdalena* gives the impression of being continuously in giddy motion. In Colombia, there is apparently no letup in communal fiestas, tribal ceremonies, and semi-pagan dancing parties. Even a native insurrection—against the tyranny of a general who owns the emerald mines in which the Muzos work—takes on the quality of a ballet."

Given all the excitement over Leonard Bernstein's *Candide* having entered the opera repertory—effectively putting an elitist seal of approval on it—and claims for *Sweeny Todd* and even *Evita* as works of music-theatre worthy of a place on the opera stage, it's regrettable that such a remarkable show as *Magdalena* has been completely forgotten, both by opera impressarios and by producers of those frequent Broadway revivals. Reading the San Francisco reviews, you could well believe that you had missed the show of the century if you weren't at the Los Angeles Philharmonic or the Curran Theatre on Geary Street in San Francisco to marvel at it.

The wonderful San Francisco reviews, however, may have soured the New York critics against *Magdalena* well before opening night. While the show train was thundering across the nation toward Broadway, the New York critical fraternity found in its morning mail huge sheets covered with the Bay City raves. If there's one allergy almost all New York critics share, it's being exposed to favorable out-of-town reviews before they've had a chance to judge a show for themselves.

That *Song of Norway* team, Wright and Forrest, agree. They were the songwriters charged with adapting Villa-Lobos' themes for the stage, so they are walking fact-books on *Magdalena*.

"Would you like me to level on *Magdalena*?" Wright asks. He says sending the New York critics those reviews was a serious mistake. He sighs: "They were the *best* notices one could get. I was so saddened by it, but I said nothing to the producers. Fantastic notices, for everyone, as they should have been. . . . If only the New York critics had known what they were seeing! As Dick Rodgers said, the show was twenty-five years ahead of its time. Not everyone understood what they were looking at."

Major national magazines such as *Life, Colliers,* and important Sunday supplements ran photo-essays and admiring reports on the show, even after the Manhattan critics had insensitively attacked it. Bruce Downes, in a feature titled "Jungle Jamboree," which Jack Cole tucked away with his *Magdalena* keepsakes, noted that despite the critical panning of the show, a perverse public was flocking to the Ziegfeld Theatre, itself an exercise in opulence and luxury. One spectator who hurried along to catch the show before it closed was Agnes de Mille: "Jerry Robbins advised me to go see it. He'd gone *five* times."

Whatever bitterness Cole may have felt, even long after *Magdalena* had been fatally wounded by the New York reviewers, he kept one memento of the experience with his most treasured papers. It was a letter from Agnes de Mille reproduced in her introductory notes to this book.

Seeing the text of her letter recently, Agnes de Mille said, "I'm so glad I wrote him. I didn't always have the gumption to do what I felt inclined to do, and this was a stunning show, a brilliant triumph. The New York critics were inexcusably carping, and the show did not succeed, but it was very fine, and Jack's work was memorable." Looking back, surveying the broad expanse of Jack Cole's choreography, de Mille says, "It didn't influence me, but I admired it tremendously. One or two of his shows were masterpieces. His *Magdalena* contained some of the most beautiful things I've ever seen. . . . It's a Villa-Lobos score after all."

Magdalena is not exactly a forgotten masterpiece. The book by Homer Curran and Frederick Hazlitt Brennan may not be by itself worthy of such status, but its score is remarkable and the lyrics by Wright and Forrest—which some critics complained were "too poetic"—are appropriate, often ingenious, and indeed poetic, but not excessively so. Cole's choreography was not notated, unfortunately, but then no commercial producers had—or have—a budget for preservation of the show's original choreography for posterity. Still, there are those, like de Mille and the artists who danced in *Magdalena,* such as Matt Mattox, Buzz Miller, and Paul Steffen, who have vivid memories of Cole's work. Photographs survive of Irene Sharaff's brilliant costumes and Howard Bay's luxuriant settings. No, *Magdalena* is not a forgotten masterpiece, although it may at the moment be a neglected work of the musical theatre.

Wright and Forrest hope for the proper circumstances which would make possible its revival. As Wright recalls, the collaboration with Heitor Villa-Lobos was, and remains, a high point in the team's long career of working in films, theatre, and superclubs. The idea of a musical by Villa-Lobos, based on native South American traditions and problems, came from Homer Curran. Surprisingly, Villa-Lobos, who disliked opera, agreed. Bob Wright remembers: "When Villa-Lobos arrived in New York, he was under the impression he was supposed to compose for an operetta. When he came, there was no book, but some ideas. And he met two young men who knew every note he'd ever written—over 1,170 compositions! He couldn't get over it. We showed him all our research: this four bars *very good*, that passage just good. We told him about our contract to adapt his music for the show."

In the program the Wright and Forrest credit read: "Pattern and lyrics by Robert Wright and George Forrest." For the composer, the credit was simply: "Music by Heitor Villa-Lobos." Wright and Forrest knew very well the special demands of the American musical theatre and the inherent difficulties in the Villa-Lobos music, especially for dancers who need to count to be able to coordinate their dancing with the score. *Magdalena,* unlike many musicals, would be cast with trained voices—Irra Petina was a Metropolitan Opera veteran—but even for such skilled artists, the music would pose problems.

"It was an adaptation," Wright explains, "with the composer between us, being told what to do. If he controlled the copyright to a piece, he'd deliver that and rewrite it. If he didn't own the copyright to some of his own music, we'd say, 'You need so many bars of music that do such-and-such. And we'd make that and show it to him. That's how 'The Broken Pianolita' was done. We'd say, 'Maestro, we have to take so much of this, that part of that, this section here, and those bars there.' " Wright explains, "To my knowledge, nothing's been done that way." There is some musical folklore that Villa-Lobos wrote all of the *Magdalena* score but in fact composed too much.

Wright says, "No, it was quite different. It was a 'living adaptation.' "

But then Villa-Lobos became critically ill. Doctors in New York apparently didn't want the responsibility of operating on him and the United States government thought he should be cared for in Brazil. He was flown back, but Brazilian doctors also refused. President Roosevelt was asked to intercede, according to Wright, to let Villa-Lobos have the operation in America.

"All this while *Magdalena* was going on. When he was critical, we were going into rehearsal, and we needed six to ten minutes of music. There was no possibility he could compose it. So *we* had to write it, but we were by this time so steeped in his music that no one in Los Angeles or San Francisco knew the difference. Or in New York. It was seamless.

"When he got out of the hospital, we went to see *Magdalena* with him. He wasn't upset, but he knew what he had written—and what he hadn't. He said, 'I have to hand it to you. No one would know what you have written.' We'd also had to improvise for some characters and situations that had come later in the show's development. He wanted to write that part for us, so it would be all his music. But he wasn't well enough and he didn't. After the show closed in New York, we redid the score and took that out. We redid the book, using other Villa-Lobos music. Nothing was harder. His contract had called for orchestration, but he wasn't well. He did do pages and pages of orchestration though, so one can say that the orchestration is his.''

Magdalena had its world premiere in Los Angeles about the time Villa-Lobos was undergoing his operation. But he was no longer really functioning even six months before rehearsals, which introduced an added element of difficulty into shaping the show. As detailed musical analyses of virtually every second of the score demonstrate, relating the music to song, dance, dialogue, and possible stage action, Wright and Forrest were tenacious in preserving the integrity of what Villa-Lobos had wrought. Jack Cole saved these fascinating analyses, as well as various sets of notes on production improvements recommended by Wright and Forrest. Perhaps, if more attention had been paid to their suggestions, the show would have been more warmly received by the New York reviewers. It's interesting to note, among the precise timings Wright and Forrest made of every song, dance, and musical passage in *Magdalena,* that the memorable ''Broken Pianolita'' number, with its frantic dance and its counterpoint of a plaintive song, took just three minutes and thirty seconds.

Given the difficulty of the *Magdalena* score and the poetic challenge of the lyrics, this musical might also have had a better chance of survival if there could have been a cast album made in Los Angeles before the show was seen in New York. Unfortunately, opening night was the beginning of a serious dispute that brought a halt to music recording. While the dispute was under way, *Magdalena* could not be recorded. Six hours before the deadline, Wright and Forrest were able to record only a 32-bar waltz from the show, thanks to a friendly RCA A & R (arrangement and recording) person. Later, André Kostelanetz recorded their ''Magdalena Suite.''

''Not to take anything away from Jack,'' Wright says, ''but Homer Curran always said there should be an old piano on the set, falling apart. We said someone could put a peseta in and kick it. Chet said maybe we could have a sleepy old man sing a song. And that's how 'The Broken Pianolita' number came about. Jack knew Villa-Lobos from Brazil. When he heard the score, he was madly in love with it. We told Villa-Lobos we'd

get Jack for the choreography. He knew and loved his dancing.''

So that Cole would have a complete recording of *Magdalena's* score in order for him to analyze the beats, the tempos,
in performance, Wright and Forrest made a studio recording for
him, with a rehearsal pianist accompanying. "With the two of
us literally *screaming* the score," Wright says in wry amusement. What's not so amusing to the duo is the fact that copies
of the record are around. Collectors have even called them about
getting copies. "A California disk-jockey played the record on
the air as a treat for us," Wright says. " 'Outrageous!' we told
him. 'We'll sue you!' "

To illustrate the peculiarities of Jack Cole's ways of working, they recount a typical tale. "Now, you know that Jack rarely,
if ever, completed anything," Wright explains. In *Kismet,* for
example, they wrote music for a dance after the song "Rahadlakum" at Cole's request. Cole never got around to setting the
dance. In *Magdalena,* it was more important. "When you think
of a dear friend doing something like this, it doesn't seem quite
possible," says Wright. "Even after Los Angeles and San Francisco, he put off doing the finale of the first act! I don't think
he was sympathetic to what we had to do there musically. It
was a little too romantic for Jack, but it was what we needed."
He sings the passage to illustrate the problem. "It was a seduc-
tion scene, but Jack could never get John Raitt and Dorothy
Sarnoff to be quite sexy enough."

The precious madonna was being stolen while the heroine's attention was diverted by her fiancé Pedro. Cole suggested making the scene into a dance, with boys in the background. The music, a waltz, was, says Wright, "gorgeous."
Cole's problem was that the waltz, which belonged to the leads,
was sexually seductive, but the rather different dance of the
madonna thieves had to be performed *against* that, with no music
of its own. This was incredibly complicated to do, and Cole began rehearsing this new dance only *after* the show had already
opened at the Ziegfeld. Dancers in *Magdalena* were permitted
by their union to rehearse only a few hours a day. It took him
four weeks to prepare it.

"Jack always did everything the hardest possible way," Wright says forcefully. It is a judgment with which many of his former dancers and professional collaborators will readily agree. "He worked—I've never seen a man work so hard in my life!" Wright and Forrest went to all the rehearsals; they were endlessly fascinated by Cole and his manner of working. On the day of the matinee in which the new finale would be seen for the first time, Wright and Forrest were on their way to the Ziegfeld when they met Cole flying up Sixth Avenue, running away from the theatre. It was almost curtain-time. Wright stopped him to ask what was wrong. Cole was so angry that only garbled phrases and profane words poured out. He assured Wright and Forrest that *it* wasn't their fault. He loved them, but he would have nothing more to do with the production. "I'll never set foot in that theatre again!" Cole stormed at them. "I went to the door, and they said, 'Who are *you?*' I said, 'I'm Jack Cole,' and they told me to get a pass!"

"He took the night plane back to California. We never saw him again at *Magdalena*," Wright says.

Magdalena left its mark on a number of Cole admirers. One was Harold Mattox, who changed his name to Matt when he made his debut as a Cole dancer. "I was so impressed by Jack's work," he has said, "that I changed my style and gradually developed the approach on which I have based all my choreography." Cole nearly didn't cast him in *Magdalena*, fearing his classical background might impede his performance. Mattox adapted rapidly to the sensuous style and said, "I even ended up doing all the solo spots in the show, as small as they were."

As Cole realized back in 1941, when he tried to create a Seminole Indian dance for the film *Moon Over Miami*, the ethnic dances of primitive American Indians were too simple, even uninteresting, for theatrical use. In that same year, on tour in Rio, he'd met Villa-Lobos for the first time and done some research on dances of Indian tribes in Brazil. Writing in the *Magdalena* souvenir program, Cole pointed to the same problem with South American tribal dances: "They would not be practical for the theatre. Therefore, it became necessary, and practical, to elaborate and compromise, so that I could make our dances look like what American audiences might expect South American native dances to look like. . . . The exciting, highly stylized Villa-Lobos music also needed a further development and formalization in my dances, so the net result is a highly personalized impression of ethnological dance forms. It is not peculiar to any one country of South America."

And what did the New York critics really say about *Magdalena*, after all this thought, effort, and artistry went into its creation? Some hated the show, it's true. Some disliked parts of it; few were wild about the book. Here are some representative reactions:

William Hawkins—*World-Telegram:* "It is the most beautiful thing to look at that has turned up in many, many seasons. Jack Cole's angular-limbed heathenish style of dance is highly appropriate and his ingenuity reaches a high point with the suspenseful 'Pianolita' number." This review was headlined: "Magdalena, an All-Around Hit."

Robert Garland—*Journal-American:* His critique bore the head: "South America's Grand Gift to North America." It was, for Garland, a "musical in a million," but "you have to like Villa-Lobos' music."

Richard Watts, Jr.—*Post:* "Score Is Best Feature of New Musical Drama" ran the headline. He thought the dance numbers "have an agreeable pseudo-savage frenzy about them." But the Curran-Brennan "sex tale of 1912 with Indian mysticism [is] in questionable taste."

John Chapman—*Daily News:* For Chapman, *Magdalena* was a "bold, stunning departure in the musical theatre." It was before its time, a "flaming, opulent, disturbing, and imaginative work." He counted some twenty-nine or thirty song and dance numbers, some of them worthy of popularity on the radio—that is, they could become popular hits, had it not been for troubles in the recording industry. Even those musical numbers that weren't potentials for the Hit Parade, Chapman found "just plain fascinating." His review was headed: " 'Magdalena' a Bold, Fascinating, and Dazzling Musical Adventure."

Brooks Atkinson—*Times:* The review headline read: "Heitor Villa-Lobos, Brazilian Composer, Has Written the Musical

Score for 'Magdalena.' " Atkinson thought the music might be all right by itself, and he liked a pleasant Spanish waltz and "an amusing burlesque of a broken-down mechanical piano." But he found *Magdalena:* "One of the most overpoweringly dull musical dramas of all time. Watching the slow process of the plot and the production is like being hit over the head with a sledge hammer repeatedly all evening. It hurts."

At the time, Walter Terry made a big point in print about Cole's genius in "adapting racial idioms to the language of the American theatre," especially in a sequence involving some Indians in a Colombian village. Shortly before his death, Terry still thought *Magdalena* was one of his favorite Cole shows. For Terry, its dances had the same kind of primitive mystery, energy and taste that Cole had put into his biblical epic for Ruth St. Denis at Adelphi College, a work Terry had found deeply moving. As Terry said, "With the Colombian and Indian background, it was just stunning!" At that time, though, according to Terry, "It was too *special*. Ted Shawn saw it, too. He said to me, 'I loved it, but it was too goddamned *ethnic* for the public.' Now, ethnic is all there is. . . . I think that *Magdalena* wasn't popular then because it was too remote from us. But Cole did a superb job on it!"

Agnes de Mille is strong in her admiration of *Magdalena*. "But to revive it? I don't know. You'd have to re-create those wonderful dances. I tried to do things like that with my American Heritage Dance Theatre. The American Dance Machine has tried to do it. But none of us has had the kind of money that's needed. You'd have to get all the kids who danced in that show together." Of "The Broken Pianolita" number—which de Mille insists was "brilliant! I cannot tell you how brilliant that was!"— she foresees a problem about dance reconstruction: "Everybody did different things in it, so probably nobody can remember it. It was so brilliantly put together. But the critics killed it dead. They used to be so profligate in their condemnations. Today, they'd praise *Magdalena*."

George Martin, who also admires *Magdalena*, says, "Gwen and I assisted Cole. Buzz Miller talks about reviving the 'Pianolita' number for Lee Theodore's American Dance Machine, but it was the first time he'd ever worked with Cole." Martin wonders if Miller can remember that intricate dance, in which so many different things were going on at the same time. Martin says *he* couldn't re-create the sequence, and he was so skilled in Cole's Technique, he could almost duplicate the steps alongside Cole, while he was creating. Martin is afraid that the "Pianolita" will never be seen again, not as Cole created it. "It's a well-known fact," Martin insists, "that dance is only for the moment!"

Gwen Verdon says of *Magdalena:* "The dances were truly extraordinary. Cole did one dance where all the men were trees, and all the women birds. That was fantastic. And he did a very formal Spanish number with fans, Castilian Spanish. And that fantastic 'Pianolita' sequence. . . . You know, that classical Spanish dance influence turned up again in *Man of La Mancha,* for which he no longer gets credit."

Buzz Miller has warm memories of *Magdalena:* "I'd just graduated from school. I had to wait a year to get into the Eastman School of Music, so I went out to California. I went to a Cole audition, and he grabbed me for *Magdalena.* Such marvelous music and such dancing as I've never seen since. It was crazy and wonderful. There were a lot of ritual things—and birds and trees! Just crazy. Matt Mattox and Marie Groscup did a Spanish number. There were flashbacks to Paris. But the really fun things were with the natives, the Indians. The show didn't last because it had a religious plot. Dorothy Sarnoff was trying to convert John Raitt to Christianity. In 1948, that was taboo. After *Magdalena,* I went right into Jack's nightclub act."

Wright and Forrest remember that Cole created an elaborate club act, soon after the failure of *Magdalena,* using Villa-Lobos's music and the best singers, musicians, and dancers he could find: "Today it would cost half a million to put that act together."

February 1949 found Jack Cole in Florida, staying at the Flamingo Hotel. Cole was very troubled at this time in his life, with the departure from the studios, the failure of *Magdalena,* and the need to keep his young ensemble going, both to continue his art and to feed all of his dancers.

This same month, February, Cole distilled his experiences on Broadway and in Hollywood for *Dance Magazine*. Now a stern disciplinarian, fanatic about promptness, preparedness, and personal pride, both in the dancers' appearance and carriage, Jack Cole had come a long way from the sulky Denishawn rebel and the scruffy, eccentric Humphrey-Weidman dancer he had once been. One thing hadn't changed: He was still eccentric. And some of his colleagues thought he could dress much more tastefully than he did.

Cole titled his words of advice, "Call Tomorrow." He began his article by noting the number of times belligerent dancers, after an audition was completed, would hang over the footlights—backed up by bellicose mothers, charging up the aisles—to demand why the stage manager had not written down their names. Cole said his piece would be an explanation of why the names were not taken, together with some suggestions for more successful auditions in the future. Some of the Cole cautions:

"If the call states that ballet dancers will be auditioned, arrive at the theatre with practice clothes and ballet shoes. Dancers who step forward and apologize for having forgotten their shoes are either suspect of having had very little or no school training, since a ballet dancer forgetting shoes is like dressing for the street and forgetting one's trousers, or of being so scatterbrained or undisciplined as to be of questionable value.

"Hair dressed up from the neck to show the carriage of the head indicates a dancer who is aware of the basic principles of her craft. Execute the variation as demonstrated or stated exactly; do not improve or embellish it. Do not ignore the indicated *port de bras* in an effort to jump through the ceiling or spin like a top. The director is only interested in good training and correct movement habits; the probability of a group of dancers being hired to execute five pirouettes and fall flat on their faces en masse is extremely remote . . .

"Many times you will be asked to demonstrate a figure in a style that is completely foreign to your training. Try to grasp the basic elements involved quickly and execute it with good grace and a minimum of pseudo-embarrassment. No editorial comment on the figure or your apparent inability to grasp it is of interest to the director. He is trying to approximate the probable speed at which you learn. Many dancers take ten years to acquire a passable *glissade assemblé,* and ten years are not available before the opening of a show . . .

"If the production is looking for tall blonde girls, and you are short and a brunette, it is not your fault, nor the dance director's. Preconceived preferences of type go by the board if your ability is remarkable. You are more than welcome.

"If you have a bad reputation from previous shows—late for rehearsals, irritability, laziness—you may be sure your case history is on file. That is the reason, on many occasions, why good dancers at an audition are not chosen. The director is usually well aware that this audition would be the last sign of effort or talent from the particular person for the duration of the production.

"Don't present letters of introduction. Don't try to talk to the director before the audition. Don't wear costumes, or strange or bizarre practice-clothes, and don't bring relatives or friends.

"*There are never enough well-trained and intelligent dancers. If you are well-equipped, you will be eagerly welcomed. Chance plays very little part . . .*"

11

SOME HITS, SOME FLOPS

DANCER, CHOREOGRAPHER, & DIRECTOR

In Broadway musicals in the initial years of the twentieth century, there was no talk of choreographers and choreography. The dance routines were frequently based on military drill formations, with emphasis on the precision with which the pretty chorines executed the movements. Capitalizing on the nature of the drills, attractive costumes with military elements and hand props such as rifles and flags might make audience hearts beat a little faster. The Spanish-American War had recently been quite a success. President McKinley was so pleased with the results—the acquisition of Cuba was one of them—that he in fact called it "a splendid little war!" In the midst of seeming domestic tranquility, trouble was brewing in Europe. Marching and flag-waving in Broadway musicals was expected; spectators awaited chorus lines whose talents included high kicks and the ability to perform in unison.

There wasn't much of a challenge for those who devised the dances. With the increasing popularity of ballroom dancing, sparked by Vernon and Irene Castle and Fred and Adele Astaire, audience tastes in dance changed, and the musical comedy dance component reflected that change. The popularity of the Charleston as a social dance ensured that it would be even more popular on stage, especially executed by energetic, attractive choruses of dancing boys and dancing girls, as well as by the stars and specialty dancers. But in some old theatre programs, it's almost impossible to find a credit for dance direction.

In the heyday of the spectacular revue, however, it was the dance director who did much to ensure the success of a show, staging big production numbers and providing a fluid series of dance routines linking individual specialty acts, songs, and comedy sketches. Few thought seriously of dance directors as candidates for the overall direction of Broadway musicals.

In the late 1940s though, things began to change, with both Agnes de Mille and Jerome Robbins taking on the dual tasks of directing and choreographing. Today, it's a commonplace of the musical theatre that when an admired dancer's performing days are nearing their end, he or she aspires to become a choreographer. If that is a success, stage direction of musicals—and even legitimate dramas—may be the next step.

Jack Cole was to try his hand as a director-choreographer. A former Cole dancer, who knew him well, suggests: "Jerry Robbins had done it. I guess Jack thought he had to prove he could do it, too." The 1950s found Cole fairly busy in Hollywood films, and with his nightclub dancers, but he did make time to choreograph for Broadway musicals. His two directorial efforts were made in the same year, 1961; *Donnybrook!* and *Kean,* both of them musicals that had a strong appeal for Cole. After so many years of complaining about the choreographer's relative inability to protect his dances and his dancers in a film or stage show because he lacked the control of a director or a producer, Cole was given the opportunity to demonstrate his own abilities as an artistic overseer.

Already in 1949, Jack Cole had set down his own cynical definitions of three categories of directors of movement and dance. He was a keen analyst—and an expert critic of the creations and performances of others. Because the term "choreographer" was coming into increasing use, and because "dance director" had long been a popular Hollywood title for the creator of film dance sequences, Cole wanted to give readers of *Dance Magazine* a vivid understanding of roles and duties:

> *Dance Director:* This title is used to designate the man who arranges the musical numbers for a show where the music is loud, rhythmic, and brassy. . . . There is little emotional drain on the Dance Director's creative reservoir since his task is merely one of rearranging.

> *Choreographer:* This form of direction is usually considered to move the action of the drama along. . . . The

Choreographer's first touch may be recognized by a fleeting use of the show's tunes, arranged out of all recognition by the orchestrators, who have convinced the composer that he is far more talented than he suspected.

Stager of Movement: This third type of director is described as being in charge of staging movement. Here, we find a curious second-rate mentality, with a residue of misinformation, half-remembered fact, and a highly personalized code of theatrical expression, based on anatomical disability.

The final comment implies that one of the favored expletives of such a director, in describing the work of his performers, would probably be "half-assed." "Two left feet" and "lame-brained" also seem likely. Cole's categories make satiric sense, but his explanations are both ironic and self-serving. Obviously, he saw himself as a choreographer, rather than a dance director—especially in his Hollywood work—or a stager of movement.

Alive and Kicking was Jack Cole's first Broadway show of the 1950s. Already in 1948, Cole had announced that he would be choreographing the revue and dancing in it as well. Then it was scheduled for 1949. He also revealed that he planned to go to Paris, where he would write, produce, direct, and choreograph a film of his own. This news was reported with the suggestion that Cole was thinking himself another Orson Welles. Cole may have had some plans to do this, but nothing came of it. In any case, the report carried this comment: "It was not explained how he would appear simultaneously in Paris and New York, but Cole will find a way. . ."

Gwen Verdon both danced in *Alive and Kicking* and assisted Cole. Bobby Van was also in the company, as was Matt Mattox. The show opened at the Winter Garden on January 17, 1950. Cole, heading his dancers, was the hit and mainstay of the revue. His numbers included *Abou Ben Adhem,* suggested by Leigh Hunt's poem and danced with Hindu influences; *Calypso Celebration,* which was a Trinidadian divorce, calypso-style; *Propin-*

quity; and the *Cole Scuttle Blues.* Cole had a problem in the show. He'd been asked to do some kind of interesting dance routine as a backup for a romantic song, "One Two Three, I Love You." He told Verdon it was "a dreary love song, and I have to take the curse off it."

Cole had an inspiration. Behind the young lovers there would be room enough for some saucy kids to clown and make fun of them—without their ever knowing what was happening. Gwen Verdon and Marie Groscup impersonated the kids, all dressed up in mother's old clothes, parading and fighting. Cole even had them walk on a fence, upstage behind the singers. It certainly took the curse off the song—and the romance as well—as audiences giggled and laughed to see Verdon's and Groscup's juvenile mockery of the two lovebirds. Cole liked it so much himself that he reworked it for the film *Meet Me After the Show.*

Pictures Cole saved from this production show him and Verdon richly costumed in Hindu garb, with the figure of a god looming behind them on an ornate pedestal. The Trinidadian number is colorfully costumed; its vibrant, exciting choreography looks compelling, even in still photos. *Alive and Kicking* was certainly an apt description of Cole and his dancers. For the show itself, it was a mockery; the production was dead after only eight weeks. A review in *Dance Magazine* said what was so often said of Cole's work in shows whose other elements didn't measure up to his inventiveness and vitality: "*Alive and Kicking . . .* proved to be of little interest save for the presence of Jack Cole and his dancers, but in this respect at least, its interest amounted to the galvanic. Cole has been absent from the stage so long that one began to wonder whether or not the star had not already begun to wane. The instant sight of Cole in *Alive and Kicking* now makes such a thought absurd. The magic is still there. He appears in this revue with a new and remarkable partner, Gwenneth Verdon, a gifted dancer and a style nicely complementary to that of his own."

In 1953, there were two Cole-choreographed shows on Broadway; both of them, like *Magdalena,* were linked to Edwin Lester's West Coast Civic Light Opera. *Carnival in Flanders* was the first of these; it opened September 8 at the New Century Theatre, where it closed within the week. Dolores Gray played the wife of the mayor of a small Flemish village, overrun by the occupying army of Hapsburg Spain.

And what do invading soldiers do when they seize an enemy or a rebellious town? *Carnival in Flanders* presented Jack Cole with a notable and eminently justifiable opportunity to stage a Rape Ballet. And that's what audiences got. There were epic disagreements, however, so that Cole, who was credited with the choreography when the show was in Philadelphia at the Forrest Theatre, was replaced by Helen Tamiris for the New York opening. George Martin says Cole left *Carnival* to work on *Kismet*, but essentially his work was already done anyway. Martin remembers, "Tamiris did nothing to the Rape Ballet, nor to the Trio: Matt Mattox, Jimmy Alex, and I—which is the same dance you see in *The I Don't Care Girl*, or at least was based on it. That was, as I remember, in *Commedia* costumes. We stopped the show with that every night. In New York, on opening night, the audience wouldn't stop applauding. Dolores had an upstage center entrance, and she had to wait. Helen Tamiris didn't change the choreography; she just took over and helped. They took out the dirty ballets."

Dirty ballets? Martin grins as he re-creates one: "The boys were all skeletons, in gray tights with bones appliquéd. The girls were dressed like Botticelli's Three Graces. But we had red witches' brooms, with bells on the ends of the broomsticks. Everyone was in a state of shock. We'd stick these things between our legs and shake them at the girls. When Cole left, they took that out."

Some critics were moved to refer to Cole's choreography as, among other things, "satanic." Over the years, former Cole dancers have also described him as a devil, a demon, or at least demonic. He was occasionally credited with possessing "demonic energy." Apparently, Cole decided to let some of that dark power loose in *Carnival in Flanders*. If he had to be on liquids for *Bonanza Bound*, upset because his producers were worrying about their investment in that show, his innards must have been in continual upheaval during the *Flanders* rehearsals and tryouts. Matt Mattox has commented on the transformation of

Cole when working on a live production—from a relaxed person to a man looking drawn and haggard. Cole was having all kinds of problems and arguments with the production staff of *Flanders*. It's rumored there were also clashes with the show's star, Dolores Gray.

Dolores Gray remembers *Flanders* very well: "A disaster for all of us! People were pulling so much against one another in that. Nothing worked right." Recently, Gray talked about Cole as a choreographer and colleague. "The few times I had a chance to work with Jack later, they were the highlights of my association with *any* choreographer. He was the best! He had a very strange, very special style, all his own." A Cole dance trademark, Gray points out, was the trio-form. In *Kismet*, there were the three Princesses of Ababu, not to forget a trio of dervishes. "As in *Carnival in Flanders*, he liked to use threes. He felt that you should mirror something that was very intricately choreographed and done with precision, so it would be like one body, but twice reflected. That was one of his trademarks, one of his tricks—and it was always very exciting."

Paula Stone, the director, had asked Cole for a religious masque at one point in the plot. Gray says, "And that's what Jack gave her. He did a lot of research on it. The girls were in virginal-white veil things, and the men were almost like beasts. In one of the sections, the girls bent over, and it looked as if the men were raping them from behind. Paula had a roaring fit and went screaming up the aisles. Jack refused to change it. He said, 'You asked for an authentic religious masque, and this is what I have given you. And I will not change it!' I think Tamiris softened that, but the Rape Ballet that was so exciting, that was totally Jack's, and there was nothing changed . . . Everyone was fighting with everyone else on that show. Preston Sturges came in, and Paula Stone lost all control. And I never even got to record 'Here's That Rainy Day.' " Dolores Gray laughs at the memory: "But I got a Tony for the part!"

The New York critics had lots of praise for Cole's dances, but it was all directed at Helen Tamiris, whose name was on the program. William Hawkins, of the *World-Telegram & Sun*, commented: "In a huge and demonic carnival toward the end, a trio of Matt Mattox, George Martin, and Jimmy Alex got the evening's most spontaneous outburst, dancing Miss Tamiris' sharp adaptations of some swift Spanish figures." The praise should have been Cole's.

Walter Kerr, reviewing for the *Herald-Tribune*, lauded Tamiris's "several flashes of driving dancing." He also admired Gray for striding "through it all with aplomb, even though the evening is coming down around her ears." Matt Mattox he admired in the trio and also as the Courier in "The Plundering of the Town." Kerr pointed out to his readers: "Though there is no program credit to say so, I am informed that this last is the invention of Jack Cole; it is one of the show's brightest assets."

After opening the decade of the 1950s with two Broadway failures, Cole had the vindication only three months later of a major hit, *Kismet*. On opening night at the Ziegfeld Theatre, December 3, 1953, *Kismet*'s star, Alfred Drake, sent Cole a telegram of thanks: "My one complaint is that you could never see me as the fourth [Princess] Ababu." *Kismet* had been a very successful 1911 stage vehicle for Otis Skinner, father of the monologist Cornelia Otis Skinner. With a score adapted from themes of Alexander Borodin by the *Magdalena* team, Robert Wright and George Forrest, the old Edward Knoblock script came alive with some refurbishing by Luther Davis and Charles Lederer. Lederer sent Cole a message when the show opened in Los Angeles at the Philharmonic Auditorium: "You'll find that being associated with me leads to a steady flow of successes." That was true for *Kismet* at least; it had a Broadway run of 583 performances, a national company, a London one as well, and countless productions all over the world. There was also a Hollywood film, which Cole choreographed.

In its original Middle Eastern setting, however, *Kismet*'s lavish staging and beautiful costumes made it one of the most handsome Broadway shows in years. The Wazir, Henry Calvin, even had some well-known muscle men as his retainers, one of them the fabled Steve Reeves; this was definitely a Cole touch. Major magazines such as *Colliers* and *Life* gave *Kismet* big picture-spreads. It was indeed a photogenic show, from many angles.

Alfred Drake became an admirer of Jack Cole's not only because of his knowledge about dance and his skill as a choreographer but also because, despite his reputation for terrorizing dancers and throwing tantrums with producers, Cole could also listen to reason. Drake remembers their working on the *Kismet* song "Gesticulate." As performed, it had a great many body and arm movements. As Cole had designed it, however, it was originally much more complex. Drake says, "He literally wanted a gesture for almost every phrase all the way through. He gave them to me. I worked on them. I struggled with them. I couldn't manage them." Drake was working on the song alone; he was, after all, a professional, a star. In any case, Cole had a lot of other work to do on the show. Finally in desperation, Alfred Drake went to Cole. "I said, 'All right, Jack. Don't sing the song at the same time, but if you *can* just do the movements, then I *will* learn how to do it.' And he couldn't do them. He said, 'I've overloaded it. I'm sorry.' He cut the number in half, and then it was possible to do. So he was amenable, even malleable, when you could convince him about something."

As have others who worked with Jack Cole, Drake noticed that Cole never completed some of the indicated choreography. A section of dance music had been composed for the song, "Rahadlakum." Somehow the dance was never choreographed—even though, in some recent revivals, it has been set under the mistaken impression that it was done that way by Cole. "It's true he had a lot of other work to do on *Kismet,* and we made a lot of changes before we got to New York," says Drake. "All right. So when we did it in London, I thought, 'Well, we'll add it on now.' We didn't. When we did the first revival, he didn't do it either. Nor on the second revival. So, either he got tired of the number and said, 'That's good enough. I don't have to do anything more to it.' Or he never had a finish in mind."

Cole had some interesting ideas about *Kismet:* one, of presenting the Princesses of Ababu—another trio of dancers, Reiko Sato, Bonnie Evans, and Patricia Dunn—not just as oriental beauties, but also as *hunters,* literally and figuratively; another, to have no dancing boys in *Kismet* at all. Cole told everyone he was sick and tired of them. He wanted the greatest ladies in the world on the *Kismet* stage. He agreed to four strong men to bear the beauties when required, but aside from those playing male roles, there would be no men. The show's composer-lyricists, Wright and Forrest, were horrified. Their years of working in clubs and casinos had taught them the necessity of having men to complement the women, no matter how beautiful. The contrast of the men, admiring and supporting the women, made all the difference, they insisted.

Jack Cole didn't agree. Wright recalls, "When *Kismet* opened in California, there were no male dancers. We had ladies and ladies. Well, when they did 'Not Since Nineveh,' it just *lay* there. It didn't work at all—throughout the show. It was a flop. The notices were terrible. A Los Angeles critic said there wasn't a tune in the show."

Alfred Drake's lively interpretation of the song "Gesticulate," devised by Cole, was, the duo maintained, the closest thing to dance in the entire show. "And that was perfectly marvelous! Oh, everything Jack did was fine, but it wasn't *exciting*," Wright explains. The problem, as they saw it, was the lack of dancing boys, especially in the harem. "The idea of a harem without males coming into it! The idea of Baghdad without males is awful!" he told Cole. He must have made his point, but Cole had already agreed to pay top salaries for the women and the body-builders. The show had proved to be much more costly than projected. Cole didn't think Edwin Lester would allow him to hire some male dancers at that point. Wright and Forrest asked, and Lester granted. Wright is convinced this reversal of Cole's original concept helped make the show a hit. He also stresses that Cole's subsequent contributions "played an enormous part in the salvation of *Kismet.*"

Initially, the show opened with Drake as Hajj, elevated on some stairs, singing the song "Fate." The Arabs were being called to prayer. Wright was also praying, but for something different—a more interesting opening. Cole seemed satisfied and wouldn't change things for anyone. Wright begged him, saying, "It's boring, boring, boring!" Cole asked why, and Wright said there was nothing really to *look* at, and Drake's song was, in fact, a difficult one to get across. Wright suggested some whirling dervishes, but Cole, steeped in ethnic and religious lore, worried about the authenticity of such an addition. Wright insisted, "Don't get a specialist. *Don't!* Don't worry about authenticity. Just let them turn a little." Wright's point in relating this, he says, is that this improved the show—since then, every production has had someone on stage at the opening turning around. And it's also an indication of Cole's ability to listen to the ideas of others and be willing to make changes.

Actually, the San Francisco and Los Angeles notices for *Kismet* were fair to good. Charles Lederer took over the production from Lester. Lederer thought the show wasn't sexy enough, that it looked too arty. He discussed this with Cole. As Wright remembers, there was a very artistic Cole sequence, *In the Oasis of Delightful Imaginings.* Cole decided this could be transmuted into the harem number with Lalume, the Wazir's seductive but neglected wife, and Hajj, whom she attempts to entice. He saw it as a big dance number, with Hajj as a song-and-dance man. Cole told Wright and Forrest about the notorious candy, *rahadlakum,* in which opiates or aphrodisiacs could be concealed. It was, Cole said, used in harems to excite the girls or to stimulate the flagging potency of their master. Cole wanted the songwriters to create a song for such a number, one that would "kill the audience dead in the second act." Could they do it?

Wright and Forrest had based their show score on themes from Borodin, notably *Prince Igor* and the "Polovetsian Dances." They thought the "musical account" was exhausted, but they found "three pretty tunes of Borodin" they still could use. They wrote four songs, including one of their own, "I'm Going Moroccan for Johnny." Cole liked that best: "That's it! Why have you kept that back?" The song became "Rahadlakum."

"Cole Porter called it the dirtiest song he'd ever heard," Wright says with impish pride. "He called us up and said he didn't know how we'd got away with it." Although Cole didn't finally create the dance for it, the accents he wanted are all present in the score. Now, when a dance is set at that point, says Wright, "it stops the show."

Walter Terry saw *Kismet* on Broadway. He saw also the influences of Uday Shankar, La Meri, and Ted Shawn in Cole's choreography and musical staging. "A lot of Denishawn came through, but updated. Having those muscle men as dervishes worked very well. That certainly came from Ted Shawn. Shawn's dervish was one of his major solos. And Shawn used to teach the principle of non-spotting turns in class, so Jack must have learned that from him." Cole also drew on such Indian forms as Kathak, Kathkali, Bharat Natyam, with footwork on heel or flat foot. Lee Theodore, of the American Dance Machine, asks, "What would *Kismet* have been without authentic folk dance? It would have been a bloody bore! Those were Jack Cole's dances, of course, but he knew how to use ethnic sources, but with imagination. He could take any dance and theatricalize it—and still make it credible."

Working on *Kismet*, Cole was briefly helped by Gwen Verdon, who was herself performing eight times a week. "I'd sit with him all the time and remind him of things he'd done with East Indian dance. I'd work on that with him, because I'd studied East Indian with him, La Meri, and Uday Shankar. I loved that so much I even went off and studied it on my own," Verdon says. Cole also engaged two of his partners for *Kismet*. One, Florence Lessing—Princess Zubbediya—had recently been dancing with Cole in his club act in Chicago. Also on hand was one of the Kraft twins, the lovely Beatrice—Princess Samaris. Buzz Miller, also in the show, realized that some of Cole's inspirations for *Kismet* choreography came from earlier dances he and Beatrice Kraft had performed with or for Cole.

Kismet opened in New York on December 3, but the reviews didn't appear for nearly two weeks owing to a newspaper strike. Critic William Hawkins repeated the popular comment that *Kismet* was a hit only because the reviews couldn't be published when it opened. Cole's work with the "trio of barbaric princesses" was, Hawkins thought, "an evening-long, three-ply hit." John McClain found Cole's dances bright and stylized. Walter Kerr was pleased with the dances, as was John Chapman, who thought them the best elements in a generous show. Brooks Atkinson, of the *Times*, praised Cole's contribution: "There is an exquisitely beautiful oriental dance by Beatrice Kraft as a princess from Bangalore. In fact, all the dancing is excellent, especially a garlanded wedding march. . ."

Despite any Manhattan critical reservations, *Kismet* was a solid hit, ultimately an international success. George Martin was asked to stage the national company, and then a second national company after that. He also helped in London and carried on when Cole had to go to Hollywood to work on the film version. A bit ruefully, Martin now says that although he worked with Cole on many shows and danced for him as well, he never really got to know him. "I was at his right hand, as far as the dancing was concerned, but otherwise . . ."

When Cole was rehearsing in London, Donald Saddler was also there, choreographing a show called *When In Rome.* Saddler remembers all-night talk sessions with Cole: "He was such a fascinating talker and on so many subjects. A number of Cole-trained dancers were then wowing audiences in Italy and France. I said how wonderful it was they were having success with his work. But he said they should have gone back to the ethnic sources the way he did. Otherwise, they were just cheating themselves. He also said he borrowed only the good steps. His ideas on ethnic dance, and the way he used it in his own work impressed me," says Saddler.

In April 1956, Jack Cole was rehearsing dance sequences for a "Jubilee" edition of the *Ziegfeld Follies,* starring Tallulah Bankhead and scheduled for a late spring Broadway opening after tryouts. Arthur Knight dropped by the rehearsal hall to chat with Cole about the work for *Dance Magazine.* He found Cole surveying the rehearsal from a perch on the Coke machine. Knight described him as a "slender, withdrawn man who looks like a wispy edition of José Ferrer."

Cole was busy engineering a typical Ziegfeld routine, but with a Cole difference: Boy dancers and Julie Newmar were to descend a grand central staircase, holding outsize candelabras in each hand. Knight described the dance as a Cole specialty, in which the torso remained erect and rigid, while everything from the pelvis on down was in intense movement. Cole counted eight beats, followed by a "bop bop," at which the dancers ground their pelvises as though they meant to detach them from their spines.

When the number was over, Cole moved on to a trio, centered on his assistant George Martin, with two pig-tailed blondes in sneakers and dungarees. As Knight described it: "This was one of Cole's swift-eccentric dances, filled with light, tiny steps and sudden changes in direction that demanded the utmost precision on the part of the performers. Its effect was one of carefree improvisation, but each detail had to be painstakingly acquired. Cole demonstrated a new addition, a bird-like hop that brought giggles from the two girls. Cole's face remained a sad mask as he hopped along." Knight watched Cole spend over half an hour, constantly repeating that step until it was integrated into the rest of the dance.

This was followed with a big production number with Carol Haney, Matt Mattox, and other Cole regulars. It was a fast, muscular affair, with many diverse bits of business going on simultaneously. Cole moved in and out of the dance, helping this dancer and that with individual variations. He ran it through five or six times. But, in spite of all Cole's efforts, the show closed in Philadelphia in May. It did limp into Manhattan the following season, but minus both Bankhead and Cole.

Cole had better luck with *Jamaica*, starring Lena Horne. Set in the Caribbean, with ample opportunity for native dances and songs, the show's book nonetheless encouraged Cole to whip up a dream ballet for the heroine, Savannah, played by Horne. Dissatisfied with her humdrum and necessarily simple life on Pigeon's Island, a natural paradise off the Jamaican coast, Savannah dreamt of life in New York. In the song "Push the Button," she outlined her fantasies of life with labor-saving conveniences.

Largely thanks to its radiant star, with support by Ricardo Montalban, *Jamaica* achieved 555 performances. Josephine Premice, herself an expert in ethnic dance, was also in the company. Cole's dances weren't sufficiently integrated into the show for some of the New York critics, but he still got good notices. Robert Coleman thought the dances were "top-shelf." Richard Watts, Jr., found them "staged with proper pace, humor, and sense of the exotic." Walter Kerr grumpily suggested that the main reason for producing *Jamaica* was simply because everyone was hoping to record a cast album. As for Jack Cole's incidental dances, they had "flare and vitality, but they are decidedly incidental." Brooks Atkinson, that longtime foe of ballet and serious modern dance on Broadway, gave an approving nod:

"Jack Cole's choreography is expert and colorful without pretending to be ballet."

In 1959, London audiences had the opportunity to see *Candide*, with a Leonard Bernstein score and book by Lillian Hellman doctored somewhat by Michael Stewart. It had not been a financial success in New York, although aspects of its artistry rapidly made it a cult favorite. Availability of a cast album helped. Hellman's book was blamed for many of the musical's problems. In London, the complaints were similar. The gifted visual satirist and stylist Osbert Lancaster designed the show. Robert Louis, a Group Theatre alumnus, staged it. The talented cast included Denis Quilley as Candide, Mary Costa as Cunegonde, and Laurence Naismith as Dr. Pangloss. Two gifted comedians, Victor Spinetti and Ron Moody, were also on hand. Jack Cole was invited to choreograph. He got to try his hand again on something like a Rape Ballet, this one occurring in the middle of a wedding, as the bloodthirsty and lustful forces of the King of Hesse overran Cunegonde's father's little fiefdom. He also choreographed some dreadful rites of the Inquisition, related to a sequence with flagellants, which he later tried to integrate into *Man of La Mancha*, though that was never seen on Broadway. There was also a Paris ball at the home of the Marquis Milton; "Glitter and Be Gay" involved a luxurious and corrupt Parisian gambling sequence. But with all the effort and ingenuity from Cole, from Lewis, from Lancaster, and the entire cast, *Candide* would have to continue to win admirers from album cultists, until the Harold Prince production, with a book by Hugh Wheeler, ensured its stage success.

Frank Loesser's rural American fantasy, *Greenwillow*, opened on Broadway for a three-month run on April 8, 1960, at the Alvin Theatre. Cole was originally supposed to choreograph, but he abandoned the project in its early stages. Had he remained, he could have worked closely with the star, Tony Perkins, whose father, Osgood, had been the star of Cole's first Broadway show, *School for Husbands.*

Given Cole's feeling about Ireland, the opportunity not only to choreograph but also to direct a Broadway musical set in the Emerald Isle was a special kind of artistic and ethnic fulfillment. Among Cole's personal papers there is a scrapbook he prepared for this show. He'd gone to Ireland to immerse himself in the atmosphere, to study the countryside and the villages, and to talk with the Irish.

John Ford had made an admired film called *The Quiet Man.* This was to be the basis of Cole's musical, *Donnybrook!* Cole's agent at that time, Josh Meyer, still insists *Donnybrook!* was "a pretty good show; it really was! Too bad it didn't run." Maureen O'Hara had been in their minds as the heroine; she'd created the film role, but she wasn't cast. Meyer thinks the show would have worked with different casting of that role, someone with more magnetism. What most concerned him in *Donnybrook!* he says, was to protect his client's royalties. Cole had often *owned* the choreography used in earlier shows and was owed royalties every time the shows were performed or revived anywhere, using his dances. But it wasn't easy to police this and ensure proper payment. Meyer arranged for Cole to be cut in on *Donnybrook!*'s subsidiary rights for a percentage. He says there was no chance for Cole to make anything substantial from his choreography fees.

After its Broadway opening, May 18, 1961, at the 46th Street Theatre, *Donnybrook!* had only sixty-eight performances. *Dance Magazine,* customarily a strong supporter of Cole's work, ran a review by Leo Lerman, who described Cole's choreography as "monotonous." Perhaps Cole's interest in his own Irish roots and establishing ethnic authenticity misled him. Irish folk dances are, in fact, notably monotonous, though the Irish understandably cherish them.

The *New York Daily News* had long nourished a fondness for things Irish. Thus, it was not surprising to find this praise in John Chapman's *News* review: "This set-to, as staged by director Jack Cole, is as good as any of the slugging matches they put on in TV westerns—and right at the beginning of the show, there is a real donnybrook involving the excellent dancers of the cast. Cole's dancers, as a matter of fact, may be the best since Jerome Robbins assembled his remarkable crew for *West Side Story,* although they do not work in such modernistic patterns. Their opening number, with the lads in their Irish kilts and the lassies in their pony-tails, gives an immediate lift to *Donnybrook!*" Walter Kerr had good things to say about Cole's work: "Is it the simplicity, almost the shyness of *Donnybrook!* that makes it the likable bit of malarkey it is? . . . Jack Cole's opening footwork for a kilted chorus spins a mesmerising web of its own."

Virtually every critic liked the opening dance. The fight was admired. A wedding also won some praise, recalling Cole's Carnegie Hall studio success years before with his *Irish Wake* for his and Anna Austin's Ruth St. Denis Dancers.

Some of Cole's former partners have their own explanation about the show. Gwen Verdon says, "I don't know what happened with *Donnybrook!* But I'm sure it was the same problem he used to have with a lot of shows. All the people he had to work with would think he was just crazy. Like *Lolita*, which never made it to New York. The producer called me. He said, 'Jack Cole just walked out! What should I do?' I told him, 'Do nothing. He'll walk back tomorrow.' And he did!"

Florence Lessing is quick to defend Cole's reputation, even with *Donnybrook!* "This was one of his *rare* failures. After all, he was a human being. He was not a god. Even the greatest artists have their failures. I have such great respect for Jerry Robbins, but not all of his ballets are winners either. . . . Jack Cole was a genius, and I must say it: he had a real *minimum* of failures!" Ethel Martin remembers *Donnybrook!* with affection. "It had a lovely *quality*. It wasn't earthshaking, certainly, but it had wonderful moments. He adapted Irish dances effectively."

One close Cole associate has an explanation for the problem at the core of *Donnybrook!:* the failure of the romance to strike sparks, the lack of appeal in the supposed lovers. "When you saw Jack Cole's works—and it's also true of Bob Fosse's—if you're talking about human beings, you will not see the *tender* side of people coming out. I don't think Jack could do that. Something inside him kept that from being expressed. Take a story like *Donnybrook!*, which is essentially a love story and a contest of male-versus-female. I don't think it was within Jack's ability to create that. Oh, *wanton* love, yes! But that's very different. Jack Cole had a great talent and he was dynamic; he did all kinds of unique things. But *heart* was something else."

The magnificent though erratic and self-destructive nineteenth-century English actor Edmund Kean has fascinated theatre folk and fans ever since he made his debut. Alfred Drake understandably longed to play Kean, as dramatized by Jean-Paul Sartre, but he says there was no producer willing to hazard a professional Broadway production of the play. But a musical was a different matter.

Jack Cole was again chosen for director and choreographer of a Broadway show, even though *Donnybrook!* didn't run. Josh Meyer says, "The producers were looking. I said, 'Jack Cole's your man!' Obviously, they agreed. *Donnybrook!?* I guess everybody was disappointed. In retrospect, if you follow Broadway shows, you need a little bit of luck, too.

"I remember *Kean* vividly. Reports came back from Boston that it was a smash. I made the deal, the contract. . . . People in the business whom I respected said it would be a big success. It wasn't," Meyer says regretfully.

Another Cole associate who regrets *Kean*'s fate is the now director-choreographer Larry Fuller. He was also in *Donnybrook!*, and remembers how strict Cole's technique was in executing the Irish dances that he had theatricalized. *Kean* similarly drew on English social dances of its period. "We did a gavotte in that, and some balletic stuff," says Fuller. "I played a street-busker—one of two. I spent half the show walking on my hands."

The Boston reviews were generally raves, especially for Alfred Drake in the title role. In the *Boston Globe*, the head was "Alfred Drake Superb in Enchanting *Kean*." The dean of Boston critics, Elliot Norton, had a few reservations, but found most of it fine. *Variety*, on September 20, had some advice: the show wasn't ready yet. It ran three hours; cutting was in order. Cole needed "to be somewhat more ruthless in his direction."

Kean opened at the Broadway Theatre, November 2, 1961. Visually, it was a rich evocation of the period, the world of London theatre and society of the early nineteenth century, Edmund Kean having died in 1833. There was certainly dramatic potential in Kean's life, not to mention in Sartre's play. Perhaps Peter Stone was not yet ready for such a challenge as writing a musical book. The songs of Robert Wright and George Forrest had—and still have—appeal and potential, largely unrealized in that production. Thanks mainly to Alfred Drake's popularity, the show survived three months.

But it was also at least partly owing to Drake that *Kean* did not enjoy the success it might well have had. Not that Drake had done anything deliberately to harm the show; far from it. *Kean* was a fulfillment for him of his longing to play this great actor. As Drake himself says, "Partially, I was responsible because I was ill. I missed quite a few performances. I hated doing that, but it happens. You can't do anything about it."

Wright and Forrest, who express their affection and admiration for Alfred Drake in the strongest terms, nonetheless were distraught with this unforeseen misfortune. They rightly foresaw disaster. The producers had planned the show around Alfred Drake. Wright and Forrest insist there wouldn't even have been an appropriate understudy if they hadn't found Lawrence Brooks, a six-year-long *Song of Norway* stalwart. He did it as a favor, they say, for he was a leading man, not an understudy. "There's never been another Alfred Drake!" Wright says. "I don't know when there will be. Brooks wasn't Drake, and he didn't pretend to be. He was excellent, and no one asked for his money back."

Brooks sang the role of Kean more in the out-of-town tryout than Drake did, say Wright and Forrest. Nonetheless, Drake performed for the Boston critics, and they were impressed. Drake prided himself on *not* using a mike, even though he was ill. The Sunday after the opening, as Wright and Forrest recall, Goddard Lieberson recorded *Kean*—with a doctor and nurse in attendance. They realized that Drake's voice was almost a whisper. He told them and Lieberson he'd sing the songs as best he could.

The songwriters had their problems with Cole as well, dear friend though he was. *Kean* opened with some twelve minutes of song and speech, to establish the time, the place, and the character of the action. Cole wanted to cut that, replacing it with a dance. And *how* would they get the plot action under way? They didn't agree with Cole. Wright says he told him: "It's wrong, wrong, wrong, wrong!"

Some other Cole suggestions for turning pure dialogue into

musical scenes were, however, very effective. "But our biggest problem with *Kean* was always the opening. He was wrong. Maybe we weren't right, but we were closer. We're going to redo *Kean*; it's one of our strongest scores." Wright pauses: "If you go out and buy an album, let me know if you can get one for less than $50. I know people who've paid $400!

"Jack was a wonderful director for *Kean*. Forget that there was no real dancing in the show. He didn't have time to *do* the dancing. We ended up with an opening that was a Polonaise. It wasn't really a dance, just a lot of walking. That was it, and it didn't work very well. There was no way to make it exciting."

Understandably, Alfred Drake remembers the *Kean* experience from a rather different perspective. Drake comments on Cole's methods: "Jack was not good with words. He was not articulate. So, perhaps as director of the book there were things lacking. His ideas—he *had* ideas, but his expression of them was not always very clear." An inarticulate Jack Cole seems a contradiction in terms if the testimony of many other Cole friends and co-workers is to be believed, but it may well be that the problems Cole faced with *Kean,* so soon after the debacle of *Donnybrook!,* were overwhelming him.

"It bored him," Drake explains. "He really didn't want to play around with the book, or discuss the book, or think about the book." Then *why* did Cole agree to direct the show as well as choreograph? "I think, because he was ambitious and thought it was about time that he did direct a show. I believe, given time and a little more self-discipline, he would have been capable of doing it," Drake says.

Cole did a lot of research, particularly on England and the theatre of Kean's time, Drake emphasizes. "He invented a character for the play, a young boy, which was marvelous. He was Kean's idolator and sang that lovely song, 'Penny Plain, Tuppence Colored.' Cole was *not* lazy. He had this concept, with regard to the attack on the play. He *convinced* me." Drake says Cole said they had to musicalize Kean's story, to put something splendid on stage. Now, Drake thinks Cole's idea of what to do with the show may have been wrong. But he also says that he and Cole were "seduced" into doing the show.

Drake thinks the central problem in the book, or at least in Cole's interpretation and visual development of it, was showing Kean drowning in self-pity. "We made a big thing of this— in Jack's staging of the end of the first act—in which the puppet-actor feels himself to *be* a puppet and behaves like one. It was a marvelous kind of mimetic movement, and I must say, I enjoyed doing it. But it was wrong. He was a very convincing man, when he wanted to be."

New York critics generally found *Kean* a handsomely designed show. Some of Cole's dances and musical stagings were praised, but the book was leaden and lethargic. John Chapman complained that the show couldn't make up its mind whether it was a musical, a music drama, or a biography with songs. Cole was also complimented for scenes that evoked the bustle of London crowds in front of the Drury Lane Theatre and the theatre life inside. As Walter Kerr viewed it: "The pavement outside Drury Lane leaps and skitters with the energetic antics of London's poor," but, for him, the "visual glory and jumping-jack numbers" were only "way-stations on an overburdened journey. . ." Howard Taubman lauded *Kean:* ". . . so imaginative, touching, and gallant that one can forgive it for not making the final leap to glory." He thought it would have been almost perfect, had it not been marred by some Broadway vulgarity in *Kean*'s otherwise "flashing elegance and robust rowdiness of the early 19th century." Despite the folklore that a good review from the *New York Times* was like money in the bank, Taubman's appreciative rave for *Kean* couldn't save it.

Among souvenirs Cole preserved of his involvement with *Kean* was an amusing artifact. It was an old photo of himself, naked to the waist, performing one of his East Indian dances. Just as an English lad of Kean's time might have done with a penny-plain picture of his stage idol, Cole embellished the photo with a splash of colored sequins and paste jewels.

Jack Cole's luck on Broadway changed with the opening of *A Funny Thing Happened on the Way to the Forum,* which ran more than two years, had an extended tour, a successful Broadway revival, a London company, innumerable foreign productions, and a film version. The show starred Zero Mostel; Stephen Sondheim provided both words and music for the show's ingenious songs; George Abbott, the veteran author-director of Broadway comedy and musicals, staged the book, and Jack Cole created the choreography and actually staged the songs for Abbott, some of them incredibly inventive in their split-second timing. Cole had program credit, but reviewers either ignored his contribution or damned him with faint praise. Walter Kerr gave Abbott full marks for his deft direction, noting Cole only to comment that he was not called on very often. The *Times's* Howard Taubman told readers: "There is choreography by Jack Cole—it says here—but not much." He extolled Abbott for having "engineered a gay funeral sequence to a relentlessly snappy march by Stephen Sondheim." This was Cole's work, and it bore his stamp.

Funny Thing, which opened May 8, 1962, at the Alvin Theatre, was a working reunion for Cole and Hal Schaefer. Schaefer, now settled in New York with his own career, didn't want to work for Cole and Abbott as a rehearsal pianist, but he welcomed the opportunity to compose the music for the dance sequences, so part of the score is actually Hal Schaefer's work.

Working on his next Broadway-bound musical, *Zenda,* Cole must have been thinking about Aladdin and his wonderful magic lamp. Or at least about the wonder-working genie that could be summoned by rubbing the lamp. One of his more curious keepsakes was a restaurant paper place mat, a testimony to Cole's out-of-town jitters. The mat is covered with Cole's frantic word-doodles: ZENDA, ZENDA . . . HELP, HELP, HELP . . . Genii, Genii, Genii . . . Unprepared . . . Not Ready Yet . . .

The show was a musical version of *The Prisoner of Zenda,* a novel of romance and adventure. The year was 1963, and it starred Alfred Drake and Chita Rivera. Drake remembers his pleasure at working with Cole again. "You see," he says, "there was one thing Jack loved. He didn't want anyone to mark anything at any point. He wanted a full-blown performance, nothing held back, every time! In rehearsal! He came to me and said, 'I admire you. You always do a performance. You don't just walk through it.' I said, 'It's not wise on my part. A singer shouldn't do that. I should be holding back some of the time.' He said, 'Well, maybe, but that's the way to do it.'

"He loved Chita. She never marked anything. She always

performed full out. All the time! Chita very quickly picked up his methods, his system. She could use her body in any way imaginable. That's another reason he loved her—she was quick! They got along like a house afire. . . . Chita had some important dances, and she and I had a duet. . . . there was a bench, like a park bench—and he invented an entire dance for the two of us, which really meant acrobatics, going round that bench. It was quite amazing. Chita is a dancer, but again, he had *me* doing things I didn't know I was capable of," Drake says in admiration. Unfortunately, despite all their efforts, Cole's genie failed to come to their rescue. The show never made it into New York.

Foxy was Jack Cole's next effort for Broadway, in 1964. The show had had an early out-of-town tryout in Dawson City, in the Yukon Territory, on July 2, 1962. The reason for this remote initial venue was the fact that the musical was set in the Yukon during the Klondike Gold Rush. In *Foxy*, Bert Lahr appeared for the last time on Broadway, playing the role of a wily fellow in a time and place where owning rich mining claims was everyone's hope or dream. Lahr was hilarious in a variety of guises and poses. Larry Blyden was admired as a foil. Robert Emmett Dolan's score had charm, with Johnny Mercer's lyrics. Cole's dances were lively and colorful. Even the idea of transposing Ben Jonson's *Volpone* from Venice to the Klondike wasn't in itself a bad one.

Foxy open on February 6, 1964, in the cavernous Ziegfeld Theatre, designed more for revues than for musicals. *Foxy* didn't project well in this space, despite Lahr's most frantic clowning. Critics praised Lahr's efforts, but some thought the entire show was trying to appeal with a somewhat desperate outpouring of energy rather than cleanly focused comic conception. Norman Nadel, for instance, found Cole's choreography "more feverish than exciting." Walter Kerr put his finger on the show's central problem. As he saw it, *Volpone* had been borrowed without having been believed in. And there were other disappointments: "We watch and watch for choreographer Jack Cole to cut loose with the whiplash severity that is characteristic of him—and would be good for the show this starts out to be—but only find him dictating the usual high kicks to the gold rush girls."

For decades, composers and choreographers for the Broadway stage have justly complained that their creations are not judged by experts in music and dance, but by drama critics, many of whom have little background in those arts. *Dance Magazine* sent one of its own editors, Doris Hering, to review *Foxy*. Hering, like Kerr, saw little of the "rhythmic acuity and definition" of the Cole style. "The 'big ballet' of the first act—a scramble of prospectors and saloon girls—had little focus and no recognizable climax. Since we saw the show, Mr. Cole is reported to have added a 'sexy' second act dance. We doubt whether it could rescue *Foxy* from being more a series of skits than a unified sequence of events." Cathryn Damon, Alice Glenn, Marlena Lustik, and Sueanne Shirley were among Cole's dance-hall girls.

Who would have thought there was a musical inside Miguel Cervantes's picaresque novel *Don Quixote,* waiting to get out? The creators of *Man of La Macha* did, and its subsequent worldwide success vindicated their belief. On November 22, 1965, the new musical opened in Greenwich Village at the now extinct ANTA–Washington Square Theatre after its premiere presentation at the historic Goodspeed Opera House in East Haddam, Connecticut, a charming old Victorian playhouse that has sent a number of musical productions—new or revivals—on to Broadway. Dale Wasserman made the adaptation, with songs by Mitch Leigh and Joe Darion. Albert Marre, who worked with Cole on *Kismet*, provided stage direction and the staging for the musical numbers. Cole had choreographic credit for the New York premiere, but was not involved with it at the Goodspeed. There, dance captain Eddie Roll was listed as choreographer, with Laura Toledo credited for Spanish dance material. These varied credits would later be the basis of a heated controversy about Cole's choreographic credits for *Man of La Mancha* when the show was revived on Broadway in 1977. For the revival, Cole's name had disappeared from the program credits. There was no choreographer listed at all. Marre, as usual, was billed as director and the stager of the musical numbers, which of course is *not* quite the same as choreographing a dance. With Cole's own song-stagings, however, it was often difficult to see where the artful visualization of the song stopped and the at-

tendant dance sequence began. Cole's inventive use of movement for singing stars frequently created the illusion that they
also were dancing.

Man of La Mancha almost didn't make it to Broadway. Its
Goodspeed producer, Albert Selden, apparently was dubious
about its prospects, but his wife loved the show and, it's said,
encouraged him to take the New York plunge. It proved to be
a shower of gold. The public loved the show.

The New York drama critics were also elated. Some didn't
mention Cole's contribution, but Taubman of the *Times* noted
Cole's and Marre's collaboration in conjuring up "some impressive pictures in action and repose." Walter Kerr paid Cole
an extended tribute: "Mr. Cole has no trouble at all in pacing
the proceedings at full gallop as Quixote and Sancho Panza take
off on two skeletonized nags. The clatter of hooves is brisk, the
farewell song cheery, the whip of the wind in the air distinctly
noticeable. Though the production has the depressing habit of
chopping off Mr. Cole's gypsy-style frenzies before they have
quite whirled about full circle, there is never any question about
making a song-number move."

The question came later, in 1977. It was: Who should get
the credit for *Man of La Mancha*'s choreography? Cole had been
dead since 1974; who now was making the song numbers move?
Albert Marre, as previously, was taking credit for directing the
show and staging the songs. No one was taking—or given—
credit for *La Mancha*'s choreography. Not only was Jack Cole
not getting credit, but his estate wasn't getting any royalties,
as a result. Cole's agent, Josh Meyer, decided to do something
about this. "There'd be no lawsuit possible if it weren't for me,"
he says. "Jack was dead. I was outraged at what had happened. . . . I was outraged for Jack, and I wouldn't let it happen. I raised a lot of hell."

Meyer took Cole's original contract for *Man of La Mancha* and
an outline of the steps he'd taken thus far to a New York lawyer, J. Edward Townsend, who agreed to pursue the complaint
for Cole's heir and longtime companion David Gray. As Meyer
recalls, "All the dancers just wrung their hands about *Man of
La Mancha*. David was just sitting there, not ready to be an ac-
tivist about it. I made it happen. Jack wasn't here to defend

himself. But once David was gone . . ." With Gray's death, the case seemed to lie dormant, but it remained a subject of impassioned comment by Cole's admirers. Gwen Verdon, like Meyer, was outraged: "He used the same style he used in *Magdalena*. It was mostly Spanish, of course, but there were also Afro-Cuban influences. But the Spanish is *Jack's* Spanish. . ."

Agnes de Mille was also angry at Cole's vanishing credit. "The usurpation of Cole's work is terrible in *Man of La Mancha*. . . . That was Cole's creation, absolutely. But his name has disappeared from the programs. I've tried to get our union to do something. I'm not strong enough to fight these fights anymore, but I went to the union. I made a speech and I wrote a letter, which was sent to every member. The union's not worth its salt if it doesn't stand up for Cole. . . . I was instrumental in forming the union, and it's intended to protect choreographers, even dead ones!"

Jack Cole's supporters remain ardent on his behalf. They want to protect his memory, his work, his credits. Before his death, David Gray, being interviewed for this account of Cole's life and career, refused to discuss anything but the missing choreographic credit—and the attendant royalties which he, as heir to Cole's estate, believed he should have been paid. The choreographic convolutions involved in the evolution of *Man of La Mancha* are so complex, however, that it may not be the best test case to establish a choreographer's rights to credits and royalties in subsequent revivals. Albert Marre contends, for instance, that there were two choreographers—neither of them Cole—credited at Goodspeed, but in fact ideas for dances and movement came from others as well. Marre has even made available a copy of the letter he sent to Cole's union, answering charges made.

In a cover letter, Marre explained: "You must know that I did not write this to denigrate Jack. I consider him the most originally gifted choreographer I have ever encountered. He not only made up the whole amalgam of jazz, ballet, modern, and oriental dance which is now loosely called 'Broadway' choreography—but he was better at it than anyone else!" Interestingly, some of Jack Cole's close friends have commented that Cole worshipped Marre. Nonetheless, Marre was, he says, aware of shortcomings in this brilliant choreographer. Whether they were the result of a lurking lack of confidence, or Cole's famous impatience with dancers who couldn't fulfill his dance visions, they were there.

"The mad part of all this is that Jack and I remained friends after *La Mancha*, despite our artistic differences. His preoccupation with physical violence had become silly in *La Mancha*. I asked him to choreograph and appear himself in *Chu Chem* a year after the *La Mancha* fiasco," Marre says. Marre's letter to Cole's union is very long, but some excerpts will present the basics of his view of what happened. For the New York production, it was judged ". . . desirable to insert two 'dance' pieces of material into this second, continued production of the play." Marre thought Cole could do the job. His letter comments: "It should be made very clear that Cole was engaged by the producer, Selden, solely to 'choreograph' 1) a new piece of material for Aldonza and the Muleteers (to replace the song and Spanish dance movement that had been staged in the original production at Goodspeed), and that 2) he was to 'choreograph' a 'black mass' sequence (a replacement for the 'gypsy' sequence done originally at Goodspeed)."

Marre's letter insisted Cole didn't choreograph or stage "dances or dance sequences." In Marre's view: "He did rehearse a new piece of dance material for Aldonza and the Muleteers. When the authors, the producer, and the director saw the material that Cole had arranged, they rejected it immediately; they felt it was entirely too violent and did serious damage to the characters as conceived and to the thread of the story. Not one moment of it ever appeared on stage at any public performance."

The "black mass," which was to replace the original "gypsy" number, also proved a problem, according to Marre. Cole began it but could not conceive further ideas to bring it to completion. He rehearsed the beginning over and over, apparently blocked. For this reason, says Marre, the Goodspeed gypsy number had to be reintroduced. Marre claims he himself staged the forefront of the gypsies' action, asking Cole to "illustrate" some ideas for the upstage gypsies. Cole drew on an idea from *Kismet*, says Marre. In *Man of La Mancha*, he insists, ". . . there was no choreography in the accepted sense of the term, except for the two minor sequences above mentioned." But the rape sequence was hardly minor; anyone who saw the New York production may recall its violence, even after supposedly being softened by Marre. Perhaps to extricate himself from the fuss about Cole's missing choreographic credit for the revival, Marre told the union he regarded the *La Mancha* sequences, which others have seen as dance, as being actually "heightened or stylized physical activity."

Cole was certainly under contract, and Marre maintains he was being paid a substantial fee. Marre asked him to heighten and improve the activity in the "Abduction Scene." Marre told the union: "Once again, he began to take this activity too far in terms of violence; indeed, the activity began to verge on the ludicrous." When this was pointed out to him by Marre and the authors during the preview period of the November production of the play, Cole stormed out of the theatre, saying words to the effect of, "All right then, do it your own way." Cole was never seen or heard from again. Marre claimed the Abduction was thereafter worked out by a kind of committee: Marre, Joan Diener, Eddie Roll, John Aristides, and Fernando Grabel.

Because Cole had a contract he was given choreographic credit. But he wasn't asked, says Marre, to reproduce the choreography for London or the national company. In any case, that wouldn't have been necessary; Cole had able assistants. When Cole was in Beirut with his show at the Casino du Liban, he saw a news item about *Man of La Mancha* opening in Paris, with a Cole choreographic credit. "But I'll never see any royalties from that," he said.

A close study of Albert Marre's lengthy reply to the union makes it clear that Cole's presence counted for something—that he did have some influence, no matter how it may have been softened or diluted by Marre, on the quality of movement in *Man of La Mancha*. Rod Alexander states "Albie Marre sort of gave up on Jack and just let him do as much choreography as he wanted to do. Jack loved the show and went overboard and did too much. So when Jack left, he cut and edited. It was Jack's choreography, but Albie never intended to use all Jack did—he just let him go. Jack could get carried away." Alexander, along with Gwen Verdon, Ethel Martin, and Agnes de Mille, insists that one could tell the rape sequence was Cole's, just by looking at it. As he says, "I've seen some other rape scenes he did. I know the movement."

John Aristides was one of the vital and violent dancers in *Man of La Mancha*. He says the big change in the choreography really took place when the musical moved from Washington Square to Broadway. "It got mutilated. The pattern of everything Jack Cole did is what remained in the show. Albie Marre mutilated the steps, the feelings, the direction of things. He removed all Jack's technique and feeling. The dynamics of what Jack did in the show was much more overpowering. . . . Albie used to get very uptight about that, because Jack was very powerful about what he did."

In Cole's "black mass," in which Aristides danced in rehearsal, there was, he says, the same power, the dynamism. But it was too powerful in conception; it would have been out of balance with the rest of the show. The sequence was to have been a dream fantasy, in which semi-nude monks came to torment the old Don. Aristides remembers it as being exciting and traumatic, something the strong religious feelings of the time would have prevented some potential viewers from understanding. "It was a little too profound," Aristides insists.

After the resounding success of *La Mancha*, no matter what was left of Cole's work in it, he and Marre were together again in November 1966. This time the show was *Chu Chem* at the New Locust Theatre in Philadelphia. The time and place were eleventh-century China, with the focus of the story an "itinerant Jewish family." Stars of the old Yiddish theatre, Menasha Skulnik and Molly Picon, who also had a Broadway public, played these indomitable Jews in one of the most remote reaches of the Diaspora. Cole choreographed and also played the Mongol, Lord Hoo Hah, with Buzz Miller one of his dancing attendants. The choreography was described as "limited." Albert Marre says of Cole's work on *Chu Chem:* "In this show, Jack behaved with total professionalism, and while he could never bring himself to finish the show's final, climactic number, he supplied the show's other choreography, as well as performing the finest, funniest five minutes of dance activity I have ever seen on any stage, at any time, at any place." The show's producers didn't need fortune cookies to tell them what the Philadelphia critics had already suggested: The show was not going to make it on Broadway. It died in the City of Brotherly Love, like so many musicals before it. "Chu Chem" means Wise Man. Critic Ernie Schier said the show should have been called *The King and Oy*.

Cole's next musical was David Merrick's *Mata Hari*. The producer gave the show its *coup de grace* in Washington, D.C., where it was in tryouts, prior to Broadway. At a Democratic fund-raising benefit performance, everything that could go wrong technically did. One wit remarked to a gossip columnist: "They should make a musical out of this!"

Analyzing the failure of *Mata Hari*, a musical saga of the notorious German spy operating in Paris prior to World War I, Cole told readers of *Dance Magazine* that a number of factors contributed to the success—and to the failure—of Broadway musicals. He said he couldn't discuss them without getting personal. So Cole got personal: ". . . the real Mata Hari was a dull dancer, a dull woman, even a dull lover. She was bottom-heavy and wore a stiff corset. Historically, the only interesting thing she ever did was to get herself shot. So the musical's book concentrated on the man who fell in love with her, having become perilously bored by twenty years of marriage. He was also the man who unmasked her and turned her in.

"Why did I take on the job to choreograph it? Well, I read the script, and I knew it was weak, but I imagined the whole thing could be done in a low key. I imagined those Paris salons cluttered with the preposterous furniture of the 1910s, that look so great in the subdued French light: drapes and heavy Persian rugs and closed-in walls and intimate trimmings to convey a sick, sinful atmosphere. Maybe this way *Mata Hari* would have come across."

Unfortunately for Cole—and also for the show, he implied—he wasn't the director and his ideas weren't followed. The results, he thought, were rather like the cover of a paperback James Bond novel in a drugstore: "Mata Hari, a great big dark woman with great big dark eyes, waving her arms over her head, against a bright orange background." Cole was contemptuous of the idea; James Bond was for lonely people who fed themselves on wild fantasies. To make such gaudy unreality work, ". . . you need someone as preposterous as James Bond himself." The production concept came, not from Cole, but from its director, Vincente Minelli, supported by producer David Merrick, who was, he thought, launching a new Broadway star in the person of Marisa Mell. Cole found her overwhelmed by the demands of the role—she was neither a singer nor a dancer, in his view, but rather a "cinematic personality," as he phrased it. She had some thirty costume changes, and her wardrobe had cost Merrick $155,000. "Who wants to see beautiful dresses?" Cole asked derisively.

Velerie Camille was chosen by Cole for the Vivian Darkbloom character in the 1971 musical, *Lolita, My Love*. She recalls the brief moments of working with him: "For me, he danced the first morning's rehearsal full-out with the boys, then broke for lunch—and did not return. He was upset that the music had not been ready in time for rehearsal, and worse, he was already behind in rehearsals—before he'd had a chance to begin!" Danny Daniels took over, only to have his work discarded and replaced by a number set on Camille and Leonard Frey by Danny Stradella. It was the only song and dance left in the show by that time. But New York was not to see this mounting of Vladimir Nabokov's novel on Broadway. It died in Philadelphia.

Jack Cole's last potential Broadway project was a musical based on the Lafayette Escadrille. Initially titled *Escadrille*, it later was renamed *Shooting the Bad Guys Down*. In April 1973, in the midst of casting—Lana Cantrell had just been auditioned—Jack Cole suddenly left New York, flying to California without saying anything to the frantic producer. Writing Cole to beg him to return for the final auditions—Rita Moreno, Cathryn Damon, and possibly Elizabeth Ashley—the producer described himself and the whole production staff as "stunned." He reminded Cole that the work at hand could have been done the previous October, but Cole had then also decided he had to be in Los Angeles and had departed, leaving his obliging colleagues to wait until he was ready to work with them. Now, as often in the past, he had again walked out.

Jack Cole didn't answer the letter, which was followed, six days later by another, special delivery registered. Cole certainly received it, because this correspondence is preserved among his papers, along with a script for *Escadrille*. In the second missive, the producer noted: "I tried to find out from Josh Meyer exactly what you are doing at UCLA that might supersede our effort here. He did not seem to know." Cole was in fact teaching at UCLA, but in this case it's apparent he was only using that as an excuse.

More than a month later, Josh Meyer anxiously wrote Cole and enclosed a copy of the *Escadrille* contract, to remind him of his artistic guarantees and also of his obligations. Meyer didn't mince his words: "Upon careful consideration and reflection, I can only say to you that there is nothing more important to your career than getting a successful show on the boards as soon as possible. Everything else worthwhile follows from such an accomplishment. . . . If you must be abrasive to achieve the result, so be it, but I hope because of the indignity you feel was contained in the letter you just received, you don't become discouraged to the point of wishing to disassociate yourself from the show. . ."

Today, Meyer says Cole's death in 1974 put a stop to further plans for a production of *Escadrille*, a.k.a. *Shooting the Bad Guys Down*. Velerie Camille concurs. Cole had wanted her in the show. After his death, the producer told her he'd dropped the show because he couldn't envision anyone but Jack Cole doing it. Apparently, Cole saw walking out in a huff as a tactical weapon. After the failure of *Mata Hari*, on which he'd worked very hard, Cole told *Dance Magazine*'s Ric Estrada what it was like to be a choreographer working under a director: ". . . there's a limit beyond which you are powerless, unless you get nasty and walk out. Then people say you're a horrible person."

12

COLE'S CHARACTER COMPLEXITIES

A MAN OF MOODS & MYSTERY

J ack couldn't stand any kind of negative criticism," Hal Schaefer claims, suggesting that, although he could certainly dish it out, he didn't like to be on the receiving end. "I never heard Jack Cole say, 'I'm sorry,' to anyone. I *never* heard it, and I have great respect for him. I never heard a real apology from him. Jack Cole would never use the word 'apologize.' That I'm sure of. He could have done the most rude thing. He could have slapped a dancer. He wouldn't apologize, but he'd do something to make up for it," Schaefer explains. The token might be a small gift, an invitation to dinner, a drink, a pat on the back.

Cole as a man remains a mystery. Many who worked with him over the years and honor him and what he achieved still say they hardly knew him as a person. Others, who felt they had been admitted to his circle of close friends, realized there were parts of his life he kept sealed off from them. A number of Cole dancers, for instance, never knew that he'd been married and had a son. Some, on hearing this news, were plainly incredulous. Asking Cole's former colleagues to describe his personality, his character, or his ambitions is a bit like that proverbial exercise of asking five blind men, each clutching a different part of a pachyderm's anatomy, to describe the elephant. Cole takes on a different character, depending on the relation of the teller to the master and also given the problems of memories fading over time. George Martin was one of Cole's favorite dancers, and Martin acted as his assistant many times. Yet today, Martin feels that he didn't really get to know Cole as his wife, Ethel, did. Martin points out that Cole was the first "very large personality" he ever worked with—followed rapidly by Kay Thompson, and more recently by Harold Prince. "All very strong people! And I was never close to them, so it might be me; that I never allowed myself to get that personal. Maybe so I wouldn't get hurt. It irked Jack a lot that I wouldn't fight with him. I never argued with him—but I also did not bow down or scrape. Ethel had many arguments with him—many of them screaming. So perhaps she understood him more than I did," says Martin.

Cole's dancers and co-workers were hardly blind to his faults. For some, when the great artist was behaving like a madman, love and admiration conveniently dimmed their sight, though it's surprising, after talking about Cole for a while, how much can be dredged up from memory that is not all adulation. Virtually all of his former dancers who have described their experiences share a mingling of respect, admiration, awe, and fondness for him. Yet there is also a darker mixture of emotions, inspired by memories of explosions of anger, cutting remarks, gruelling practice sessions, and, every now and then, some totally irrational behavior, later redeemed by some spontaneous gesture of generosity or reconciliation. One admiring Cole dancer shook her head: "It was like he was forgiving *you*, when he was the one who'd done the injury in the first place."

For those who never knew Cole, it's too much to ask to think of him as both Saint and Devil, but both images hover spectrally in the background whenever his friends talk about him. The diabolic is more often invoked. Ethel Martin illuminates this paradox of good and evil existing side by side. At least Cole's more devilish impulses, she insists, weren't insidiously disguised as something else, such as solicitude in helping, while actually destroying a young dancer. For Martin, there are other noted choreographers, still among the living, whose "evil is more insidious than Jack's ever was. It's refined so much you find it difficult to combat. Irrational, yes, but also quite cruel. Jack was cruel, too, but it was a volatile cruelty. You could fight it, if you had the guts to do it. And he didn't hate you for trying. He'd even admire you.

"With Jack, you see, he wouldn't accept anything short of perfection from a dancer. Well, we weren't perfect. I don't think we ever came up to his standard. We all tried very hard; I think it wrecked many of us. I mean, we stayed around Jack too long. We began to expect of ourselves what Jack expected. So, if we couldn't be as great as Jack, then we thought we weren't talented. With such a high standard in our heads, it was very hard to go on to become choreographers—to dare to be anything—knowing it wouldn't be as good as Jack Cole was. And the damn truth was that we *weren't* as good as Cole!" Martin admits.

Even people who worked with Cole only once or twice suffered from intense feelings of inferiority. Ethel Martin insists it wasn't so much a matter of Cole's making his dancers *feel* inferior, as the fact that they really were inferior to him. Malcolm Goddard remembers the sense of fear he and the other English dancers had of Cole: "It was a real fear. Maybe awe—maybe . . . But in those days—a generation ago—it wasn't so difficult to fire dancers. There was a clause in the contract: If the option wasn't taken up in fourteen days of opening, you could be fired. And there were plenty of people waiting in line at the stage door for jobs. There I was, an unknown, working with people like Jane Russell and Matt Mattox. I thought: 'Oh, *help!'* "

There was a strange paradox in Cole's way of dealing with dancers. To English dancers like Goddard, it was incomprehensible. He could be cutting; he could fire people abruptly, and, at the same time, he could show great kindness. Once Goddard watched Cole fire a good dancer and retain one who wasn't nearly as competent. Later, when he became friends with Cole, he asked why he'd done this. The good dancer wasn't trying; he wasn't working at anywhere near his potential. Cole despised such laziness, especially when one had talent and training. The other dancer was, as Cole said, "giving it all he had." Cole respected that and wanted to help him become a better dancer. No matter what the pressures in rehearsing for the opening of a show or the beginning of shooting on a film, Cole was constantly and concurrently operating a training school in Cole Technique, in the same studio with the same dancers. No wonder Goddard today asks: "Is it possible to be completely terrified of somebody, respect him, like him, and work your guts out for him all at the same time?"

When Cole told Walter Terry—who'd accused him of mellowing—that it was because he was growing older, and "being evil" took a lot of energy, he was not merely joking. It's quite clear, from many remarks he made to intimates as well as from comments recorded in newspaper or magazine interviews, that he fostered the legend of his terrible temper, his awful wrath, when a dancer, a conductor, or other professional colleague fell short of his expectations. He told one reporter: "I don't say I haven't been a horrible person at times. To get things done, you often have to jump down into the pit and smash the conductor's baton in half. 'Now, did you get the message?' You must somehow get through to people, to dancers especially. Sometimes you have to slap them. It isn't like painting or writing or something that can be done in solitude. The trouble with choreography is that you have to get the person out of the way before you can bring out the dancer."

These are, of course, sentiments calculated to freeze the blood of dance novices and raise the hackles of union shop stewards. As for smashing batons, Cole broke Eddie Le Baron's in two in front of astonished Rainbow Room patrons. Cole even got his message across to unruly customers. Once, one of them had done something during a performance to offend his partners Florence Lessing and Anna Austin. When the audience had left, Cole helped this man through the club's glass doors—without the formality of opening them. Cole made himself into a one-man Reign of Terror. And yet, his colleagues are quick to add that he could be so tender, so thoughtful, so amusing—as though nothing had happened.

Cole's childhood had been marred by his defective eye, by enforced stays in a convent school and a military academy, and by loneliness. He felt unloved by his mother and ill-used by his stepfather. His Roman Catholic religion offered only a temporary refuge for his sensitive, questing spirit, surrounded by so much insensitivity.

Those who knew Cole really well comment on his basic shyness, his easily wounded feelings. Cole's physical toughness, his mercurial temper, his biting sarcasm, and his aggressiveness were obvious compensations and concealments, behind which the real Jack Cole was often cowering, sick at heart—and also at his stomach, ready to vomit from inner anxiety and outer pressures. But Cole's compensations were also his weapons in dealing with those who irritated or threatened him. For an artist who had such a clear vision of perfection, it was ironic that he chose to be a commercial dancer-choreographer for much of his life. It almost always placed him at the final mercies of directors, stars, and producers, whose wishes and notions took precedence over his own ideas and standards of excellence. Had he been a serious choreographer with his own concert company, he would have had to answer to no one—except audiences and critics. At least he would have been, in a real sense, his own boss. But when that wasn't possible, Cole kept his ultimate weapon at the ready: walking out in a huff or a rage. Since he had a house he loved in Los Angeles and a cozy apartment in New York City, it was no problem for Cole to take a walk and then take a plane, whether the project at hand was in Hollywood or Manhattan. His early agent, Jack Davies, was always trying to patch up misunderstandings Cole had made worse with outbursts of temper. His last agent, Josh Meyer, had to remind him of the importance of getting along with others if he was to work.

Dancers, of course, took the brunt of the Cole sarcasm and displeasure. The performing arts have long been a haven—or a hideout—for some of life's underachievers: those whose misfortune it is to be spoiled in childhood, attractive in youth, indolent in nature, narcissistic in temperment, and accustomed to adulation. While Cole also admired beautiful people, he had no patience with anyone who possessed a good body and an intelligent, responsive mind, but who showed no real inclination to make the effort needed to master the Cole Technique. Some would-be dancers who retreated from encounters with Cole told their friends he had "destroyed" them. Even colleagues and dance teachers accused Cole of that. For Cole, however, this was not destruction at all. Anyone who was so easily wounded would never make a good dancer.

All he wanted to do, Cole said, was to "touch the dancer at the center of his emotion. I try to remind him of what he is— a dancer, an actor, a real person. If you're ashamed of this or that emotion, you can't dance. . . . When you dance, you must bring real emotion to whatever you're doing. Isn't that what dancing is about—emotion, life—and not just patterns in the air?" Cole continued: "The funny thing is, bad dancers hate me.

Good dancers love me. Bad dancers don't want to find out things about themselves. I say to them, 'Baby, you don't want to dance. Get out!' I've got no use for them. Good dancers love the process of self-discovery.'' Cole fostered this growth in unusual ways. He had an excellent Japanese dancer in the company for *Mata Hari*. Cole noticed that she didn't like to be touched. He privately urged other members of the company to touch her, even to fall on her, as often as possible. She got Cole's message. He said she opened up once she understood that no one resented her for being Japanese. How he had arrived at the conclusion that that was the root of her problem remained unclear.

Josh Meyer emphasizes what was at the heart of Cole's ways of dealing with dancers and other professionals. "He was a perfectionist in working. And—there's no getting away from it— he had a very volatile temperament. Personally, I got along with him fine. It's a two-sided coin. I know some people who actually worshipped him; others will tell you how difficult, how demanding he was. As far as dancers were concerned, he *was* difficult; he was demanding. He was a taskmaster. He'd drive people to the point of exhaustion—and tears. But those who couldn't call him enough names, later, on the street, they'd talk about him as if he were a deity. He commanded great respect."

Apparently, Cole couldn't accept the reality that most dancers would never be able to do what he could do. Hal Schaefer is convinced this created a problem for Cole in his professional life. "He was such a fantastic dancer—you couldn't believe what he could do; he was so extraordinary! But try as they would, others couldn't do it. Oh, Gwen, Matt Mattox, Carol Haney, Ron Field, Lee Becker—they could approach it. But he worked with hundreds and hundreds of dancers. Most of them couldn't even get near what he wanted. Even though he'd hand-picked them. . . . He had this sense of artistic perfection always with him. It made him crazy. It was too severe. There was no compromise. He'd rather see someone do something badly, or as slapstick with a funny nose, than dance in a mediocre fashion. He hated mediocrity! He was a very severe man, hard on himself and very hard on others. When it came to his work, he didn't know *ease*. He didn't know how to relax. Only after he was through for the day, or apart from his work, would he relax. Then we'd tipple a bit."

Alfred Drake had ample opportunity to observe Cole at work. He agrees, "He might have been considered cruel when he was working with dancers, because he fully expected them to be able to do anything. Anything that he could do, they could do! That was his theory. After all, the whole training for dancers is quite different from that of actors. I rather admire their discipline. I think the rest of the theatre could profit from it. When he was working with people, of whom he knew he could not expect true dancing, he was very understanding and very forgiving."

But Drake stresses Cole's care for inexperienced dancers in *Kismet*. He preferred to use his own trained dancers when he could, but if he had to use non–Cole dancers he then retrained them during rehearsals, while choreographing waited. They couldn't dance the routines he was setting unless they had mastered at least the basics of Cole Technique. As Drake recalls, "He would teach them—literally—in separate dancing rehearsals, *not* while the rest of us were waiting. I happened to watch some of them, so I knew. It's not an easy technique, so the kids were finding it very difficult. He made no bones about it: 'If you don't know how, you're going to have to learn. Now!' He only taught me a few techniques I might need in the show. I wasn't called upon to do any of his kind of dancing." For the London *Kismet* production, he'd hired a girl who wasn't up to his standard. Drake knew Cole would fire her, so he suggested a chorus girl he'd noticed following every step of the dance. "I could see she wanted to understudy that role; she was learning it. So I went to Jack and said, 'Take a chance on that one.' It was Juliet Prowse—and she was excellent!"

Dolores Gray, like Drake, was fascinated by Cole at work. Whether on a Hollywood set or a Broadway stage, she loved watching Cole rehearse his dancers. "Whenever anything was wonderful, and Jack was teaching it, you'd sit at the edge of the set—or in the rear of the house—and watch them do it! And you'd think it was really wonderful. But the instant that Cole got up and did it, it was like a miracle! His work was so strong, so clean. His moves were so clean that the dance took on a whole new meaning. Always! No matter how wonderful his dancers were, he always did it a hundred times better," she says.

Jane Russell also respected Cole's amazing talent and his drive for perfection. She agrees that he was "difficult on people's egos. If they didn't want their feathers ruffled—well, they were going to get ruffled around Jack. . . . When Jack got angry with them, it was because he was demanding that they do their very best. If they didn't feel like it at that moment . . . he wouldn't let up. And they'd get annoyed then, but later, they'd know he was right. And then he'd be very friendly and dear with them."

By the time Cole was working with Russell and Marilyn Monroe, he didn't have a regular dance workshop with contracted dancers. He of course had Cole-trained dancers he could call on, but for a large movie chorus there would always be those new to the Cole Technique and his own mystique. As Russell says, "If you have that many people, and they're all doing something almost mechanical, they have to be exactly the same. It's got to be precise. You'll find the same thing with an orchestra conductor as with Jack Cole. At work, he insisted that there be perfection. And then they'd get mad. He told me some stories . . . one about Gwen. She got so mad at him one night, she took off her high heels and beat the hell out of him!"

More than once Cole's closest co-workers turned on him in anger. Hal Schaefer was furious with Cole during an engagement in Havana. "I threatened to kill him! I broke a mirror in his dressing-room, and I put a piece of the broken glass at his throat," Schaefer admits, because Cole had driven him too far. Then, says Schaefer, "a year later, when Jane Russell called about doing a club act, she said, 'I want Jack, and Jack wants you.' So I did it. We buried the hatchet."

Francine Ames Kuney still has painful memories of some Cole jibes: "Jack had a cruel streak. He had an uncanny ability to sense people's vulnerabilities and to use them. I mean as punishment. If he didn't like the way you were dancing, he wouldn't comment on that. Instead, he'd use something very personal, to get back at you for your bad performance." The young Francine Ames, as she sees herself now, was very innocent and very vulnerable. It was during World War II. She was recently married, and her husband was fighting in the Pacific. "He made fun of the fact that I was loyal, faithful to a young man who was in the Pacific. For him, that was high camp—a piece of *kitsch.* He made me cry," Ames remembers.

Some dancers took Cole's needling less sensitively. Larry Fuller remembers, "He never picked on me much, but, when we were doing an East Indian dance number, I was trying to do a specific step. He looked at me and said, 'You look like Ann Miller trying to make a comeback in houseshoes.' I started to laugh, and after that, we got along terrifically. Sometimes he'd pick on the person I was dancing with, and that got to me, and I'd lash back. He seemed to appreciate that. He respected it. I learned tremendously from him."

In his last months of life—which he devoted to teaching dance at UCLA, as though he knew this was his last chance to pass on what he'd mastered to younger dancers—he also used such piquant images. Spider Kedelsky emphasizes that these dancer-images that Cole would suddenly coin were actually appropriate as well as amusing. In an odd way, they often captured the essence of what a dancer was doing wrong, or of a major physical or mental problem impeding his work. The purpose of these verbal barbs was not to humiliate the dancers in front of their friends—though they sometimes had exactly that effect—but to remind individual dancers in a very vivid way that they had to keep their minds on controlling such things as fluttery fingers or wobbling ankles.

Cole defended his use of such phrases, as well as curses and suggestive expressions. They were used to wake up the dancers. John Aristides empahsizes: "If he had to curse, swear, or use pornographic expressions, it was to make you understand about yourself. About what you weren't doing, weren't thinking. If Jack saw you were really trying, he'd be so patient. But if he knew you didn't give a shit. . . . He'd say, 'The first thing is to forget you know anything about dance, if you want to work with me. If you want to learn!' You had to retrain completely. He demanded maturity; otherwise, you wouldn't want to work and accept what he had to give." Aristides, like so many other Cole dancers, is still in awe of him. Not only dancers, says Aristides, but also singers, actors, all kinds of performers could learn from Cole. "Although he wasn't a musician, he had a marvelous musical sense. And his insights into everyone's ways of movement! He was very patient. . . . There was a whole *presence* about him. He had so much energy. He couldn't always put things into words for everyone. Some people were jealous, but he was a genius. An incredible man. . . . He was before his time, way before! There will never be another," Aristides says regretfully.

A production stage manager, who worked with Cole, remembered his impatience with dancers who weren't getting the steps mastered fast enough. "And he wasn't terribly happy about taking breaks. He himself didn't require them, but he would do it, grudgingly. He was always dancing. He had a never-ending supply of energy. He could just go on forever, full-tilt. He couldn't understand why other people couldn't do the same. He told me he slept three hours a night and really didn't need any more than that. He was always highly energized, but he never seemed to me to be hyper."

Ron Field believes that Jack Cole gave him a lot, and not just the Cole Technique he mastered as a Jack Cole dancer. Cole's vision, his unusual ideas, his breadth of knowledge about the dance, partly gleaned from his remarkable dance collection and partly from experience, and his ability to know what the varying potentials of different dancers were—all these made deep impressions on Field. But he also learned some negative lessons, as well, he says. He watched how Cole worked, how his search for perfection drove him on—and sometimes drove young, inexperienced dancers to tears. As Field says of Cole's rehearsals, "Some people would decide they weren't going to be energetic. Jack needed 100 per cent. If you came in with 95 per cent, guess what? He'd say, 'Thanks, but maybe people with fat asses shouldn't be dancers.' That was it. He'd sensed 95 per cent that day. He only went for people with bad attitudes, attitudes he didn't like. A lot of times, it's the people you love most who may be disappointing you. Or there are three people whose work you don't like at all, but you are almost afraid to correct them. So you pick on someone you love. If you started on the others, you'd go crazy. I don't do that anymore. I'm able to talk about it. Jack helped me that way; now I don't pick on people."

There is at least one famed Broadway director who is known for his habit of picking some relatively minor member in a new cast and using him or her as a scapegoat for the sins and omissions of others. Reluctant to offend or fight with his stars, he takes it out on this underling. Everyone understands perfectly well what's going on, so if the stars have any compassion at all they try to avoid difficulties and spare the scapegoat the director's wrath. Cole could do such things, but he seldom did. It was his custom to attack the offending dancer, not a surrogate, but as has been noted, usually not directly in terms of what really needed correction or improvement. If this artful displacement of blame in Cole's sarcasm seems a bit sadistic, it may well have been. Several of Cole's former dancers have commented, almost without thinking, "I guess dancers are masochists anyway."

Jack Cole was able, however, to demand much from his dancers that they'd never have given another choreographer. One thing he was always longing to try was a nude dance rehearsal. Whatever the psychological basis of his interest in such an activity, he had the idea direct from Ted Shawn. When Cole was still at Jacob's Pillow, just before the men's group was firmly founded, he took part in some of Shawn's sessions of nude sunbathing, recreation, farmwork, and rehearsal. Cole preserved some photos of these seemingly innocent adventures in the Berkshire sunshine. Urging his dancers at the Columbia dancers workshop to try a nude class, Cole was turned down by the women. As Francine Ames makes clear, they were a little terrified of Cole and also respected him very much, but the women were all too horrified at the idea to cooperate. Cole had his way with the male dancers, however.

That was the day Cole fired Paul Steffen. He was at the back of the room, and the whole group of men, jaybird naked, were doing stretch exercises. In the crucial one, dancers first had to squat on the floor, then balance on their hands and push their rumps up in the air. Way up in the air. Steffan told Francine Ames about this odd experience later. As she tells it: "Because Paul was at the back of the rehearsal room, his only vision, when he put his head up, was to see every male dancer with genitals waving! He fell to the floor, clutching his stomach, and started to howl with laughter. Jack fired him. He said, 'This is serious!'" As with many other Cole firings of favored dancers, Steffen was back at work the next day.

Some of Cole's women dancers seem to have felt much closer to him than did most of the men who worked with him. But even they have difficulty explaining Jack Cole. Florence Lessing, long a partner and a friend, says, "He was a strange mixture of ego and lack of ego. I can't explain it, but I think it was compensation. I don't want to use psychiatric terms, but I think most people compensate now and then. Go off in the opposite direction to make up for some lacks. With Cole, it was outbursts of ego, and then periods of deep self-doubt.

"He was not a handsome man, but with makeup and his intense personality, he really was magnetic. He didn't like his looks, even aside from the fact that he had a cast to his eye. At the beginning of his career, he was very conscious of it, and it made difficulties for him. He tended to project in a different way because he was unhappy about it. A lot of people found it very interesting, and it certainly did give him a very intense expression. In the photos, he often looks ferocious. That's not just makeup. He *was* ferocious. When it came to the performance, his emotions were so sharpened that an explosion could occur at any minute. And it often did. He rehearsed and worked with such intensity. If the music went off or the tempos were wrong, he was ready to kill. He really was!"

Lessing sighs. "He was a fury! But he was a doll at the same time. . . . I loved him a lot. We were good friends, so he seldom exploded at me. But, where others were involved, I've seen him explode with people in a way that was scary, scary. He was so manic, so bursting with energy. He didn't seem to need rehearsals or exercises for himself, so much energy was coming from some inner core. But he had a lot of things suppressed inside him. If he could have got rid of it, life would have been much easier for him, I think. I don't know what it was, but he suffered a great deal from it. He was full of hostility and defensiveness. I said I wasn't going to use psychological terms, but I have to. He was also obsessive."

Whatever was suppressed, Jack Cole had been trying to deal with it, handle it, control it, exorcise it for years. Before he could accept an acting role in *Designing Woman*, he had to ask his psychiatrist's advice, so at that point in his career he was apparently having regular help. A decade before that, shortly after the close of the chapter with Columbia Pictures, which he'd designated as "A Period of Great Emotional Stress" in one of his astonishing full-page scrapbook doodle-collages, Cole was seeking aid from a distinguished psychiatrist. This man was the brother of an author who hoped Cole might work on a film version of one of her novels. She sent her brother a letter of introduction regarding Cole, begging him to spend "long hours in which to discuss what he wants and what is to be done." She didn't want Cole referred to others. It would be hard to find "another doctor who can match his intellect anyway."

She sent two of Cole's articles to the doctor so that he could know more about him and "sense the nature of his problems." Introducing him, she wrote: "He is Jack Cole, a dancer. Not just another one—and not just a fellow with problems—not someone mediocre, but an enlightening personality. Someone of the utmost refinement and a prominent artist in the real sense of the word." She came closer to one aspect of Cole's complex character in her final paragraph: "It is a spiritual, intellectual, and aesthetic pleasure to speak to this superbly artistic creature who is on the borderline between being human male and feminine, though he is not effeminate. This has made him the creator of fantastically erotic and, above all, highly artistic dance forms. He expresses through movements what others are unable to express in words."

Cole kept a copy of this letter. But there is another paper also preserved, of a more disturbing nature. It is only a set of mimeographed instructions, and there's no indication of whom they were intended for. The instructions are for coming to Grafton State Hospital, near Worcester, Massachusetts. There is some mention of mental illness, but the text stresses that the hospital is not a jail nor a penal institution. Apparently voluntary patients were accepted, as well as those who had no option. But whether this directly related to Cole or a close friend is unknown. Nor is it possible to know the year these instructions were given to him.

Cole's tremendous fund of energy, sometimes lacking adequate outlets and fueled by his impatience when things were not going as he wished, could expend itself on occasion in physical outbursts—in addition to verbal assaults—directed at dancers. As mentioned before it must be stressed that he seems to have been incredibly patient with students and dancers whom he could see were actually making their utmost efforts to learn the Cole Technique or steps he had set. But when he was dealing with a capable dancer who was *not* really working hard or paying attention, he could unleash an intimidating fury. How many girl dancers Cole dragged across the floor by their hair is difficult to establish. Most of his colleagues have at least one such story. Florence Lessing remembers an occasion or two when Cole seemed to have lost control. "He had a tremendous temper," she says. "He was famous for losing his temper."

Gwen Verdon says she never heard about Cole dragging a dancer by the hair, "but I do know he tried to throw a girl out of a second-story window. . . . I had fistfights with Jack, though. I'd grown up with an older brother, so I'd already learned to duck the punches. He never landed one on me! But he wasn't joking when he took a poke at me. He was mad. Most people wouldn't fight back. I did because I was just as mad as he was!

"We knew that when he got really angry, he could become deranged," Verdon says. "Absolutely deranged. And he had no patience with stupidity. He thought there was no excuse today for people to be uninformed about things. It has become so easy to get an education. But worse than being ignorant about things which could be learned, he thought, was being dense, aggressively stupid. He couldn't stand that. He couldn't understand, for instance, why people, after coming out of a revolving door or off an escalator, will just stand there, with all the people behind them bumping into them. He thought that was stupidity.

"When someone is as creative as Jack Cole was," Verdon insists, "I figure he deserves to be a little eccentric—whatever you want to call it. If he hadn't been so talented, I don't think anyone would have accepted how angry he could become. He could be so violent. But you didn't accept it in the sense of, 'Well, I *have* to have this job.' You accepted it because you knew you were really learning something. I think working for Jack Cole was the toughest work I've ever done in my life. Yet, for me, it was also the preparation for anything and everything I've done since!"

Gwen Verdon pauses, thinking about the monumental anger of talented choreographers. "I wanted to learn, even if he was angry. And I knew he didn't understand the anger himself. I mean, I've seen Bob [Fosse] get angry. He's no pussycat either. I saw him try to attack a guy who'd had a few beers and dropped a set on my feet. He was a stagehand in *Redhead*. So I've seen Bob get deranged, too. Jack wasn't the only one.

"When I first met Jack," Verdon remembers, "I thought he was terribly weird-looking. He scared me! I think he was blind in one eye then, so he'd cock his head in a funny way. He did have a rather strange body and a weird little head. He was really strange-looking. On stage, he looked about six feet tall. That's the first way I saw him: on stage, in performance, in makeup, in a nightclub. But then I met him with no makeup on. He was a strange-looking man.

"You could say I was in shock. But he was terribly shy. As he spoke with you, he could get very red in the face, almost apoplectic. Yet he was absolutely determined to get the very best you could give—even if you didn't think you could give anything special. *He* knew whether you could, and he'd drive you until he got it," she says. Although Cole could be both verbally and physically violent, Verdon can't remember a dancer ever suing him. "That means," she explains, "that they must have thought they deserved it. You became very aware of Jack's values. And he never drove anyone harder than himself!"

As a footnote to the infamous Cole temper and its visible manifestations, Verdon mentions his interest in religions, especially mystical and contemplative faiths of the Far East. He was, she says, catholic with a small *c*. Raised a Roman Catholic, he became interested in many beliefs, cults, and philosophies—perhaps another heritage from Denishawn. "He found truth in all religions," Verdon says. "We had to learn all about that—about reincarnation, about Buddha, Krishna. Jesus is the twenty-seventh incarnation of Buddha, and Krishna is the sixth. Many of the dances we did in nightclubs had that as their basis. *Big Noise from Winnetka?* Well, that was Krishna! A lot of the movement was based on old carvings of those stories."

Ethel Martin remembers his furies well. But, before discussing that aspect of his character, she insists on the importance of people in general—audiences for films, club acts, and shows, and not just dancers—knowing about the basis of Jack Cole's work and its pervasive influence on dance today. "It's unforgivable that there are so many books on modern dance, and Jack is never—or almost never—mentioned. If you care about dancing . . . if you care about contributions and influences, you should want to know about his life and career," she says.

"Well, I adored Jack. But I was also furious with him very often. You couldn't work with him and not be. He'd fire me six times and then rehire me two days later. We fought, Jack and I! Oh, he had a terrible temper. I wouldn't say that Jack's disposition wasn't evil enough to do you in if he could, but that was only part of it. I was feisty and fought him. We fought terribly, but I loved him. When I was very young, I couldn't separate the man from the talent," Martin admits.

"I thought he was a god, in his talent, and I expected him to behave like a god. But he didn't. Now I hope I've grown wiser about people. Then, he expected slavery from us—and he got it!," says Martin. She has her own Cole hair-pulling story: "The most violence I ever saw involved me. Jack and I met head-on during a rehearsal of *Kismet.* I had my hair in a bun and I let it down. It was very long. He grabbed it. We stood there, nose to nose, snorting at one another. I said, 'I'm not afraid of you!' He said, 'What do you mean, you're not afraid of me? I'll kill you!' 'Oh, you think you'll kill me, do you?' We screamed and snorted at each other. The next day, we met in the hall and he laughed and laughed about it. That's what I liked about Jack. He'd be furious, but overnight, he'd rethink the situation, and the humor of it would all take over." Apparently, just as Hal Schaefer has said of Cole's way of dealing with unpleasant situations he had provoked, Cole had decided to forgive Martin for the fight or have a good laugh about it. This was less embarrassing than to admit he'd been wrong.

Working with Cole, of course, was not all dance-slavery and insults. "He loved jokes," Florence Lessing recalls. "He used to laugh a lot. We had great jokes together. He loved Marcus Blechman for his sense of humor. Marcus was a close friend of both of us and he was one of the great wits. There are many stories about Marcus, very funny ones. Jack learned a lot from him, in many ways. Marcus was older and had this coterie of brilliant artists, dancers, singers, and musicians of all kinds. Jack was exposed to this circle of friends, so Marcus was a great influence on Jack's life."

Lessing recalls Cole in a wide range of situations. They used to date, and they even went on holidays together. "He'd be so wonderfully funny. We'd go out all night—nothing to do with dance—and roar with laughter at his jokes. We had such good times together!

"It's not easy to sum up Cole's life," Lessing says thoughtfully. "He was a lot of people—there were many facets to his personality. Some people, those who know only one aspect of him, may paint him as an ogre, saying he was cruel, a terror. And many people have said just that. On the other hand, he could be warm and funny in certain situations. . . . Well, not always . . . he had such a tense personality—but a many-faceted personality. So you will meet many Jack Coles if you talk with many people about him," says Florence Lessing.

"If it's a kid who worked with him, a lightweight with no talent, well, he would have had very bad treatment from Jack. If it was someone who was really beautiful, he would have gotten very good treatment. My! Jack admired and adored beautiful people! He really did! I say it in all modesty, but when I first met Jack, I was young, and he was taken with my looks. I knew very little about dancing actually, but I learned a lot from him. Oh, I had danced, but I was raw. His influence on me was terrific. He would forgive a lot of people lack of talent, if they were beautiful. . . . The reason he admired beautiful people so much was that he always considered himself very ugly. In fact, he was fascinating-looking. Not handsome, but certainly striking."

Asked for some Cole anecdotes, violent, humorous, or otherwise, Buzz Miller is shy about repeating any. "They're all unprintable," he says, with an elfin grin. "Cole was wonderful. He'd invite you to dinner and tell a string of very funny, often obscene, stories. He had a terrific sense of humor; he was very verbal, very articulate. But he could work you very hard, too. When I first joined him, he threw a difficult ethnic dance at me. I wasn't used to picking up steps. He was in a rage, but I was in a rage, too, so it canceled out. As a matter of fact, I threw a chair at him! But that was it, and then it was over." Miller recalls the agonies of rehearsing and performing film choreography, as well as the nightclub work. It took only six minutes, says Miller, to perform the show-stopping routine *Sing, Sing, Sing,* but its aftermath for the dancers was harrowing. "Everyone came off, gasped, and then threw up. It was a number which asked the impossible of you," says Miller.

For all Cole's genius, say those who were close to him, he never boasted. "He never put on airs," insists Ethel Martin. "He had a great disrespect for people who pretended to be what they were not. In all the years I worked with Jack, no matter how much success he had, you could always go to his house, sit on the floor, and call him 'Jack.' . . . I've known many other dancers who, the moment they had one Broadway success, suddenly didn't know you anymore. They changed their names, their pronunciation, their behavior. If you spend an evening with them, you will hear nothing but what they are doing. People like that are in the millions. Not Jack. He didn't brag; he didn't have to. And he'd want to hear about you.

"Jack wasn't afraid of being judged. He was contemptuous of that sort of thing. In his later days, Jack took to doing some weird things. If you met him, you'd laugh at his wit and brilliance, while he tore everything down. But, at the same time, you'd say, 'Whoof! I don't know what's got into him!' People were intimidated by him. But he was so bright, so unique. Once, Jack was supposed to do a show for Jayne Mansfield at the Dunes in Las Vegas. He couldn't and turned it over to me. I went out to the coast for preliminary meetings with the writers, and Jack was there to help us get started. I was astounded. He was talking about a special kind of costume. He said, 'You'll probably find it in the 1928 issue, June, I think, about the middle of the magazine.' And sure enough, there it was! He'd remembered that from a long time ago. But then he did have one of the largest private dance libraries in the world."

This was the impressive archive of which Cole was so proud, the one possession he really enjoyed showing off to visitors. Anna Austin and others who knew Cole well insist it was his intention for it to go to the UCLA library, but his longtime companion David Gray had it sold at auction in London at Sotheby's. In one of Cole's scrapbooks, there are photos of parts of his large collection, shelved in his spacious hilltop home on Kew Drive. There are also photos of Cole's five beloved cocker spaniels. These photos, as so many others in the seven huge Cole scrapbooks, are worked into intricate visual compositions, on which Cole must have spent hours with red, green, blue, and black inks, drawing all kinds of frames, borders, pillars, cornices, pedestals, foliage, and other doodle-devices. One wonders what Cole's psychiatrist would have made of these fantasies. Often Cole would cut away the rectangular borders of a photo, reducing it to a free form, concentrating on the central subject—which was frequently none other than Cole himself. In some photos, Cole is dressed as Harlequin. In others, he's stripped to boxer trunks, his body oiled. Or in a strap—or completely naked. He may have thought his face unattractive, but he seems to have been proud of his lithe, lean, athlete's body. Some shots show him in stylized combat with Rod Alexander and George Martin, all three tanned, oiled, muscles taut, posing in white trunks. One might call these fascinating scrapbook pages "doodle-collages." They seem to have absorbed some of Cole's restless energy between jobs. But he never finished mounting the materials. Several books repeat materials in others. Others are largely empty, but almost all of them have many loose photos, letters, telegrams, reviews, and other Cole memorabilia thrust between the pages, ready for mounting.

But, aside from early photos of himself, his mother, and his family, dating from the 1910s and 1920s, and the letters he wrote his mother from school, there is no material relating to the Cole family, nothing about his mother in later years, and very little about his own private life. Several friends have noted that Cole told them he didn't save such things. In the two major collections of Cole papers that have surfaced from the Sotheby's auction, there is little. It may well be that two other auction lots that were not sold will disclose some useful information; their current location—if they have indeed survived—is unknown. One of them, according to Sotheby's auction catalogue, includes Cole's credit cards and passports. One or more of these may be issued, not to Jack Cole, but to John Richter, his baptismal name, for Florence Lessing and others have said he used to have difficulties with the authorities on reentering the United States from Brazil or Cuba because of the German name in his passport.

Perhaps in these papers there are references to Jack Cole's wife, to his son, and to his grandsons. Many who worked with Cole had no idea he'd ever been married or was a father. Hal Schaefer heard about it only obliquely. After years as a touring bachelor musician, he was thinking of marrying and settling down. He asked Cole's advice. Schaefer remembers, "He said, 'I was married once.' He said it was the wrong life-style for him. But he had to live that way with a woman to see if it would work out." Anna Austin Crane believes Cole married a girl he knew in high school, in South Orange, New Jersey, around 1934, after which a son, Maximilian, was born in 1935. Tragically, Cole's young wife died in childbirth. Austin says she had a letter—now lost—in which Cole had written her the sad details. Because of Cole's constant touring and working in nightclubs, it wasn't possible for him to raise the boy, so he was cared for by the maternal grandparents. Later, the boy married and had two sons, of whom Cole was very proud. Cole used to show Austin their photos and talk about them. Apparently Cole did what he could financially to help his son and his grandchildren. One Cole colleague remembers Cole speaking of his son as: "My son, the accountant!" But he doesn't know whether that meant the son was actually an accountant. Austin says she has not been able thus far to establish contact with Cole's descendants. She also notes that Cole said that at the time he never told his own mother about his marriage.

Parts of Jack Cole's childhood and certain aspects of his personal life remain relative mysteries, which makes all the more ironic the fact that Cole had prepared special notebooks for his memoirs—much as he had had the seven red-bound scrapbooks made—but never found the time to record all these missing links in his life and what he thought about them. Given his satiric humor, his wide-ranging knowledge and experience, his uncompromising honesty, and his closely-guarded feelings of inferiority, what a witty and scathing memoir this would have been—sparing no one, neither Cole nor the studio moguls and Broadway producers who frustrated him.

What Cole did preserve, possibly for their amusement value, were interviews in which some bizarre rumors about Cole were exploded, only to be replaced by Cole's own imaginative interpretation of his past. Cole was not Balinese, as sometimes reported, nor was he the son of a Hindu prince, another bit of press-agentry he took pains to correct. He told interviewer Dorothy Rayner, "The closest I ever got to a Hindu temple was the *National Geographic*." He told another journalist that his maternal grandfather was an Irish tugboat captain. He also said his father was a New Brunswick pharmacist, a vital statistic which recurs in stories about Cole. He told Rayner that the tugboat captain used to spend time in the corner bar, bringing home a fish as a peace-offering. "Grandma accepted it always and beat him over the head with it." This sounds like Cole's love of a good story at work.

Sometime in 1937 or 1938, when Cole was at the peak of his popularity in the Rainbow Room, he met John David Gray, who was to share his life until death parted them in 1974. Gray had come to New York from Texas. People who knew Cole and Gray well thought this was a relationship, as a famous choreographer says, "ahead of its time," especially for its durability and mutual loyalty.

Gray preferred not to discuss his relationship with Cole for this account, talking instead about the problems of Cole's missing credits and royalties for the *Man of La Mancha* revival. He did, however, talk about with friends and with some of Cole's students from UCLA. He lauded Cole, as well he might. Visitors to their home remember how Cole used to praise Gray's varied talents as well. Hal Schaefer says of Cole and Gray: "Their relationship was very honest and true with each other for a very long time. It was very uncommon in those days. It was very classy, handled very well. That's probably why David didn't want to say anything. It was not 'Hollywood Style'; let me put it that way. They'd made a commitment to each other, and that was it."

As a young man, David Gray was, by all reports, extremely handsome and well mannered. It's understandable then, that Cole, secretly thinking of himself as unattractive and always attracted to beauty, should appreciate Gray's qualities. Robert Wright and George Forrest were well acquainted with Gray before they began working professionally with Cole, even before Cole met Gray. He later gave them some helpful advice when *Song of Norway* was in early rehearsals. Gray also helped Cole produce his club acts. Wright and Forrest met Gray through producer-director John Murray Anderson, who had a professional eye for attractive young performers. Anderson had discovered Gray in Texas where he was appearing in a Billy Rose show celebrating the state's centennial. Bob Wright recalls, "He looked like an English lord in those days—spectacular looking! . . . He could dance quite well, but I don't know whether he was trained as a serious dancer. But he was a knockout to look at, and he could function quite beautifully. He had cultivated speech, and he'd traveled all over the world. David knew everybody. David was a very, very brilliant young man. . . ."

When Cole first moved to Los Angeles, Wright and Forrest were living nearby. They gave him the names of good carpenters, plumbers, and painters. Later, when he had moved to his hilltop house, Cole was continually improving his premises. Ernie Eschmann describes it: "It was all marble. The floors, the walls. Someone said, 'My god! Another piece of marble and it would be a mausoleum.' 'Well,' he said, 'it's dedicated to Josephine Baker.' It was modern; I don't know what style. With a marvelous pool. It was on the top of a mountain range. The first time I went out there, I was stunned. Such a view from there! Like being on top of the Empire State Building, with the whole city of Los Angeles below you.

"So I wondered, 'What's he doing in that dinky apartment in New York City, when he's got all *this?*' But he said, 'The action's in New York, not out here.' He preferred New York. He had only a couple of rooms, but he liked it. 'New York,' he'd say, 'is where things are happening!' But he didn't do much. He'd just sit there and do needlepoint. Needlepoint, needlepoint, needlepoint! He had a little 9-inch TV set. That was all," Eschmann says. Cole's needlepoint, like his convoluted scrapbook doodling, was an outlet for frustrated energy. Jane Russell recalls this well: "He loved a joke. He'd much prefer you to send him a rude remark. And he used to do needlepoint and write rude words like 'Fuck You' and stitch them." Rod Alexander remembers one piece of needlepoint for its poignant and entirely appropriate Cole motto: "When My Ship Comes In, I'll Probably Be At The Airport." When the Black Panthers were in the headlines, Cole stitched a picture of a huge black penis. Under it he delicately threaded this title: "Black Power." After his death, Gray sent Ethel Martin a whole tea-crate of Cole needlepoint. Martin says they are outrageous. And even the ones she thinks are amusing enough to hang have to be displayed in places where they can easily be removed if prim visitors are expected. One piece of Cole's handiwork is a rectangular pillow bearing the alarming information: "Mary Pickford Sucks." If that's not outrageous enough, Cole permitted this pillow to be used as a prop for a color photo taken in his backyard by a Los Angeles maker of male films. Squinting in the Southern California sunlight, a slack-jawed and apparently dim-witted youth stands completely naked. He holds Cole's Mary Pickford pillow in front of him, but not where common decency would suggest. Cole also kept a scrapbook in his New York apartment, but it wasn't anything like his seven Los Angeles books, filled with fascinating Cole drawings and career memorabilia. Instead, it held a collection of cutout photos of male models, mostly unencumbered by confining garments, accompanied by advertising slogans or newspaper headlines Cole had found and pasted under the proud young men. Innocent in themselves, these mottos and slogans take on an entirely new meaning, both comical and suggestive, coupled with the photos. Cole at least had a sense of the ridiculous side of pornography.

At home in Los Angeles, Cole was a kindly host. He was always eager to give strangers and friends alike the grand tour of his collection. He loved gourmet cooking and preferred to entertain at home. Wright and Forrest, who remember a number of excellent Cole-cooked meals, say he really did not like to eat out. Dinty Moore's in New York and Buchbinder's in Philadelphia were among the few restaurants he approved of. When he did go out, says Hal Schaefer, he always demanded the best for his guests—and he always insisted on picking up the check.

When Dolores Gray was at MGM, she'd have Cole over for dinner, and he'd invite her for gourmet meals. He was, she says, "homely, in the English sense of loving his home. He'd have workmen up there, month after month, year after year, refining and adding, doing things to his home. He loved his home!"

Considering all the stresses and strains of Cole's work at the film studios, it would seem only natural, after a hard day's work, for him to come home and find David Gray ready with a cool drink, Cole's dressing gown, and dinner on the stove. Friends who were often guests in the home find such an image amusing. It was Cole who did the cooking and made sure that Gray had a nice cool drink. And, while Gray was unfailingly correct to all visitors and most often cordial, some had the sensation that he was only tolerating them for Cole's sake.

Although a favorite Cole motto reputedly was, "Yea, Though I Walk Through the Valley of Death, I Will Fear No Evil, for I Am the Meanest S.O.B. in the Whole Damn Valley," this dance-director tiger at MGM or Fox was transformed into a pussycat at home. It's not, however, unusual for mates who are dominant, forceful and aggressive on the job to play a passive or servile role at home. Some think Cole was even a bit afraid of Gray, possibly of losing him. Cole was, after all, not an easy person to know or get along with, and he was riddled with insecurities. Barton Mumaw, a decade after Cole's passing, was still reminded of Cole's cavalier behavior as a member of Ted Shawn's troupe: "He would use your toothbrush as his own, flick his cigarette ashes in your saucer, leaving his unsullied—small acts, but lethal in daily relationships." Mumaw, like so many other Cole intimates, found his good qualities far outweighed either thoughtless or calculated selfishness. As he says, "Despite his ego, his vagaries, Jack Cole was eminently lovable. He had ingratiating ways, was intensely interesting as a person, highly opinionated about people, politics, religion, the arts. He was of the earth, earthy, and of the spirit, celestial."

Alfred Drake, who cherishes warm memories of Cole and his talent, was once given a birthday party in Cole's beautifully landscaped yard. *Kismet* was playing its first revival on stage in Los Angeles. A pavilion was decorated with streamers and all kinds of messages for Drake—all of it arranged by Cole. Drake marveled at the pool—80° all the time, rain or shine. He said, "It's a big bathtub! Throw in the soap!" Cole knew how interested Drake was in the history of the performing arts, as well as in fine books and artworks. "I think he was delighted when I first saw his library and told him how envious I was that a man could actually build a cottage to store his books in, when I've done nothing but build bookcases all over my home," Drake says.

Even when Cole had been drinking, Drake found, he was never very revealing about himself. If he said anything about himself, he'd do it in a deprecating way: "Isn't *that* a joke!" But Drake understood it wasn't a joke to Cole at all. He spoke of his unhappy childhood and his Catholic upbringing. He mentioned his marriage and his child in passing. "Jack Cole was not someone you felt you were ever going to get terribly close to," Drake explains. Nonetheless, he says, he felt very warm toward Cole. "And I had the feeling that he liked me. I did admire his talent tremendously, of course. I loved it anytime he would illustrate something and do a little dancing. He was electric to watch. But I also felt about him that there was another Jack Cole underneath that we were never going to get to know very well. But I think I would have liked that man. . . ."

Even when Cole was in New York, doing his X-rated needlepoint and watching his 9-inch TV, he was bursting with nervous energy. As in Los Angeles, he worked out at a gym daily. Often he asked Ernie Eschmann, a professional masseur, to join him at the gym. He had told Jane Russell that he had to work out every day or he'd go berserk. "I get absolutely crazy," he said, when he'd missed a day's exercise. Once he told Eschmann to drop by Jane Russell's apartment to pick him up for a workout. Russell was hoping to do a musical revival and had asked for Cole's advice, but he didn't want to miss his gym appointment. Eschmann called from downstairs for Cole, but Russell insisted he join them. "Russell and Cole and some friends were 'holding court.' Once he got started, he could never stop. I wished I'd had a tape recorder. We didn't get out until six o'clock! It was entertaining as hell. She'd decided to do *Lady in the Dark*—or was it *Company?* Cole said he'd help her but she'd have to knuckle down and work seriously. It came to nothing."

From the workouts, it became clear to Eschmann that Cole really did have bad knees, and a bad foot as well. There were times when he feared Cole would have to give up his work, but Cole had such determination he mastered the suffering and kept on going. From the masseur's standpoint, aside from these disabilities, Cole had no special physical problems. He recalls however that Cole had very high arches. Cole said that only Martha Graham had higher arches than he did, Eschmann remembers. Cole would tell student dancers he wanted them to stand when he came in, says Eschmann, as a mark of respect, just as Cole stood when Martha Graham entered a room. Watching some of Cole's warm-ups for dancers made Eschmann glad he didn't have to do them daily. They were often at the Henry Hudson Gym on the West Side. "He was very tough," says Eschmann. "He wouldn't do weights. He'd do stretching. He could do that at home, but he went to the gym for it. 'Take it easy!' I'd say. 'You're doing too much.' He also liked to walk fast. He'd say, 'People get out of your way when you're coming and they see you're walking fast. If you just saunter along, they'll get in your way.' "

Cole didn't let much get in his way in a brilliant—if uneven—career and a tempestuous life. Five months before his brief, final illness with cancer, he had his gall bladder removed. Heading his comical, if groggy, letter, "In the heart of beautiful downtown Burbank," he wrote to Eschmann about the experience. He'd never be able to eat pickled pigs' feet again, he said. He was worried about meeting his UCLA modern dance class, for the university's fall quarter would begin soon. Recurring pain brought recurring shots of something to send him on a little trip. Cole wrote Eschmann in a large, painstaking hand. He told him he didn't know why they didn't keep him that way the whole time because it was such a wonderful feeling. The pain was gone in about the slow count of twenty, and he felt wonderfully warm and snoozy.

Cole was eager to get out. He thought he could manage that, he said, if he played the second act curtain of *Stella Dallas* in full sets and costume for his doctor. His fellow patients were getting on his nerves, when he wasn't all warm and snoozy. He told Eschmann that an old man down the hall who was senile was out roaming the hall again. The nurses were trying to get him back in the room while he kicked and screamed. They finally had to get him in a straitjacket and sedate him. A nurse was trying to cover up the old gentleman, Cole told Eschmann, when the old man announced that his balls hadn't been much to look at for fifty years and he didn't care who looked at him now.

Even in pain and nearing the end of his long fight for recognition and perfection, Cole hadn't lost his ability to be outrageous and humorous at the same time.

13

DANCE AS HIGH ART

COLE'S TRIBUTE TO TERPSICHORE

Jack Cole's most ardent admirers often wished he had chosen to serve the Muse of Dance as seriously as had Martha Graham. His own research into ethnic dance was never questioned, and he had compiled one of the largest private collections of dance manuscripts, references, and artworks. He kept extensive notes on aspects of dance history and practice. Cole's ferocious dedication to the discipline which dance demands is legendary. Today dancers, directors, conductors, and dance critics still testify to Cole's angry outbursts at any kind of imperfection in rehearsal or during performance. He set the very highest standards for both himself and his dancers in physical fitness and in performing.

And yet, Cole's fans and those many reviewers who admired his talents found themselves apologizing for his commercial success on Broadway, in films, and in nightclubs. His ideas for dances, his innovations in patterned movement, his adaptations of classical ethnic forms to jazz, and his inspirations in creating milieus for his choreography all argued a kind of genius.

There were few professional dance critics in the early 1930s when Cole first began to attract attention with his nightclub performances. John Martin and the late Walter Terry were, at that time, the best-known and the most widely respected of dance critics. Although they were mainly concerned with chronicling and critiquing the serious dance scene in America, once in a while Terry and Martin found time to see Cole in a supperclub performance. Their admiration for Cole's ingenuity, fantasy, intensity and astonishing technique is a matter of record. They often felt, however, that Cole's amazing skills were in the service of dances—and perhaps audiences as well—that simply were not demanding enough. Despite Cole's obvious brilliance, Terry occasionally wrote that he sensed something was missing. When Cole's choreography won rave reviews for his work on Broadway or in Hollywood musicals, the praise was usually bestowed by critics who had little or no knowledge of dance. Their appreciation was genuine enough, but these critics were not well-informed. As a result, aside from giving Cole a moment of ego-gratification, their reviews could not have spurred Cole on to new challenges. He had to be his own spur.

Enthusiasts for Cole's Technique and choreography did not have the reservations of Martin or Terry. Even today Cole dancers and fellow choreographers insist that his choreographic achievements and critical raves would have been even greater, if only he had made an effort to work part of the time in the arena of serious American dance rather than restrict himself to commercial ventures. Such an attitude may seem odd to non-professionals; in fact, many dancers and choreographers themselves would be happy to achieve success in merely one of the several areas in which Cole was effective.

Movie buffs and aficionados of Broadway musicals may be pardoned for regarding Cole's major film and stage choreography as outstanding examples of serious American dance. Even the Charleston has become an American classic. But this usually takes years, and Cole's commercial choreography has largely disappeared, except for that filmed in Hollywood or reconstructed by Lee Theodore's American Dance Machine.

When Cole was at the height of his creative and physical powers, serious dance critics could take *him* seriously, but not most of his choreography. It is clear that Cole longed for their approval. He kept a letter from John Martin inviting him to participate in the fourth annual Dance Festival at Carnegie Hall to benefit the Spanish Refugee Appeal. It must have been flattering to be asked. Other related items he preserved were notes from La Meri, from her School of Natya at the Ethnological Dance Center, and a report about Walter Terry having resigned after a relatively brief period as director of the Jacob's Pillow Dance Festival. Cole must have understood very well Terry's dilemma. He wanted to program exciting, innovative work, but the board, which Ted Shawn dominated, insisted he guarantee that each season would at least break even. Terry knew he couldn't promise that. Cole treasured a newspaper report that cited him for breaking the path for serious dance at the Rainbow Room, making the way clear for others such as Agnes de Mille, Hugh Laing, and Ruth Page and Bentley Stone. Also among Cole's souvenirs were photos of Uday Shankar, performing and informal, relaxing with his son; Van Damm portraits of the famed Chinese classical actor Mei Lan Fang, and many photos of Eugene Loring's choreographic work for American Ballet Theatre.

Ron Field succinctly explains why Cole didn't make a major effort to mount serious, non-commercial works: "He took the jobs that came along." Hal Schaefer agrees, saying, "Jack Cole was a genius, but he had to pay a high price for it, being in the commercial field rather than on a concert stage." Barton Mumaw notes that Walter Terry, who was fond of Cole, was always urging him to work more in the serious, classical areas of dance. Asked if Cole did not in fact do more for popularizing dynamic modern dance by bringing his work before an audience of millions, via motion pictures, television, stage musicals, and even club acts, rather than choreographing precious works for necessarily limited audiences of dance enthusiasts, Mumaw emphatically agrees. Proof of the strength of Cole's choreography, says Mumaw, is the success he enjoyed in the commercial arenas. "I think a nightclub stint would be good for every dancer who is classical," Mumaw says quite seriously. George Martin says, "I don't know a person who ever saw a Cole dance—even the nightclub patrons—who didn't know he was seeing something fabulous! To watch Cole dance was a staggering experience. There are few like that: Baryshnikov, a few others. Jack was also an intellectual, but he was more than that. With some geniuses in musical theatre, it's all from the neck up. With Jack, it also worked down here." Martin indicates the groin. "His work had balls! And it was even more powerful up close on the nightclub stage."

Jack Cole aspired to becoming a choreographer of serious works as well as the founder-mentor of a concert ensemble. But there were always prior commitments, other engagements, the jobs that "came along," as well as personal detours and deflections. On occasion, when friends or admirers would ask him why he hadn't already launched a serious concert group, if he

didn't lose his temper at the implied challenge, he'd be quick
to refer to his early fear from the Denishawn and Humphrey-
Weidman days: starving to death while performing at the 92nd
Street "Y" and on college campuses around the country. In the
1930s and 1940s, there was only a small, if appreciative, dance
public. Big national tours of dance and ballet troupes in major
regional theatres were virtually unknown—until the late 1940s
at least. College touring meant weeks and months of dreary
travel and often unrewarding one-night stands. That Cole already commanded top fees in clubs, films, and stage musicals
must surely have reinforced his idea of the kind of poverty and
starvation serious concert touring would involve.

Endless touring and performing for large, often undiscrim-
inating, audiences was wearing down Cole's limited fund of
patience. He told Marie Mesmer: "When I was young in the
dance, I wanted to do 'jumps,' and the larger the audience, the
higher I wanted to jump. Now, I have a personal idea about
the dance. And while the cross-country tour of eight months
has provided the opportunity for my group to work for technical proficiency, the opportunity for creative work, planning,
and thinking has lessened. . . .

"Ruth St. Denis once told me that giving a performance was
like making love to an audience. There is a vibration one feels
coming from the audience and, in our particular type of dancing it is a needed factor or else we 'turn in' and give a routine
performance." Excitement in the audience, generated by the
excitement of Cole's dancers, in turn spurred them on. But such
was the concentration and involvement required for a dance like
Cuban Nanigo—where the dancers were working up to the climax of feeling "possessed"—that the slightest disturbance in the
audience "disturbs the unity of the mood and its completion,"
he explained. Cole admitted that he understood from long experience what the distractions of a tinkling glass can be, but now,
he felt, "an environment can move in on you." Cole told Mesmer
that he'd reached artistic fulfillment in the club medium. If he
did not now do what he wanted to do and in the way he wanted
to do it, "I may as well be planting geraniums," he said.

Cole told Mesmer that Miss Ruth was his spiritual mother.

He recalled some of her early advice: "When you go on stage, dance as if it were the last time you will ever dance." With such a high standard for himself and his dancers, Cole insisted, "I must provide the stimulating atmosphere in which the dance can be fully nurtured." And Cole was not alone in this feeling. "Whenever I get an idea, I look at the 'kids' to see if they think differently. We all agree crowding seven or eight dances into a night's performance and working in high gear as we do is bound to tear down the standards we want to maintain."

This was in 1948, but Cole did nothing positive about fulfilling himself artistically on the concert stage. The following year, he did get a serious credit, but it wasn't what his previous statements would have led a dance addict to expect. *Dance Magazine* reported: "Jack Cole's first appearance on a concert stage in New York in many years occurred October 28th at the Ethnological Dance Center. Mr. Cole lectured and had a demonstration on artistic considerations for ethnic departures. . ."

In the early 1950s, Cole wrote to Arthur Todd, explaining— or excusing—his inactivity on the dance concert stage: "I have been asked to do a series of concerts here and abroad, all of which will have to wait on the development of a school." Cole was clearly still missing his Columbia Pictures dance workshop. Nor did he take the necessary steps to establish his own school. In the same letter, just before this comment, Cole said, "My teaching was interrupted by long transcontinental tours, several of which took me from home for a period of a year or so. For the past two years, I have taught for short periods of time at Eugene Loring's school. I intend to stay out here and organize a permanent school. California is a real frontier, and there is an entire world open for pioneering. Eugene Loring, Carmelita Maracci, and Lester Horton just about covers the active field, and, if we might even get together, we might move things. The sun does shine, and it is slow." Even then the pace of Southern California was "laid-back."

When Cole was on the defensive about his seeming neglect of serious dance, he'd respond, with some justification, that the work he was doing at any given time, in whatever circumstances, was always the best he could do. His reviews certify that. The flaw in Cole's defense was that his choreography was also conditioned, at least in films and on stage, by the quality and the quantity of the plots and non-dancing performers with which he had to work. Nor should it be forgotten that both Broadway and Hollywood musicals were then being created under the most pressured, chaotic, and, occasionally, sordid of circumstances. That something sometimes approaching *art* was able to emerge at all is astonishing. Producers and audiences were, after all, quite content if musical films and shows were nothing more than entertaining. No one expected a serious message from *Eadie Was a Lady,* nor did they get one. Even when Cole specifically invoked the classical Muse of Dance, Terpsichore, in *Down to Earth,* achievement of High Art doesn't seem to have been a conscious goal, even though Cole helped Rita Hayworth dance like a goddess in the film.

Somehow, Cole always managed to put off that fateful day when he might have to show his talents as a male Martha Graham. Some of Cole's co-workers insist he was always too busy. Others think having a concert ensemble was only a pleasant pipe dream for Cole, and that he used his commercial commitments as an excuse to avoid a critical confrontation with serious dance reviewers, had they been allowed to judge such a venture. In 1950, however, Cole did make an abortive effort to establish a concert repertoire, when he created *Harlequin's Odyssey.* It was featured in both *Parade* and *Dance Magazine.* Cole played an anguished Harlequin, a role with which he identified, balanced by Gwen Verdon as the "Golden Woman," who represented Fate.

The article in *Parade* noted that the dance was produced in Cole's backyard for the magazine's cameras in a total of six hours, with a cost of $5 for materials and props. Cole used a *Santo,* a religious image recalling the holy figures in *Magdalena.* There were some giant tarot cards. Verdon was garbed in what seemed lengths of cheap cheesecloth. Cole told *Parade* he thought the clown character, in the framework of this story, would have wide appeal, even if toured abroad. As he said, "Basically, it's simple. The Clown is a symbol of all people. He leads a wonderful and brave existence. If I can really become Harlequin the Clown,

I can speak to people anyplace in the world and be understood."

At this point in his career, Cole was obviously at loose ends. A new spate of film-making was shortly to begin, but he didn't yet know that. He had been performing in *Alive and Kicking* on Broadway during its short run. He'd turned down—all in the same day—a Michael Todd offer to choreograph on Broadway and a Hollywood proposal to act a film role. He even said, "Betty Grable is very attractive indeed, but, just the same, I don't feel like dancing with her." With the abandonment of the Columbia dance workshop and his other cinema dance obligations, Cole had quit at the height of his career; he said he'd been earning $5,000 per week, very good for the mid-1940s. He said he'd given up his club dancers because "I want to dance my own dances." But he also had five cocker spaniels, "and they've got to eat." So a concert tour at least seemed attractive. "I want to be a sort of 'eternal clown,' being comic or sad or gay to any audience anywhere," Cole explained. This feature was headed: "Jack Cole: An Interpretive Dancer's Lot Is a Hard One." In addition to the photos illustrating *Harlequin's Odyssey*, *Parade* reproduced a photo of Cole and a colleague in nothing but boxer trunks. Cole seems to be giving the other dancer a KO, a knockout. *Parade* editors noted: "Rigors of dancing are more strenuous than ten rounds in the ring."

Ten rounds in the boxing ring is an interesting comparison for Cole choreography. No wonder some of his dancers continually refer to their aggressive character. At least Cole completed this one in six hours. Some Broadway dance sequences he never managed to finish.

It's fairly easy to understand a self-pitying Cole seeing himself as Harlequin in this little symbolic dance. On a page of his scrapbooks, he pasted tiny photo cutouts of hands and arms swathed in cords and bonds. These were illuminated by a welter of hand-drawn red and green arrows. Did these images symbolize Cole's fettered and restricted talent, lured—or driven—constantly here and there, instead of being focused on one important goal? The photo images from the *Odyssey* that Cole used in his doodle-collages certainly suggest this dance was significant for him. And yet, on the evidence of these photographic images and Cole's outline of the action—admittedly without the actual dance movement to animate the conception—the piece seems to be high-minded aesthetic *kitsch*.

It's entirely possible that Cole's reluctance to choreograph serious works and to establish a concert ensemble was conditioned by his own inferiority complex. He may have feared that he did not have sufficient inspiration, learning, or understanding to create a major serious dance work. He was very intelligent; that has been made abundantly clear by those who worked with him. He was largely self-educated, in no small way through the amazing dance collection he'd been building up. Cole respected learning, but he'd only had two brief semesters at Columbia before joining Denishawn. In his work, he had a genius for detail, for polishing to perfection. He was immensely clever in devising steps, relating them to specific situations, costumes, props, or performers. He knew how to explore and boldly project the movement and emotive potential of a dancer's body. But in most of his dances, there is little evidence of an overriding philosophy or an intriguing comment on human follies beyond the domain of satire.

Cole's choreography was crammed with energetic action and teeming with details, as though he hated pauses and contemplation. There was little time for thought in a frenzied dance that had to "flash" by a nightclub audience in a few minutes, or make its visual effect in a film or in a Broadway musical in a similarly short span. As things were, kitsch was very much at home in Hollywood film production. Had Cole not been so closely bound to his three or four commercial dance arenas, he might have risen above the demands they imposed, the habits they fostered, to take a longer view of human life and emotion in dance. Had he possessed a different kind of intellect, had he been able to control his own passions more effectively, he might also have created some really serious works of dance. Fortunately for him, some of his major film and Broadway dance routines are being considered "classics" by knowledgeable dance folk.

Before Cole died in 1974, Lee Theodore dined with him at

his Hollywood home. She told him about her plans for the projected American Dance Machine and her hopes of reconstructing and preserving some of his once-celebrated but now forgotten Broadway dance sequences. "He said he thought it was a swell idea," she recalls. "But now, whenever I'm struggling to make it work, I think of him and his bizarre sense of humor. I think he must be laughing at me. But he did say he should have formed his own company: a concert company. He didn't manage it; he was always too busy." If he had been able to assemble and train such an ensemble, Theodore thinks it could have preserved much of Cole's work in a way that would have enabled critics and audiences to see it as serious choreography, standing on its own.

George Martin shakes his head at Cole's excuses, recollected a decade after his death. "When he had the nightclub act, Jack could have said to any of us, especially to Ethel, me, Rod Alexander, and Bob Hamilton: 'Listen, I *can't* do this anymore. I'm not making any money.' He couldn't have been making money with all the expenses he had—and insisting on the best costumes and musicians. He was paying six to eight dancers $125 per week, with transportation back and forth across the country. We never played more than eight weeks. That was a long engagement. But he could have said: 'I can't do it anymore, kids. We're going to have a serious group. If you have to make a living, you can work in pictures, and we'll do some serious work at night.'

"We would have done it! Eight hours in pictures, and then we'd have worked with him. We did that, really, when we were studying with him. When we were in the Columbia workshop from 9 to 5, we'd go to classes with Carmelita Maracci at night. But he got angry. He didn't form a serious group. Instead, he said we were bleeding him. He said, 'I'm dissolving the act.' We always thought he was angry at *us*." What Martin finds especially sad, in retrospect, is that in Los Angeles at that time, even with so many talented choreographers, teachers, and dancers working in films—and later in television—there was no major classical company of the first rank nor was there yet an outstanding modern ensemble. There was virtually a dance performance vacuum, with a potential audience of thousands; Cole could have helped fill this void.

Like Martin, Buzz Miller remembers frequent Cole comments about a concert group. "In fact," says Miller, "he talked incessantly of having this wonderful concert company in New York. But he never got around to it. There was always a movie to do, and there was good money in nightclubs. He was a driven man, filled with energy. He was just too impatient. It's probably as simple as that."

Florence Lessing has another explanation for Cole's failure to realize his dream of a concert ensemble. "He was such a great creative talent," she insists. "I do think it was a shame he never went into the concert field, but that had to do with some feelings of inferiority. In his prime, he couldn't have choreographed for ballet companies because they were doing a real minimum of modern pieces—modern dance, I mean. But Jack had wonderful ideas. We did an *Irish Wake,* for instance. What an interesting piece it was! Jack could have become a great concert artist."

Gwen Verdon repeats Cole's complaints about modern dancers in his day being condemned to starvation and performances at the 92nd Street "Y." Cole's major commercial work was being created at a time when there were few foundations and even less funding for the arts. To form and sustain a concert troupe, Cole would have had either to find a gold-lined patron or to search endlessly for grants. "Jack said you'd either have to prostitute yourself to get a patron or settle for Kaufman Hall," reports Verdon. "Jack wanted to make money so he could pay his dancers. If he couldn't pay well, he would not be able to get the best dancers. Like me—and I had a son to support. Art was wonderful, but I had to buy milk and lamb chops!"

Cole often talked about the idea of a company with Ethel Martin. She was one of the last of the Cole nucleus to work with him professionally, helping recreate his dances in musical revivals. When Cole put together a club act for the Casino du Liban in Beirut, Martin says she told him: "There's not one of us who wouldn't drop what we're doing and give you six months of our time—if you really want to do this. We'll just put what we're doing on hold."

Looking back, she suspects that Cole's problem was oddly similar to that of another dancer Martin considers to have been great, Carmelita Maracci. Like Cole, Maracci was a dancer of power and invention; she had trained her company beautifully, something also typical of Cole. "She put together some wonderful programs out on the West Coast. Her company was excellent, and she drilled it diligently. Then she'd announce she was bringing it to New York, but, as the time drew near, something would always happen to prevent that. She'd suddenly fall ill and have to cancel. I think there was something of that in Jack's behavior, too." Considering the number of times Cole confessed to interviewers that he could hold down only liquids because his stomach was so nervous when he was working on a show or a film, this is more than mere speculation. Even without the demands a serious repertory and ensemble would have made on him, Cole put himself through more than enough stress and strain in the commercial arenas of dance.

For Ethel Martin, it is "the hurt of my life, the most stupid thing the dance world has ever allowed to happen," that Cole's contributions as a teacher-trainer and as a choreographer seem to be sinking from sight without leaving much of a trace and almost no critical comment. Martin is not the first to suggest the dual importance of Jack Cole and Agnes de Mille in changing the nature of dance on Broadway. De Mille's contributions have been justly and widely celebrated and chronicled; they are now part of theatre and dance history. Not so with Cole's work.

Instead of being satisfied with giving Broadway audiences what Martin calls "a nice fun time," Cole and de Mille both insisted on providing exciting, artistic, and meaningful dances. When modern dance in America was just beginning to emerge into prominence, and Denishawn disciples were able to create serious works which were noticed by critics and the public, there was still very little in the way of either public or private arts subsidy for non-profit dance ensembles. So Cole took the route which would at least enable him to pay his dancers. Thus, Ethel

Martin sees Cole as fearful of failure in the arena of serious dance, but, at the same time, anxious to feed his troupe. The second may have been a covering excuse for the first.

There is real irony, with current subsidies for the performing arts, how little there is in the way of impressive dance creativity, although there are certainly a great many choreographers at work. This is especially painful to former Cole dancers who still wish he'd formed a troupe. Ethel Martin speaks for them all when she forcefully says, "It's astounding how *many* dance companies are being sponsored in America. They really have very little to say, very little! I'd have no trouble now getting a grant to form a company if I'd say that I wish to speak in my dances about the inner cosmos of the outer energy of our time whereby extreme energy is expanding throughout. I could say this in six different ways, and I'd get a grant. Why? Because they'd say, 'She really had something important to say!'" Gwen Verdon characterizes a lot of this fashionable avant-garde dance activity as *loft-dancing,* the kind one does in one's loft.

Actually, dance subsidies are not so easy to get now as they were in the 1960s and 1970s. Still, if Jack Cole were alive today, one can speculate whether the arts panels of various foundations would really believe he had something important to say. Since he hated both pretension and amateurishness, for him loft-dancing would be an impossibility. But, while de Mille and Jerome Robbins won plaudits both on Broadway and on the ballet stage, Cole never achieved the latter. If he had been invited to choreograph for the New York City Ballet, or if he had formed his own concert company, one can only imagine what might have been.

It is just possible that nothing would have come of either venture. To understand why, it is necessary to go back to Cole's earlier attempts to do really serious work. In his younger days, Cole once offered his own interpretation of Baudelaire's *Les Fleurs du mal* in a studio performance before his peers. They may have appreciated it, but a critic who wrote about the dance was most unkind to Cole, finding him "a symbol of vague sexuality."

In later years, he was careful not to expose himself, either as a dancer or a choreographer, to such criticism. He had much better luck with critics when he choreographed the New York City Opera's production of Alberto Ginastera's opera, *Bomarzo*, in 1967. This was a mordant musical tale of the physically and mentally warped Duke of Bomarzo, whose fantastic garden of grostesque stone figures still stands on his estate near Viterbo, in Italy. Buzz Miller and Barbara Sandonato were the opera's featured dancers. Cole created movement for them which evoked the elegant dances of the story's historical period but, at the same time, echoed the distortion and torment in the strange sculptures in the garden of Bomarzo, carvings that mirrored the deformities and twisted passions of the duke.

Ginastera was Argentine. So was the opera's stage director, Tito Capobianco, and its designer, José Varona, creator of a number of important American opera, ballet, and stage designs. It was always very important to Cole that the choreography and the stage milieu, the settings, the costumes, the lighting, should complement each other. They ought, Cole thought, to enhance the total effect, rather than to impede or work against one another. Varona was entirely in agreement. "It was such a great pleasure. He was such an intelligent, gifted man. A genius! There was such taste in what he did."

During the rehearsals, Cole's taste did not always extend to his choice of words or images in helping the performers arrive at a tasteful solution to the opera's varied staging problems. Cole enjoyed telling friends about several incidents during production that indicated he'd lost none of his Hollywood bluntness.

For an orgiastic dance sequence, a kind of exciting and frightening dream ballet, Cole wanted dancers who weren't overly modest. One girl protested she wasn't a stripper. He told her not to worry. She wouldn't have to. He'd get someone else. She could go home; she didn't get the job. Apparently Cole wanted some of the dancers in this sequence to bare their breasts. Then there was the problem of the foreign soprano who sang the role of the duke's disappointed wife. She habitually sang with her right arm extended and her left hand on her breast. Cole watched this with some interest, perhaps previously unaware of how appalling much operatic "acting" was and is. He knew the singer admired his work and he thought she respected him, so he called the translator to tell her what he thought of her performance. Cole asked him to tell her that ninety per cent of the audience wouldn't understand a word of the sung Spanish text. "But they understand gestures. Now the duke is hunchbacked. When he comes over to you, hunched over like that, and you stand there with your right arm out that way and your hand on your breast, the audience is going to think you are singing: 'My tit is tender, and if you come any closer, I'm going to slap you across the face!' "

The translator was aghast. "I cannot tell Madame such a thing!" he protested. "Tell her *Mr. Cole* said it," Cole directed. When the translator relayed this message, the singer's eyes rolled. But, boasted Cole, she never did that again!

Bomarzo was given its world premiere in Washington, D.C., May 19, 1967. It had been banned in Argentina owing to some of its perverse and erotic subject matter, which only made it more attractive to Cole, who could also sympathize with the duke. The following season, the New York City Opera's then artistic director, Julius Rudel, brought the production to the New York State Theatre in Lincoln Center.

If ever Jack Cole longed for a splendid critical tribute to his choreography as a serious work of art, he certainly achieved it in the glowing critique of Paul Hume, the distinguished music critic of the *Washington Post*. He said in part: "Special praise, too, must go to Jack Cole for creating choreography that flowed through and around the central action, lascivious in the erotic ballet that is the acme of the opera, of courtly grace at the coronation." For Hume, something very important had happened to dance in *Bomarzo:* "Both in the central role they fill and the singular responsibility that is theirs, the dancers in this opera occupy an historic position." Hume noted that *La Traviata* can survive quite well in production, even if the dancing in Act III is indifferent. *Carmen* can succeed without great dancing in Lillas Pastia's tavern. He might well have added that some operas seem improved by the deletion of their ballets, which were originally often nothing more than diversions for the members of Paris's Jockey Club.

"But in *Bomarzo* there are dream sequences in which an

idealized figure of the Duke dances, freed from the weight on his back, able to mix in the joy and the sexual equality with the beautiful women upon whom, in actual life, he can only look with impotent longing." For Hume, Cole's dream choreography was a scene of "amazing power." Also, Cole was choreographing with unaccustomed subtlety. "Often, during the opera, the dancers must suggest by the subtlest gesture or movement, that there is more beneath the surface of their dancing than outward appearances present," Hume wrote. He judged that all the elements of music-theatre had been welded into a "totality of overwhelming power." Unfortunately for the historic position of Cole's dancers in this opera production—and for Cole's dances—*Bomarzo* didn't stay in the New York City Opera's repertory. Jack Cole's highly effective choreography and orchestrating of other stage movement vanished.

Buzz Miller was cited by both Herbert Kupferberg and Harriett Johnson for his dance as a grim, floating skeleton. Kupferberg's attention was captured by the visions of devils and various monsters. He told his readers there was "a good deal of orgiastic dancing." Johnson, writing in the *New York Post*, praised "the company of dancers who, in their multi-colored fusion of red shades, go progressively from staring into space to rolling on the floor—all accomplished with art and nuance." She also said, "Sex-wise, *Bomarzo* is subtle." Gene Shalit, the TV critic and personality, was excited more by Joanna Simon, an American soprano, in the role of a courtesan. "Her costume (but not her voice) was just about topless," he wrote.

Douglas Watt, the *Daily News'* drama critic, who is also knowledgeable about music-theatre, commented: ". . . Jack Cole's lavish deployment of dancers is so striking, perhaps his finest work, that you feel you have never before seen dancing in an opera." Given the ancillary role dance has historically been accorded in opera, it usually doesn't take much for inventive opera choreography to stand out. But, from the various appreciative critical observations about Cole's use of dance and movement in the entire production, it is apparent that he had finally managed to make a very special, valid, exciting, contribution to serious dance, even though his *Bomarzo* ballets were part of a larger work rather than existing in isolation.

Some music critics refused to be impressed by anything about *Bomarzo*, which may explain why it vanished so rapidly from the City Opera's repertory. Irving Kolodin, of the *Saturday Review*, didn't care for the dances and didn't mention Cole. The *New Yorker*'s Winthrop Sargeant saw *Bomarzo* as "a great dramatic spectacle," but "nowhere did either its story or its music involve me in any way." He found Cole's choreography ably done, with such dancers as Buzz Miller, Robert Powell, and Carmen de Lavallade. Sargeant noted that the music for the Erotic Ballet was aleatory. By definition, such music involves elements of chance in composition or performance, so it may have been a challenge to Cole's dancers to count this part of the score. As for the sexuality and shock generated by the Erotic Ballet, Sargeant thought it was "no more lurid than a country square dance." The *Times*'s Harold Schonberg was also not about to let his readers think Cole could shock him: "There was a ballet which was actually prim compared with some of the stuff the Joffrey Ballet and others have been doing."

Nineteen sixty-seven was an important but not entirely auspicious year for Jack Cole in the arena of serious dance. This was also the year in which he began work—in January—on a ballet commissioned by Mrs. Rebekah Harkness for her Harkness Ballet. Cole worked for weeks on this, leaving the young dancers in September, with the dance still incomplete. A newspaper report implied that he had left to work on David Merrick's ill-fated *Mata Hari* musical. The Harkness Ballet had already paid Cole $1,500 for the work he had done, so it was decided to include the fragmentary ballet in the Harkness fall repertory under the title of *Requiem for Jimmy Dean—A Work in Progress*. The company performed it in fragments in the sequence in which Cole had been working on it.

Among Jack Cole's papers are some interesting letters relating to this curious episode. On September 23, 1967, Brian Macdonald, then the director of the Harkness Ballet, wrote a friendly letter to Cole, advising him that he, Mrs. Harkness,

Donald Saddler, and Jeannot Cerrone had looked at the *Requiem* in a "private showing" and it had made "a very strong impact on us all." Macdonald wrote that it was planned to present the incomplete work in New York, "as a 'work in progress,' as you suggested." It's not clear from the context whether Cole in fact had suggested to Macdonald that the *Requiem* could be performed as long as it was identified as still in the process of development. The Harkness was going to perform the work first in Indianapolis. Macdonald asked Cole to come out to Indiana if he could and to let him know what the ballet's continuity should be, as well as Cole's wishes about costumes and lighting. Macdonald concluded with another affirmation of the enormous impression Cole's work had made on them.

On October 2, Cole responded in apparent bafflement. He thanked Macdonald for his "kind words," but feared there had been a misunderstanding. *Requiem* may have been a work in progress, but Cole stated firmly that it had never been his intention for it to be publicly performed prior to its completion. Cole assured Macdonald of his intention of finishing the choreography "as quickly as possible." But in the meantime, Cole didn't want the work to be seen. He wrote that a performance of the unfinished ballet in its present stage of development would be "grossly unfair to the work, your company, and to myself, and that I cannot permit." He concluded by specifically forbidding the Harkness Ballet to perform *Requiem for Jimmy Dean.*

Two days later, Cole's attorney, Jerome Berger, wrote Mrs. Harkness to make it quite clear that the *Requiem* was not to be performed. Cole had directed him to say that he hoped the matter could be resolved in a mutually agreeable fashion, without recourse to legal action. In extenuation of Cole's rigid position about the ballet, Berger pointed out that Cole had informed Mrs. Harkness "over a period commencing six to eight weeks ago," that the work could not be completed by the time originally set. Cole further complained that the Harkness Ballet had failed for a full month to provide him with music he needed for the ballet, not to mention its failure to provide "an adequate number of performers." He did not mention, though Cole was later to do so, that the young Harkness dancers were so unused to the strenuous demands of Cole Technique, that he spent most of his rehearsal time training them, instead of developing and completing the dance.

Macdonald then wrote Cole a cheerful letter to announce the success of *Requiem for Jimmy Dean* in Indianapolis. George Bardyguine had done the lighting. The dance had been done with simple black velours the first time, but, for the second performance, some of the velour "legs" were flown to give the stage and the work more of an "in progress look," as Macdonald phrased it. He assured Cole that the ballet had been intensively rehearsed. After the New York engagement of the Harkness, Macdonald could make the dancers available to Cole for almost six weeks of rehearsal to finish the dance. The tone and the content of Macdonald's letter were very positive, very friendly. But there was absolutely no mention of the fact that Cole had forbidden the Harkness to perform his unfinished work.

Immediately after this, Cole sought an injunction to prevent the *Requiem* from being shown in New York. A New York State Supreme Court justice denied the injunction. Cole, working out of town on *Mata Hari*, had claimed "irreparable damage" to his reputation if the ballet were presented in its incomplete state. The judge found for the Harkness Ballet, on the basis that Cole had not satisifed the terms of his contract with the Harkness. The ensemble opened its New York season at the Broadway Theatre.

Frances Herridge, reviewing for the *New York Post*, wrote that she could see why the Harkness Ballet insisted on showing *Requiem for Jimmy Dean*: "It's the most exciting work that's come into the repertory so far." Herridge, usually favorably disposed toward Cole and his work, continued: "Though brief and incomplete, it has the jazzy zing, the tension, the whiplash movement that Cole does so well. There's no attempt at story. The boys wear black boots, but otherwise the costumes are work leotards. No other outer show is needed, because the inner spirit is there. The current Cole conveys of the rebel generation that loved Jimmy Dean is electrifying. And the Ronald Herder jazz score keeps pace."

Clive Barnes, then the resident dance "maven" at the *New York Times*, was more temperate in his enthusiasm. He noted of *Requiem* that it ". . . certainly makes a swinging title, but quite what it has to do with the dead film star and in what way it is a requiem is never explicit." If Barnes didn't have high marks for Cole as an effective conceptualist choreographer, he at least praised Cole's technical proficiency: "Mr. Cole's choreography, with its swinging legs and taut pelvises, elastic jumps, and happy bounce, is good Broadway stuff, hand-crafted by a master technician."

Requiem for Jimmy Dean: A Work in Progress was given its New York premiere on November 3, 1967. The role of Dean was danced by Lawrence Rhodes. Cole kept among his papers a program for the premiere at the Broadway Theatre, as well as a cordial card from Rebekah Harkness and Donald Saddler. He preserved reviews of the premiere and a number of photos of his Harkness House rehearsals for the *Requiem*. Also among these mementoes was an unused ticket for the premiere—obviously one of a pair of aisle seats: No. 102. Did Cole use No. 101? Was he actually present at the premiere? There is no other indication among these papers that he was.

Shortly after this, Cole talked to *Dance Magazine* about the event: "I could say a few things about Rebekah Harkness . . . who won't wait 'till I complete the modern ballet in six parts she commissioned me to do. Oh, no! They'll play two parts out of six. . . . You can't show two parts of anything and expect it to hold. It makes me look ridiculous. . . . I hope to complete it later this month. They'll probably call it 'Work in Progress Number Two.' "

Donald Saddler has an especially vivid memory of this encounter with Jack Cole, whom he greatly admired. "Although unfinished, it was splendid! It was a scrap, a fragment, like Schubert's 'Unfinished Symphony.' But a masterpiece. I was working with the Harkness Ballet then, and I thought it would be a wonderful experience for the dancers to have Cole choreograph a piece for them. It took me a long time to get him to do it.

"He was really leery of working with ballet dancers," con-

tinues Saddler. "He said they'd be so busy with their pirouettes that they'd have no time to dance for him. And yet, of
his own dancers, he demanded classical training for control. He
liked the majority of the Harkness dancers. They were flexible;
they'd been exposed to many choreographers and styles; exposed to jazz dancing and its sources. Cole worked with them
for six weeks. But he didn't do more than twelve bars of music
in all that time. The dancers did perfect what he gave them,
but he had to go away."

At this point, one of Cole's close friends had been asked to
Florida for a vacation. Cole was clearly blocked and frustrated
by the Harkness experience, so he invited himself along. At the
end of the holiday, the host told Cole's companion, "You're
welcome anytime, naturally. But don't *ever* bring him along
again." Cole, as was often his wont, had been difficult.

He returned to the Harkness Ballet. Today, Saddler cannot
remember whether he stayed with the dancers ten or twelve
weeks, but it was for an extended period of time. "We hoped
he'd finish the ballet. I think he only finished seven minutes of
it. He'd jump around, doing sections of the piece. He finally
got the Harkness dancers to move just the way he wanted them
to, but the discipline was terrible for them. Some just couldn't
stand the drilling and the repetition.

"To get the isolation that he wanted, with *no* variations,
everything had to be exact. All those dancers who really tried
to get what he had to offer emerged as the best in the Harkness. They learned from Cole the power of selectivity of a
movement; what's effective *in* that movement; how to rivet every
ounce of concentration on just doing that. *Not* overdancing, but
pulling back, almost being still. I felt it was all worthwhile,"
Saddler insists, "even though the ballet never was finished.

"It was very effective. We had the dancers do the first part—
then everything was coal-black—after which the group did another section, then a blackout again, as the music continued.
There were three sections of dance: three minutes, two minutes, and one and a half minutes. The music played throughout, but the lights were up only during the choreographed portions. It was just beautiful—like cuts from a film. If you knew

Cole's Technique, it was the essence of his work." As much as Saddler, Mrs. Harkness, and the dancers wanted Cole to complete the dance, it would have taken a year at the rate at which he was working.

In the aftermath, according to Saddler, there were no hard feelings, only regrets that the dance was not finished. Since the performance of the fragments was not filmed, and Mrs. Harkness later disbanded her company, this incomplete version of a serious Cole choreography was not preserved.

Undaunted by this experience—after all, he had not worked directly with Cole—Saddler continued to want to work more closely with the tempestuous choreographer. When Saddler launched his Dance Repertory Theatre at the North Carolina School of the Arts, in Winston-Salem, he invited Cole and Alvin Ailey to join him on the project. Although Cole said he would, neither he nor Ailey finally did so. "It would have been a tremendous trio," says Saddler, "but it wouldn't have held together with three tremendous egos."

Agnes de Mille, Jerome Robbins, and George Balanchine had had no qualms about choreographing for both Broadway and the ballet stage. Cole, however, had definite misgivings about mounting serious ballets, possibly because he feared he lacked their training and strengths in classical ballet. Although he insisted on some Cecchetti classical work as part of his own dancers' training, he tended to make fun of classically trained dancers—such as the Harkness youngsters—when he had to work with them. A decade earlier, in 1958, Cole was still publicly viewing serious dance as a very risky proposition for any performer who really "wanted to work." In the next two decades, of course, all this changed dramatically, but time was running out for Jack Cole.

Cole had enjoyed notable success with choreography that was innovative, if ultimately repetitive. Late in his commercial career, with work in films at an end and a string of Broadway disappointments, Cole may not have had the energy or the courage to attempt a new career move into the arena of serious dance. He did not take failure well, and even success was not so easily digested. Also, in the late 1950s and in the 1960s, there were various indications that his fountain of ideas and his capacity for improvisation were drying up.

Things were not made any easier for Cole when he was blocked or frustrated in developing a dance sequence and a well-meaning colleague or friend pinpointed the difficulty. As Hal Schaefer has said, "Jack couldn't stand any kind of negative criticism." Schaefer still thinks Cole was terrified that he might lose his authority and control over his dancers if he gave even an inch. And to be criticized or, worse, ridiculed by a reviewer could be seen as a very visible public attack on Cole's authority and abilities. That's why he was so concerned about the "irreparable damage" performing the unfinished *Requiem* could do to his reputation. Certainly Clive Barnes's critique didn't do it any good. As Schaefer says, "He had a lot of successes, but it never really changed this exaggerated fear of failure, this curse he had." Also, Schaefer notes, Cole could not bring himself to admit he'd failed or made a mistake.

Bob Wright and Chet Forrest were all too aware of this, especially when it was necessary for all the collaborators to be flexible, to make compromises for the survival of a musical that was in trouble out of town. Wright remembers: "Unless driven to it, he'd never admit he was wrong." Wright cites some important moments in all three of the musicals in which he believes he and Forrest were right—or at least "more right"—and Cole was not. But, he agrees, choreographers all have their awkward moments, those crises in the development of a dance or a production when they get stuck. For most, the easiest thing is to fall back on their "vocabulary" of dance steps and routines, those distinctive aspects which—if they are really good— tell the knowledgeable spectator that he's looking at a Kidd, a Robbins, a de Mille, or perhaps a Fosse choreography. Wright insists: "Jack wouldn't do that. He wouldn't repeat himself." That seems to have been Wright's actual experience in working with Cole. In Cole's films, however, if the dance routines are seen one after another, in rapid succession, and not, as originally created, spread over two decades, it's easy to see where and how Cole repeated himself, despite his boundless ingenuity and innovation.

"There are very few gifted people, when they're jammed in shows and not supported creatively, who can bring it off." One of Cole's best-known dancers testifies to that. He's Ron Field, the director-choreographer, who has *Applause* and other Broadway hits to his credit. He says it's a fact of life that directors and choreographers get jammed, or blocked, a creative impasse well known also to writers. "Jack got jammed. Teeth clenched, eyes crossed, brain in a spasm: all he wanted to do was run—which he did, a lot!" Trying to explain Cole's temper, tensions, and inner doubts, Field draws on his own experiences, which he believes are typical. "People just don't know what choreographers go through! The difficulties, the insecurities! It all has to come out of our heads. We can't pull it out of a book. It's all in your head, and when anything goes wrong, it can drive you crazy. The music didn't arrive; they didn't bring the flourescent lights when they said they would; two dancers didn't show up; the star is sick. Anything can jam us. Everything's our responsibility.

"So we are amazingly insecure. On the way to rehearsal, we don't know what is going to come out. And Jack had to deal with that all the time, but he couldn't say, 'People, I'm scared today. We shoot the day after tomorrow, but I have no ending for this number. I feel so untalented.' Well, you cannot say that, even if you really feel it," Field says. "They are all depending on you. You *have* to make it work."

Toward the end of his career, Cole was finding it more and more difficult to make it work. Sometimes ideas refused to come; nothing worked. He blamed distractions; he indicted the derelictions and failures of others. Working with the Harkness Ballet, working with young dance students at UCLA, working with comparative novices in a Broadway show, Cole often announced that he would first have to train them to become Jack Cole dancers, before he could get on with the choreography. And in fact, it was so. In a number of cases, even with expert dancers, however, some Cole choreography did not get finished.

Even in Cole's early days in the casinos and clubs, he occasionally had difficulties pulling a routine together in time for the opening. Once at Chez Paree in Chicago, even the waiters were watching the fascinating Cole rehearsals, but as things progressed, and the dance wasn't ready, they became increasingly worried. The better the show, the better their tips, for one thing. The day before the opening, Cole told them the dance was finished.This is a story Cole told on himself. When he told them the act was ready, he said, the waiters banged jubilantly on dishpans, pounded on the tables, and cried "Whoopee!"

"Choreography was very hard for him!" insists George Martin. He was certainly in a position to know, since he worked side by side with Cole, prepared to rehearse Cole's new sequences of steps and body movements over and over with the dancers. Martin remembers: "He pretended it wasn't difficult, but we would work all day on eight counts. That was not unusual." For many years, Martin says, the core of Cole dancers, those who were in the Columbia Pictures dance workshop, thought this slowness in developing the dances was really their fault, not Cole's; that they had to master his style first. Martin says, "Rightly so, because we must have looked like bloody fools." Every muscle counted; he admits, "He had us there. Granted, we were all young and not the best dancers in the world. But at that point, after two and a half years with Cole, we were better dancers than most he'd find. I think he used it as an excuse!

"Jack found choreography the most difficult thing in the world!" Martin insists. "I'm not talking about his steps or about his style." Martin means creating a complete dance entity, using steps and style, to project a concept, a vision, a mood, an emotion. But no matter how difficult this kind of creation was for Cole, Martin is convinced he could have done serious work, if he'd wanted to pursue it. He believes that, in the late 1940s, Cole wanted to "put himself on the line," alongside Charles Weidman and Martha Graham. That was some fifteen years after he'd left Humphrey and Weidman and immediately after his association with Columbia was terminated. To Martin, Cole's group of hand-picked thoroughly trained dancers became very important to him. It was, in a sense, his artistic center, now that he no longer had the protection of the studio and his subsidized workshop. So it was important to Cole, but as Martin sees it, "not important enough for him to put himself on the line."

Regarding his failure to finish the *Requiem for Jimmy Dean* for the Harkness, Martin asks: "Well, how many shows do you think he tried to put that in? He started to put it in all the wrong shows! He tried to do part of it in *Zenda*." Martin says it's only folklore, however, that Cole was fond of choreographing rape sequences for shows that would never need them. "We had a rape scene in *Carnival in Flanders* and one in *Man of La Mancha*. That's *all* I remember!"

For George Martin, what's important about Jack Cole is not that he created some specific dances, but rather his tremendous influence on modern theatre dance. Agnes de Mille has made the same point. Martin suggests: "I think Jerome Robbins is the greatest theatrical choreographer we've had, but I don't think he's influenced dance *this* much." Martin's thumb and forefinger measure half an inch. "Let's face it! You saw his *Opus Jazz*. Is that not Jack Cole? Practically step by step? Jerry's a theatrical genius. He knows what he's doing. But I'm talking about *influencing* dance—about the actual physical thing of *dancing*. And look at Bob Fosse: he got his Cole influence from Gwen Verdon!"

Pressed repeatedly for a comment on Jack Cole, Robbins had this to say: "I never worked with Jack Cole, but I had infinite admiration for his work. I feel he had tremendous influence on theatrical dance in America!"

At UCLA, where Cole finally completed his *Requiem*—shortly before his death, so that it was, in effect, *his* requiem—Carol Scothorn, current head of the dance program, observed Cole choreographing. Watching Cole work on it, Scothorn came to the conclusion that "he was a wonderful choreographer when he was surrounded by *context*, as in a Broadway show. When you took away that context, and ideas had to come entirely from him, from Step 1, and be entirely self-contained and self-pronouncing—that kind of choreography was more difficult for him."

Cole found it hard to believe that other choreographers could achieve interesting professional results with student dancers who lacked the skills he thought any dancer needed to perform his work. He told Professor Scothorn he found one dance he'd seen remarkable, considering that the student body "turned over every year like the football team. One year you have winners; the next year, you don't." Cole insisted that the young UCLA enrollees in the Graduate Dance Center had to do his exercises and master his techniques before they could become artists. "He didn't recognize," says Scothorn, "in college students who are only half-trained, there could be some degree of artistry."

Scothorn explains how Cole worked: "He wouldn't let anyone go on to Step 2 until they'd mastered Step 1—which means you never got very far. So, unless he had perfect dancers—which he didn't—he couldn't get his choreography out. His problem with the students was that they just couldn't do Step 1 soon enough to move on to something else. If he'd known how college students are, and he'd sketched out the ballet a bit, they'd eventually have gotten it. He wanted to start out on performance, before he had any choreography. He wanted perfect, *perfect* mastery of everything before there was anything to perform." Scothorn thinks George Martin is accurate in suggesting that this rehearsal pattern was Cole's way of deferring the agony of actual choreographing.

Nonetheless, the dance was finally performed at UCLA. "The local critics gave it a terrible reception. The critic for the *Los Angeles Times,* who wasn't well informed about dance, panned it. As director of the company, I'd lost my perspective a bit," Scothorn admits. The *Time's* man, Daniel Cariaga, found it "slick but uneventful," resembling "nothing so much as leftover group choreography from *Kismet.*" Scothorn believes Cole worked very hard to achieve what he'd envisioned. This level of excellence, she says, was not reached until the very last performance of the dance. "But, by then, he was gone."

Madeleine Scott, an assistant professor of dance at Ohio University, was at that time one of Jack Cole's most dedicated students and disciples in the UCLA program. She recalls the experience of working on the dance, which she refers to as *Requiem for a Dead Hero.* The specific reference to Jimmy Dean had disappeared, perhaps chased away by Clive Barnes's slighting comment on Cole's failure to invoke this name—and image—effectively. Cole held no auditions, for the work was to be performed by students in the subsidized Dance Center program. Seventeen of them showed up to work with Cole. Madeleine Scott says fifteen survived.

Rehearsals began in September 1972 for the March performance date. Scott says this rehearsal period was twice what was customary. At first, they rehearsed twice weekly, followed in January by sessions four or five times a week. In all this time, Cole worked only on the first third of the dance. "The final two-thirds and introduction material," Scott reports, "seemed to happen in the last three weeks in *very* long, arduous hours of rehearsal. But Jack was not fitting the dance to us and our capabilities; he was fitting us to the dance. His rehearsals were more about drilling to find good dancing—excuse the pun, but with Jack it *felt* like the search for black gold."

Cole's *Requiem* at UCLA opened very formally, with live music by Pia Gilbert. Audiences saw a row of dancers on one knee across the proscenium opening, their backs turned to the auditorium. The girls had long ponytails hanging down their backs. They were clad in black bodysuits, bare across the shoulders except for a "crown of thorns" made of pipe cleaners that framed the chest. Cole thought this also would improve the dancers' *port de bras*. They wore black pants, tied with paisley sashes, hanging Jamaican-fashion around the hips. These women faced a single man standing center stage in what Scott calls a "modified Samurai-warrior dress." This was made of deep, long black culottes, with a single slash of purple in it as a design element. This dancer, Keith Marshall, with a strong jaw and curly blond hair, bore a resemblance to James Dean.

"He performed a slow solo, while the women watched and the live percussion and horn music continued," Scott remembers. She was in the performance, so she didn't see the dance unfold in the way a spectator would have. This initial passage was followed by all the dancers clearing the stage, reentering to taped Santana music. "At this point, the dance became a cir-

cle dance. Five lead women, each flanked by two women, began the smooth, undulating walk around the stage which was
accentuated by falls and knee-drops. The dance broke up into
smaller groups, not all of which I saw. I led a small stationary
group in *bharat natyam* movement, the gestures of which were:
'The Universe Sparkles with Miracles, but none of them shines
like man.' Other dancers swept through the space diagonally,
cutting the circular illusion.

"We thought he was pushing for the maenads in us all,
whipping both us and the dance into a wild frenzy, throwing
ourselves on the floor, hurling ourselves through the dance.
Truly, we had the most unbelievably colorful bruises all over.
The dance concluded with a brief return to the 'hot/cool' opening mood and music," Scott explains. "However puzzling or
inconclusive the dance may have been, it was meant to be the
raw pure power of being, a wild desire of energy which was
Jack Cole."

Requiem for a Dead Hero was farther along in March 1973 at
UCLA than it was with the Harkness Ballet, but it was never
really completed. (Slightly less than a year later, Cole would be
dead of cancer.) Looking back on this memorable experience,
Scott says, "If one considers Jack's reputation for unfinished
work, perhaps our less than 'good' dancing was an easy out,
an excuse for not completing the work. For us, working with
Jack was all-consuming. Most other things and people pale in
comparison. Even his own work did not deflect the attention
of his dancers from him. I think, for us, *what* we danced was
not the issue; *how* we danced was the primary concern.

"With Jack's *Requiem*, he had an idea of what he wanted to
create, but not how to create it. He'd work for two hours on
eight counts of movement frequently. He rarely could get past
our dancing, it seems. After we studied with him, I believe he
had more faith in us as dancers. He talked at points about a
small company of five to seven dancers, even telling me who
he'd chosen and why."

At the very end of his life, keeping his pain and suffering
to himself, Jack Cole was still talking about that serious concert
ensemble he always meant to create.

14

JACK COLE'S FAREWELL

EXIT DANCING & TEACHING

G iven Jack Cole's varied achievements as a dancer and choreographer, it's easy to overlook his function—his dedication, even—as a teacher. Almost any group of dancers he worked with immediately became Cole's students. While valuable rehearsal hours spent in exercises and mastering technique might have seemed a terrible waste of money to a harrassed producer, or have been viewed as Cole's own curious way of delaying the moment of truth when he would finally have to complete a difficult choreography, it is apparent, from repeated testimonies of dancers and colleagues, that Cole wanted all his performers to be as well prepared as possible. In this he was quite sincere. Even when he complained that "the stars can't dance," he did everything he could to make it look as though they could. More than that, he often made himself available to help coach them for subsequent films or to aid them in creating their own club acts.

Early in the decade of the 1950s, Cole had talked about setting up a school in Southern California. He had been working intermittently at Eugene Loring's school, but he found the work boring, possibly because the students weren't as eager, talented, or dedicated as he wished. He was never to found this dream-school, but he did spend time in the 1960s and 1970s actively involved in various teaching roles. His final commitment was to the dance program at the University of California at Los Angeles.

In the 1960s, Cole accepted several such challenges. In 1965, for instance, he was in Dallas, on the faculty with Violet Verdy for the Texas Association of Teachers of Dancing—TATD—for their convention. Ted Shawn had been invited to lecture as well. In one of the Annual Letters he wrote from Jacob's Pillow to special friends, he described the encounter: "I had not really had a chance to be alone with Jack, to have long talks with him, for over thirty years. The very first evening I arrived, Goodloe Lewis [president of TATD] left us alone in his suite at the Sheraton, and we sat and talked for hours. . . . The next day, I watched him teach—he is amazing! He has the slim, wiry body of a twenty-year-old, moves more excitingly than ever before in his life, and is a fabulous teacher!" The talks continued, and after the convention banquet, Shawn, Verdy, Cole, and Camille Long Hill, Houston's "great lady of the dance," talked until the early morning hours, each trying to top Cole's hilarious stories. Shawn paid tribute to his "fiendish sense of humor." He said Cole had the group rolling on the floor. If that were literally true, one can imagine the temptation for Cole to put "Papa" Ted Shawn through some reclining exercises.

The Texans must have liked Cole's contribution, for he was invited back in May 1966. The TATD Bulletin advised members that "Mr. Jazz returns to teach at the 18th annual Normal School jazz classes." Earlier that spring, Cole again had met with Shawn at the Southeastern Regional Ballet Festival in Orlando. This interest in conferences, festivals, and dance workshops may seem out of character for the individualistic and iconoclastic Jack Cole, but he was now a man in his fifties, looking back. His film triumphs were past. He no longer appeared in clubs with his dancers. Recent Broadway experiences had been disappointing. But there was one thing he could still do, and that was teach.

In 1971, the last summer Ted Shawn was director of Jacob's Pillow, Jack Cole, the teenaged troublemaker of long ago, was invited back to teach. Barton Mumaw remembers the experience. Cole had, in many respects, mellowed, Mumaw thought, "but he was disrespectful as ever of accepted forms of action or thought which he considered sham or bigoted, and he had no compunction about making a scene, acting forcefully, or emitting a phrase amounting to shock tactics to underline and make very clear his meaning or position." Jack Cole was getting older, but the leopard wasn't about to change his spots.

After the Jacob's Pillow teaching stint, Cole accepted a part-time assignment at UCLA. Originally, it was for one quarter only and was designed to permit Cole to prepare a concert work with talented students on special Rockefeller scholarships at the Dance Center, a graduate-level program. His agent, Josh Meyer, explains: "He took the job in one of those times when there were no other offers. That happens now and then—no work. I don't care who the performer is, if you stay in the business long enough, there are highs and lows. There was a time when even Frank Sinatra couldn't get a job."

The Rockefeller Foundation was then assisting dance groups and programs around the nation, hoping to develop strong regional dance companies. UCLA's Graduate Dance Center was one of these experiments in aspiration and subsidy. It was a two-year program, in which highly talented dance and choreography students worked with an outstanding faculty and guest artists. Cole was brought in to work on technique. Mia Slavenska was teaching ballet. One of Cole's students during this period says that Slavenska's classes got even better, thanks to the challenge of Cole's dynamism.

Alma Hawkins was then chairman of the UCLA Dance Department, and she remembers Cole's sense of urgency in passing on what he had learned of technique. "He talked with them a great deal about what he believed and about his theories," she recalls. Setting up the program, Hawkins had insisted on having professionals who would be with the students for more than just a few days. She says she really didn't know Cole at that time, but she certainly knew of him and his work and that he lived in the Los Angeles area. Hawkins called Cole and found him eager to go to work. Although he had a reputation for a tart tongue, the student complaints Hawkins received were made, she says, "in a laughing way." He wasn't as sarcastic as in his earlier days; these were, after all, only students, not professional dancers working under contract. "He did expect a great deal," Hawkins admits, "and he pushed them. But he was fond of them. He had some of them to his house; he was interested in what they were doing. As I understand it, this was at a time in his life when he'd not been busy for quite a while."

As Cole and Hawkins got to know each other, he lowered his guard somewhat. Before and after class, he'd drop by her office to talk about the students and their progress, as well as ideas about dance. She liked to visit Cole's classes and watch for a while before getting back to her duties.

One of Cole's inner group at the Dance Center was Linda Gold, who now teaches dance at Santa Monica Junior College. For her, working with Cole was a "love-hate relationship, but more often love." She remembers especially his tendency "to drive you beyond your limits—or what you *thought* your limits were." At the same time, however, Gold was surprised to find that this tough dance taskmaster was also, underneath, a very sensitive gentlemen. Her impression of the UCLA version of *Requiem for a Dead Hero* was that it was indeed not complete. It didn't come to completion in the way that Cole wanted, but this had to do with the lack of preparation of the students in Cole's techniques. "He'd go over and over and *over* something. That's what took the long hours in rehearsals and extra classes," Gold says. It may have looked complete to the audience, but, having worked through the process with Cole, she says there were sections of the dance which "were just let go."

Gold believes this was not an excuse to avoid choreographing, but Cole's determination that his dancers would be just right in what they did execute. She especially admires his technique: "Not showy technique, but a very honored use of the body. He talked of form following function, of making turns in terms of your own body's alignment." Considering some of Cole's difficult mirror-dance sequences, which required absolute precision, he may also have been thinking privately about some body realignments. That's what the long hours of Cole rehearsals had basically been about over the years.

At the time Cole was working at UCLA, Carol Scothorn was supervising the Graduate Dance Center program. She succeeded Alma Hawkins as chairman of the Dance Department. In addition to Cole's varied talents, which she appreciated, now she wishes she could find more dance teachers with Cole's "enormous energy . . . Just an enormous, explosive intensity that was wonderful for them!" But there was another side of the Cole experience that worried Professor Schothorn: "He also destroyed some people. Absolutely! A couple of people who were brilliant dancers just walked out and said, 'I won't go back to that class!' Some can learn under that kind of prodding. Others can't function; they just fold up," she says. "Perhaps it

works better in the theatre—with which Cole had a lot of experience," Scothorn suggests. "A lot of actors can be intimidated into a performance," she explains. But there were at least
three gifted young western dancers who couldn't endure Cole's
criticism. New Yorkers, she says, take such things with ease.

Apparently Cole didn't destroy Kimberly Susan Kaufman.
She did her M.A. thesis on him and his work. David Gray even
permitted her to study the Cole archives as they were being
prepared for sale in London. "From personal experience, I know
that Jack found turning dancers away at auditions painful, no
matter how poorly they danced, if he saw they were really
trying. It seemed as though his years of hardship remained clear
memories. I think it was one of Jack's dreams that he could use
every dancer who auditioned for him, and that every one of
those dancers would be intelligent, beautiful performers," she
wrote.

Some of Cole's last students are carrying on the tradition
he passed to them. One of the most dedicated is Madeleine Scott,
who recalls: "He was a very ethical man and an emotional one.
Dance was his love, and I believe he knew we'd be his last students. He worked passionately to make us understand. He told
a great many anecdotes which alluded to things close to him;
some were about dance, some not. But, in the second year of
working, they were less about anger and more about what and
how he loved. It took us a very long time to realize that when
he said, 'You make me weep,' he verged on tears."

Another fervent convert was Spider Kedelsky, studying
choreography in the Dance Center program. After working with
Cole, he became a choreographer and a producer, inspired by
Cole's teaching, and today is on the dance faculty at Amherst
College. Talking to Kedelsky, it's clear that even at that time he
realized he was "participating in an event few would ever have
in their lives." He knew nothing like Cole and the classes would
ever happen to him again, he says. For Kedelsky, Gold, Scott,
and others of the most dedicated dance students, there was also,
as he phrases it: "the sense of *giving* ourselves to a teacher!"
Working with Cole was "a process of learning about dance—
and about Life on Earth." Kedelsky thinks it's unfortunate that

Cole has not been accorded the position in American dance annals he deserves. Cole told Kedelsky: "I've *always* been a modern dancer." "Cole was," says Kedelsky, "a giant in popular culture!"

When Cole arrived at UCLA, most of the students didn't know who he was, but they knew about Bob Fosse and Michael Kidd. For these students, Cole Technique was something new. Most had classical or modern training. Instead of the initial quarter term, Cole's teaching time stretched from 1972 until late in 1973, when he could no longer meet his classes. Kedelsky and Scott were so taken with Cole and his teaching, they conspired to get him back on campus after that first quarter and his *Requiem*. Looking back, Kedelsky thinks the administration may not have been too happy to have students interfering in programming, but the student plot succeeded. Cole even arranged to teach the most devoted students privately.

Scott explains that Cole's rule, even for the young graduate students, was simple. She says: "Dance till you throw up—go out—throw up and come back and do it again." And it was a gruelling dance regimen. "We did Cecchetti pushups and Cecchetti hitch kicks and Cecchetti handstands. We did much of what you see in *Gentlemen Prefer Blondes* as the Olympic team's workout. We got strong and flexible and began to grasp what Jack had been talking about in rehearsal," says Scott. Cole would demonstrate stylized movement, but he did not usually show his students how to do the combination of gymnastic and balletic movement which was the core of classwork.

"All floor work was done as if standing up. It made sense to do it this way," Madeleine Scott says. In fact, anything Cole gave them proved, to her at least, to be sensible and helpful. "To him, good dancing was a law. It was the most logical, efficient, functional, and aesthetically pleasing way of using the body, or so Cole taught them. Today, Scott thinks Cole was really desperate to pass this perception on to the UCLA students. As in his stormy past, when Cole made difficulties for himself because of his ever ready tongue, he treated students to his lively, often comically mocking analyses of people, students, and other dance teachers he had known. Some of this may have simply been venting old rages and fights that still rankled Cole, but his tart critiques were often designed to illustrate points about performance or teaching dance. Cole could not understand, for instance, dance teachers with no personal energy. How, he wondered out loud, could they hope to inspire a class?

For Spider Kedelsky, "Cole was the last of his kind," but even more interesting than that was the fact that he was, in Kedelsky's opinion, the only Denishawn dancer who made an important, successful commercial career. Others, such as Martha Graham, Doris Humphrey, and Charles Weidman, certainly achieved distinction in the American dance, but largely m the serious, non-profit concert areas. Describing some of the classes with Cole, Kedelsky notes that he fired his accompanist almost immediately, preferring to beat time for the UCLA students with a Wigman drum. Much of the Cole Technique was very new to these young dancers. In the second or third class Cole showed them what he wanted the class to do the next day. The classroom was Studio 18, a very long room, perhaps 50 to 60 feet long and Cole was at the time, in his early sixties. "He dropped down on his knees so fast I couldn't see how he did it, and did a knee-slide halfway down the room," Kedelsky says. The class was open-mouthed to learn that that was the next day's exercise.

Cole was trying to make the Dance Center's students much better as dancers, but there were those who took offense and departed. Others were intimidated and stayed—even though they weren't happy with Cole.

Cole felt a special kinship with Kedelsky, who was planning to choreograph. After a year, Kedelsky injured a knee and couldn't dance anymore. He became closer to Cole, who could talk more objectively about the UCLA work now that Kedelsky was an observor rather than a participant. Spider Kedelsky was always very interested in ethnic and traditional dance, another likeness to his dynamic mentor. Even now, he marvels: "I don't think we knew anyone who was so directed, so demonic, so pithy—and who cursed so much!"

When Kedelsky created two of his own works, he invited Cole to see them and comment. One was a male solo which Cole liked very much. The other was principally ballet techniques, with some Bach preludes and fugues. Instead of attacking it and its choreographer, Cole sat down with Kedelsky and asked him to think carefully about the ballet vocabulary—its distinctive positions, movements, and attitudes—and from what origins it had evolved. Cole stressed the *logic*, the *precision*, and the *science* of classical ballet. If Kedelsky wanted to use balletic material in an innovative, eccentric way, as Cole had done with ethnic dances, then he first had to understand the ballet on its own terms—which Cole had done with East Indian, Afro-Cuban, and other ethnic materials.

"That statement alone had a very great influence on how I worked for the next few years, even on what I *didn't* use," Kedelsky reports. Cole had made his point about the logic of dance and the sense of "things dancing right" so that his student wouldn't forget it. Despite Cole's great interest in traditional dances, in ethnic rituals, and other dance sources in the lives of the world's peoples, Kedelsky is convinced that he really had established no dance categories other than good dancing and bad dancing. The classes at UCLA, and the extramural sessions, were moving away from Cole's earlier concentration on gymnastics toward more and more Cecchetti ballet work. For Cole, Cecchetti was a *fundamental* training for young dancers. At this stage of training, Cole was interested in styleless dance, an almost abstracted training of the body. When this had been mastered, then style could be added so that, as Cole believed, his dancers "could dance *anything!*"

After Cole's death, Spider Kedelsky got an NEA grant to study how Cole worked in training dancers. Walter Terry and Alvin Ailey helped him on the project. Today, he says, he was probably too young to understand just how such research might be done, but at the time he was struck with the attitudes of such Cole contemporaries as Bob Fosse and Jerome Robbins, both of whom owed clear debts to Cole's innovations. He found they "very grudgingly had any kind of generosity toward the man," but he also thought he knew why: "If nothing else, probably because Cole was such a son-of-a-bitch—and not overly generous to anyone else."

When Kedelsky had distilled all that he uncovered in his NEA Jack Cole investigation, he found what some of Cole's favorite dancers and assistants had already learned and what Walter Terry also came to realize: "The heart of the matter was *Jack!* The core was *him*—and what he did, integrating all this dance material."

In 1971, when Cole and Barton Mumaw were teaching at Jacob's Pillow, Mumaw noticed that Cole was terribly thin, even though his body was working wonderfully well. "I thought something was wrong, but he was full of life, his usual self. I was concerned, but there was nothing you could put your finger on." Then in September 1973, at the beginning of Cole's next academic year at UCLA, he had his gall bladder removed in a Burbank hospital. Alma Hawkins remembers that in the fall of 1973 Cole's energy level was lower, but she had no hint he was ill. He taught, she recalls, almost until the end. She believes he must have known he had very little time left. Hawkins remembers one day watching Cole walk to his car in the parking lot, but she had no idea she was seeing him for the last time.

The last six months of his teaching, says Spider Kedelsky, "had a great sense of urgency . . . as though he were desperately trying to pass on what he knew to the last students he would ever have." At first, those close to Cole thought he was only concerned that they'd soon be finishing school. "Come on, kiddies!" he'd say, "come on! You gotta work harder. You can't suck energy off me. You have to work hard. We haven't much time!" Both Madeleine Scott and Kedelsky wonder how much Cole knew about his impending fate; a man so sensitive to his body *must* have known something was very wrong with it. But, on the other hand, perhaps the same fanatic determination, the same manic energy which would not permit him to apologize, may also have prevented him from recognizing that his days were numbered.

Near the end, Scott recalls Cole teaching his last classes sitting down. He was wearing tennis shoes "rather than his beautiful black boots, because his feet were too swollen." Professor Carol Scothorn one day found it impossible to get her own class's attention. "I said, 'What's the matter with you?' They told me, 'Jack is dying.' Everyone knew he was ill. They were enormously affected by his presence and his inspiration. We didn't know what was wrong, but we knew he was struggling with something. . . . Suddenly, he disappeared. That's when we realized he was terribly ill. He wouldn't see anyone."

Cole always hated hospitals and visiting people in hospitals. He didn't want his friends to see him as he then was. He was briefly in the UCLA Hospital, where his illness was diagnosed as terminal. Since nothing could be done for him there, through the intervention of Gene Kelly and Gwen Verdon, he was moved to the Motion Picture and Television Memorial Hospital, in Woodland Hills. He died there on February 17, 1974. His UCLA dance disciples sent his obituary to the *Los Angeles Times*, but it was not published. The *Los Angeles Herald-Examiner*, *Variety*, and the *New York Times* did, however, honor his memory with obituaries.

Anna Austin Crane, who had cherished her Denishawn-spawned friendship and sometime partnership with Jack Cole since the late 1920s, first heard of Cole's death on the radio. She phoned his companion, David Gray, to ask when he would have the memorial service. She says Gray told her he'd had the body cremated, and there would be no service.

It was ironic that Jack Cole's UCLA core of dancers was never quite sure what his final sense of urgency really meant. At its simplest, they thought it was his concern that they would soon leave school. There were, however, also some intimations that he wanted to groom them for a new Jack Cole club act— or for his long-dreamed-of concert ensemble. At least six of the UCLA dancers had agreed to continue working with him after graduation, possibly in this club act. The summer before he died, he and Alma Hawkins had a wide-ranging talk about Cole's hopes of raising money to give the UCLA students some real professional touring experience, as well as developing serious concert work on campus, which was the goal of the Graduate Dance Center.

Shortly before his death, however, Cole had another serious project in mind, one which might have been his last bid for critical acclaim. He wrote an urgent letter to Robert Wright and Chet Forrest, asking for permission to use their musical adaptations of the Villa-Lobos themes used in the magnificent but failed 1948 musical *Magdalena*. He wanted their musical score and their help in mounting *Magdalena* as a ballet in Rio de Janeiro. Not long before this, the three longtime friends and collaborators had been discussing another new project, a musical version of Edmond Rostand's romantic drama *Cyrano de Bergerac*.

Even at the end, Jack Cole was looking forward to devising new dances, incorporating his familiar materials. More important for posterity, however, was passing on the Cole Technique—and Cole ideas about dance—to gifted young students, the dancers, choreographers, and teachers of tomorrow. And most important of all was the survival of Jack Cole's remarkable dance archive, destined for UCLA.

Cole was already trying to ensure the preservation of Ruth St. Denis's memoirs at UCLA, both for posterity and to help Miss Ruth pay her bills. Ted Shawn, who never divorced her even though they had parted at the breakup of Denishawn in the late 1920s, had provided a small annuity. But Miss Ruth was generous and improvident. Cole told Walter Terry of his philanthropy: "So I send her money, but the main thing is to have her journals transcribed, journals she began in 1896. They're historic!"

Terry reported that Cole had been very impressed by the journals. He'd said, "We use the word genius too loosely, but when you read what that girl from a New Jersey farm saw in the theatre in the 1890s—and what she dreamed of—you know you are in the awesome presence of a genius. So I want them transcribed. Miss Ruth is so awful about things, throwing them away, giving them to people. I want them kept at UCLA."

Frequently, if not monthly, Cole sent Ruth St. Denis a check for this work. Cole told Terry that Miss Ruth was honest but forgetful. From time to time, he'd drop in on her and find that some had indeed been transcribed by a "flunky," but he was afraid that she often forgot what his check was for. "Well, if she wants to buy four hundred yards of gold lamé," he told Terry, "she's earned the right." Another St. Denis request astonished her former student. As he confided to Terry: "She wants a *temple!* Why the hell anyone wants a temple in California . . . but she's earned the right. So she can have her temple and do anything she wants with it—have Buddhist rituals or pee on the floor. I'll pay for it because she's a genius!"

This and other evidences of his thoughtfulness show that Cole did have a tender, sentimental side. But it wasn't one he often showed. Rod Alexander says he doesn't believe Cole was at heart so hard and cold as some thought. "I remember very well the day that President Franklin D. Roosevelt died; Jack was very shaken and told us to take the rest of the day off. He also went home, and I thought I detected tears." His firm friends and admirers, Wright and Forrest, see him as a very shy man, who did not like to talk to people. He knew how to maintain a distance between himself and others, whether dancers or fans, unless he wished to bridge that gap briefly. Hal Schaefer emphasizes how very difficult Cole could be, as a man and as a choreographer. But, at the same time, he was "the best in the business," as well as an extremely well-read man, an intellectual in Schaefer's estimation. Cole's aloofness and his aggressiveness were both strategies to keep people from getting close to him, so for Schaefer and many others who admired and respected him, to love Jack Cole was also often to hate him.

The noted costume designer Irene Sharaff worked with Cole on several musicals, among them *Magdalena* and *Mata Hari*. She is reluctant to talk about him, saying she knew him as a friend, but "not that well." And was Cole then a nice person away from the rehearsal studio or the stage? "No, he wasn't a nice person," Sharaff says, "but then *few* people are." She laughs, making this point. "He was an extremely interesting person, and he had a very definite point of view about things." Admiring of Cole's talents and achievements, Sharaff thinks "a lot of people have missed the point about Jack and his place in dance."

Even today, Barton Mumaw is a bit aghast at Cole's own relish of his contrived tantrums. "He once described to me in great detail and with glee how he brought an entire airline to ground in order to silence his ranting and screaming in the center of an airport ticket area, until his every just demand was granted. The rages for which he was famous were absolutely genuine, governed with control worthy of a great actor."

Looking back, Mumaw has phrased a summation of the Cole character which is most telling: "Jack always reminded me of the beautiful archangel Lucifer, whom God tossed out of heaven, for with all his talents, Jack was impossible in 'real life.' 'Opalescent' and 'quicksilver' are words that come to my mind when I think of him. On the surface, he could seem calm and controlled, yet I always felt extreme tension underneath, ready to break through. Even his skin was unnaturally smooth, stretched closely over his musculature. Rebellion was deep in his consciousness. I became aware of this when he would speak to me of having had to carry out certain chores while still a schoolboy living at home. I did not realize until I had come to know him better what terrible resentment was behind these, to me, rather childish confidences. I believe he never lost this quality of resentment."

Jack Cole, unlike George Balanchine, did not arrange to leave his artistic footprints in the cosmic concrete. Like many dancers and choreographers and indeed most mortals, Cole left his in the shifting sands of time. Soon after Cole's death, Alvin Ailey dedicated a season to his memory. In 1976, Lee Theodore and her American Dance Machine—with the aid of Cole's own dancers such as Buzz Miller, Florence Lessing, Ethel Martin, Gwen Verdon, and Bob Hamilton—reconstructed some of his dances, with close attention to steps, style, and interpretation. A videotape was made—*Jack Cole: Interface 1976*—showing some Cole choreography from films and television and including a discussion about Cole's work and significance with such people as Miller, Pat Dunn, Beatrice Kraft, Martin, Verdon, and Lessing.

Viewing the ADM Cole videotape, Deborah Jowitt, dance critic for the *Village Voice,* commented on Cole's image, an "exotic, slightly cruel face." Echoing what earlier critics—even some of his own dancers—had said, she noted: "Cole's dancing always strikes me as immensely aggressive . . ." She stressed the immense counter-efforts needed to stop certain powerful Cole dance gestures and movements. "No flaccidity or softness is permitted: Cole dancers are warriors. The most frequent image he presents of women is that of the sexy tiger kitten, soft of skin and sharp of claws. The men are more overtly menacing. They dance as if holding out the promise of arduous, rather cruel sex."

Then, in 1982, in Tokyo of all places, the American Dance Machine premiered an evening of some sixteen reconstructed Cole choreographed works, in the framework of a show called *Jack,* subtitled "A Musical Fantasy." Wayne Cilento played Cole and danced his roles, looking at times astonishingly like the man who has been called "The Father of American Jazz Dance." Lee Theodore certainly agrees with that accolade for Jack Cole. It's the reason she wanted to produce *Jack,* as a tribute to this "visionary innovator." Theodore enlisted Hal Schaefer to work on the score and Irene Sharaff to create the costumes.

Not only is there apparent aggression in Jack Cole's dances, but Barton Mumaw detects it also "to this day in the theatre dance style he established. There is the thrust, the intensity, the loaded physicality, as well as the sheer enjoyment of moving in today's theatre dance [that is] so characteristic of Jack's teaching. From his great interest in, and use of, the jazz idiom of our country, he believed an 'Urban Folk Dance' would develop. His conception of such a happening seems to be visible today in the 'Street Dance' now springing up in our cities." But, impressive though this Cole heritage may be, Mumaw has another cause to thank Jack Cole. As he says, "He would laugh to hear me say this, but Jack gave me courage through the years, for I knew his standards. His driving force was ever an inspiration. He taught me that the quality of the work was the most important part of a creative life. His own spirit demanded perfection and drove all else before it." Mumaw adds that he can well believe the story—though not verified—that Cole died sitting up and raging that he was not yet ready to "meet his Maker."

George Martin, like Mumaw, thinks Cole's influence on modern theatre dance was tremendous, "more than anybody's in the whole world." Martin prefers theatre dance to jazz dance as a name for Cole's works. What George Martin, Gwen Verdon, and Florence Lessing want to know is: "Why doesn't the world know about Jack Cole?" They believe he did more than anyone else for modern theatre dancing, but "why isn't it up there in lights?"

Velerie Camille, a former Cole dancer who often charmed Parisian audiences, recently wrote *Dance Magazine* to ask: "I have always felt we were spiritually fed by his exciting dance form. We earned our salaries from his work, and the thrill of working in his style formed many of us as dancers. Why not give this great man his due? Why not acknowledge him?"

Donald Saddler thinks it is sad that more people don't know the Cole Technique, but sadder still that they didn't know Cole, the real source. He thinks Cole's most innovative work was actually done in the nightclubs, where he was seldom reviewed—or, if so, by cabaret critics. Walter Terry, who did survey the Cole work in all its aspects, always found it artistic and created and performed with integrity, no matter what its potential public. Jack Cole's innovations and those of Agnes de Mille, notes Ethel Martin, helped banish the pony chorus kickline and the glamorous showgirls from the musical stage. Cole's influence on fellow choreographers such as Jerome Robbins is very real. Gwen Verdon, who was often on the spot, says: "Jerry Robbins used to hang around with Jack, watching him choreograph nightclub shows, his own troupe, and movies. I mean, Jerry was always there. So something *had* to rub off on Jerry."

"Jack Cole's work is living again," says Lee Theodore. "It will live! We need seminars on his work. Young performers have to have a history. Without history, there's no continuity. Oth-

erwise, we are always reinventing the wheel! We need a platform of excellence, to go on from there. Given a heartbeat, the
material can now be taught." The American Dance Machine has
preserved some of the major dances both on tape and for live
performance. The Cole Technique is also taught; it's given in
Manhattan at Harkness House in workshops. On college campuses, the ADM offers it as a four-week workshop.

In his time, Jack Cole won *Dance* and Donaldson Awards,
but he never got an Emmy, an Oscar, or a Tony. Cole's most
anticlimactic dance honor must surely be one accorded him after
his death. In 1975, after Jack Cole had been dead for a year, a
large manila envelope was forwarded—not mailed directly—to
his Los Angeles address. It brought the less than exciting news
that Cole had been "nominated" to the Entertainment Hall of
Fame. Unfortunately, each year only ten really outstanding
nominees could be elected from all the many deserving candi-
dates. Of course, Jack Cole was not among the lucky ten, but
the envelope did contain a transmittal letter from Howard
Barnes, the Hall's executive director, plus a "citation" for Cole
to show his friends, proving he'd been at least a nominee.

Cole's surviving companion and heir, John David Gray, did
not bother to frame it—or even throw it away. He left it in the
original envelope and bundled it up with a number of real Cole
treasures and shipped it off to London. There, on Monday,
November 12, 1979, Jack Cole's Entertainment Hall of Fame
nominee citation was sold at auction at Sotheby's. Its buyer had
no idea he had bought it. He bid £35 for a heap of large envelopes containing Cole's personal working papers and souvenirs
from such productions as *Bomarzo, Kean, Magdalena, Kismet,
Ziegfeld Follies, Donnybrook!,* and other shows Cole choreographed.

The only items in this pile of Cole papers that the bidder
really wanted were a pencil sketch, by the distinguished designer Rouben Ter-Arutunian, for the *Donnybrook!* front curtain, some reproductions of the show's costume designs by Irene
Sharaff, and copies of its set designs by Howard Bay. They were
well worth the bidding price. Had this buyer wished, it would
have been the easiest thing in the world to have dumped the

rest of the Cole memorabilia in some London rubbish bin. It would also have saved a lot of money in postage. Fortunately, the purchaser, Paul Stiga, realized how valuable these Cole papers could one day be to researchers. He brought them back to America and preserved them. They have since proved invaluable in preparing this account of Cole's life and career.

In the future, their permanent home will be the UCLA Research Library, where Jack Cole wanted them to be, along with other Cole papers now either lost or scattered to the four points of the dance collector's compass. When Cole proudly showed his impressive collection of original dance manuscripts, drawings, dance first editions, and other choreographic rarities to visitors, he often mentioned his wish that, after his death the collection not be broken up but instead deposited at UCLA, where his interest and financial aid had already made possible a collection of Ruth St. Denis papers, and where his final months had been so satisfyingly spent with his last students ever.

Once again, this sad miscarriage is but another instance of failure to make full and proper legal arrangements before death for such bequests. If Cole was serious about making this benefaction to UCLA, it should all have been worked out with the university authorities beforehand. It appears no such arrangements were made. He left his entire estate to his friend John David Gray.

Gray did, in fact, offer the Cole library to UCLA, but he also offered it to the Dance Collection of the New York Public Library's Lincoln Center Library of the Performing Arts. There was a small catch; the collection would cost the buyer $100,000. Wright and Forrest remember Gray's disappointment when Genevieve Oswald, Curator of the New York Dance Collection, looked over the treasures in Los Angeles. Gray hoped to keep the archive intact, but Oswald wanted only certain books, manuscripts, and other dance items that weren't in the permanent collection in New York. Some very rare and valuable books in Cole's collection were already on the shelves in Manhattan, copies the library had acquired in the past. In any case, the New York Public Library did not have the $100,000, even if it had wanted to buy the collection entire and later profitably dispose of duplicates. Nor did UCLA have $100,000 for a single collection, no matter how valuable and attractive. Dance research was at that time not a top scholarly priority on campus.

Some of Cole's friends tried to raise the money to keep the collection at UCLA. The sum was too great. If Gray needed money, however, it's curious that he chose to have the entire Cole archive auctioned off, not in Los Angeles or New York, where Cole was well known and where friends, fans, and collectors would be extra alert to the values offered, but instead in London—where Cole was relatively unknown. Many of Jack Cole's close friends, his former partners, and his assistants were not told where and when the collection would be sold. Anna Austin Crane, who says Cole told her "many times that he was willing all this to UCLA," was especially hurt not to know about the auction, so she could try to save something. The fact that Gray himself died not so many months afterward makes the London sales even more sad.

Among unsold lots of Cole's personal papers were: Lot 97—some 600 photos of Jack Cole and his dancers from the 1930s through the 1940s; Lot 98—95 photos, some by major photographers, other film and theatre stills; Lot 100—photo album of Cole's family, letters, passports, notebooks, photos, reviews; Lot 101—1,000 pages of musical scores marked by Cole for his dances; Lot 103—73 photos of Cole, many signed by his friend the photographer Marcus Blechman; Lot 105—101 photos and other memorabilia of La Meri; Lot 108—53 American playbills and posters for major musicals and dance ensembles, and Lot 184—22 very decorative Jack Cole costumes worn on tours of Brazil, Cuba, and America. Sotheby's does not know what may have become of these valuable archival materials relating to Cole. Customarily, the auction house packs up unsold lots and returns them to the seller. What David Gray may have done with them is at present unknown. Some or all of them may come to light.

One unsold lot, Cole's seven large red scrapbooks, did not go back to Los Angeles. It was bought after the November auction by the Theatre Museum, housed in the Victoria & Albert Museum in London. These extremely fascinating Cole artifacts—especially his full pages of wild doodle-collages—thus have been preserved for study by serious researchers. To the suggestion that it would be more fitting if the scrapbooks were back in Los Angeles where Cole intended they should be, a most helpful museum official pointed out how many invaluable books, manuscripts, and artworks relating to the history of dance in Great Britain are now hidden away in American university libraries. He jested, "You've got so many of our rarities, it's only fair that we keep something of yours!"

Early and late in his unusual career, Jack Cole had cause to think that "Life Was Unfair." Often, his difficult personality and his insistence on perfection helped guarantee that life indeed would seem to be unfair to him. And he, in his own turn, managed to make life unfair for some others, especially rejected dancers. Life was still unfair to Jack Cole five years after his death. Not only was he largely forgotten by many, but at the Sotheby's sale, only two out of nine lots of his personal papers sold at all: one for only £30, the other for £35.

But his album of Isadora Duncan photographs brought £222 on the auction block. Most impressive of all was the photo album devoted to the legendary personality that Cole helped create—Marilyn Monroe. This trove of thirty-seven photos and other souvenirs won a high bid of £600. The irony would not have been lost on Cole. He might have laughed, wherever his perturbed spirit was on November 12, 1979.

THE THEATRE
OF
JACK COLE

1933

THE SCHOOL FOR HUSBANDS (Empire Theatre) □ *Opened:* October 16, 1933 (15 performance weeks). *Producer:* Theatre Guild, Inc. *Director:* Lawrence Langner. *Rhyme adaptors:* Arthur Guiterman, Lawrence Langner. *Music:* Edmond W. Richett. *Lyrics:* Arthur Guiterman. *Settings:* Lee Simonson. CAST: Osgood Perkins, June Walker, Michael Bartlett, Flora Le Breton, Doris Humphrey, Charles Weidman Troupe with Jack Cole, Marcus Blechman.

1934

CAVIAR (Forrest Theatre) □ *Opened:* June 7, 1934. *Producer:* Patrick A. Leonard. *Director:* Clifford Brooke. *Book:* Leo Randole. *Music:* Harden Church. *Lyrics:* Edward Heyman. *Settings:* Steele Savage. *Choreography:* John E. Lonergan. CAST: Nanette Guilford, George Houston, Violet Carlson, Franklyn Fox, Dudley Clements, Alice Dudley, Jack Cole.

THUMBS UP (St. James Theatre) □ *Opened:* December 27, 1934 (5 performance months). *Producer:* Eddie Dowling. *Director:* John Murray Anderson. *Sketches:* H. I. Phillips, Harold Atteridge, Ronald Jeans, Alan Baxter. *Music:* James Hanley, Henry Sullivan. *Lyrics:* Ballard MacDonald, Earle Crocker. *Choreography:* Robert Alton. CAST: Bobby Clark and Paul McCullough, Hal LeRoy, J. Harold Murray, Eddie Garr, Ray Dooley, Pickens Sisters, Paul Draper, Jack Cole, Alice Dudley.

1935

VENUS IN SILK (National Theatre, Washington, D.C.) □ *Opened:* October 7, 1935. *Producer:* Laurence Schwab. *Director:* Zeke Colvan. *Book:* Laurence Schwab, Lester O'Keefe. *Music:* Robert Stolz. *Settings:* Raymond Solvey. *Choreography:* William Holbrook. CAST: Nancy McCord, Jack Young, Audrey Christie, Gilbert Lamb, J. Harold Murray, Joseph Macauley, Alice Dudley, Jack Cole.

ROSE MARIE (revival) □ Jack Cole did the choreography for Ruth St. Denis.

MAY WINE (St. James Theatre) □ *Opened:* December 5, 1935 (213 performances). *Producer:* Laurence Schwab. *Director:* Joe Ruben. *Book:* Frank Mandel. *Music:* Sigmund Romberg. *Lyrics:* Oscar Hammerstein II. CAST: Walter Slezak, Nancy McCord, Walter Woolf King, Leo G. Carroll, Robert Fischer, Jack Cole, Alice Dudley, Vera Van, Earle MacVeigh.

1937
PRINCESS TURANDOT (Westport Country Playhouse) □ *Opened:* August, 1937. CAST: Anna May Wong, Jack Cole, others.

1939
NICE GOIN' (Shubert Theatre, Boston) □ *Opened:* October 23, 1939. *Closed:* November 4, 1939. *Producer:* Laurence Schwab. *Associate:* Dick Berger. *Book:* Laurence Schwab, Nunnally Johnson. *Sets:* Harry Horner. *Musical director:* Don Walker. *Dances:* Al White. CAST: Mary Martin, Bert Wheeler, Lee Dixon, Pert Kelton, Carol Bruce, Tom Ewell, Jack Cole, Florence Lessing, Anna Austin, Letitia Ide.

1942
KEEP 'EM LAUGHING (44th Street Theatre) □ *Opened:* April 24, 1942. *Producer:* Clifford C. Fisher, in association with the Messrs. Shubert. A Vaudeville Bill. *Scenery:* Frank W. Stevens. CAST: William Gaxton, Victor Moore, Paul and Grace Hartman, Hildegarde, Zero Mostel, Jack Cole and His Dancers, Kitty Mattern, Miriam La Velle, Shirley Paige.

1943
SOMETHING FOR THE BOYS (Alvin Theatre) □ *Opened:* January 7, 1943. (422 performances). *Producer:* Michael Todd. *Directors:* Hassard Short, Herbert Fields. *Book:* Herbert and Dorothy Fields. *Music and lyrics:* Cole Porter. *Choreography:* Jack Cole. CAST: Ethel Merman, Bill Johnson, Betty Garrett, Paula Laurence, Allen Jenkins, Betty Bruce, Anita Alvarez, Murvyn Vye, Dody Goodman.

ZIEGFELD FOLLIES (Winter Garden Theatre) □ *Opened:* April 14, 1943 (553 performances). *Producers:* Messrs. Shubert, Alfred Bloomingdale, Lou Walters. *Directors:* John Murray Anderson, Arthur Pierson, Fred De Cordova. *Music:* Ray Henderson. *Lyrics:* Jack Yellen. *Choreography:* Robert Alton. CAST: Milton Berle, Ilona Massey, Arthur Treacher, Jack Cole, Sue Ryan, Nadine Gae, Tommy Wonder, Dean Murphy.

1944
ALLAH BE PRAISED! (Adelphi Theatre) □ *Opened:* April 20, 1944. *Producer:* Alfred Bloomingdale. *Directors:* Robert H. Gordon, Jack Small.

Book and lyrics: George Marion, Jr. *Music:* Don Walker, Baldwin Bergersen. *Settings:* George Jenkins. *Choreography:* Jack Cole. CAST: Mary Jane Walsh, Patricia Morison, Milada Mladova, John Hoysradt, Joey Faye, Edward Roecker, Evelyne and Beatrice Kraft, Sheila Bond, Anita Alvarez, Jack Albertson.

1947

BONANZA BOUND! (Shubert Theatre, Philadelphia) □ *Opened:* December 26, 1947. *Closed:* January 3, 1948. *Producers:* Herman Levin, Paul Feigay, Oliver Smith. *Staged by:* Charles Friedman. *Book and lyrics:* Betty Comden and Adolph Green. *Music:* Saul Chaplin. *Choreography:* Jack Cole. CAST: Adolph Green, Carol Raye, Allyn McLerie, Gwen Verdon, George Coulouris.

1948

MAGDALENA (Ziegfeld Theatre) □ *Opened:* September 20, 1948. *Closed:* December 4, 1948. *Producer:* Homer Curran. *Director:* Jules Dassin. *Music:* Heitor Villa-Lobos. *Book:* Frederick Hazlitt Brennan, Homer Curran. *Pattern and lyrics:* Robert Wright and George Forrest. *Choreography:* Jack Cole. CAST: John Raitt, Dorothy Sarnoff, Hugo Haas, Irra Petina, Matt Mattox.

1950

ALIVE AND KICKING (Winter Garden Theatre) □ *Opened:* January 17, 1950. *Closed:* February 25, 1950. *Producers:* William R. Katzell, Ray Golden. *Director:* Robert H. Gordon. *Music:* Hal Borne, Irma Jurist, Sammy Fain. *Lyrics:* Paul Francis Webster, Ray Golden. *Choreography:* Jack Cole. CAST: Jack Cole and His Dancers, David Burns, Jack Gilford, Lenore Lonergan, Carl Reiner, Bobby Van, Gwen Verdon, Jack Cassidy.

1953

CARNIVAL IN FLANDERS (New Century Theatre) □ *Opened:* September 8, 1953. *Closed:* September 12, 1953. *Producers:* Paula Stone, Mike Sloane, Burke and Van Husen. *Director:* Preston Sturges. *Book:* Preston Sturges. *Music:* James Van Husen. *Lyrics:* Johnny Burke. *Carnival Ballet and musical staging:* Helen Tamiris. *(Original choreography: Jack Cole.)* CAST: John Raitt, Dolores Gray, Pat Stanley, Kevin Scott, Matt Mattox.

KISMET (Ziegfeld Theatre) □ *Opened:* December 3, 1953. *Closed:* April 23, 1955. *Producer:* Charles Lederer of Edwin Lester's production. *Director:* Albert Marre. *Book:* Charles Lederer, Luther Davis. *Music from:* Alexander Borodin. *Musical adaptation and lyrics:* Robert Wright and George Forrest. *Choreography:* Jack Cole. CAST: Alfred Drake, Doretta Morrow, Joan Diener, Richard Kiley, Henry Calvin.

1955

KISMET (Stoll Theatre, London) □ *Opened:* April 20, 1955 (648 performances). *Producers:* Meryn Nelson, Albert Marre. *Director:* Albert Marre. *Book:* Charles Lederer, Luther Davis. *Music from:* Alexander Borodin. *Musical adaptation and lyrics:* Robert Wright, George Forrest. *Choreography:* Jack Cole. CAST: Alfred Drake, Doretta Morrow, Joan Diener, Nigel Burke, Juliet Prowse.

1956

THE ZIEGFELD FOLLIES (Shubert Theatre, Boston) □ *Opened:* April 16, 1956. *Closed:* May 12, 1956 (Shubert Theatre, Philadelphia). *Producers:* Richard Kollmar, James W. Gardiner, by arrangement with Billie Burke Ziegfeld. *Sketch director:* Christopher Hewett. *Choreography:* Jack Cole. CAST: Tallulah Bankhead, Joan Diener, David Burns, Mae Barnes, Elliott Reid, Matt Mattox, Carol Haney.

1957

JAMAICA (Imperial Theatre) □ *Opened:* October 31, 1957. *Closed (for vacation):* June 28, 1958. *Resumed:* August 11, 1958. *Closed:* April 11, 1959. *Producer:* David Merrick. *Director:* Robert Lewis. *Book:* E. Y. Harburg, Fred Saidy. *Music:* Harold Arlen. *Lyrics:* E. Y. Harburg. *Choreography:* Jack Cole. CAST: Lena Horne, Ricardo Montalban, Josephine Premice, Ossie Davis, Erik Rhodes, Adelaide Hall, Alvin Ailey.

1959

CANDIDE (Saville Theatre, London) □ *Opened:* April 30, 1959 (60 performances). *Producers:* Linnet and Dunfee Ltd. *Director:* Robert Lewis. *Book:* Lillian Hellman, Michael Stewart. *Music:* Leonard Bernstein. *Lyrics:* Richard Wilbur. *Other lyrics:* John Latouche, Dorothy Parker. *Designer:* Osbert Lancaster. *Choreography:* Jack Cole. CAST: Denis Quilley, Mary Costa, Laurence Naismith, Victor Spinetti, Ron Moody.

1960

GREENWILLOW (Alvin Theatre) □ *Note: Cole was originally set to choreograph, but left the show in its early stages. This for the record: Opened:* April 8, 1960. *Closed:* May 28, 1960. *Producer:* Robert A. Willey in association with Frank Productions, Inc. *Music and lyrics:* Frank Loesser. *Book:* Lester Samuels, Frank Loesser. *Director:* George Roy Hill. *Choreographer:* Joe Layton. CAST: Anthony Perkins, Cecil Kellaway, Pert Kelton, Ellen McCown, William Chapman.

1961

DONNYBROOK! (46th Street Theatre) □ *Opened:* May 18, 1961. *Closed:* July 15, 1961. *Producers:* Fred Hebert, David Kapp. *Director/Choreographer:* Jack Cole. *Book:* Robert E. McEnroe. *Music and lyrics:* Johnny Burke. CAST: Art Lund, Eddie Foy, Jr., Susan Johnson, Joan Fagan, Philip Bosco.

KEAN (Broadway Theatre) □ *Opened:* November 2, 1961. *Closed:* January 20, 1962. *Producer:* Robert Lantz *Director/Choreographer:* Jack Cole. *Book:* Peter Stone. *Lyrics and music:* Robert Wright and George Forrest. CAST: Alfred Drake, Joan Weldon, Lee Venora, Oliver Gray, Alfred De Sio, Christopher Hewett.

1962

A FUNNY THING HAPPENED ON THE WAY TO THE FORUM (Alvin Theatre) □ *Opened:* May 8, 1962. *Moved:* March 9, 1964 (Mark Hellinger Theatre). *Moved:* May 12, 1964 (Majestic Theatre). *Closed:* August 29, 1964. *Producer:* Harold Prince. *Director:* George Abbott. *Book:* Burt Shevelove, Larry Gelbart. *Music and lyrics:* Stephen Sondheim. *Choreography:* Jack Cole. CAST: Zero Mostel, David Burns, Ruth Kobart, Jack Gilford, Brian Davies, Preshy Marker.

1963

ZENDA (Curran Theatre, San Francisco) □ *Opened:* August 5, 1963. *Closed:* November 16, 1963 (Pasadena Civic Auditorium). *Producer:* Edwin Lester. *Director:* George Schaeffer. *Book:* Everett Freeman. *Music:* Vernon Duke. *Lyrics:* Lenny Adelson, Sid Kuller, Martin Charnin. *Choreography:* Jack Cole. CAST: Alfred Drake, Anne Rogers, Chita Rivera, Earl Hammond.

1964

FOXY (Ziegfeld Theatre) □ *Opened:* February 16, 1964. *Closed:* April 18, 1964. *Producer:* David Merrick. *Director:* Robert Lewis. *Book:* Ian McLellan Hunter, Ring Lardner, Jr. *Music:* Robert Emmett Dolan. *Lyrics:* Johnny Mercer. *Choreography:* Jack Cole. CAST: Bert Lahr, Larry Blyden, Cathryn Damon, John Davidson, Julienne Marie.

1965

KISMET: Revival (New York State Theatre) □ *Opened:* June 22, 1965. *Closed:* July 31, 1965. *Began national tour:* August 2, 1965 (O'Keefe Theatre, Toronto) *and closed:* November 18, 1965 (Fisher Theatre, Detroit). *Producer:* Music Theatre of Lincoln Center, Richard Rodgers. *Director:* Edward Greenberg. *Book:* Charles Lederer, Luther Davis. *Music and lyrics:* Robert Wright, George Forrest. *Choreography:* Jack Cole. CAST: Alfred Drake, Anne Jeffreys, Lee Venora, Richard Banke, Henry Calvin.

MAN OF LA MANCHA (Anta Washington Square Theatre) □ *Opened:* November 22, 1965. *Moved:* March 19, 1968 (Martin Beck Theatre). *Moved:* March 2, 1971 (Eden Theatre). *Moved:* May 25, 1971 (Mark Hellinger Theatre). *Closed:* June 26, 1971. *Producers:* Albert W. Selden, Hal James. *Director:* Albert Marre. *Musical play by:* Dale Wasserman. *Music:* Mitch Leigh. *Lyrics:* Joe Darion. *Choreography:* Jack Cole. CAST: Richard Kiley, Irving Jacobson, Joan Diener, Ray Middleton, Robert Rounseville, Jon Cypher.

1966
CHU CHEM (New Locust Theatre, Philadelphia) □ *Opened:* November 15, 1966. *Closed:* November 19, 1966. *Producers:* Cheryl Crawford, Mitch Leigh. *Director:* Albert Marre. *Conceived and written by:* Ted Allan. *Music:* Mitch Leigh. *Lyrics:* Jim Haines, Jack Wohl. *Choreography:* Jack Cole. CAST: Menasha Skulnik, Henrietta Jacobson (replaced Molly Picon), Marcia Rodd, Jack Cole, James Shigeta, Robert Ito.

1967
BOMARZO (New York City Opera) □ *Premiere:* May 19, 1967, Washington, D.C. 1968, New York State Theatre, Lincoln Center. *Composer:* Alberto Ginastera. *Director:* Tito Capobianco. *Design:* José Varona. *Conductor:* Julius Rudel. *Choreography:* Jack Cole. CAST: Salvador Novoa, Joanna Simon, Richard Torigi, Isabel Penagos, Claramae Turner, Buzz Miller, Barbara Sandonato.

MATA HARI (National Theatre, Washington, D.C.) □ *Opened:* November 18, 1967. *Closed:* December 9, 1967. *Producer:* David Merrick. *Director:* Vincente Minelli. *Book:* Jerome Coopersmith. *Music:* Edward Thomas. *Lyrics:* Martin Charnin. *Choreography:* Jack Cole. CAST: Marisa Mell, Pernell Roberts, Blythe Danner, Bill Reilly, Martha Schlamme.

1971
LOLITA, MY LOVE (Shubert Theatre, Philadelphia) □ *Opened:* February 16, 1971. *Closed (for revisions):* February 27, 1971. *Reopened:* March 23, 1971 (Shubert Theatre, Boston). *Closed:* March 27, 1971. *Producer:* Norman Twain. *Staged by:* Tito Capobianco. *Book and lyrics:* Alan Jay Lerner. *Music:* John Barry. *Choreographer* (after Jack Cole left): Danny Daniels. (Dan Siretta took over in Boston.) CAST: John Neville, Annette Ferra, Dorothy Loudon, Leonard Frey, Velerie Camille.

1973
ESCADRILLE (Renamed: SHOOTING THE BAD GUYS DOWN) □ April, 1973. Jack Cole left in the midst of casting. Show was never done.

THE FILMS
OF
JACK COLE

1941
MOON OVER MIAMI (20th Century–Fox): 91 minutes □ *Producer:* Harry Joe Brown. *Director:* Walter Lang. *Screenplay:* Vincent Lawrence, Brown Holmes. *Music and lyrics:* Leo Robin, Ralph Grainer, Joe Burke, Edgar Leslie. *Dances:* Hermes Pan. CAST: Don Ameche, Betty Grable, Robert Cummings, Carole Landis, Jack Haley, Charlotte Greenwood, Cobina Wright, Jr. Specialty number by Jack Cole and Company.

1944
KISMET (Metro-Goldwyn-Mayer): 100 minutes □ *Producer:* Everett Riskin. *Director:* William Dieterle. *Screenplay:* John Meehan. *Dances* (uncredited): Jack Cole. CAST: Ronald Colman, Marlene Dietrich, Edward Arnold, James Craig, Hugh Herbert, Joy Ann Page, Florence Bates.

COVER GIRL (Columbia): 107 minutes □ *Producer:* Arthur Schwartz. *Director:* Charles Vidor. *Screenplay:* Virginia Van Upp. *Songs:* Jerome Kern, Ira Gershwin. *Dances:* Stanley Donen, Gene Kelly, Seymour Felix, Jack Cole. CAST: Rita Hayworth, Gene Kelly, Lee Bowman, Phil Silvers, Jinx Falkenburg, Eve Arden, Otto Kruger, Anita Colby.

1945
EADIE WAS A LADY (Columbia) 67 minutes □ *Producer:* Michel Kraike. *Director:* Arthur Dreifuss. *Screenplay:* Monte Brice. *Songs:* Saul Chaplin, Sammy Cahn, Phil Moore, Buddy De Sylva, Nacio Herb Brown, others. *Dances:* Jack Cole. CAST: Ann Miller, Joe Besser, William Wright, Jeff Donnell, Jimmy Little, Tommy Dugan, Marion Martin, Jack Cole.

TONIGHT AND EVERY NIGHT (Columbia): 92 minutes □ *Producer/Director:* Victor Saville. *Screenplay:* Lester Samuels, Abem Finkel. *Songs:* Jule Styne, Sammy Cahn. *Dances:* Jack Cole, Val Raset. CAST:

Rita Hayworth, Janet Blair, Lee Bowman, Marc Platt, Leslie Brooks, Jack Cole.

1946

TARS AND SPARS (Columbia): 86 minutes □ *Producer:* Milton H. Bren. *Director:* Alfred E. Green. *Screenplay:* John Jacoby, Sarett Tobias, Decla Dunning. *Story:* Barry Trivers. *Songs:* Jule Styne, Sammy Cahn. *Dances:* Jack Cole. CAST: Alfred Drake, Janet Blair, Marc Platt, Sid Caesar, Jeff Donnell, Ray Walker, James Flavin.

GILDA (Columbia): 110 minutes □ *Producer:* Virginia Van Upp. *Director:* Charles Vidor. *Screenplay:* Marion Parsonnet. *Songs:* Doris Fisher, Allan Roberts. *Dances* (uncredited): Jack Cole. CAST: Rita Hayworth, Glenn Ford, George Macready, Joseph Calleia, Steven Geray.

THE THRILL OF BRAZIL (Columbia): 91 minutes □ *Producer:* Sidney Biddell. *Director:* S. Sylvan Simon. *Screenplay:* Allen Rivkin, Harry Clork, Devery Freeman. *Songs:* Doris Fisher, Allan Roberts. *Dances:* Jack Cole, Eugene Loring, Nick Castle. CAST: Evelyn Keyes, Keenan Wynn, Ann Miller, Allyn Joslyn, Tito Guizar, Veloz and Yolanda.

1947

THE JOLSON STORY (Columbia): 128 minutes □ *Producer:* Sydney Skolsky. *Director:* Alfred E. Green. *Screenplay:* Sidney Buchman, Stephen Longstreet. *Dances:* Jack Cole, Joseph Lewis. CAST: Larry Parks, Evelyn Keyes, William Demarest, Bill Goodwin, Ludwig Donath.

DOWN TO EARTH (Columbia): 101 minutes □ *Producer:* Don Hartman. *Director:* Alexander Hall. *Screenplay:* Edwin Blum, Don Hartman. *Songs:* Doris Fisher, Allan Roberts. *Dances:* Jack Cole. CAST: Rita Hayworth, Larry Parks, Marc Platt, Roland Culver, James Gleason, Edward Everett Horton, Adele Jergens, George Macready, William Frawley.

1951

ON THE RIVIERA (20th Century–Fox): 89 minutes □ *Producer:* Sol C. Siegel. *Director:* Walter Lang. *Screenplay:* Valentine Davies, Phoebe and Henry Ephron. *Songs:* Sylvia Fine. *Dances:* Jack Cole. CAST: Danny Kaye, Gene Tierney, Corinne Calvet, Marcel Dalio, Ethel Martin, Gwen Verdon.

MEET ME AFTER THE SHOW (20th Century–Fox): 86 minutes □ *Producer:* George Jessel. *Director:* Richard Sale. *Screenplay:* Mary Loos, Richard Sale. *Songs:* Jule Styne, Leo Robin. *Dances:* Jack Cole. CAST: Betty Grable, Macdonald Carey, Rory Calhoun, Eddie Albert, Fred Clark, Lois Andrews, Irene Ryan, Steve Condos, Gwen Verdon.

DAVID AND BATHSHEBA (20th Century–Fox): 123 minutes □ *Producer:* Darryl F. Zanuck. *Director:* Henry King. *Screenplay:* Philip Dunne. *Music:* Alfred Newman. *Dances:* Jack Cole. CAST: Gregory Peck, Susan Hayward, Raymond Massey, Kieron Moore, James Robertson Justice, Jayne Meadows, John Sutton, Gwen Verdon.

1952

LYDIA BAILEY (20th Century–Fox): 89 minutes □ *Producer:* Jules Schermer. *Director:* Jean Negulesco. *Screenplay:* Michael Blankford, Philip Dunne. *Dance sequence:* Jack Cole. CAST: Dale Robertson, Anne Francis, Charles Korvin, William Marshall, Luis Van Rooten, Adeline de Walt Reynolds, Carmen de Lavallade, Jack Cole.

THE MERRY WIDOW (Metro-Goldwyn-Mayer): 105 minutes □ *Producer:* Joe Pasternak. *Director:* Curtis Bernhardt. *Screenplay:* Sonya Levien, William Ludwig. *Music:* Franz Lehar. *New lyrics:* Paul Francis Webster. *Dances:* Jack Cole. CAST: Lana Turner, Fernando Lamas, Una Merkel, Richard Haydn, Thomas Gomez, John Abbott, Gwen Verdon, Jack Cole.

1953

THE I DON'T CARE GIRL (20th Century–Fox): 91 minutes □ *Producer:* George Jessel. *Director:* Lloyd Bacon. *Screenplay:* Walter Bullock. *Dances:* Jack Cole. CAST: Mitzi Gaynor, David Wayne, Oscar Levant, Bob Graham, Craig Hill, Hazel Brooks, Bill Foster, Gwen Verdon, George Jessel.

THE FARMER TAKES A WIFE (20th Century–Fox): 80 minutes □ *Producer:* Frank P. Rosenberg. *Director:* Henry Levin. *Screenplay:* Walter Bullock, Sally Benson, Joseph Fields. *Songs:* Harold Arlen, Dorothy Fields. *Dances:* Jack Cole. CAST: Betty Grable, Dale Robertson, Thelma Ritter, John Carroll, Eddie Foy, Jr., Gwen Verdon.

GENTLEMEN PREFER BLONDES (20th Century–Fox): 91 minutes □ *Producer:* Sol C. Siegel. *Director:* Howard Hawks. *Screenplay:* Charles Lederer. *Songs:* Jule Styne, Leo Robin. *Dances:* Jack Cole. CAST: Jane Russell, Marilyn Monroe, Charles Coburn, Elliott Reid, Tommy Noonan, George Winslow, Marcel Dalio.

1954

RIVER OF NO RETURN (20th Century–Fox): 90 minutes □ *Producer:* Stanley Rubin. *Director:* Otto Preminger. *Screenplay:* Frank Fenton. *Songs:* Lionel Newman, Ken Darby. *Dances:* Jack Cole. CAST: Robert Mitchum, Marilyn Monroe, Rory Calhoun, Tommy Rettig, Murvyn Vye, Douglas Spencer, Will Wright.

THERE'S NO BUSINESS LIKE SHOW BUSINESS (20th Century-Fox): 117 minutes □ *Producer:* Sol C. Siegel. *Director:* Walter Lang. *Screenplay:* Phoebe and Henry Ephron. *Songs:* Irving Berlin. *Dances:* Robert Alton, Jack Cole (uncredited). CAST: Ethel Merman, Donald O'Connor, Marilyn Monroe, Dan Dailey, Johnnie Ray, Mitzi Gaynor, Richard Eastham, Hugh O'Brien.

1955

THREE FOR THE SHOW (Columbia): 93 minutes □ *Producer:* Jonie Taps. *Director:* H. C. Potter. *Screenplay:* Edward Hope, Leonard Stern. *Songs:* George and Ira Gershwin, Gene Austin, Hoagy Carmichael, Harold Adamson. *Dances:* Jack Cole. CAST: Betty Grable, Marge and Gower Champion, Jack Lemmon, Myron McCormick, Paul Harvey.

GENTLEMEN MARRY BRUNETTES (United Artists): 97 minutes □ *Executive producer:* Robert Bassler. *Producers:* Richard Sale, Robert Waterfield. *Director:* Richard Sale. *Screenplay:* Mary Loos, Richard Sale. *Dances:* Jack Cole. CAST: Jane Russell, Jeanne Crain, Alan Young, Scott Brady, Rudy Vallee, Gwen Verdon.

KISMET (Metro-Goldwyn-Mayer): 113 minutes □ *Producer:* Arthur Freed. *Director:* Vincente Minelli. *Screenplay:* Charles Lederer, Luther Davis. *Music and lyrics:* Robert Wright, George Forrest. *Dances:* Jack Cole. CAST: Howard Keel, Ann Blyth, Dolores Gray, Vic Damone, Monty Woolley, Sebastian Cabot, Jack Cole.

1957

DESIGNING WOMAN (Metro-Goldwyn-Mayer): 118 minutes □ *Coproducers:* Dore Schary, George Wells. *Director:* Vincente Minelli. *Screenplay:* George Wells (Academy Award winner). *Dances:* Jack Cole. CAST: Gregory Peck, Lauren Bacall, Dolores Gray, Chuck Connors, Sam Levene, Jack Cole, Mickey Shaughnessy.

LES GIRLS (Metro-Goldwyn-Mayer): 114 minutes □ *Producer:* Sol C. Siegel. *Director:* George Cukor. *Screenplay:* John Patrick. *Music:* Cole Porter. *Dances:* Jack Cole. CAST: Gene Kelly, Mitzi Gaynor, Kay Kendall, Taina Elg, Jacques Bergerac, Leslie Phillips.

1959

SOME LIKE IT HOT (United Artists): 120 minutes □ *Producer/Director:* Billy Wilder. *Screenplay:* Billy Wilder, based on an unpublished story by R. Thoeren and M. Logan. *Musical staging (uncredited):* Jack Cole. CAST: Marilyn Monroe, Tony Curtis, Jack Lemmon, George Raft, Pat O'Brien, Joe E. Brown, Joan Shawlee, Mike Mazurki, Nehemiah Persoff.

1960

LET'S MAKE LOVE (20th Century–Fox): 118 minutes □ *Producer:* Jerry Wald. *Director:* George Cukor. *Screenplay:* Norman Krasna. *Songs:* Cole Porter, Sammy Cahn, James Van Husen. *Dances:* Jack Cole. Cast: Marilyn Monroe, Yves Montand, Tony Randall, Frankie Vaughan, Wilfred Hyde-White, David Burns, Bing Crosby, Milton Berle, Gene Kelly.

SELECTED BIBLIOGRAPHY

Chujoy, Anatole, and Manchester, P. W. (eds.). *The Dance Encyclopedia.* New York: Simon and Schuster, 1967.

De Mille, Agnes. *America Dances.* New York: Macmillan, 1980.

Halliwell, Leslie (ed.). *Halliwell's Film Guide.* 3rd ed. New York: Charles Scribner's Sons, 1981.

Hirschhorn, Clive. *The Hollywood Musical.* New York: Crown Publishers, 1981.

Kaufman, Kimberly Susan. "A Biographical-Bibliographical Study of Jack Cole." Los Angeles: Unpublished UCLA M.A. thesis, 1976.

King, Eleanor. *Transformations: the Humphrey-Weidman Era.* Brooklyn, NY: Dance Horizons, 1978.

Loney, Glenn (ed.). *Twentieth Century Theatre.* 2 vols. New York: Facts on File, 1983.

Mantle, Burns, and others (eds.). *Best Plays* (annual series). New York: Dodd, Mead.

Manville, Roger (ed.). *The International Encyclopedia of Film.* New York: Crown Publishers, 1972.

McDonagh, Don (ed.). *The Complete Guide to Modern Dance.* Garden City, NY: Doubleday & Co., 1976.

Michael, Paul (ed.). *The American Movies.* Garden City, NY: Galahad Books, 1969.

Pickard, Ray (ed.). *A Companion to the Movies*. London: Lutterworth Press, 1972.

St. Denis, Ruth. *An Unfinished Life*. New York: Harper & Bros., 1939.

Shawn, Ted, with Poole, Gray. *One Thousand and One Night Stands*. New York: Doubleday & Co., 1960.

Shelton, Suzanne. *Divine Dancer: A Biography of Ruth St. Denis*. Garden City, NY: Doubleday & Co., 1981.

Sherman, Jane. *Denishawn: The Enduring Influence*. Boston: G. K. Hall, 1983.

———. *The Drama of Denishawn Dance*. Middletown, CT: Wesleyan University Press, 1979.

———. *Soaring: the Diary and Letters of a Denishawn Dancer in the Far East, 1925–1926*. Middletown, CT: Wesleyan University Press, 1976.

Siegal, Marcia B. *At the Vanishing Point*. New York: Saturday Review Press, 1972.

Stearns, Marshall and Jean. *Jazz Dance*. New York: Schirmer Books/Macmillan, 1979.

Terry, Walter. *The Dance in America*. New York: Harper & Bros., 1956.

———. *I Was There*. New York: Audience Arts/Marcel Dekker, 1973.

———. *Ted Shawn: Father of American Dance*. New York: Dial Press, 1976.

INDEX

DATE DUE